D1008825

GRAND ILLUSION

GRAND ILLUSION

THE MYTH OF VOTER CHOICE IN A TWO-PARTY TYRANNY

Theresa Amato

THE NEW PRESS

NEW YORK
LONDON

Published in the United States by The New Press, New York, 2009
Distributed by Perseus Distribution

LIBRARY OF CONGRESS CATALOGING-IN-PUBLICATION DATA

Amato, Theresa A.
Grand illusion : the myth of voter choice in a two-party tyranny / Theresa Amato.
p. cm.
Includes bibliographical references and index.
ISBN 978-1-59558-394-9 (hc. : alk. paper) 1. Political parties—United States.
2. Two party systems—United States. 3. Voting—United States. I. Title.
II. Title: Myth of voter choice in a two-party tyranny.
JK2265.A67 2009
324.273—dc22 2009000593

The New Press was established in 1990 as a not-for-profit alternative to the large, commercial publishing houses currently dominating the book publishing industry. The New Press operates in the public interest rather than for private gain, and is committed to publishing, in innovative ways, works of educational, cultural, and community value that are often deemed insufficiently profitable.

www.thenewpress.com

Composition by Westchester Book Services
This book was set in Janson Text

Printed in the United States of America

2 4 6 8 10 9 7 5 3

To the builders of democracy everywhere
and
to my family

Contents

Foreword

by Ralph Nader

Party is not mentioned in the Constitution. George Washington and Thomas Jefferson, among other Founders, despised political parties, calling them "factions" bent on self-perpetuating their own narrow interests.

How prescient were these Founders! Today the country is saddled with a two-party dictatorship that commercializes elections, picks its own voters by gerrymandering most congressional districts into one-party-dominated enclaves, and proceeds to turn our federal government—department by department—over to the control of big business.

The consequences of subordinating civic democratic values to the supremacy of corporate, commercial dictates are lethal to the objectives of justice and freedom that our Constitution reserved for "We the People." Where the Republicans and Democrats manage to offer voters a two-candidate choice, they increasingly have been converging their agendas, policies, and taboos closer together. After all, they are dialing for the same commercial dollars from corporate lobbies and executives.

What remains to challenge this two-party duopoly are third-party and independent candidates who have had to surmount the highest barriers to getting on the ballot in many states since our Republic was founded. During the nineteenth and early twentieth centuries, these parties and candidates could place themselves on the ballot with few restrictions, if any. With each election cycle, additional draconian barriers, partisan judges, and harassing litigation are employed against candidates viewed by one or the other major parties as affecting margins in this winner-take-all duopoly system.

This book takes a hard, firsthand look at the neglected but serious violations of civil rights and civil liberties that deny voters more choices of candidates and deny more candidates their desire to give voters such choices. Year after year of two-party domination has created an aura of inevitability, through passage of restrictive laws and exclusions from debates, that daunts both the expectations of voters and the willingness of candidates to confront these costly and draining hurdles so as to generate a competitive electoral democracy.

Our minds need to be liberated and our expectations launched to higher levels if we are to grasp how suppressive electoral conditions have become in the pretentious democratic image that the U.S. government presents to the rest of the world. The last major frontier of systemic political bigotry is that directed against the ballot access rights of minor-party or independent candidates. As was the case decades ago with minority voters, this bigotry is entrenched in law, tolerated by lawmakers, accepted by most of the media, and largely ignored by the federal judiciary. There is an additional prejudice in the minds of many voters partisan to one or the other of the major parties, including those who vote for whom they perceive to be the "least worst" of the two. Wittingly or unwittingly, they lash out and demand that the smaller upstarts, who may "take away" votes from their least-worst choice, not run—that is, not speak, petition, or assemble inside elections.

Do they know how censorious their suppressive words are? Do they realize they are demanding that these potential or actual candidates not exercise their First Amendment rights? Don't they see that they are captives of this 220-year-old winner-take-all Electoral College system and that the course of freedom of speech is to break out of that prison through long-advanced electoral reforms? Are they not glad that some citizens went to the polls in the nineteenth century and declined to be least-worst voters between the Democrats and the Whigs or between the Democrats and the Republicans on the matter of slavery, women's right to vote, or the historic efforts to start expanding justice for industrial workers and farmers? Some of the voters, having choices on the ballots, were able to pioneer these critical shifts in power that jump-started national agendas sooner because of the efforts of parties and candidates who never won a national election and only rarely a state election.

I wrote my first article in 1958 on the many barriers to third-party and independent candidates erected by the Republican and Democratic parties in state after state through their legislatures. Recalling my words in that edition of the *Harvard Law Record*, I never dreamed that the situation today would be much worse—higher signature requirements for ballot access and scores of other obstructions, regulatory trapdoors, and arbitrary power exercised by partisan government officials. The more third-party and independent candidates overcome the obstacles—at great cost and time to them in particular states—the more the two-party duopoly raises the bar for the next election or tries in various ways to bully away any competitive challenge to its rooted hegemony.

Such candidate rights under existing legislative, executive, and judicial frameworks are reminiscent of the plight of minority voter rights back in the 1920s, 1930s, 1940s, and 1950s. Then the statutes were stacked against African Americans in many states, along with the biased decisions and inflammatory language of judges, secured by the executive glue of the respective secretaries of state.

There is little or no official or public recognition—and inadequate sensitivity even by most civil liberties advocates—that more voices and choices by diverse candidates clearly give voter rights more meaning as well. In short, candidate rights and voter rights to express their First Amendment freedoms of speech, petition, and assembly are inextricable. After all, Western observers were often treated to the Soviet Union's boasting over 90 percent voter turnout, but they were not fooled because there was only one candidate on each ballot line.

Severe limitation of candidate choice in our country is assured not just by ballot access barriers. Widespread partisan redistricting (gerrymandering) has left voters in most congressional districts (about 90 percent of them) with the certainty of coronating the incumbent. Many state legislative districts are dominated by one party. In Massachusetts, 60 percent of the state legislative districts have Democratic incumbents and no opposition at all by the Republican Party.

These exclusionary barriers act to the detriment of competitive political activities and energies as well as to the right of the underdog to have a chance to have a chance. We know what happens in nature when seeds are not given an opportunity to sprout. We know what happens to our economy, concentrated as it is, when entrepreneurs and small businesses find that their freedom to compete is squelched. There is little regeneration and much decay in both arenas. Indeed, were these two major parties operating in the market economy in such a collusive manner as to deliberately exclude competitors, they would be indicted and convicted under the antitrust laws.

Enter Theresa Amato with this groundbreaking book from the recent battlegrounds of ballot access struggles. As my campaign manager for the 2000 and 2004 presidential campaigns, she studied, saw, participated in, litigated, and contemplated this mockery of any democratic theory or practice. Our challenges of these state barriers—that remain latent until provoked—brought out the bigotry and corruption lying beneath the surface.

I first heard of Ms. Amato when she was a practicing lawyer, having graduated from New York University Law School and completed a federal judge clerkship, at the Public Citizen Litigation Group. Her supervising attorney David Vladeck told me: "I don't know any other young lawyer who can keep so many balls up in the air at the same time." This trait—now called multitasking—served her well in 2000 and 2004. It left her with a sense of urgency, without peer in our nation, regarding the blockades, harassments, delays, manipulations, and outright Jim Crow–like tactics perpetrated by the Democratic Party, its retained corporate law firms, and its political and judicial allies.

What started out in 2000 to be an alternative Green Party electoral path and a deep progressive reform agenda for voter choice found us by the end of 2004 deep into a major civil liberties and civil rights mission. This drive for candidates' rights is a logical ally of the emerging pressure to confront the myriad messes gravely affecting voter registration, voter turnout, and voter counts that erupted most visibly in Florida (2000) and in Ohio (2004). For if the duopoly cannot be challenged from the outside, the malaise and cynicism that settle in among voter expectations leave citizens with an interminable least-worst (of the two major candidates) option that gets worse every four years. The pull by corporate interests on these candidates day after day is not countervailed by a pull in the opposite direction, because least-worst voters, with nowhere to go, are signaling they can be taken for granted by the least-worst candidate.

From the broader context internationally, there is no Western democracy that erects such impediments to smaller parties and independent candidates, impeding them from merely even getting on the ballot. Not even close! Does it make a difference? Ask the Canadians about the initiatory role of the New Democratic Party (NDP) in establishing, decades ago, universal health care for our northern neighbors. Or ask the smaller parties either in coalitions or going it alone to pioneer for social democratic services and facilities for the people of Western Europe. In these places, there are more vibrant candidate debates and by far more numerous parties, leading to far higher voter turnouts and nonpartisan, accurate vote counts.

In *Grand Illusion: The Myth of Voter Choice in a Two-Party Tyranny*, there is a wealth of detail that has not been disclosed or reported—call it empirical reality that exposes the political myths we were taught in history classes. The evidence, events, and rules that Ms. Amato connects in this engrossing but worrisome narrative should bring political scientists, whose vocabulary starts and stops with the contemptuous word *spoiler*, down to earth, along with reporters, editors, and pundits who possess similar tunnel vision. Voters themselves will have their expectation levels elevated about political choice and benefits as they read these pages. They will find irrefutable evidence of how far ballot access for small-start candidates has been undermined.

To those unduly depressed by the rigidity of the existing barriers, Ms. Amato is not tilting at windmills. She is devoted to turning windmills into renewable political wind power to blow away the barriers restraining the most elaborate use of the First Amendment, namely, running for elective office as a ballot-qualified candidate.

She understands that the lesson of history is so often one of having to strive, strive, and strive, lose, lose, and lose, until the victories begin appearing on the horizon. Such a prospect must include the U.S. Supreme Court, whose knee-jerk habit routinely denies petitions for *certiorari* from adverse, sometimes preemptory decisions of the lower federal courts against non–major party candidates who seek ballot access. In one case they did decide, *Timmons v. Twin Cities Area New Party* (1997), Chief Justice William Rehnquist even provided some dicta, declaring that ours is a two-party country juridically, not just politically, such that the states "may, in practice, favor the traditional two party system."

As you proceed through the pages of *Grand Illusion*, you may find yourself saying, "What?" or "This can't *be*!" or "Not in America!" or "No way!" or "Why haven't I heard about this before?" One reaction I doubt you will be having: "This can't be true." Ms. Amato is a meticulous and very precise author with specific documentation for her research, her recollections, and her recommendations for change.

The plight of a nation that presumes to be structurally democratic can be traced back to the concentration of economic power in the hands of a few over the many. Such concentration of corporate power in our society seeks to take over more and more of electoral and governmental power for the purpose of expanding and perpetuating its power and the spoils that are its objective. As Franklin D. Roosevelt warned in a message to Congress on April 29, 1938, "The first truth is that the liberty of a democracy is not safe if the people tolerate the growth of private power to a point where it becomes stronger than their democratic state itself. That, in its essence, is Fascism—ownership of Government by an individual, by a group, or by any other controlling private power." This "fascism" is far more a reality in today's multinational corporate world. Washington, DC, is now corporate occupied territory.

As a Harvard Law School student in 1956, I was a member of a standing-room-only audience who came to listen to a middle-aged attorney by the name of Thurgood Marshall. He was describing his and the National Association for the Advancement of Colored People's (NAACP) many lawsuits, including their recent victory in the celebrated desegregation case of *Brown v. Board of Education*. All of us sensed the beginning of a major social justice movement in America, which extended to the Civil Rights Act of 1964 and the Voting Rights Act of 1965.

Ms. Amato's book may be a precursor of a comparable movement for minor party and independent candidates' rights, remedies, and other related electoral reforms. Its gripping details may presage the awakening of those traditional tools of litigation, regulatory actions, and comprehensive legislation. Long overdue! This complementary civil rights movement will open doors of opportunity to vigorous candidates and start-up parties determined to show the nation how to bring about a responsive politics that improves the well-being of its citizens and—together with the electoral reforms discussed herein—liberates posterity from the present exclusionary, stagnant, indentured two-party dictatorship.

As Theresa Amato concludes, what is urgently needed is a comprehensively reformed electoral system. Genuine ballot choices through clean competition and the accurately counted votes of the people constitute no small start toward elevating the quality of our federal government. Only organized people can give themselves this future, and that can begin with the readers of this book visiting the Center for Competitive Democracy at www.competitivedemocracy.org.

Acknowledgments

> Human virtue demands her champions and martyrs, and the trial of persecution always proceeds.
>
> —Ralph Waldo Emerson, "Heroism"
> *Essays: First Series* (1841)

This book was written for all the past, present, and future third-party and independent candidates in the United States, their supporters and parties, and the election law reformers and chroniclers, as well as those who have tried, or will try, to grapple with the stunning incompetence and injustice of the broken, two-party-dominated American electoral system. It is written for all those around the world who strive to build democracy and establish the right—not just in theory but in practice—of all people to vote freely for, give informed consent to, and hold accountable responsive leaders.

This book was written in particular for Ralph Nader, an American hero. History will record his incessant, breathtaking efforts to fight for more justice on behalf of consumers, taxpayers, workers, and voters and to make this country—its government, citizens, institutions, and protocols—live up to the promise of democratic ideals. For nearly two decades, it has been my privilege to work with this great man.

In addition to Ralph, I am indebted to the many lawyers, students, volunteers, activists, party members, independents, journalists, and scholars who have helped by exposing and documenting the injustices, undertaking the litigation, supporting third-party and independent rights, and seeking reform of the electoral system. Any errors in the recounting of these barriers to entry in the electoral arena and the many challenges are, of course, mine.

Special thanks go in particular to Bruce Afran, Mark R. Brown, Basil C. Culyba, Oliver Hall, Harry Kresky, Michael Richardson, and Richard Winger. Additional thanks to Steve Conn, Jason Kafoury, Smita Khatri, Carl Mayer, Dan Meek, Darcy G. Richardson, and Kevin Zeese. To the legions of lawyers around the country too numerous to name here but who were galvanized by the injustice of it all to help Nader/Camejo 2004, thank you. You were remarkable. The necessarily abbreviated descriptions of your cases and legal heroics contained herein and on my Web site do not do justice to the amount of effort and talent that you dedicated.

Additional thanks to the lawyers during the 2000 campaign who took on the Commission on Presidential Debates, the Federal Election Commission, the ballot access laws, and MasterCard. Special thanks to Jason Adkins and Howard Friedman; John Bonifaz, Gregory Luke, and Bonnie Tenneriello, all formerly of the National Voting Rights Institute; Scott P. Lewis at Palmer & Dodge; David Kairys; Glenn Moramarco and Elizabeth Daniel of the Brennan Center for Justice at New York University School of Law; Anthony Fletcher, Stacy Grossman, and Lawrence Kolodney at Fish & Richardson; Mark Lemley at the University of California, Berkeley; and our counsel Michael Trister, who almost every day in 2000 patiently taught me something new about the federal election laws. Additional thanks to Jamin B. Raskin, Steve Cobble, Bill Hillsman, and North Woods Advertising for their counsel, and to election reformers Rob Richie and Steven Hill for their ongoing education about, and devotion to, fixing our electoral system.

To the dedicated staffs, party members, petitioners, donors, and volunteers of Nader/LaDuke 2000 and Nader/Camejo 2004, there are no words adequate to express my gratitude. You are too numerous to mention, but you know who you are and how you each contributed to history. Thanks in particular to those who contributed recollections or who were interviewed for this book. Very special thanks go to the unflappable Monica Wilson (2000) and the indefatigable Marcia Jansen (2004) for their incomparable efforts to make my role in each campaign possible.

To vice-presidential candidates Winona LaDuke (2000) and the late Peter Miguel Camejo (2004) and the few "stand-ins" we had, such as Jan Pierce: you are champions in the fight for justice. It was an honor to run your tickets. To the only two members ever of the nonexistent "fan club," thank you for bringing me into it all.

A heartfelt thanks to my superb editor Diane Wachtell, the executive director of The New Press, her entire team, and David Bruce Wolf. To the members of the unofficial "Chicago Populist School," Thomas Geoghegan, John Wasik, and most especially Brian Conlon, your advice, encouragement, and/or edits were invaluable. To my fellow public interest activists, lawyers, staffs, interns, and students—my gratitude for your dedicated efforts to advance justice and for having taught me so much on the road. And to my in-laws, the Main/Mead/Berwick/Fry families, and my friends and relatives who suffered through my involuntarily drafted focus groups, including those who babysat (me or my children), thank you—you have been so kind. I also thank John P.C. Duncan and Duncan Associates Attorneys and Counselors, P.C., for their patience, Cathy Konas for proofreading, and Loyola University Chicago School of Law student Donato Latrofa for his valuable citation assistance. To the Heinrich Böll Foundation, especially Sascha Mueller-Kraenner: thank you for generously inviting me to witness elections and discuss political parties throughout Germany, Paris, and Brussels. A special shout-out to Reinhardt Bütikofer and Renate Künast of the German Greens, Pascale Girard of the French Greens, Arnold Cassola of the Italian Greens, Bob Brown of the Australian Greens, Annie Goeke of the U.S. Greens, and the many other Greens I have met since 1998 from a variety of countries (especially our own) who are dedicated to building a more sustainable planet and politics.

I am eternally grateful to Alan B. Morrison, the brilliant co-founder of the Public Citizen Litigation Group, and my fellow lawyers and advocates throughout Public Citizen for teaching me at the beginning of my legal career, in Alan's words, "If you aren't losing, you aren't taking the hard cases."

Finally, this book is written with love for, and gratitude to, my extended family, especially for my parents and grandparents for their love and support and the many sacrifices they made to give me and my brother John the best education possible. I owe everything to them for shaping my character and personality so that I could both undertake and understand the unique experiences contained herein. They and so many dedicated and "subversive" schoolteachers, my mom first among them, taught me the inherent value of confronting injustice.

I am indebted in the writing of this book to many but above all to my partner in life, Todd Main. We met on the 2000 campaign, and every day since has been an improvement—even through our plane ride over the Pentagon on the morning of 9/11, the anthrax, "the snipers," and the diapers. With unfailing good cheer and devotion, he has kept me sane and alive, for better and for worse, and even worse, while "fighting the bad guys" together, as he would say. No one could ask for a better foxhole compatriot either in a campaign or in life. In particular, I write for our daughters Isabella Rosina and Vittoria Teresina, because "mommy" missed some story hours to live through and write about our presidential elections—but, more important, because I want them to live in a world where all people can vote freely and where all children, including little girls, can have a fair chance to grow up, run for, and become president.

Introduction

Port-au-Prince, Haiti, December 1990

It took days to get across the border to Haiti. The Lawyers Committee for Human Rights had sent me to the Dominican Republic (DR) to investigate whether the government was using Haitian children to cut sugarcane for export to the United States. I had arrived in Santo Domingo in late November 1990, only to discover that the conference I was to attend had been abruptly canceled. None of Haiti's human rights advocates were going to show. They were reluctant to leave Haiti for fear they would not be allowed back into their country in time to vote: Haiti was about to hold its first free election in 125 years.

I didn't want the mission to fail, but I wasn't sure what to do. I was only twenty-six. The city streets were filled with potholes. It was hard to go anywhere. The electricity would go off for hours at a time. I didn't know anyone—all the project's contacts were supposed to come to the canceled conference. With the lights blinking on and off, I decided to call the bishop of the Anglican Church. He was supposed to be the conference's keynote speaker, and I hoped he would know where to start. When he was kind enough to have lunch with me, I asked him if he could loan out a priest to introduce me to the cane-cutting community.

He delivered. With a savvy Anglican priest and a worried trade unionist guiding my journey, I hopped across the DR from one armed-guarded, state-owned *batey*, or sugarcane plantation, to another. Working conditions were appalling—the labor was tantamount to indentured servitude. Some children were born into these cane fields; others came lured by the promises of work picking tomatoes or gold or free radios on the streets of Santo Domingo.

I went to Haiti to find out why the children of Haiti were in the back-breaking Dominican cane fields. And so it was in this pursuit of documenting the labor rights conditions of children that I came to witness the importance of free and fair elections.

When I arrived in Port-au-Prince, I knew precisely nothing about Haiti's history and even less about its politics. Most of what I knew came from Graham Greene's *Comedians*. Unlike virtually every other foreigner there during those historic days, I was *not* in Haiti to "monitor" the elections, and my timing could not have been worse. The election frenzy meant that there wasn't a room available in downtown Port-au-Prince. Perfect strangers were doubling up at the relatively posh Holiday Inn—in rooms where rats ran through the wicker headboards—just to have front row seats across from the National Palace. The place was crawling with journalists and Jimmy Carteresque "election monitors."

My Haitian contact assumed I wanted to go to *the* campaign. He took me on arrival straight to Jean-Bertrand Aristide's "Lavalas" headquarters. "Titid," as the often-called "radical former priest" was affectionately known, was running for president. He and his colleagues were champions of the poor, orphaned children in particular. Meeting some of them was crucial to understanding the plight of Haiti's young cane cutters.

When we arrived at the Aristide campaign headquarters, the driver parked the car a healthy distance from the building. He explained that either the car or the building could be bombed at any time: "So why tempt fate," he said, "by parking close?" Indeed. Why tempt fate by being there? I made light of the remark in the way a young American with no concept of mortality does.

I had never been to a national presidential campaign headquarters anywhere in the world, but I didn't need a law degree to tell me something was very strange. There weren't any bodies stuffing envelopes or answering phones. Aristide had been the target of assassination attempts already, so the message was meant as fair warning. The last time the Haitians had tried to vote, paramilitary forces came out and shot down or chopped up the prospective voters. Aristide's church and parishioners had been attacked by former dictator François "Papa Doc" Duvalier's bullies, the Tonton Macoutes. Many of Aristide's followers died or disappeared. In a few days, the fate of this country would be determined, and most of the world had sent observers there to watch or "help"—amazed that the upstart candidacy of a preacher to the poor had so energized the country. The campaign headquarters was a ghost town. I would have more luck on the streets, talking to destitute children in the slums of Cité Soleil.

I started interviewing children about recruiters, *buscones*, who were luring them on a per capita reward basis to the DR to cut cane. Within five minutes of talking to anyone—young or old—on any Haitian street, anyone could see the hope in the hearts of the poor that Aristide would win, be "their" leader, remove their suffering, improve their lives, and turn their country around. Even I, an ignorant foreigner, could tell that if the people were allowed to vote, Aristide was going to win this election by a landslide.

On Election Day I watched tanks go by on the square in front of the National Palace. The whole place was jittery. I was traveling around the region in the backseat of a dark SUV with human rights observers who were still debating who would win. As we drove, the observers would check to see whether ballots had been delivered both in downtown places and in the more remote periphery. Electricity wires were jerry-rigged all over the place. In some places, people were still voting by candlelight, late into the night, in tiny makeshift polling huts. We went into these huts one or two at a time to watch the process. I will never forget the sight of Haitians getting their thumbs stained with red ink to prevent fraud and the elderly with tears streaming down their wiry faces. Their smiles reflected their surging pride: they finally had a chance to vote in their lifetimes—in *their* country.

The Haitian people were brave. They wanted so badly to vote that they would risk the threat of another militia-interrupted, voter-mutilated election. Some people had stood in line ten hours or more, waiting for ballots to come. Some had begun standing at 6:00 A.M. to have this first-in-a-lifetime experience. Many took a long time to vote, carefully viewing the options. The ballots were larger than placemats—and colorful, with animals, names, and slogans to identify each of the many candidates to a mainly illiterate population.

Aristide had massive popular support and won with a two-thirds majority. If Haitians controlled the Vatican, he would have been canonized rather than defrocked. This was not a state secret, but the intelligentsia I observed—the media, the international monitors—were in a state of elitist, inside-the-Beltway denial: a black, Marxist preacher of "liberation theology" was going to become president of the most destitute country in the Western Hemisphere. A country only 500 miles from Florida, where corporate America did not even let its planes park overnight, where the U.S. government had backed the Duvalier dictatorship, was going to have a radical president, beloved by the poor. For me, the 1990 Haitian election was an amazing introduction to incipient democracy in action.

Caracas, Venezuela, January 1991

I wrote the DR/Haitian human rights report in a tiny room in Altamira Norte in downtown Caracas, Venezuela.[1] Consuela, the effervescent, generous woman whose spartan room had become my rental home for a month, was urging me in Spanish to stay in Venezuela and write more reports—many more reports. She was particularly concerned about South American police whom she said locked up or shot children just for existing. Because "there are too many of them," she explained. But I had to go.

Departing Venezuela, I got searched—excessively—at the airport. Consuela explained that this was because I was American, because George H.W. Bush was currently bombing Iraq: "Who knows, he may be coming to invade Venezuela too because Venezuela has oil." She then added that it was "impossible to know who is telling the truth—Saddam, Bush." They were "all the same" in her experience. Politicians were "todos ladrones"—all thieves.

In far-from-perfect Spanish, I spent an inordinate amount of time trying to convince educated, middle-aged, president-of-her-condo-association Consuela that there was a real difference between what the U.S. government says and what Saddam Hussein says. I promised that there wasn't a snowball's chance in hell that the United States would be invading Venezuela or any country for oil anytime soon. And I was outraged to be treated practically like an enemy in the Venezuelan airport!

I thought Consuela was naive to make no distinctions between the U.S. government and Iraq's. By the time I went to Haiti and Venezuela, I had already worked or interned for all three branches of the federal government. I believed in the intent and power of the U.S. government to do good things for people. I grew up steeped in Midwest, immigrant family Americana. My grandparents and father came from Italy through Ellis Island to find a better life in America. I set records selling Girl Scout cookies in the Chicago suburbs. Apart from the three years my brother John and I attended Divine Infant, where we wore plaid uniforms and dedicated every paper to Jesus, Mary, and Joseph, I mainly went to public schools, reading positively sanitized textbooks on American history.

By the time I got to high school, I was playing John Philip Sousa songs on the piccolo in a marching band and dancing around the flag at pro-government camps such as Girls State and Girls Nation. I ran for "youth governor" of Illinois in the YMCA's Youth and Government program and even entered a beauty contest, marching around in a short red skirt and a white blouse with blue sequins, waving Old Glory and singing, "You're a grand old flag." I watched the Watergate hearings after school every day, somewhere in between Chicago Cubs games and *Speed Racer*; so in 1974, at age ten, when my dad brought us into the living room to watch Richard Nixon get on a plane and leave the White House, without tanks in the background to ensure the orderly transition of power, I took this as another confirmation of how democracy works in the United States.

I confess all this to convince you, the reader, that I am not someone who wants to just throw rocks at our political system. I don't hate all government and ours in particular. Before I left college, my pro-Americana bona fides were in complete order: I had both a security clearance from the U.S. State Department and a license to buy and sell securities on Wall Street.

And so there I was telling Consuela in January 1991: My government does not recklessly invade countries because they have oil. My country doesn't make people wait hours on end to vote. My country does not try to prevent populist candidates from becoming president. My country does not randomly lock up, torture, or shoot people. And my country certainly doesn't search people as if they are criminals just because they present a foreign passport at the airport. Alas. Despite the best education in the world, I was naive, with a remarkably skewed and deficient sense of U.S. history. Charitably, you could say that a crucial part of my education was unfinished.

This book is a result of part of the education that followed: It is a firsthand account of the barriers to running for president as a citizen candidate, outside of the two major parties, in the United States at the beginning of the twenty-first century. The content is derived from what I learned in my role as the national campaign manager of Ralph Nader's 2000 and 2004 campaigns for the presidency of the United States, first as a third-party candidate for the U.S. Greens, then as an independent, and from decades of citizen advocacy and paying close attention to what I read about our electoral system from the media, the bloggers, the courts, the reformers, and the scholars.

What happens when ordinary people—citizen candidates outside the Democratic and Republican parties—actually seek to exercise their rights to run for president of the United States? I'll share with you what I have learned the hard way, up close and personal: it is a myth that anyone can grow up and successfully run for president—outside the two major parties. Our system is so exclusionary and undemocratic that not even an Ivy League–educated, white, male American icon like Ralph Nader can effectively run for president outside the two parties.

Washington, DC, 2005

On the wall in my office hangs a sign from 1919 that says, simply, "Let Women Vote." It could just as easily say: "Let Blacks Vote," "Let 18-Year-Olds Vote," or "Let People Vote Directly for Senators." It could also say: "Let Ex-Felons Vote," "Let Noncitizens Vote," "Let Puerto Ricans Vote," or "Let the Citizens of Washington, DC, *Really* Vote."

The United States has an inglorious history of denying and diminishing the vote. As a country we are still struggling with democracy, equality, and voting rights.[2] When I began this account in 2005, I lived in Washington, DC, where the license plates say, "Taxation Without Representation"; the residents routinely refer to DC as the "last colonial capital" because its 570,000 taxpaying denizens have no voting representation in the U.S. Congress. Today, "more than 8 million American citizens, a majority of them racial and ethnic minorities, still belong to communities that are absolutely or substantially disenfranchised by law."[3] Even though the 1948 Universal Declaration of Human Rights recognizes the right to "universal and equal suffrage," the United States remains one of only eleven electoral democracies in the world whose constitution has not joined the other 108 electoral democracies whose constitutions explicitly guarantee their citizens an affirmative right to vote.[4]

So when I look at a sign like "Let Women Vote," I reword it in my head. To me the sign in shorthand screams: *Let All the People Vote!*

But that is only half the sentence. After running two national presidential campaigns, I then add an essential, highly ignored corollary: *Let All the People Vote for Whomever They Want!*

The flipside of voter rights—which we are still far from fully achieving—is candidate rights. After all, people in many dictatorships can vote. But what good is any election if the slate is predetermined by the state? What good is the right (or requirement)[5] to vote if you have only one choice? What good would perfect election machinery and administration be if your choice has been artificially limited by the state to just one or two candidates? Voting under such restrictions is an exercise in futility even if the votes get counted accurately. The outcome is predetermined by the government without the consent of the governed because *the choice* is unfairly narrowed.

Our country puts out human rights reports and loudly scolds countries that lock up, kill, or shut out the political opposition so that every election is really only a referendum on a slate of government predetermined choices.[6] After two presidential campaigns, one for a third-party and another for an independent candidacy, I have concluded that the laws, regulations, and barriers we have in place against political competition in the United States are only one *short* step removed from countries where the state itself predetermines the slate. Our electoral system could be called "supply-side politics," with very little diverse trickle-down to the people. We have an infinite choice of limited supply, from only two increasingly converging and yet rancorous and stagnating parties. Other providers of political supply and thought are effectively barred from entry and so denied the right to compete effectively in the political arena—or even to be in demand.

If you think this conclusion is hyperbolic, then I invite you—challenge you—to read this book. It contains the empirical and anecdotal data I have collected from having been in the political arena twice for a political minority. If you have not lived through a campaign for a third-party or independent candidate, as every minor-party candidate, independent, and their campaign teams, staff, volunteers, and parties alike have, it is hard to believe. The experience does not comport with any sense of fairness, rationality, or Americana that we grow up thinking is our heritage, our unique image of ourselves—our "American democracy."

I have tried to explain the discriminatory barriers to my friends and family in understandable terms. Invariably, I use analogies: Imagine a country where thirty-three ice cream flavors are manufactured for sale, but every time you go to the store, you are only allowed chocolate or vanilla. Imagine a country where in order to get any investment capital you must already have 5 percent of market share or don't bother to apply.[7] Imagine a country where if you don't already have 15 percent of market share, you are not allowed to advertise on television.[8] Imagine a country where all the rules of the road changed when you crossed from one state line to another, and you had to take another driving test and get a new license before your car could cross the border—even though it is a national highway system. Or imagine if you had lived in the state once, graduated high school there, and left the state, but in order to come back—even if you were fifty or eighty years old—the state insisted that you spend another four years going back to high school.[9]

The equivalents of these circumstances, which our nation would never tolerate in the economic arena, are the kinds of inanities that third parties and independent candidates face routinely in the political arena when they try to offer themselves in the American electoral market. In other arenas, millions of Americans respond to innovation, entrepreneurship, competition, transparency, mobility, and regeneration. But "more is better" and "free competition"—the reigning economic ideologies—simply do not apply in political or legal scholarship.[10]

This book is not a political memoir or a campaign tell-all. It is only my inside scoop on the electoral injustices I have observed up close in two presidential elections. Readers looking for anecdotes about, or insights into, Ralph Nader or all the strategic inner workings of either historic campaign may well be disappointed. Instead, I describe in great detail why—even if we come up with a less dysfunctional electoral system where everyone who wants to is capable of being registered to vote, even if we remove the modern-day Jim Crow laws, and even if we manage to count and account for the votes properly—all this "election perfection" would still not render democratic elections if we are left with only one or two major-party-sanctioned candidates. Fixing the mechanics of voting and voter registration would be meaningless if we still have no real choice at the polls or if we get to the point that no one is willing to run because we have made it impossible or unappealing for alternative candidates to participate in the democratic process.

In this country, we are just beginning to understand the flaws of our electoral system. Attention is now placed on the mechanics of registering to vote or being able to vote or having every vote counted accurately by a machine of better-than-dubious programming or security. Some 800 laws allegedly designed to address these problems were passed in state legislatures just in the first two years following the Florida debacle of November 2000![11] There are perennial discussions of the undemocratic Electoral College; the extension of the franchise to others, such as the residents of DC, Guam, and Puerto Rico and ex-felons; and the relatively newer lines of advocacy regarding how alternative voting systems are more likely to reflect the will of the people.

But virtually none of the current attention is on the rights of third-party or independent candidates to compete on a level playing field with the major parties so that all voters have a chance to vote for whom they want. Every time a legislature, an agency, a court, a media outlet, or a corporation makes it tougher for candidates (even disfavored major-party candidates) to get on a ballot, to get public financing, to comply with the election laws, to get exposure, or to get into the public debate, we diminish our democracy.

If you have not lived as a minority, it is hard to appreciate fully the kinds of discrimination that minorities face. Similarly, the discrimination against political minorities is not recognized fully, and certainly third parties and independents have not yet been legally assigned anything like protected status. Indeed, since the "Red Scare," when the reigning groups feared a Communist takeover if just anyone were allowed to throw his or her hat into the political ring, this country—the courts, the legislatures, even public understanding—has moved in the opposite direction: we have made it much harder to be a political minority, with a half-century of the electoral, judicial, and legislative equivalents of *Dred Scott* and *Plessy v. Ferguson* serving to solidify second-class or "noncitizenship" as well as "separate but equal" for third parties and independents.

We now have quasi-institutionalized political discrimination against third parties and independents, which we euphemistically label "bipartisanship." To the 33 percent of the country that self-identifies as independent, and to those who belong to a party that is not one of the two major parties, the term *bipartisan* can sound like fingernails on a chalkboard. Bipartisanship is political apartheid to third parties and independents. Bipartisan means fair to a Republican and a Democrat. Bipartisan translates into manifestly unfair to those who have no intention of running in or voting for either major party. *Bipartisan* to third parties and independents is a term akin to *all white* if you are black and trying to buy housing in a neighborhood or facing a jury; it is a term akin to *all male* if you are a female trying to get a job, into a club, or on a sports team. In short: it is not a system "of your peers"; it has a "Do Not Enter" sign on the door; it is "separate and unequal"; and chances are that whatever is being described has been statistically, historically, and routinely stacked against you.

Commissions and boards that are set up supposedly to be fair to all parties are often tagged as bipartisan. For example, the Federal Election Commission is often referred to as bipartisan—three Democrats, three Republicans—though the law only requires that no more than three commissioners come from any one party. Yet no independent, Libertarian, Green, Socialist, Constitution, Natural Law, or Reform Party people sit on it. The Election Assistance Commission is also bipartisan. State and local electoral boards tend to be bipartisan. The Commission on Presidential Debates was established as bipartisan. These entities may not be codified as bipartisan—but that is all they are, all the time.

The political segregation and discrimination against political minorities has to stop. Nothing in our Constitution or founding dictated that we should be a country of only two parties.[12] The U.S. Constitution does not even mention political parties. Indeed, some of the framers viewed parties on the order of cabals. Under Article II of the Constitution, one can, theoretically, run for president if one is at least thirty-five and a natural-born citizen. But in practice there is nothing near a level playing field if one is not also very, very wealthy or among the sanctioned favorites of one of the two major parties. So why do most Americans today accept this two-party system as natural? Because their exposure to third parties is limited by the extensive barriers to entry for anyone outside the system.

The United States is unique among democracies. No other country regulates their parties and candidates the way we do.[13] No others treat third parties and independents the way we do. According to Paul S. Herrnson, director of the Center for American Politics and Citizenship at the University of Maryland: "The anti-minor-party bias of American elections stands in sharp contrast to elections in other countries.

Multimember proportional representation systems, used in most other democracies, virtually guarantee at least some legislative seats to any party . . . that wins a threshold of votes. Public funding provisions and government-subsidized broadcast time ensure that minor parties have a reasonable amount of campaign resources at their disposal. The media provide significant and respectful coverage to many minor parties and their candidates."[14]

And yet in the United States, most people grow up believing that the natural order of a well-functioning electoral system is only a two-party choice. The well-known French Sorbonne sociologist Maurice Duverger claimed that "the natural movement of societies tends toward the two party system" just because "throughout history all great factional conflicts have been dualist," citing the Guelphs and Ghibellines, the Catholics and the Protestants, the Bourgeois and the Socialists, and so on. He claims that "whenever public opinion is squarely faced with great fundamental problems it tends to crystallize round two opposed poles,"[15] as if we had only binary brains. (Or even pols who opposed each other.) I'm surprised he didn't cite Noah's Ark. Duverger is famous for his law correlating the two-party system with first-past-the-post or "winner-take-all" elections. It seemed to be his prism when he ordained two-party systems as "natural" in the 1950s.

Giovanni Sartori, a former dean of the Political Science Department at the University of Florence and now a professor emeritus at Columbia University in New York, famous for his multiparty classification system, debunked Duverger—by looking at the numbers. Decades ago, Sartori pared the list of two-party countries down to only three: New Zealand (which is now multiparty), Great Britain (which now has a third party), and the United States.[16] He articulated "the paradox of having the most celebrated type of party system [two-party system] running out of cases."[17]

With some minor, mainly small island, exceptions,[18] the United States is the only major country left standing practicing "two-partyism" at the federal and state levels, and it is on life support at that. As Theodore Lowi puts it: "One of the best-kept secrets in American politics is that the two-party system has long been brain dead—kept alive by support systems like state electoral laws that protect the established parties from rivals and by Federal subsidies and so-called campaign reform. The two-party system would collapse in an instant if the tubes were pulled and the IV's were cut."[19]

We are the only country with an Electoral College fetish in combination with a federal election system for president. For the last four decades, there has been a global trend away from winner-take-all systems to proportional representation in the 120 or so countries counted as electoral democracies.[20] But we in the United States live under a grand illusion that somehow our democracy is the model for the world. As democracy scholar Robert Dahl wrote in 2003, "Many Americans appear to believe that our constitution has been a model for the rest of the democratic world. Yet among the countries most comparable to the United States and where democratic institutions have long existed without breakdown, not one has adopted our American constitutional system. It would be fair to say that without a single exception they have all rejected it."[21]

To get an empirical sense of how badly propped up American two-partyism really is, I bought a book published in 2004 by the University of Toronto Press on election laws in democracies, hoping it would tell me if we were, in fact, the last two-party country.[22] What did it say? Well, there has been a burst of democracies in the last few decades, and the book's authors wanted to compare the election rules of all of them. But guess what? The United States has so many rules, which are so varied, that they wouldn't fit into any of the book's charts. We are such an aberration that we can't even be counted in the scholarly studies because we have fifty-one different sets of rules!

I did learn about other countries from this book. Most of them (83 percent) vote for their presidents on a holiday. We vote on Tuesday because in 1845 that was when farmers went to town for Wednesday's market.[23] In most other countries the government takes responsibility for people registering to vote.[24] Not us. It's opt in here, with a vengeance. You, the citizen, have to figure it all out. None of the other countries require their minor-party presidential candidates to collect the volume of signatures that we do to get on the ballot. As Richard Winger, publisher of *Ballot Access News*, writes, England and Canada have within their respective countries the same ballot access rules for all parties.[25]

Other countries also manage to centralize and codify their rules and regulations. Daniel Lazare, in his book *The Velvet Coup*, uses India as an example. This country with "more than 600 million voters, sixteen major language groups, and a dozen-and-a-half major parties," manages to have one "all-powerful commission [that] sets the dates for elections, arranges for security at thousands of polling places, distributes the ballots, and then takes responsibility for gathering and counting them up."[26] We ought to send Jimmy Carter around the world like Marco Polo to collect useful election tips he could bring back here. Ironically, the Carter Commission would never agree to monitor our elections because we don't even meet the four minimum criteria of a democratic process that they would undertake to monitor! And yet we faced the 2008 elections with more of the same threats to our electoral legitimacy, under the widespread and mistaken popular notion that we are the Alamo of democracy.

Once people find out that I ran the Nader 2000 campaign, they often ask me if I am "sorry" that my first venture into electoral politics was to "help elect" George W. Bush. To the contrary, given how the two-party-imposed structural barriers have operated against third parties and independents in the last half century, I could not be more proud of our efforts to reveal and break down this exclusionary system and to help provide more voices and more choices to the American people. Third parties and independents are arguably the only remaining defenders of real political choice in the United States today. The fact that they continue to exist in a system so rigged against their participation, as this book will demonstrate, is nothing short of miraculous. Am I sorry? Oh yes—I am sorry that we have a broken and uncompetitive electoral system that traps Americans into poor choices and delivers worse government in almost every political cycle, failing for decades to fix, and sometimes even to discuss, intransigent problems like access to health care, poverty, immigration, global warming, fair trade, drug policies, a fossil fuel–dependent economy, racism, corporate crime, civil liberty violations, and many more.

That said, am I sorry that against all odds, with no money, no experience, a ragtag team, and an embryonic Green Party, we put an alternative choice in front of the American people? Hell no. I would do it all again. And did. In 2004, I helped run the only major antiwar candidate for the general election when the Democrats lost their collective nerve and let George W. Bush march the United States into Iraq. And I hope third parties and independents of every stripe will run again and again and again. It doesn't matter if I don't agree with a word of what they say. Just like exotic animals I would never make an effort to see, I want third parties and independents to run because I fear for their extinction. It reassures me to see them—like planet ecodiversity. I have never really gone out of my way to see a bird, though millions of Americans apparently do every year. But I wouldn't want just two bird species or brands of toothpaste or flowers, even if I always do order the red roses. And I don't want just two-party candidates on my ballot, even if I were never to vote for a third party or an independent such as John Anderson, Ross Perot, or Ralph Nader. I want all individuals to have a fair chance to run—for as long as it takes to get a better electoral system and better leadership for the American people.

Third parties and independents pollinate our political discourse; they offer alternative thinking on, and discussion of, major issues often ignored by the two parties. They instigate election reform and they offer broader choice, even if you don't choose to vote for them. As Steven J. Rosenstone and co-authors note in their book *Third Parties in America*, "The power of third parties lies in their capacity to affect the content and range of political discourse, and ultimately public policy, by raising issues and options that the two major parties have ignored. In so doing, they not only promote their cause but affect the very character of the two-party system."[27]

I show in this book how the two parties have developed barriers to political competition from third parties and independents to ensure the two parties' continued preeminence. I have personally seen this, from the application of byzantine ballot access laws to the federal financing system to the presidential debates. Scholars including A. James Reichley and Theodore J. Lowi have been saying this for years. Writing in *The Life of the Parties*, Reichley states, "It is no accident that no enduring new major party has emerged in American politics for more than 130 years."[28] And Lowi wrote in "Deregulate the Duopoly" in *The Nation*, "It is not Providence that takes an energetic social movement and crushes it as soon as it chooses to advance its goals through elections. It is the laws of the state here on earth that keep the party system on life support by preferring two parties above all others."[29]

Lowi goes on to list the single-member districts, the antifusion laws, the gerrymandering, and the "countless state laws that prescribe higher thresholds for the number of correct signatures required on third-party nominating petitions than for regulars on two-party ballots."[30] He notes that

> [e]ven the laws that apply equally to all parties are discriminatory, because they are written in such detail that ballot access for third-party

> candidates requires expensive legal assistance just to get through the morass of procedures. That mind-numbing detail is doubly discriminatory because the implementation of these laws thrusts tremendous discretion into the hands of the registrars, commissioners and election boards, all staffed by political careeristas of the two major parties, whose bipartisan presence is supposed to provide "neutrality with finality"—but it is common knowledge that they *can* agree with each other to manipulate the laws for the purpose of discouraging the candidacies of smaller and newer parties.[31]

This book demonstrates in concrete detail the accuracy of these Lowi conclusions.

Our zero-sum, winner-take-all voting system cements the institutional barriers against third parties, protects the incumbents, and at the end of the day, primarily protects the predominance of the two major parties. The Democrats and Republicans have been unresponsive to making our voting system resemble more enlightened, choice-maximizing systems because such a bold move would allow third parties to gain a foothold among voters and thus threaten two-party supremacy. Consequently, the current structural system continues to dictate how our elections are conducted, in which states the presidential candidates will campaign, which voters they cater to, and thus which issues are raised or solutions discussed to move our country forward.

Political economist Albert O. Hirschman in *Exit, Voice and Loyalty* has a theory about the behavior of oligopolists in the economic arena that author Alan Ware in *The Logic of Party Democracy* applies in the political context to party competition.[32] In short, when you get only two oligopolists, the lack of diversity leaves both competing over image and branding, as they both make lower-quality products. When our presidential contests devolve into discussing Hillary Clinton's or John Edwards's hairstyles, whether Barack Obama or Hillary Clinton is the more "likable," or how much money Sarah Palin spends on clothes and makeup, this is exactly what I think Hirschman and Ware are talking about.

As a result, we get the canned, polled, three-message-point speeches, and a Fourth Estate focused on the placement of stage props. We have a highly developed economic system that prides itself on competition (falsely and securely in the expectation of socialistic corporate welfare, handouts, and bailouts for the "too big to fail," *e.g.* banks), and a neo-Neanderthal, uncompetitive political system that has been dumbed down to squash any enlightened discourse. Voters are left to distinguish between two boxes of soap, each resting on a branding strategy to sell their political product even as they erect barricades against entry to the market for all other suppliers of political thought.

In the political as in the economic arena, the lack of competition produces inefficiencies, and these are most pronounced when the two market leaders collude to keep others out. How many more election cycles will it take until real progress is made on some of our more outstanding problems, such as access to health care or global warming? Why must we suffer through these inefficiencies of a political marketplace when no competitor is allowed to tell the reigning two-party front-runners that their policies have failed? What cost has it been to the American people, not to mention the Iraqis, that neither major party in the presidential debates or on prime-time news would stand up and oppose the Iraq war in the 2004 election, or that both major party candidates supported a massive government bailout in 2008?

Because the structural barriers against third parties and independents are numerous, this all adds up to a self-fulfilling prophecy: third-party candidates do poorly in large part because people think that they will.[33] Moreover, third-party scholars show how the barriers, the electoral outcomes, the lack of judicial rectification, the lack of knowledge of American history, and the media have all confirmed this "prevalent belief . . . that the two-party system is a sacred arrangement. . . . Third party candidates are seen as disrupters of the *American* two-party system."[34] Shut out from the bipartisan political cartel in our country, third parties and independents are labeled erroneously as "spoilers" of a fossilized, entrenched incumbency class—instead of as "defenders" of the right to freedom of electoral choice in the United States.

In *Third Parties in America*, Rosenstone, Behr, and Lazarus conclude: "A citizen can vote for a major party candidate with scarcely a moment's thought or energy. But to support a third party challenger, a voter must awaken from the political slumber in which he ordinarily lies, actively seek out information on a contest whose outcome he cannot affect, reject the socialization of his political system, ignore the ridicule and abuse of his friends and neighbors, and accept the fact that when the ballots are counted, his vote will never be in the winner's column. Such levels of energy are witnessed only rarely in American politics."[35]

I hope to demonstrate in a kind of gruesome detail typically absent from academic books how difficult the two major parties have made it for third parties and independents to compete in the electoral process, from ballot access barriers and biased deadlines to partisan election administration, elimination litigation, dense election regulations, and faux presidential "debates." Throughout this book, I explain the many hurdles third parties and independent candidates must overcome just to have a chance to offer their candidacies in our current electoral process, and I ask why we treat our third parties and independents this way when most of the rest of the civilized world has embraced multiparty democracy.

Two-party dominance was not always the standard in the United States. In the first half of our country's existence, we didn't let the government tell us who could be on the ballot, and we certainly didn't let two parties set the terms of existence for all their rivals. Up until the late 1880s, at about the same time we started eradicating cholera epidemics, the United States had no ballot access laws. Instead, political parties just printed their own ballots, hoping to get citizens to vote for their slate of candidates.

Throughout the nineteenth century, with no ballot regulations, all kinds of political parties flourished in the United States. We had the Equal Rights Party, the Anti-Masons, the Liberty Party, the Greenbacks and the Free Soil Party, the American (Know Nothing) Party, the Silver Party, the Readjusters, the Southern Rights Party, the Single Tax Party, the Peoples (Populist) Party, the Prohibition Party, the Farmers Alliance, the Socialist Labor Party, the Union Labor Party, and the Labor Reform Party. These parties (and those of the early twentieth century) were free to participate in our elections, unhindered by the obstacle course of modern-day ballot access laws. And they were able to put substantial public agendas with issues like the abolition of slavery, women's suffrage, the forty-hour workweek, child labor laws, social security, unemployment compensation, sick leave, the direct election of senators, and more, before the American voter, unimpeded by state-imposed ballot access lunacy.

Indeed, according to history professor Peter H. Argersinger, from 1878 to 1892 "minor parties held the balance of power at least once in every state but Vermont, and from the mid-1880s they held that power in a majority of states in nearly every election, culminating in 1892 when neither major party secured a majority of the electorate in nearly three-quarters of the states."[36] At the end of the nineteenth century, Americans elected twelve senators from minor parties (five Peoples

[Populist] Party, five Silver Republican, and two Silver) and filled nine seats in the U.S. House with minor-party representatives (five Populist, two Silver Republicans, one Independent Populist, and one Silver).[37] In 1911, at least thirty-three U.S. cities, including Milwaukee, Wisconsin, and Flint, Michigan, were led by Socialist administrations.[38] In the early part of the twentieth century, third parties routinely continued to win seats to office. Teddy Roosevelt's Bull Moose (Progressive) Party won nine seats in the House of Representatives.[39]

So how did we get to a point where we have completely eliminated a level playing ground for third-party and independent candidates? Once the state governments started printing the ballot to combat vote buying and overbearing political machines, the seeds for third-party and independent candidate disenfranchisement were planted. Along with the state's power to control access to the ballot came the power for the incumbents to control the terms of access for all others. Prior to 1889 there were no government-printed ballots in the United States, and until 1907, an independent presidential candidate could make a choice to run even after the two parties had chosen their respective nominees.[40] Two waves of restrictive ballot access periods then occurred in the first half century—after the third-party candidacy of Teddy Roosevelt and the first post–World War I "Red Scare," then during the second Red Scare of the 1940s and 1950s because of rampant fear of the rise of the Communist Party.[41]

Between 1912 and 1924, "ten states significantly increased" the number of petition signatures required for a candidate to get on the ballot, and prior to World War II states introduced filing fees and shortened filing deadlines.[42] Nineteen states barred Communists or any party advocating violence against or the overthrow of the government.[43] Add the natural incentive of the incumbents who made the rules over six more decades—the two-party-dominated state legislatures whose seats were at stake in a real political competition—and the restrictions started to pile up. Early ballot access laws ranging from 500 to 1,000 signature requirements gave way to more and more onerous requirements until 1968, by which time at least seven states had created massive burdens for those trying to offer a choice outside the two parties.[44]

Additionally, to further burden the process, deadlines by which candidates were expected to turn in those signatures were being moved earlier and earlier, thus whittling the field by forcing third parties and independents to declare candidacies *before* either of the two parties had settled on its nominee. By 1980, twelve states had deadlines for independent presidential candidates before July, two (Maryland and New Mexico) as early as March.[45] John Anderson, the 1980 independent candidate for president, helped reorient the lower courts for about two decades with his 1983 Supreme Court victory in *Anderson v. Celebrezze.* He challenged the state of Ohio's March deadline and got the Court to declare early deadlines unconstitutional, as they burdened the First Amendment rights of voters and candidates. But starting in 1993, ten states moved their deadlines to earlier than July.[46] Through 2001, lower courts struck down all the early deadlines. Yet it appears that after the third-party candidacy of Ralph Nader in 2000 (as with Teddy Roosevelt in 1912), courts once again permitted more restrictive independent presidential ballot access deadlines, allowing some states to keep early deadlines even though there has been no Supreme Court ruling on ballot access since the *Anderson* case to permit this outcome.[47]

The power best equipped to stop these myriad injustices is the judiciary. Whither the courts? Designed to act as an independent branch of the government and to uphold the First Amendment's protection against government regulation of core political speech, the courts have not lived up fully to their role. To the contrary, they have increasingly bought into the notion that *the two major parties need to be protected* from outside forces—namely those citizens of the United States outside the two parties who are also trying to exercise their First Amendment rights to speak, petition, and associate.[48]

As a result of the many lawsuits filed by George Wallace (1968—four lawsuits),[49] Eugene McCarthy (1976—22 lawsuits),[50] and John Anderson (1980—11 lawsuits),[51] ballot access law improved. But in the last decade, especially during the 2004 Nader campaign, the standards that emerged from some of these prior rulings were in part undermined by state and federal courts unwilling to balance the interests of the parties as set forth in *Anderson v. Celebrezze.* The Supreme Court is not only no longer the remedy for third parties and independent candidates seeking to enforce their rights; it has become, as discussed in Chapter 5, a supporter of the duopoly.

In the first part of this book, I describe the hurdles that exist now, at the start of the twenty-first century, after decades during which both major parties took full advantage of their dominance of state legislatures to craft and control the election process. I expose the gauntlet of obstacles a third-party or independent candidate must run, including entering awkward political alliances with other minor parties to gain ballot access, bringing affirmative litigation to protect basic rights, and fending off endless frivolous lawsuits from whichever major party feels threatened by the existence of a third-party or independent candidacy. The second part of the book looks at the special impediments faced by third parties and independents in the regulatory process, the media, and the presidential debates, as well as the overall incompetent, partisan administration of our elections.

Ultimately, I ask in this book why we continue to have a federal electoral system of fifty-plus different sets of rules. We have antitrust laws to prevent market power concentration in the economic arena but not in the political one. As long as control of the ballot remains in the hands of two-party-dominated state legislatures with no incentive to change the system, and as long as the federal regulations are made only by two parties, with a Supreme Court favoring "two-party stability" as opposed to open competition, the only electorally viable candidates outside those two parties will be the superrich, able to buy their way around the barriers of ballot access restrictions and nonexistent media coverage. I doubt, though, that even the superrich could completely overcome the kind of unprecedented effort to remove their candidacy from the ballot faced by Ralph Nader and Peter Miguel Camejo in the 2004 campaign. And as Ross Perot found in 1996, even the superrich can't pay their way into the debates or buy themselves nonpartisan election administrators, much less an electoral vote.

A number of scholarly books have been written on third parties and on our exclusionary, uncompetitive, and broken electoral system. I try to integrate these topics by arguing that if we want democracy in practice, not just in theory, then we need to federalize key components of our federal elections both to remove the discrimination against third parties and independents and to eliminate some of the current dysfunction and discrimination that occurs from state to state that do not serve any of the voters—be they two-party, third-party, or independent.

This book is in some ways a cri de coeur, in the hope that, as Ralph Waldo Emerson said, "sometimes a scream is better than a thesis."[52] I have tried to provide both and, in so doing, to add to the many other voices that have written and preached about the need for election reform in the United States. Our electoral system is broken: its inadequacies are manifest in election jurisdictions throughout the country, on the front pages of newspapers, and in the eyes of the world.

Because I have read history, I have hope that we as a country can fix these problems. It was less than forty-five years ago that people would be beaten unconscious for standing up for the right to vote, at a time when some states made African Americans count jelly beans in a jar, take literacy tests, and pay poll taxes to vote. I am hoping that it doesn't take us another forty-five years to let Americans vote for third-party and independent candidates, even if they are not "sitting in" at lunch counters and marching on Montgomery but are simply refusing to be gagged, or told to "drop out" or "don't run."

We need to come to terms with the fact that our democratic machinery, protocols, and election law framework are deeply flawed and discriminatory. But not only that. We deserve a functional electoral system, with real choices for the American voter. We have to remove the discrimination against political competition—what Ralph Nader calls "the last frontier of political bigotry": the discrimination against third parties and independent candidacies.

Our national conversation must occur now, because, to borrow a line from a favorite Leonard Cohen song, "Democracy is coming . . . to the USA." The making of this pro-democracy movement now exists: from conscientious election officials who know well the state of the rot to nonprofit organizations filled with dedicated public advocates to the citizen blogosphere of reformers and chroniclers, Americans are getting informed and organized about the systemic disarray of their electoral system and its outdated, undemocratic methods.[53] Third parties and independent candidacies continue to forge ahead despite the odds, hoping that this country will once again permit them to flourish.

It may take a long time. But as my talented friend Sam Smith reminds us, of the 300 women who went to Seneca Falls, only one signer of that historic declaration lived to cast a vote.[54] And in that spirit I offer this book, because I believe that one day in the United States we may all eventually vote and have our votes counted, accurately, for the candidates of our choice in an America that continues, however imperfectly, to strive to live up to its democratic ideals.

PART 1

THE FANTASY OF FAIR PLAY

Chapter 1

Ballot Access Laws Since the Time of Cholera

> The two major parties are in the business of winning elections rather than promoting democracy, and elections can be won by disenfranchising opponents, making it procedurally difficult for them to vote or not counting their votes at all.
>
> —Alexander Keyssar, "Reform and an Evolving Electorate"[1]

"Are You Registered to Vote?"

In August 2004, on the steamy streets of Washington, DC, I found out firsthand that asking whether someone is registered to vote may be one of the more complicated questions in the United States. Registration to vote in a U.S. federal election is not a federal requirement. We let the states dictate the terms of registration. Thus you don't have to be registered to vote in North Dakota, the only state with no registration requirements,[2] but in all the other states you do, by state-imposed criteria. In most states, including North Dakota, you must be a resident at least thirty days before the election. As of 2007, seven states would let the voter register on the same day as the election. Some states limit eligibility because of criminal status. All states now require you to be at least eighteen and a U.S. citizen, though this was not always the case.[3]

In Canada, citizens are automatically registered to vote in a National Register, continuously updated by the federal government, but citizens may opt out and are protected by privacy laws. In the United States, however, all of our voters have to "opt in." We have opt-out policies in the commercial sector for phone solicitations (the Do Not Call List) and privacy violations, but opt-in policies in the public sector for the civic act of voting.

As one of the few DC residents on the Nader campaign in 2004, and with just a few days to go before the DC deadline to collect valid signatures to put Ralph Nader and Peter Miguel Camejo on the ballot, I decided to help out in the sweltering heat to get a taste of what the valiant circulators were experiencing in trying to collect signatures for the Nader campaign.

I was asking this question—"Are you registered to vote?"—because if you run for president as a third-party or independent candidate (a candidate who is running as the nominee of several minor parties or no party at all), you are forced to comply with an unimaginably arcane set of rules that are different in each of the fifty states, the District of Columbia, the Commonwealth of Puerto Rico, and the three territories.[4] The two-party-controlled state legislatures pass laws and the election administrators—usually through a board of elections or a secretary of state's office—apply the laws and establish the regulations that determine how a candidate gets to be on the ballot. The Supreme Court has said that this process cannot be "overly burdensome" and that the regulations, if they are severe, have to be "narrowly tailored" to meet state interests because these state rules butt up against a candidate's competing First Amendment constitutional rights to petition, to speak, and to participate in free association.

Our goal in DC was to collect 5,000 signatures to meet a 3,600 signatures state requirement. If DC were a battleground state, we would have aimed for between double or triple the signature requirements to inoculate against multiple efforts—by Democratic partisans or partisan officials—to strike Nader and Camejo from the ballot in the states where the vote could be close, as described in Chapter 4.

So when you need to collect 5,000 signatures of registered voters in the District of Columbia, or in any state, what do you do? Like a good scout, I first made sure I was wearing the appropriate outfit—comfortable shoes and clothing that made it less likely I would be taken for a nut or a mugger! Armed with clipboards, petitions, campaign buttons, and pens, I went to a metro exit, figuring that this would be a very highly trafficked place. Rookie mistake! Of course it is highly trafficked—but with people who live in Maryland or Virginia and thus are not registered to vote in DC, if they even know where or whether they are registered to vote.

For the 2004 election, approximately 142 million people, or 72 percent of the voting-age citizen population in the United States, were registered to vote, which was the highest since 1992 and up 12.5 million people since 2000.[5] So even assuming everyone you meet on the street lives in the state in which you are circulating (an unwise assumption in a place as cosmopolitan as DC), you are already starting with the significant disadvantage of having 28 percent of people not registered. On the order of 15 percent of the eligible voters, or more than 9 million Americans, also move from one state to another each year, and 40 million total move (the difference being those moving in state), making it difficult for both the voters and the state to keep track of voter eligibility in any particular local jurisdiction.[6] And if you were registered at one address and moved, you may no longer be registered to vote, even if you moved in the same jurisdiction. Modern-day mobility, coupled with the lack of ability by the states to maintain accurate voter registration databases, creates registration chaos. Finally, factor in the general lack of citizen interest in voting—only 64 percent of the citizen voting-age population turned out in the 2004 presidential election, which was higher than the 60 percent in 2000—and you will have some sense of the challenge third-party and independent candidates face just getting over the ballot hurdle. Even in 2004, billed as a "high-stakes" presidential election, "more than one in three eligible voters did not participate."[7] Now add the aversion of most people on the street to being confronted by anyone with a clipboard.

So on the hot August nights I was out collecting, I tried to find registered DC voters willing to sign our campaign's petition. The first thing I noticed is that as a society we have evolved from congregating on the street corners to discuss whether to take on King George III and subject ourselves to taxes to blogging on the Internet and reading "Politico." People are more likely to be in front of their computers posting a critique or making a YouTube video than plotting a Boston Tea Party. Indeed, a third of the people I encountered could not even be physically approached because they had on headphones or were talking on their cell phones.

Unlike candidates in Britain and most other countries, third-party and independent candidates in the United States have to spend substantial percentages of their time and resources petitioning their fellow Americans just to get on the ballot. And if you are not on the ballot, your candidacy does not exist. No ballot access, no votes.

Candidates for office are able to put their names on the general election ballot either by being the nominee of their party, if they are major-party candidates, or by having to collect signatures on a petition if they are third-party and independent candidates whose party does not have a ballot line. Sometimes third parties have ballot lines because they petitioned to obtain one or received enough votes under the laws of their states to retain an official party line on the ballot from one election to the next. If the third-party candidate does not obtain the threshold number of petition signatures or did not obtain the state-required minimum number of votes during the previous election to qualify, the third-party candidate has to start petitioning all over again, each subsequent election. Thus, even though the Libertarian Party has petitioned onto the ballot in virtually all of the states for most of the elections since it was formed in 1971, because its candidates only obtain the threshold for ballot retention set up by the two-party-dominated state legislatures, in about half of the states (twenty to twenty-five) the Libertarians have to start all over again each election cycle in the remaining states.

Third-party and independent candidates must often petition to be on the primary election ballot as well, if they are seeking the nomination of a minor party. Some states do not permit a person who has voted or will vote in a primary to also sign a third-party candidate's petition for the general election. (I didn't write these rules; I just had to learn all of them!)

When we started the Nader 2000 campaign, the Green Party had twelve ballot lines earned from having petitioned or run candidates in prior races that reached a requisite threshold that allowed the party to keep its line. Ultimately, thanks in large part to the petitioning work of the local Greens and the campaign's fieldworkers, Ralph Nader and Winona LaDuke, his 2000 running mate, made it onto the ballot in forty-three states and the District of Columbia. In 2004, the Greens started with twenty-two lines, in part because of the showing of popular local Green candidates and Nader's showing in the 2000 race, which allowed the Greens in some states to keep or gain more ballot lines.

In 2004, however, Nader had decided not to seek the Green nomination and their ballot lines. He chose to run as an independent. So on February 22, when he declared his candidacy on *Meet the Press*, the campaign had to start the ballot process from scratch. We had no ballot lines, and we were facing fifty-one deadlines—ranging from May 10 to September 16, 2004—in all the states, many of them with onerous conditions for collecting the requisite number of petition signatures to be able to have ballot access. In 2004, a third party or independent had approximately six and a half months to collect 634,727 valid signatures across the United States. That's almost 4,000 valid signatures a day. A campaign really has to collect almost double the number required to protect against spoilage—invalid signatures from incorrect voter information (the voter is not really registered to vote) or incorrect voter registration records (the state cannot tell whether or not the voter is registered)—to assure the campaign will net the required number of valid signatures.

If you are a campaign that is subject to a massive major-party attack and partisan administrators in control of the local election, as the Nader campaign was in 2004, you have to collect between double and triple the required number of signatures to inoculate against lawsuits and challenges, as I describe in detail in Chapter 4. So a third-party or independent campaign really has to collect 8,000 to 12,000 signatures a day. Now, if you have ever tried to circulate a greeting card in your office or among family members to get people to sign on time for a birthday, or if you have tried to get signatures for a block-party permit, you may have a ten-thousandth of an idea of how difficult it is to collect this many signatures across fifty states and the District of Columbia.

Accordingly, the Nader campaign divided the country into three segments and had three national field coordinators at the headquarters in DC responsible for each of three lists—what we called the first-, second-, and third-tier states, based on levels of difficulty. There were thirteen states in the hardest (most difficult to succeed in) Tier One; fourteen in Tier Two; and twenty-four in Tier Three. (In 2000, we divided them into extremely worrisome, very worrisome, and worrisome.) The first deadline was Texas, a first-tier state, which required in 2004 64,011 valid signatures to be collected—exclusively from voters who *did not* vote in the primary!—in the sixty days from March 10 to May 10.[8]

As we started the laborious process of trying to get signatures, I kept thinking that Ross Perot spent more than $18 million to get on the ballot in 50 states in 1992.[9] We knew we were not going to come close to having that kind of money. By March 2004 we had about $260,000, and most of that came from Ralph's February 22 *Meet the Press* announcement. At first we were lucky to be able to pay even one person per state in about half the really tough Tier One states to help coordinate a group of volunteers. Even most of our coordinators were volunteers.

Each of our three national field coordinators was in charge of a list of states that combined some top-tier and some lower-tier states. The first priority was to confirm each and every ballot access rule, procedure, curlicue, or unpublished policy with the state authorities. Michael Richardson, an activist and former paralegal I had worked with a decade ago in a ballot access lawsuit in Illinois, was brought on board to help with this process. He read the statutes in each state, attempting to confirm the often vague and conflicting laws to ensure that we began the petitioning process properly. (There is nothing worse than spending time and energy collecting signatures on a defective petition!) He called the head of elections in each state to confirm the current laws because many of these states have a procedure for ballot access or some other facet of third-party or independent participation that is known to be against the law as interpreted by the courts. As Richardson wrote in his publication *Voter Voice*, as of October 2005, there were at least six "Footnote States"—states in which the state legislatures did not amend their election codes even after a judicial declaration of unconstitutionality.[10]

After confirming the requirements, each state coordinator had to develop a valid petition, recruit qualified circulators to help circulate the petition, and collect the required number of signatures in each state from qualified signers. This is much, much more difficult than it sounds.

Let's start with the actual physical requirements of the petition. Some states have prescribed petition forms; other states leave minor-party candidates to their own devices to come up with something resembling what is "required" based on trial and error. Does the state provide an actual petition or a sample petition? Some states do; some don't. Some states will let the third-party or independent candidates photocopy forms to circulate. Others require that the candidates obtain an original form (sometimes rationed) from the state. California will take petitions on 8½ × 11-inch or 8½ × 14-inch paper or on a napkin, whereas Maine's petition is provided by the state and is 11 × 17 inches and on pink paper. We had to beg Hawaii in writing for additional petitions, as they would ration them, costing us crucial days and lost opportunities to collect signatures.

A campaign must also be aware of whether information needs to be filled out or presented in a certain way on the face of the petition. Disputes arise because of ambiguity. When the petition says "candidate address," for example, does that mean domicile, residence, mailing address, street address, or the address at which the candidate is registered to vote? Is the proper terminology for an independent on a petition in a given state *Independent* or *Unaffiliated* or *Disaffiliated* or *No Party*? Ohio requires each petition to bear a photocopy of the signature of the candidate.[11]

Often, details about how to craft or fill in the face of the petition are not specified, leaving the window open for challenges by political opponents or partisan administrators down the line. For, unlike a birthday card, a candidate's petition must conform with every minuscule requirement in each state in which it is being circulated. The District of Columbia printed a sixty-page guide titled "Elections 2004, District of Columbia Candidate Qualification and Ballot Access Guide." Woe to those who fail to do *exactly* as the guide instructs. The entire candidacy can be voided in a state for failing to meet any one of the requirements.

Then there is the question of whether the candidates must designate a party on the petition or whether candidates who are a member of a party may actually run as an independent. Though running as an independent with Ralph Nader, Peter Miguel Camejo was a member of the Green Party. In some states, that simply wasn't allowed, so the campaign either had to seek another party's state party line—for example, the Independent Party in Delaware[12]—or offer a "stand-in" vice-presidential candidate in that state, as we did in Oregon.[13]

In addition, there is the question of whether the vice-presidential candidate "must" appear or "may" appear on the face of the petition. And if the petition circulating starts before the presidential candidate names the vice-presidential candidate, or there is a nominating convention to select a vice-presidential candidate, then there may be a question of whether a stand-in vice president (VP) on the petition can be substituted later by the formally chosen vice-presidential candidate. Most states don't say anything about this issue in their laws; some states specifically prohibit this substitution and refuse to substitute other candidates. Jan Pierce, a retired Ohio union leader, had to be our vice president in Alabama because the Democratic secretary of state's office apparently overlooked the substitution papers and then refused to allow us to substitute Peter Camejo after he was selected to be Ralph's vice president in June, claiming it was then too late in October.[14] Some states allowed a substitution only after they were sued or threatened with suit. In 2000, Pat Buchanan had to get an administrative ruling from the state of Illinois to have his actual vice president, Ezola Foster, replace the VP named on his petition, Tom Piatak.[15] Some states, like Ohio, have internally inconsistent laws.[16]

There is also the question of electors. Voters do not vote directly for president, no matter what your ballot says. In *Bush v. Gore*, the U.S. Supreme Court made clear that voters vote, at the grace of their state legislatures, for electors, the people who actually get to cast their votes for the president via the Electoral College.[17] How many electors or alternate electors does a candidate have to line up? This varies from state to state. The Nader campaign had to find fifty-five people who would be electors in California, and each one of them had to go in person to a local governmental office to register to be an elector. Do the electors' names then have to appear on the petition? Well, in Illinois and Pennsylvania, yes. Thus each petition form in those states had to have all twenty or twenty-one electors, respectively, along with their addresses, on the petition sheet before it could be circulated.

Must electors be registered to vote in a certain area of the state? (Yes, in Nebraska, they must be from every congressional district;[18] and in New Hampshire and Virginia, the voters who sign must be from a particular part of the state.)[19] Must they also be registered as independent by a certain date in order for the candidate to run as independent? (Yes, in Pennsylvania and Maine.) Must they have lived in the state consecutively for a certain number of years? (Yes, at least two in Idaho;[20] seven in New Jersey.)[21] Take out your spreadsheet!

In Missouri, the state requires notarized elector declarations of candidacy; there we had to do a round-the-clock stakeout of an elector's home to get her to notarize the paper in time.[22] If an elector decides to sabotage a candidate's effort, as one did in Massachusetts to the Nader/Camejo campaign by refusing to fill out the paperwork after the petition had been in circulation, then you have to start the petition drive all over again. Lining up electors who fit the requirements in each state was such a grueling, time-consuming process that we actually had to compose an in-house "Treatise on the State of Nader Electors" to guide staffers on how to recruit eligible electors.

Then there are criteria for the person circulating the petition; the circulator also has to conform with specific laws. As of 2004, about 20 percent of the states, including states such as California, New Jersey, New York, Michigan, Missouri, Nebraska, Pennsylvania, and Washington, DC, had the requirement that the circulators of petitions also be registered voters. This is true even though the U.S. Supreme Court ruled in 1999 that this restraint on circulators is unconstitutional. Another handful of states require the circulator to be eligible to vote in the state, thus imposing a residency requirement (Missouri, Arizona, Idaho, Virginia, Wisconsin). This requirement has been invalidated in Wisconsin in *Frami v. Ponto* and is probably also unconstitutional. (We lost cases initiated in 2004 in Ohio and Arizona contesting this residency requirement, though we appealed Arizona and refiled in Ohio to make the challenge anew and in 2008 won unanimous decisions in both of these challenges in federal appellate courts.)[23] Some states don't allow ex-felons to circulate petitions, even if they are registered to vote and have served on juries, until the state says they are officially "rehabilitated," as we found out in Arizona, to the detriment of our petition drive there. In 2003, even though the state of Wisconsin lost the challenge to its residency requirement, the law requiring circulators to be residents was still on the books until 2005.[24]

West Virginia had a requirement that the petition contain language informing voters that signing the petition would prohibit them from voting in the primary.[25] This was struck down in *McClure v. Manchin* in December 2003 but was still on the books when we were preparing our petition in June 2004.[26] Now, why do states have blatantly unconstitutional laws on the books? Well, most of those in charge of administering the election laws or serving as counsel to election administrations know, and will even admit, that their laws are unconstitutional and out of compliance with reigning Supreme Court precedent, which is binding on their actions. What is their response? They have to wait until their legislatures fix their state's defective laws! The election administrators are powerless to do anything about this sorry state of affairs. They just dance around the discrepancies, hoping not to be sued, waiting term after term for the legislators—who have no incentive whatsoever to change the law—to overcome their inertia and provide a more level, legal playing field for third parties and independents.

Some fair-minded secretaries of state or heads of election administrations will acknowledge that their laws are out of date and patently unconstitutional. Some will beg candidates, as they did us, not to sue them, in exchange for their acknowledgment that our petitions were circulated with the correct language. Others will just exploit the situation and offer no interpretation, much less advice, to disfavored candidates of how best to avoid the nightmare.

For a long time, in some states such as Alaska, there was *no way* to run as an independent, a limitation that was undeniably unconstitutional.[27] Before June 2005, the only way independent presidential candidates could get on the ballot in Alaska was by starting a new party. The state legislators there must have thought they had the right to force political association, contrary to the First Amendment. Their election administrators, knowing their law was a First Amendment fiasco, required independents to become "a Limited Political Party under AS 15.30.025" solely for the purpose of selecting candidates for electors for the offices of president and vice president of the United States. In 1980, in Alaska, John Anderson had to create the artificial "Anderson Coalition Party"; and in 1992, Ross Perot, as an independent candidate, had to create the "No-Party Party." The 2004 Nader independent campaign went with the Populist Party. By June 2005, Alaska finally established the state's first set of procedures allowing an independent presidential candidate to get on the ballot.[28]

In some states the circulators have to swear that they live in a particular county and fill in their county in a circulator affidavit that is notarized on each petition.[29] California, prior to our intercession, was requiring that only people who live in a county could circulate petitions in that county.[30] The DC petition has an ominous warning on it before the affidavit of the person circulating the petition page: The circulators must swear that they are registered, qualified electors in DC, that they personally circulated the petition sheets, that they witnessed the signing of each signature thereon, and that they have determined from each signer that he or she is a duly registered voter in DC. This is followed by bold capital letters:

> **WARNING! READ THE ABOVE AFFIDAVIT AND MAKE SURE IT IS TRUE BEFORE YOU SIGN BELOW. IF YOU ARE CONVICTED OF MAKING A FALSE STATEMENT, YOU CAN BE FINED UP TO $1,000 AND/OR JAILED FOR UP TO ONE (1) YEAR (D.C. CODE SECTION 22-2514).**[31]

Talk about a disincentive to becoming a volunteer circulator! You basically have to trust that the signers know whether they are registered to vote. Most people don't walk around with a voter registration card in their pocket, and it might insult even those who do to ask them to flip it out to prove to the circulator that they are indeed registered. One of our circulators in Ohio, middle-aged state coordinator Julie Coyle, had all of the signatures she collected thrown out because her signature as a petitioner did not perfectly match the signature on her voter registration card—which she had signed at age eighteen!

Here is another grim truth: some people *think* they are registered to vote, or are ashamed that they are not, but will tell you that they are and sign your petition. Other people have moved since they last voted or registered to vote, which in some states means that they are no longer registered, often unbeknownst to them. Some people who were registered to vote sign the address of where they currently live, instead of where they are registered to vote, thinking it doesn't matter; but it does. Often, even when the candidate can prove the signature is from a legitimate voter registered elsewhere in the state, if a state claims it cannot find the registration of a voter or circulator, the voter, and/or all those signatures circulated by an improperly registered circulator, get struck.

Then of course there are the people who sign "Mickey Mouse" or "Donald Duck" or the name of your candidate; or the people who will walk off with your clipboard because they are hostile to your candidate; or the ones who will circle you with some thugs and pull out a shotgun, as one Nader petitioner encountered in West Virginia. Jason Kafoury, one of the national field directors in charge of some of the most difficult states, wrote in a post-campaign memo dated May 26, 2006, that petitioners "were sometimes physically assaulted (spit on, shoved, had their boards ripped out of their hands, had their petition sheets ripped up, etc.). In such a climate, we were forced to teach petitioners how to deescalate conflicts by walking away and focusing on the next potential signer. It had an element of civil rights non-violence trainings. The mental and physical abuse took a toll, especially on volunteers." I didn't face any weapons, but I did have a lot of angry people pointing their fingers in my face and looking for a physical encounter. I circulated just for a few hours, but some of our professional circulators and longtime road crew met with unbelievable abuse all through the campaign.

Moreover, petitioners had to worry about being arrested by police who didn't understand the law. Our petitioners were often issued citations and warnings and faced arguments from public officials and the police who believed public places were "private property." We sent people around with an actual copy of the Supreme Court's *PruneYard* decision on how it might be okay to exercise your First Amendment rights in "private" malls in your state (about five states) so that we could ask the police to read it before they threatened our people with arrest and forced them out of places where the Supreme Court has said the state may say it is permissible to circulate. Still, according to Kafoury, "many of our petitioners were afraid to confront the police and our more brave souls had to launch guerilla style operations of darting on and off [publicly funded places] without being caught."[32]

Even in a place as basic as a public sidewalk, our petitioners had "countless fights" with police, especially, to our surprise, in liberal places such as Austin, Texas. Petitioning is often erroneously mistaken for soliciting. Many localities have antisolicitation regulations to prevent everything from door-to-door sales to prostitution. But collecting signatures on a petition—a constitutional right of political speech and association—is apparently not in some local officials' ordinance or code books and thus not something for which their police get any proper training. The exercise of constitutional rights is sometimes mistakenly considered to be a local code misdemeanor.

Some of the more peculiar or arcane requirements we encountered in individual states include the following:

- Some states, like New York, Michigan, and Missouri, don't allow a citizen to sign a petition for more than one candidate for the same office.[33]
- Nebraska requires a signer's date of birth. Alaska, Virginia, and Hawaii ask for Social Security numbers, though all three state in fine print on the petitions that these are optional.[34]
- Ohio petition signatures must be written in from only one county on each petition, requiring circulators to carry around multiple county petitions.[35]
- Washington State requires advance publication of a notice in the newspaper that you will be petitioning.[36]
- West Virginia requires the circulators to go to a county clerk and get credentials, which must be displayed and not just carried in their pockets, a curlicue over which the Nader campaign faced a lawsuit.
- Nevada requires that each petition be notarized.[37]
- Pennsylvania still had mandatory candidate filing fees in 2000, with no waivers for indigents, even though the U.S. Supreme Court had held mandatory filing fees without indigent waivers illegal since the early 1970s![38]

- Nevada and Oregon require the candidates to submit the petition to the state for approval before petitioning begins.[39]
- New Hampshire and Rhode Island require candidates to submit declarations of intent to file a petition in the states, months before the actual deadline for the signature petitions. If the candidate misses the deadline for filing his or her statement of intent, the state can preclude the candidate from circulating petitions.[40]
- Nevada and Michigan will disqualify signatures on petitions if the signer signed the petition before the signer's voter registration card was actually received and/or processed by state officials.[41]

Assuming the petition, the circulator, and the signer are all correct, the circulating candidate still has to get the required number of signatures. Now this can be relatively manageable in some states. New Jersey requires a total of 800 valid signatures; Mississippi, 1,000; and Iowa, 1,500.[42] Minnesota and Wisconsin require 2,000.[43] These are reasonable state requirements, proportionate to the state's goal of requiring a candidate to show that they have some legitimate public support and merit ballot placement.

But in many states the number of required signatures is outrageously high, either on its face or in relation to the population of the state. In 2004, North Carolina required 2 percent of registered voters, or more than 100,532 signatures.[44] This was reduced by their legislature, finally, in 2006. California requires 1 percent of its registered voters during the last general election, which in 2004 was 153,035 valid signatures.[45] Texas requires an independent candidate to collect 64,076 valid signatures (1 percent of the last presidential vote) from registered voters who *did not vote* in the state primary—and all by May 10. (Worse, you can't start circulating until March 10!)[46] So one has sixty days for 64,000-plus *valid* signatures of people who didn't bother to vote in the primary.

Wyoming requires 2 percent of the votes in the last presidential election, or in 2004, 3,634 valid signatures.[47] This may seem like a low number, but the state capital of Cheyenne, the most populated place in the state, only has 53,011 people. Oklahoma has the worst per capita requirement in the country. It requires 3 percent of the votes cast in the last presidential election, or in 2004, 37,027.[48] Imagine trying to collect 37,000 valid signatures (or double that number for protection) in Oklahoma. Oklahoma has 2 million more cows than people. (And now

Oklahoma's attorney general, in an attempt to criminalize circulation, is prosecuting some veteran activists, even though they had consulted with state authorities, for bringing in out-of-state petitioners to get a statewide initiative on the ballot.)[49]

Finally, the turn-in or submission process has to conform with the state's deadline and intricate processes. Some states have requirements about which corner must be stapled or bound and which pages must be numbered or not, consecutively or not, by noon or by 4:30 or by midnight or on an unspecified, "rolling" basis, so that the local clerks have enough time to process them before their deadline for getting them from the local level to the state level. In states such as Massachusetts, Maine, and North Carolina, where circulators had to carry a separate petition for each town, city, or county, those petitions must be hand delivered, or mailed and received, in each and every town, city, or county where there are signatories to the petitions—thus necessitating, in some states like Massachusetts, delivery to one hundred or more turn-in locations. In North Carolina, all the petition signatures that have been validated by each county must then be picked up and redelivered by the campaign to the state capital a few weeks later.

To complicate matters further, in a Kafkaesque way, many of the election officials are afraid to say exactly what provisions of their state law mean; they do not want to be implicated in a legal battle—so they often claim that they do not know, that they cannot say, and that you cannot rely on anything they say. Alternatively, you may get different opinions, based on whom you ask, or encounter election officials who just don't know the law they are enforcing, even in some of the biggest states, as we found in 2004 in California.[50] Candidates in California can start circulating 193 days before the election and must turn in by 88 days before the election.[51] From April to early July, an elections analyst at the secretary of state's office was insisting to our coordinator that we couldn't have any circulators circulating outside the county in which they were registered to vote, until we pointed out the Supreme Court case declaring this type of restriction to be unconstitutional.

The director of the Bureau of Elections in New Mexico tried to rule out presidential write-ins on grammatical grounds, saying that the law permitting write-ins says "candidate," but the president and vice president run together and thus constitute "candidates," so write-ins do not qualify as the law is written. How's that for statutory construction? My rule throughout the 2004 campaign was that any campaign representative who conversed with anyone in any elections office should get them to confirm their discussions in writing and memorialize it immediately as high up the ladder of authority as possible because, as we were to find out and as you will in Chapter 4, relying on public officials to tell you what the state law is would not necessarily get you closer to ballot access.

Now, what goes into determining whether a signature is valid? Whether a citizen can vote and is properly listed to vote on state databases is controlled by the state—even for federal elections. Your right to vote is conditioned on the laws of the state where you live, on the quality of the voter registration databases in that state, and on how the state determines whether you are entitled to a provisional ballot, which is discussed in Chapter 9.

No Federal Database, No Federal Standards

A handful of states permit voters to register to vote up through the day of the election. In other states, if you have failed to fill in your form thirty days in advance of the election, forget it. If you are a current felon, you can vote only in Maine and Vermont. If you are an ex-felon, it depends on where you live. For example, in Alabama, you might be stripped of your right to vote for a crime of "moral turpitude," which, according to the *New York Times*, may or may not be a DUI (driving under the influence) felony. But no one in Alabama seems able to define this crime consistently.[52] If you are not guilty of vicious murders by reason of insanity, you may get to vote in Rhode Island. But if you can't regulate your own meds (even if you *can* research who should be president or governor), you may not get to vote in Missouri.[53] So if Alzheimer's runs in your family, you may want to check your state laws and pack your bags for a state that will allow you to vote. Seriously, eligibility to vote for federal office varies—beyond rationality or comprehension—from state to state.

If the states themselves can barely tell who is registered, imagine the situation for a candidate—who is at the mercy of the quality of those very same state or local databases to determine whether he or she can get on the ballot. It is nearly impossible, without spending untold amounts of human time and dollars, to crosscheck petitions with the state database—assuming there is one, assuming it is accurate, and assuming it is accessible.

Under the Help America Vote Act (HAVA) of 2002, Congress required every state to have a statewide voter registration database by January 2004. But because the enforcement body created in HAVA was not set up in a timely fashion, the federal government said that it was "okay" for the states not to be in compliance until January 2006. As a consequence, forty-one states and the District of Columbia got waivers from compliance in 2004.[54] Only fifteen states had statewide voter registration databases up and running in time for the November 2004 election.[55]

There is no federal government database of registered voters. In 2004, this information—approximately 142 million registered voters—was primarily recorded and maintained in databases in more than 13,000 local election jurisdictions in the United States.[56] In 2004, and even still in 2008, chaos and disarray reigned in many states for anyone trying to identify whether someone was actually registered to vote. Often our circulators had to travel to numerous counties or towns, some far less hospitable than others, some making their databases available only during certain hours or for purchase! Ohio's assistant general counsel personally told me on the phone, after the Democrats challenged our petitions, that Ohio had eighty-eight county databases, *none* of which matched the information in the state capital's database.[57] In 2008, the blogosphere here was abuzz with stories of people trying to confirm their registrations and then showing up to vote only to be told they were not registered.

Even after HAVA, there are still no federal standards on how to maintain these databases. (In the half year between June 2005 and January 2006, there were at least three General Accounting Office reports discussing how—if they desired to—state and local election officials could maintain accurate voter registration lists.)[58] The variations include those that can be purged and those that cannot; those that are outsourced to private companies (more than half) and those that are state built; those that integrate with other state databases, such as the Department of Motor Vehicles, and those that do not; and those that are immediately updated and those that have a time lag.[59]

In 2004, one jurisdiction the General Accounting Office visited reported that "*on a daily basis*" they were "30,000 to 40,000 applications behind" in data entry.[60] Indeed, 19 percent of the jurisdictions had trouble inputting voter registrations in time for Election Day, though they finally caught up after hiring lots of temporary workers to work nights and weekends.[61] What this time lag means for a petitioning candidate is that his or her petitions may be rejected for lack of sufficient registered voters, when thousands of voter registrations sit in a pile, waiting to be entered in a mad dash by hired temps just in time for Election Day but not in time for the much earlier deadline to determine whether a candidate can get on the ballot.[62]

To understand this rank incompetence, one has to comprehend how these databases work. If a county registrar goes to look up your petition signer "John Smith" and finds only John Q. Smith or Johnny Smith or John Smythe, that voter might not count on your candidate's petition as being validly registered, even if his address matches the database, because sometimes the state doesn't make that second inquiry into the address or another identifier. In 2006, and yet again in 2008, the Brennan Center for Justice at New York University School of Law reported in their nationwide survey of statewide databases the havoc that exists in keeping eligible voters off databases. According to the Center, "A 2004 trial run in New York City showed that up to 20% of eligible new applicants could have been rejected [if conditioned on matching among databases] solely because of data entry errors, and the Social Security Administration is now showing a 28.5% failed 'match' rate nationwide." That's right: 28.5 percent! In 2008, the Center concluded that "states regularly attempt to purge voter lists of ineligible voters or duplicate registration records, but the lists that states use as the basis for purging are often *riddled with errors*."[63]

In 2007, seven states used same-day voter registration, with a "leave-no-voter-behind" philosophy that obviates many of these problems. Republican and Democratic secretaries of state for Idaho and Maine, respectively, wrote a joint op-ed in the *New York Times*, urging same-day registration and citing their states along with Minnesota, Montana, New Hampshire, Wisconsin, and Wyoming as having a voter turnout average of 10 to 12 percent higher than states that require advance registration.[64] One reason may simply be that the odds of getting turned away because of database errors are smaller.

As of January 2006, the *extended* deadline for HAVA compliance, nineteen states *still* were not in compliance: for a while, the states appeared to have endless immunity on fumbling this most fundamental cornerstone of democracy. Finally, in 2006, the U.S. Department of Justice (DOJ) began to ask questions. States were at least required to provide a memo explaining their status, why they couldn't manage to come up with a statewide database on who was registered to vote, and how they planned to comply. The DOJ started to prosecute for failure to comply with HAVA, beginning with New York[65] and Alabama.[66] In the meantime, woe to the petition circulator and candidate faced with petition challenges because a major party wants to eliminate them from competition. HAVA provided the concept of the provisional ballot to cure the problem for voters when they go to the booth—but provided no similar recourse at the petition stage.[67] So what of all the wrongfully disqualified signers of candidates' petitions? They get their names struck, and candidates may get accused of fraud.

Now, assume a candidate surmounted all these daunting petitioning hurdles. In some states, just about anybody can challenge the candidate's ballot petition for any reason whatsoever. In Illinois, all an opponent has to do is fill out a form alleging that the petition doesn't conform with the rules, and, wham bam, the rival candidate is mired in a long, tedious process to prove that all of his or her signatures are valid in an excruciating administrative proceeding requiring multiple people to staff multiple computer terminal positions in which pages of challenges are examined all day long for multiple days. Alternatively, the campaign is in court, trying to prove signature validity. In Pennsylvania, the state has no administrative procedure to determine signature validity. Upon a Democratic Party challenge there, our campaign was forced to be in eleven courtrooms simultaneously, from early morning to late at night, including the weekends. We had to argue against well-heeled corporate law firm opponents disputing more than 51,000 signatures in front of frustrated state court judges, who were turned into *de facto* county clerk temps because no administrative process existed to sort through signatures.

If Martians landed and witnessed this byzantine process for putting candidates on the ballot, they would think that the United States is crazy. Who would believe that in the twenty-first century, in the most powerful country in the world, this is how political candidates have to prove some measure of modest support simply to get their candidacy on the ballot? In an Internet age, the idea that candidates' supporters have to stand on a corner accosting people, many of whom have no knowledge of their voter registration status, in a country where 13,000 local governmental units are bizarrely in charge of administering federal elections and where the states cannot manage to get their own databases in order, is, at best, arcane.

Let me reiterate: this is *not* the procedure for the Democrats and Republicans in most states. Democrat and Republican candidates usually qualify for placement on the ballot automatically, without having to go through this ridiculous rigmarole.[68] The way most states avoid subjecting their own major parties to their unfair laws is by passing laws that permit a party whose candidates received 2 or 3 or 5 percent of the vote in the last presidential or gubernatorial election to have their nominee of that party always qualify, without having to do much more beyond paying a filing fee or collecting a *de minimis* number of signatures. Sometimes an unfavored challenger within the two parties, such as Arizona senator John McCain in challenging George W. Bush in 2000, faces similar obstacles.[69] But most of the time, these rules are applied only against third parties and independents. This is the procedure concocted by the Democrats and Republicans in our two-party-dominated state legislatures around the country to haze third-party and independent candidates who dare to offer a candidacy to challenge the reigning duopoly.[70] The result of our discriminatory ballot access system is that few, if any, minor parties get on the ballot in every state nationwide, and if they do so regularly, like the Libertarians, they have to spend unconscionable resources (time, money, people, energy) just to overcome all these barriers.[71]

Even if any one state were not a particular obstacle to, or burden on, the exercise of a candidate's core First Amendment rights, the same cannot be said of the aggregate of these procedures. Not a day went by in either campaign, 2000 or 2004, in which we didn't have some ballot access nightmare procedure staring us in the face, a field director ready to pull out his or her hair in abject frustration, petitioners quitting over abusive tactics, or state officials in need of education on, or clarification of, their own law and procedures. For reasons I set forth in Chapter 5, I believe that this aggregate, fifty-state procedure for presidential ballot access nationwide is itself an undue burden that should be challenged and struck down as unconstitutional. As Richard Winger, the publisher of *Ballot Access News* and a one-person tour de force on the history of these insane procedures, says, "There is no other country in the world that has free elections that forces a candidate for chief executive to have to wrestle with 51 separate sets of laws."[72]

Chapter 2

To Third Party or Not?

> The principal shortcut that people use in deciding which candidates to vote for is, of course, the political party.
>
> —Louis Menand, "The Unpolitical Animal"[1]

Third-party myths revolve around two predominant themes—that the parties and their candidates are either "spoilers" or "kooks" who can't fit into the big homogenizing tents of the two parties. Neither is accurate, but since Florida 2000, the spoiler myth has become a national meme, despite all the facts.

In the closest U.S. presidential election since 1876, the Florida 2000 presidential ballot contained the following individuals with their respective parties and vote counts, in this order:

George W. Bush (Republican Party): 2,912,790

Patrick Buchanan (Reform Party): 17,484

Albert Gore (Democratic Party): 2,912,253

David McReynolds (Socialist Party): 622

Harry Browne (Libertarian Party): 16,415

Howard Phillips (Constitution Party): 1,371

Ralph Nader (Green Party): 97,488

Monica Moorehead (Workers World Party): 1,804

James Harris (Florida Socialist Workers Party): 562

John Hagelin (Natural Law Party): 2,281

A mere 537 votes separated George W. Bush from Al Gore Jr. *Every* third-party candidate who appeared on the ballot received more than those 537 votes. Only one candidate, though, was blamed for the outcome: Ralph Nader. Why did this scapegoating happen when there were at least a half dozen other more plausible arguments for why Gore lost the election?

Factors Affecting the 2000 Election Outcome

Gore Did Not Perform

Al Gore became the first major-party presidential candidate to lose his home state since 1972 when George McGovern lost South Dakota—and these two candidates were the only two in the last half century. Gore's failure to win his home state of Tennessee cost him the election, which—after Bush won Florida's 25 electoral votes—was decided 271 to 266. Had Gore won Tennessee's 11 electoral votes (or even the 6 electoral votes of Bill Clinton's Arkansas), he would not have needed Florida's electoral votes. Gore also failed to win the votes of more than 250,000 registered Democrats (12 percent!) in Florida who voted for Bush, not to mention the millions more registered Democrats across the country who also voted for Bush. More than ten times the number of registered Democrats who voted for Nader in Florida voted for Bush in Florida. Yet no one calls Bush a spoiler.

Gore's Failure to Challenge

Al Gore and the Democrats didn't win the legal strategy after the initial vote count in Florida, and that had nothing to do with Ralph Nader. A discussion among all of 2000's campaign managers at the Campaign Managers Forum at Harvard in February 2001 made it clear that the Republicans immediately did everything possible to hire or conflict out most of the top-notch election litigation firms in the state. This put the Democrats at a severe tactical disadvantage in a compressed time frame, which was manifested in their unprincipled strategies regarding which votes should or should not be counted.

It was Gore's position in the Florida Supreme Court that only four counties should be recounted; it was Bush's position that there should be no recount. Neither major party asked for *all* the state's votes to be counted! Ultimately, the Florida Supreme Court rejected both positions—Gore's, 4 to 3. Instead, the Florida Supreme Court ordered a limited statewide recount of undervotes. Neither of the two major parties stuck up for the principle to count all the votes. There is more irony to this, because in hindsight Gore's position of recounting just four counties would not have made him the victor under any scenario. Two newspapers—the *Miami Herald* and *USA Today*—reviewed the 64,248 "undercounted" ballots in the sixty-seven Florida counties whose recount was halted by the U.S. Supreme Court. According to the newspaper count of the undercounted votes, Bush's margin of victory would have increased—not decreased—had Gore's standard of vote counting been used in a full manual recount of the state. Instead of a 537-vote margin, Gore would have lost by 1,665 votes. Conversely, had the Republican's strict standard of vote counting been used, the papers concluded that Gore would have won by 3 votes and by much more had Palm Beach and Broward counties not thrown out hundreds of ballots that they deemed no different than many valid ballots.[2]

Only a full recount, including overvotes (when a voter casts a vote for more than one candidate per office), and under certain circumstances as done by a later consortium of eight newspapers, would have shown that Gore had won Florida. Gore's campaign manager Donna Brazile wrote about how her struggle to get her own team to count every vote and how raising the voting rights violations fell on deaf ears with Gore and inside the campaign's recount team. She knew, from calls on the ground, how people were being kept from voting with ridiculous excuses and Jim Crow–era tactics, but she lost the day on that one.[3] And Gore lost the count. Gore may have lost regardless of what he did, but as Jeffrey Toobin made clear in *Too Close to Call*, "Gore did not do nearly everything he could to secure his victory, so the nation can never know whether a more determined effort might have succeeded."[4]

Republican Vote Manipulation

What about First Brother Jeb Bush's control of all the state machinery for elections? What about Secretary of State Katherine Harris's shenanigans? The wrongfully "purged" databases, the voter intimidation, the dearth of voting machines, the inaccurate databases? There have been tomes written to lay the blame on all of these maneuvers. With the margin of difference so tiny, to determine how votes should be counted, not just whether undercounted or overcounted ballots were counted, was enough to dictate the outcome.[5] What about the *6 million votes lost* nationwide? (See Chapter 9.)

The Media, the Mayor of Miami, Ballot Design, the Weather, the Electoral College

There are an infinite number of variables in an election. If we are looking for reasons why Florida was "too close to call," we could blame the media, as *Wall Street Journal* columnist John Fund wrote in *Stealing Elections*, for airing erroneously that the polls were "closed" dozens of times before thousands of conservative voters in Florida's western Panhandle could go give Bush more votes to increase his margin of victory.[6] Or we could ask why the Democratic mayor of Miami's political posturing hurt the vote for Al Gore on the recount effort. Or we could ask why the Democrats allowed a ballot design so confusing that Palm Beach denizens wanting to vote for Gore were voting instead for Pat Buchanan.[7] If we just want to "assign blame," we could blame the weather. According to Princeton political scientists Christopher Achen and Larry Bartels, "2.8 million people voted against Al Gore in 2000 because their states were too dry or too wet. . . ." These two scientists think that weather patterns "cost Gore seven states, any one of which would have given him the election."[8] Finally, no one disputes that Gore nationally did win 543,816 more popular votes, of the votes counted, than Bush. If we had a direct vote for president and a true one-person, one-vote standard, instead of an anachronistic Electoral College, Al Gore would have been president.

Nader's Disputed Impact

Though the national myth has become that Ralph Nader, a third-party candidate, "spoiled" Gore's chances, the truth is that there is no one reason Al Gore lost, nor is it clear that Ralph didn't help him lose by *less* rather than more. CNN's exit poll showed Bush winning by *more*, had Nader not been in the race.[9] Solon Simmons, now an assistant professor of conflict analysis and sociology at George Mason University's Institute for Conflict Analysis and Resolution, posits that a share of Ralph's votes went to Gore at the last minute, thereby helping Gore to increase his totals and thus win in New Mexico and Wisconsin, and that "Gore would not have won either New Hampshire or Florida had Nader dropped out."[10] Robert Fellmeth, a professor at the University of San Diego Law School, concluded in a post-2000 election op-ed that "Democrats should thank Nader" for positioning Gore to the center and not allowing Bush to paint him as a left-winger. Indeed, Fellmeth contended that "if Democrats can be sure he [Nader] will poll below 10 percent, they should pay Nader to run [in 2004]," arguing that Nader gave Gore far more independent voters than he would have drawn otherwise.[11]

Finally, to tag any third party or independent as a spoiler is silly.[12] After reading this book, or understanding what a third party must go through to run, blaming any of these candidates for the margin of difference between the two major parties is like accusing a start-up in a garage of influencing whether Microsoft or Apple controls more market share.

The Other Myth

I should probably pause here to disclose that I am not, nor have I ever been, registered as a member of a third party. I have been registered as both a Democrat and (when young) a Republican, and I am currently registered as an independent, a member of no party. Clearly, I am on a political quest. So far, my general disposition has been "a pox on all your houses." I know there are millions of U.S. citizens, if not billions of citizens of most nation-states, who feel the same way, seeking some better way to make sense of politics in the twenty-first century and, in so doing, to make progress in our respective countries and the world.

Though I always thought I would want to serve in government some day, the closer I get to electoral politics—and having now had an opportunity at the presidential level to learn about how our current system really works—the more I want to run the other way. I consider this a healthy and sane instinct for psychological survival. However, I have not chosen to exit completely; instead, I have chosen to stand and fight for an often neglected and disadvantaged part of our political spectrum, totally outside the predominant two-party-favored electoral system. And I have written this book in the hope that our electoral system can be changed so that more candidates of various political leanings and with different ideas and platforms are considered in this process. I believe that voters should have more, not fewer, choices at the polls.

Most of my professional career has been spent as a public interest lawyer trying to open up government for citizens who want to participate, "fighting city hall," suing the federal government, and trying to stand up for the underdog. I am not a professional political operative of any stripe, and I am no expert on all third parties, nor do I speak officially for any of them.

With all these disclosures out of the way, if I were forced to generalize about the people I have met in third parties, I would describe most as downright earnest. As David Cobb notes in Micah Sifry's *Spoiling for a Fight: Third Party Politics in America*,[13] "To be in a third party you have to be intentionally outside the box—legally, culturally, historically, socially. . . . You have to be comfortable with that. And there are two types of people who are—visionaries and kooks."[14]

As a rule, the third-party people I know are much smarter than your average bear. They have to be. They have to justify themselves and their politics, over and over again, in a two-party system. The third-party or independent voters I have met are freethinkers. Many eschewed the hereditary inclination to vote as their parents did. They avoided all the grammar school indoctrination about two parties. They read history. They got over the fact that they were not going to vote for a winner or "be a winner" in most political cases. They are comfortable underdogs, not suffering from "most likely to succeed" baggage. Unfortunately, a good chunk of them have grown comfortable and have accepted their own marginalization, though I hope that stops and that they all continue to rail on in a great American tradition.

Having said all this, there are inevitably in any third party (and in the major parties, too) some who come across as marginalized in other ways. They might be viewed as a little "off" because of how they express themselves or dress or stutter or appear shy or breach some other unspoken rule of "polite society." The media is quick to pan third-party crowds of people who would never be confused for investment bankers or pinstripe-suited lawyers. They look like America—they look like the people I see every day riding into downtown Chicago on the Chicago Transit Authority and distinctly unlike the members of the U.S. House and Senate. At a third-party convention, the media tend to focus on the one person dressed as a sunflower and passing out seeds to foster the image of "nut cases." It is so easy to paint the third-party adherent with broad, condescending strokes, not bothering to understand the dedication it takes to lose, over and over again, so that you can build to win. Third-party and independent wins are few and far between, but they are there.

The framers of our government were, if anything, "antiparty." They used the words *cabal* and *faction* as condemnation.[15] Both George Washington and John Adams warned against the "spirit of party."[16] But by the early nineteenth century, as James L. Sundquist wrote in a 1988 issue of *Political Science Quarterly*, "a fledgling two-party system . . . was in operation, with two slates of candidates running nationally. The electoral college was hardly formed when it ceased to be the intended body of nonpartisan statesmen with complete discretion and independent judgment and became what it has since remained—a body of faceless partisans that merely registers the choice of the voters between or among national party candidates."[17] Even James Madison had succumbed to parties, despite his fixation on the dangers "the tyranny of the majority" posed to our democracy and the need to protect "one part of the society against the injustice of the other part."[18] This is as true today as it was in the eighteenth century.

Nonetheless, our current, deep indoctrination about being a "two-party system" causes many to think that third parties and independents are just spoilers. In 1980, when I was in high school, I remember volunteering to make calls for John Anderson to see if Illinoisans would vote for a "third party" or how they felt about "third parties." Illinoisans said yes! In the last few decades, Americans have consistently said yes, by a two-to-one majority, disfavoring "two-partyism." In July 1992, a Louis Harris survey poll "found less than one-third of the public expressing support for continuation of the present two-party system."[19] In October 1995, a *Washington Post–ABC News* poll found that "more than three out of every five respondents 'supported the formation of a third political party.'"[20] As of June 2007, according to a Zogby poll, 67 percent of Americans, two of every three, said they were dissatisfied with the "two-party system."[21] Historian Joel H. Silbey wrote in *The Parties Respond* that by the end of the twentieth century the parties "were routinely considered to be 'at best interlopers between the sovereign people and their elected officials and, at worst, rapacious enemies of honest and responsible government,' irrelevant to, or destructive of, our ability to solve the critical problems facing the nation."[22]

So how and why have we become a "two-party" system, one not only where two parties alone stand a chance of winning, as the term was originally coined to mean in Britain in 1911, but also where—with the current electoral system—the government actively squashes the other parties? And why is it an "extraordinary act" to vote for a third party, with most of them getting marginal vote tallies?

Because of "I win. You lose."

We have, in technical terms, a "single-member plurality system," a voting system where "the winner takes all." This means that a geographically defined district is represented by one elected official. This is how we elect members of Congress, for example. While most Americans take this system for granted as the only one a democracy adopts, in truth we are the *exception* rather than the rule among virtually all democracies in the world. Most other Western democracies have three or more major parties and either proportional representation, where candidates take seats in parliament in proportion to their vote; preferential voting systems (Ireland and Australia); or multiround election procedures (France).[23] Two of the most recent indictments of the winner-take-all system can be found in Steven Hill's excellent book *Fixing Elections: The Failure of America's Winner Take All Politics* and William Poundstone's *Gaming the Vote: Why Elections Aren't Fair (and What We Can Do About It)*.[24]

Hill, who is an expert on voting systems, notes that it's not the framers' fault—they were on the cutting edge for the eighteenth century. Systems "like cumulative voting, choice voting, limited voting, proportional representation, instant runoff voting, and the like had not yet been invented." "But today," Hill explains, "Winner Take All is horse and buggy technology."[25] And it is killing political choice. If you are sure to lose to the dominant political party in the area because you cannot, consistently, get 50.1 percent of the vote, there is no incentive to show up—either as candidate or voter—because if you don't get a majority in a two-party race, you lose. Everything. All the time. This is a strange voting system for a political country that has been fixated since inception on protecting the rights of minority interests (as in minority factions—not identity issues).

Winner-take-all is also why every ten years we now have a knockdown, drag-out fight called "redistricting." It's because your representatives are choosing you, whether or not you want to choose them. Some of these representatives essentially admit that they pay what amounts to "protection money" to make sure the political remappers preserve their seats.[26] All the court fighting about the legislative districts is key not just to how the Congress or your state legislature is made but also to how the spoils are divided in your state and your pull at the national level.

In *Fixing Elections*, Hill compiles the following sobering statistics about U.S. elections, which he attributes to a winner-take-all voting system:

- less than half, often only one-third, of eligible voters will participate in national elections;
- even fewer voters will participate in state and local elections;
- barely a third, often one-quarter, of all voters will cast a vote for a *winning* candidate;
- about three-quarters of U.S. House races regularly will be won by landslides (at least a 60 to 40 percent margin), and a full 90 percent of House races will be won by noncompetitive ten-point margins (at least 55 to 45 percent);
- state legislative races will be even less competitive than U.S. House races, with a whopping 40 percent of state legislative races typically *uncontested* by one of the two major parties;
- despite having primarily a two-party system, about 90 percent of voters will have only *one choice* of a candidate with any chance of winning their district seat;
- at least 95 percent of incumbents will be reelected on a regular basis.[27]

Why does the United States routinely rank in the bottom quartile of democracies in the world for voter participation, with about 90 *million* no-shows at election time? Perhaps because, among other things, people figure out from the above grim realities that their vote does not count, or that there is no *real* vote going on. What is the point of showing up when the same incumbent or party wins over and over again, or when there is only one candidate on the ballot, or where you know the election is going to be a rout—of twenty points or more? Even devoted Chicago Bears fans leave Soldier Field at that point. Whereas other representative democracies with modern voting systems have 75 to 95 percent participation, here we have to beg the people to vote, apparently mainly to keep up appearances. The same people get elected over and over unless they die or retire, and—the kicker—they design the system's rules so it stays that way! To entrench themselves. Is everyone satisfied with only two-party, or even one-party, "choices"?[28] People I talk to say they are disgusted and feel disenfranchised. And many polls bear them out.

As Lisa Jane Disch points out in *The Tyranny of the Two-Party System*, there is no inherent reason for the United States to be a two-party system.[29] Hill, Poundstone, and Lani Guinier have shown how to experiment with or change the voting system rules to make them more balanced between majority and minority political interests or to more accurately reflect voter desires. In 1994, when Guinier was nominated to head the civil rights division of the U.S. Justice Department, she was shamefully pilloried by the media and others for so much as suggesting that we look at the political impact of our current voting rules. As Guinier learned, it is nearly heretical to suggest that we can change the voting rules to make them more fair to racial and political minorities. Simply exploring this in your scholarship brings your American bona fides into question. But this is not a new idea. Guinier points out the Madisonian concern: "The problem of majority tyranny arises . . . when the self-interested majority does not need to worry about defectors. When the majority is fixed and permanent, there are no checks on its ability to be overbearing. A majority that does not worry about defectors is a majority with total power."[30]

Sounds like our two-major-party system to me. The parties maintain their power by enacting discriminating ballot access laws, by redistricting to protect their own seats, and by refusing to pass instant runoff voting (IRV), where voters rank their preferences, and the bottom choices are eliminated until a candidate with a majority emerges, or the even-less-known range voting (RV), where voters assign numerical scores to candidates, and the candidate with the highest average score wins.[31]

The Republicans and Democrats don't want a third party, because third parties or minority factions would require them to consult the country as a whole—other parties would "destabilize" the "majority" of the two-party system. A strong third party might introduce substantial unpredictability into what are now predictable outcomes in all but a few contested jurisdictions in the United States.

The rise of third parties was limited in the last century[32] and continues to be because the two dominant parties consistently and vehemently agree to keep third parties off the ballot, out of commissions, out of the debates, and off any platform that enables political defection from the major parties. Moreover, the bipartisan failure to alter voting methods ensures that third parties and independents will continue to have low vote counts, unable to hit percentages that would accrue attention, public financing, or respect. It is almost impossible to go from a start-up party to a majority winner in any state, for any partisan race,[33] as our winner-take-all system effectively requires of these parties and then stifles them when they cannot. Look at Ross Perot, who got 19 percent of the entire U.S. presidential vote in 1992. Under winner-take-all, he did not get a single electoral vote! Nor did John Anderson, who won nearly 6 million votes in 1980. Indeed, in only four U.S. presidential elections in the last one hundred years have third-party candidates ever won any electoral votes—and not exactly enough to write home about: 1912, Teddy Roosevelt (Progressive), 88; 1924, Robert La Follette (Progressive), 13; 1948, Strom Thurmond (States' Rights), 39; and 1968, George Wallace (American Independent Party), 46. A Libertarian Party candidate "received" one electoral vote in 1972, but no third party has *won one in the last 50 years.*[34]

Third parties are thus reduced to redefining success. They start to measure number of registrants signed and number of ballot lines procured. They strive for a percentage of votes that will allow them to be recognized as a "party" in between elections or to retain ballot access in the state for the next election. No matter how well they do, even if they hit double digits, if they do not do well enough to win federal financing or continuous ballot status, it is almost impossible to build momentum from one election cycle to the next.

To me, growing up during the Cold War with drills in class in case we were nuked by the Soviet Union, winner-take-all still feels like code for preventing a national takeover by Communists, Socialists, or other national bogeymen. Our historical development has encouraged this two partyism, as has the mainstream media and scholarship, tending to equate or lampoon multiparty existence as unstable and thus undesirable, lest we look like the French Fourth Republic or post-Mussolini Italy!

Back in 1950, *American Political Science Review* published a seminal report titled "Toward a More Responsible Two-Party System: A Report of the Committee on Political Parties."[35] This report was chaired by a professor who believed that "modern democracy is unthinkable save in terms of the parties."[36] To be sure, the report suggested a number of good reforms, and it criticized the two parties for not being "programmatically accountable," for essentially being too blurable. The report claimed that responsible parties would be those that "provide the electorate with a proper range of choice between alternatives of action."[37] It wanted the American electorate to be able to hold parties accountable for a national program based on voting records, noting, "When the parties lack the capacity to define their actions in terms of policies, they turn irresponsible because the electoral choice between the parties becomes devoid of meaning."[38]

The worry in the 1950s was that the failure of the two parties to develop truly alternative programs would frustrate the voter, and "the mounting ambiguities of national policy might also set in motion more extreme tendencies to the political left and the political right."[39] Given world events at the time, political scientists wanted to keep a stable America and thought the best way to do that was to make sure that the two parties presented a real choice, that they acted as opposition parties in a competitive system. Otherwise, a real programmatic choice would emerge from groups on the left and right of the two parties. On third parties the political scientists said: "The two-party system is so strongly rooted in the political traditions of this country and public preference for it is so well established that consideration of other possibilities seems entirely academic. . . . The inference is not that we consider third or minor parties undesirable or ineffectual within their limited orbit. Rather, we feel that the minor parties in the longer run have failed to leave a lasting imprint upon both the two-party system and the basic processes of American government."[40] That's it—a bunch of academics saying that to even talk about third parties was, well, "academic."

This report, which half a century later reads a bit more like a propaganda piece than a study, engendered much debate in academia. But even among its critics there was a "satisfaction with American politics" that stressed "stability as the primary virtue of a political system."[41] As political science professor Gerald Pomper wrote in 1971, "Basic consensus was presumed to be necessary for democratic government. In the United States, a nation of 'high civil-war potential' because of its multiplicity of classes, races, sections and interests, the achievement of consensus was particularly difficult. The great accomplishment of the American party system had been that it created agreement in the face of great diversity."[42]

But at what price? As professor and political scholar Paul S. Herrnson wrote twenty years later in 1992 about the effects of a political system designed to promote agreement at all cost:

> An overwhelming majority of Americans support the basic foundation of our current political, economic, and social order. Our nation's heterogeneous population, large middle class, and lack of a feudal legacy contribute to a consensual society that provides little foundation for the ideological or class-oriented divisions found in many other democracies. The outcomes of many elections depend on winning the support of voters who are located at the center of the ideological spectrum. Candidates and parties have strong incentives to become associated with middle-of-the road positions, valence issues, and favorable personal traits. They have few reasons to campaign on ideologically focused platforms, to take controversial positions on key issues, or to distance themselves from the political center. The pragmatic orientation of political candidates tends to drive the parties toward the center and to blur the distinction between them, rather than to encourage them to provide voters with what the APSA [American Political Science Association] committee referred to as a "proper range of choice."[43]

For the better part of the last century, we have all been steamrolled into a big consensus pot, harmonized into the middle, so we don't cause any revolutions. Stability *über alles.* The two parties end up fighting over sliver issues, trying to play up how likable they are, and forgetting their base whenever possible to move to the center. Our two-party politicians avoid getting too detailed about programmatic alternatives; with most people growing up to be hereditary voters—following their parents' predilections rather than choosing programmatic alternatives—should the major-party candidates take a firm electoral stance on an issue, it might actively cause voters to stop and think, rather than blindly voting their party ticket. According to A. James Reichley, "Party identification is still by far the best predictor of how voters will cast their ballots in most elections."[44]

In a December 2004 article in the *New Yorker* titled "Permanent Fatal Errors," Louis Menand wrote about the "I always order the cheeseburger" theory of voting—"partisans who choose the Republican or the Democrat no matter what. They have already picked the party, and they let the party pick the candidates. It's a reasonable and respectable labor-saving device."[45] And it is true that two-thirds of voters are hereditary voters in that they vote how their parents did, and as a consequence, they identify with one of the two major parties. But the tide may be turning. In July 2006, according to a Fox News Opinion Dynamics poll, "half of Americans think it is a good idea for a third political party to be formed to run candidates against Democrats and Republicans."[46] In a *New York Times/CBS News* nationwide poll conducted in October 2006, 58 percent of Americans would prefer "elections in which all the candidates ran without party labels."[47]

When we began the campaign in February 2004, Nader was determined to offer more choices than the two parties to the American people. Ralph's initial goal was to eschew parties and to try to get on as many ballots as possible as an independent. He would end up on seventeen as an independent in 2004, compared to five as an independent in 2000.[48] By May, however, when we saw how many states had policies still favoring minor parties over independents, we dropped the pure independent approach.[49] But rather than choose one third party to the exclusion of all others, Ralph decided to welcome other party support in a big-tent fashion while remaining independent. This was, of course, a dicey proposition. Third parties are primarily ideologically defined niches in the political spectrum, identified precisely because of their uniqueness and unwillingness to be homogenized into any other entity. But we felt these parties' ideological differences would be outweighed initially by the political discrimination they faced in common. Hence, we collaborated with Libertarians furious with Bush over the Iraq war and his anti–civil liberty behavior, as well as Socialists who believed in Ralph's candidacy as a means of forcing the Democrats to become a real opposition party. We also attracted independents who did not want to be affiliated with any party. We were, in short, a big-tent and ballot access hodgepodge.

In our courting of parties, Ralph did not want to step on the toes of other candidates who were their party's nominees or create chaos within other parties, as had happened to the Reform Party in the 2000 election cycle when John Hagelin and the Natural Law Party had battled Patrick Buchanan for the Reform nomination. Thus, we often toed a very careful line between inviting support and throwing Ralph's hat into the ring to be eligible to become a party's potential nominee. The same was true for ballot access: I made all state field coordinators sign a contract, with the last paragraph stating: "I also understand that as a state field coordinator I am a face of the campaign in my state. I will conduct myself ethically and appropriately at all times. I will not sabotage any other parties' efforts to get on the ballot or campaign in my state. I will be courteous to other third-party and Independent candidates which share our ballot access obstacles."

This was going to be the ethos of our campaign. Third parties and independents face enough problems just trying to get on the ballot to challenge the two-party system. Our campaign wanted to be allies for the third-party/independent cause; we didn't want anyone representing us to be hurting any other third-party efforts to get on the ballot.

On the other hand, we did want to compete for the support of third-party and independent voters who believed in at least parts of Ralph's platform. To ensure no blurring of ideology, we made clear that Ralph would always run on Ralph's platform, but to the extent it overlapped with other parties' platforms—antiwar; fair, nonsovereignty-reducing trade; corporate and government reform; political and economic justice; and citizen empowerment; in short, a fundamental shift in power to people—we were interested in obtaining endorsements and support. If this was acceptable to them—and as long as they knew that Ralph was not going to be any one party's exclusive nominee but the torchbearer for any who wanted to take on the system—then we wanted their support. This made for some unusual bedfellows.

Green Party

One party to which Nader owed some allegiance, and vice versa, was the Green Party. As Micah Sifry notes in his book *Spoiling for a Fight*, in 2000 the Nader campaign helped build 500 new local Green chapters and 900 college chapters, as well as bring in close to a million new voters. It was "the best showing of any progressive third-party presidential candidate since 1924."[50] The 2000 Nader campaign put the Greens on the U.S. historical map and caused the U.S. Green Party to be noticed globally.

But many people in 2004, I not among them, argued that Ralph should run as an independent, not a Green. Personally, Ralph was an independent, not a Green, and he split with the Greens on a number of matters. Pragmatically, the Greens, as they demonstrated at a DC convention during the prior summer of 2003, were a house divided. These divisions played out in print, on email lists, in public pronouncements, and in ways large and small and are for the reading in a book titled *Independent Politics: The Green Party Strategy Debate* edited by longtime New York Green and Nader supporter Howie Hawkins.[51] The Greens were not expected to resolve their divisions until their nominating convention, in June 2004, in Milwaukee, Wisconsin.

One part of the Green Party did not want to put forth any presidential candidate. They saw an unwinnable presidential race as a diversion of time and resources from local races, which they could win and had won. This argument comes up among many third parties: movement building should trump futile bids for the presidency. A second set of Greens, arguably the majority, wanted to run hard with Ralph because they saw him as capable of building the party—as he had in 2000 and thereafter—nationally. A third contingent wanted a "safe" or "smart states" approach to avoid a George W. Bush reelection. This faction wanted to campaign only in states that were solidly Democratic or Republican but not stand in the way of a Democratic Party victory in any battleground state where the election was actually in contention. They promised not to hurt the Democrats in closely divided states, in return for the Democrats promising not to hurt them elsewhere. This strategy was recognized by many as an apologia and death knell for the Greens' electoral power.[52]

Despite this internal party trifurcation, Ralph held out the possibility of collaboration with the Greens. He said that if they decided against a nominee, and if he decided to run, he would welcome their endorsement. He did not, however, want to get enmeshed in the internecine battles of personality fights and the strategic decisions of this growing party. The Greens had a mixed relationship with Ralph. Most of the grass roots supported him. Most of the leadership did not, because they could not manipulate him, despite their many efforts.[53] There were prominent exceptions in both camps.

In 2004, David Cobb, a public interest lawyer in Texas and the Greens' general counsel, sought to be the standard-bearer of the "smart states" strategy, which he believed would help "grow the party."[54] Cobb had done yeoman work for the Greens, spending time traveling the country to help build various state parties by helping them get in compliance with state and federal regulations. In doing so he earned the trust of some people in some of these states, who in turn rewarded him with their loyalty at the Green Party convention in Milwaukee.

In a preemptive move against Ralph's nomination, and in favor of Cobb's, some of the state parties sought to amend their internal bylaws to prevent the nomination of any candidate who was not a registered Green.[55] This faction believed it was fine to collaborate with Democrats at the Green Party's expense, but they were intent on banning independents from seeking Green Party nominations. Go figure! The decentralized setup of the party and the very weak national coordinating committee enabled states to determine on their own that they did not want to put the national party's nominee on the state ballot line, even after the national nominating convention. I had explored with some Green leaders—like Dean Myerson, who had worked with Nader 2000 but was avidly supporting Cobb's smart states approach—what would be the consequence of this state party "nonacquiesence" to national nomination procedures. Myerson said that a state that didn't put the national nominee on the ballot "could" be kicked out of the party. But that was a penalty without a remedy from the perspective of a national presidential campaign that would have had no other recourse to a ballot line.

I was a proponent of Ralph's seeking the Green nomination, then going "big tent" for all third parties; from my perspective, it would have been much more powerful than going big tent without the Greens, whom he had literally brought to the dance last time around after they had tugged him into electoral politics in 1996. Most important for the long run, I thought that beyond opening the political process to all and being the standard-bearer through the general election in November for getting out of Iraq, helping to build a capable, alternative U.S. party to the two major parties was a very, very good reason to run.

Ralph, however, read the publicly proclaimed tea leaves and heard from registered Greens—from Maine to Oregon—who thought it was a mistake to seek their party's nomination. Some longtime Green supporters wrote him letters or called, begging him *not* to seek their party's nomination. Ultimately, Ralph declined to seek the nomination but chose as his vice-presidential candidate the former California Green Party candidate for governor, Peter Miguel Camejo.

Camejo—a former member of the Venezuelan Olympic sailing team in 1960, a Socialist candidate for president of the United States in 1976, and an accomplished historian, social investor, and businessperson—

appealed to both the International Socialists and many Greens, along with many Californians, who viewed him as having acquitted himself formidably in the televised debates in the California gubernatorial race. After receiving 5.3 percent of the vote in his 2002 gubernatorial run and his strong showing in the recall race of Governor Gray Davis in 2003, with 2.8% in a field of 135 candidates, Camejo was one of the most prominent Greens in the party nationally.

Ralph chose Peter for many reasons: He was a tested candidate, he was rock solid on the issues, and he was a fierce advocate of opening up the political process. He would not flinch under the withering attack from the Democrats, because he had a comprehensive understanding of American history and the struggle of social and political movements. He had even written a book about third parties. Ralph also believed that Peter's nomination would help to win a Green endorsement at the convention. But it did not.

The Milwaukee Green convention rules were stacked against Ralph and Peter long before the convention; they had been primarily drafted by Cobb supporters and allowed for a disproportionate number of votes to go to itsy-bitsy delegations representing states whose entire membership was barely larger than their convention delegation. Cobb barely broke 12 percent in the Green primaries, when Ralph was not even on the ballot, and Peter received more than 72 percent of the primary vote and more than 75 percent of the California primary vote, where David Cobb also resided.[56]

The convention was held in a downtown Milwaukee hotel. We sent a team, myself included, to encourage the Greens either to leave the nomination open to state party decisions or to opt for Camejo's unity proposal—a joint endorsement of both Cobb and Nader tickets and then leave the decision open to the state parties. We did this because going into the convention we had been called by several state parties asking if Ralph would be on their ballot line, and we told them all—as a matter of principle—that we would not be contradicting the party's decision in Milwaukee.

During the Milwaukee convention, Ralph phoned in to a Friday night rally before the Saturday nomination. Despite last-minute entreaties by me and our media spokesperson Kevin Zeese, Ralph declined to appear in person and flew instead directly to the West Coast, where he had competing, previously scheduled engagements—such as the Oregon ballot access convention. I think that this decision cost him the Green nomination. A number of delegates, spurred by the Cobb campaign, kept asking, "Where's Ralph?" The question was meant to be a shortcut for bruised feelings, and that was translated into: "He doesn't care about us; therefore, we should not care about him." It was juvenile. I thought about how Woodrow Wilson did not even know—because he was not at the convention—until the forty-sixth ballot that he was the Democratic nominee![57] Cobb won the nomination in the second round of voting.

A statistical analysis done after the convention showed how, with a minority of support, Cobb and his supporters controlled the outcome of the convention in Milwaukee. Had a one-person, one-vote system (which is supported by the Green Party, along with the abolition of the Electoral College) been in place, according to the report, "Ralph Nader would have overwhelmingly carried the day and won the party's nomination."[58] Alas, that was not to be.

As a result, through the 2004 election and the convention in 2005, the Green Party was rife with internal divisions and disagreements on very basic issues. Though more Greens have won local office, and have won higher offices (state representatives), the number is still less than the Libertarians and less than the high-water mark in 2002. Cobb and Myerson's rationale for a smart or strategic states approach seemed to be a step backward for the Greens, making the Green Party irrelevant at the national level,[59] at least until they kicked into action to demand an Ohio recount after the 2004 election.

By the numbers, the party had twenty-three lines (twenty-two states plus DC) going into the 2004 election and ended up on twenty-eight state ballots but came out of the election with only fifteen. Green Party registration went up 43.3 percent in the election stretch run in 2000, while it went up only 5.4 percent during the same time period in 2004. This is inevitably due to the historic differences in the conditions of the elections, but it is also due in part to Cobb's play-it-safe campaign in which his own running mate, Pat LaMarche from Maine, was reported to have declared that if the election were close in her state, she would not necessarily vote for her own ticket.[60] She later claimed she had been misquoted.

Many questioned the prospects for the Greens. As of November 2005 and through 2008, there were just under 300,000 Greens registered nationwide and Richard Winger reported in late December 2008 that registration is now at 255,019.[61] The campus-based Greens with approximately 900 active chapters in 2000 had shrunk to about 20 active chapters in the formally organized Campus Greens of 2006, though there is now an informal attempt to rebuild them.[62] The national party, which was struggling for dollars, added back some ballot lines, while losing a few in key places like New York, Alaska, and Maryland. The Greens started 2008 with only nineteen lines, compared to the twenty-three they had to start in 2004 and managed to get on thirty-two ballots, four more than 2004, but fewer than the 2008 Libertarians (45), Constitution Party (37), and Nader ticket (46).

At their 2006 national meeting the Greens had changed course and voted for "an all-out" campaign for president in 2008, which they ran with Cynthia McKinney, a former Democratic member of the United States House of Representatives, and Rosa Clemente as vice president. In 2007, one prominent Green noted that if anyone argued for a safe states approach, they would be "laughed off the Green lists." There also has been a national resolution for political independence and a move toward a "one Green, one vote" ideal for their convention voting. This indicates a definite culture change within the party since the 2004 presidential election and may bode well for their future mission.

Reform Party

Several state chairpersons from the Reform Party started calling us early in 2004 to see whether Nader would be their nominee, because, as Nelson Foley of the Reform Party of Maine stated, they had 3,000 to 4,000 unsolicited emails over the course of the early part of the year asking that Ralph be the Reform Party candidate. Foley believed Ralph would get significant support from Reform Party members. Though there was common ground in their platform and Ralph's, not everything was compatible. We knew we would take the heat for some of the differences, such as our widely divergent views on hot-button immigration and abortion issues; but, on the other hand, there was a sizable overlap on core issues such as fair trade, campaign finance reform, and corporate reform.[63]

A survey of 1992 Perot voters who also voted in 2000 revealed that 14.4 percent of those surveyed who voted for Perot in 1992 voted for Nader in 2000. (Only 3.6 percent of those surveyed voted for John Hagelin or Pat Buchanan in 2000.)[64] Micah Sifry's claim in his book, now erroneously repeated by others, that the Nader 2000 campaign ignored Perot voters was incorrect:[65] Ralph did not seek the Reform nomination and the $12 million that came with it in deference to the already announced Reform Party candidate, but we paid close attention to Perot voters in 2000—with our Get Out the Vote (GOTV) calls and with our media buys, because we had statistically studied the substantial overlap in supporters.

In early March 2004, about a week after the campaign began, I heard from John Blare, the Reform Party's designated liaison to the Nader campaign, that the party was seeking to rebuild after the Buchanan-Hagelin chaos of the 2000 campaign, which had left many of their supporters battle scarred and the party badly in debt. There was no doubt that the Reform Party was a wounded party after 2000. They had started the 2000 campaign with thirty-three ballot lines in place after 1996.[66] Nearly 20 million people supported Perot in 1992, a number that shrank to a little over 8 million in 1996. But after the insider brawl of 2000, the Reform Party would start 2004 with just seven ballot lines. According to *Ballot Access News* they had a national registration of 63,729. They were, however, still the fourth-largest minor party in the United States of America. I was interested historically in their potential for resuscitation (they were the best third-party vote-getters in decades), and I was especially interested in two immediate campaign goals: the Michigan and Florida ballot lines.

Ralph told the Reform Party in mid-April 2004 that his campaign was about a broader fight than any one party—a collaborative effort on behalf of all third parties and independent candidates "who want a chance to have a chance" in our political process. Ralph said he would welcome their endorsement if they did not have a nominee. On May 10, Ralph spoke along with six others seeking the Reform Party's nomination/endorsement, to at least forty people on a conference call from all around the country. They had planned this telephonic call the prior year as a cost-effective way to choose a nominee, and the call went half the night and through much of the next two nights as well. Ted Weill, the front-runner, graciously bowed out in support of Ralph. In the wee hours of May 12, I accepted the nomination/endorsement on behalf of Ralph Nader and thanked the Reform Party. My understanding was that Ralph had an outright majority on the first vote but that the required supermajority was not gained until the third vote. The Reform Party was delighted that Ralph would be their standard-bearer.

I was relieved that the big-tent approach seemed to be working and that Florida was secure so early in the campaign. We may have lost Texas, as I describe in the next chapter, but there was no way this campaign was going to have an impact if we also lost Florida. The press started to accept that we were going to be on the ballot in the seven states with a Reform ballot line, and this was helpful since we weren't on the ballot anywhere at this point.

Within days after the nominating convention, I was told by John Blare that "Michigan could be a problem." What? It turns out that there were two groups claiming to be the Michigan Reform Party and that a gentleman named Matt Crehan was in charge of one of them. And then I got a fax on May 20 from a gentleman in South Carolina, identifying himself as "chairman of the Independence Party of South Carolina" and stating that he didn't view South Carolina as bound by the phone vote even though the Reform Party USA did. He was apparently aligned with Lenora Fulani's Independence movement, based in New York. My head was already starting to hurt! Third-party democracy is messy, to be sure. But as a counterpoint, I had the money-sucking vortex known as the Texas petition drive happening, and I was therefore not quite sure which way we wanted to be tortured on any given day about ballot access.

Immediately, I started calling regarding Michigan. Shawn O'Hara, the national Reform Party chairman from Hattiesburg, who proclaimed himself to be the best-known political activist in Mississippi, a licensed Southern Baptist minister, and the author of 3,600 songs and 1,112 books, 700 of which were in a series titled "Jesus One," "Jesus Two," and so on, called to let me know that maybe I should get a *man* to talk to the person claiming to be the Michigan chairman. Oh my.

Well, it was clear that the Reform Party of 2004 was not going to get the Nader/Camejo campaign the 20 million votes they got for Ross Perot, who also ran as an independent in 1992. But they wanted to rebuild, and we were going to engage in a mutual assistance program as part of our "one for all, all for one" fight for third parties against the two major parties.

Independence Party

I first heard of Lenora Fulani while clerking in the Southern District of New York in 1990. I knew relatively little about her politics but understood that the Independence Party line in New York, which she helped build, regularly filed lawsuits and was routinely courted by big-name politicians such as Democratic U.S. Senator Chuck Schumer and Republican Michael Bloomberg alike. Fulani is a player in New York. She had run in 1992 as the New Alliance Party candidate for president and qualified in forty states and received federal matching funds—taxpayer money given to threshold-qualifying candidates. She had also run in 1988, when she had become the first African American woman to appear on all fifty state ballots. These are not small accomplishments for any independent or third-party candidate, much less one with political baggage.

Fulani and her affiliation with Fred Newman, a psychotherapist, are controversial, in part because of Newman's practice and because of comments Fulani has made critical of Israeli government policies toward Palestinians and stood behind. The two have been the focus of a number of unflattering stories and are controversial even within the Independence Party, as various state leaders tried to disaffiliate them or from them, without much success in 2006.[67]

When the Committee to Choose an Independent President hosted a convention in New Hampshire in the dead cold of January 2004, Ralph went to give a speech there about the difficulty of being a third party or independent, which resulted in some columnists going off the deep end, claiming that we were in bed with the "Newmanites." The always interesting Christopher Hitchens was a chief offender (a title he may relish), writing a long rant in *Vanity Fair* claiming that the "Newman-Fulani cult more or less *is* the Nader campaign." He labeled them as "loonies," "crackpots," or "fascistic zombie-cult" members.[68] And we became transmogrified by association, because Ralph gave a talk about barriers to entry for third parties and independents!

I don't really know enough about the Independence Party or its feuds and history. Every party I have seen up close has a messy marriage at best, and it is hard to tell who threw the first stone unless you were there. But I do bristle at the idea that just because you show up to give a talk somewhere, you are complicit in anything that has ever been said by the host or another panelist.

That said, the few people I have had the occasion to talk with in the Independence Party have been eminently reasonable in their conversations with me, and they have a quarter of a million registrants in New York alone, which is more than most other third parties have nationwide.

As for Fulani, she immediately came out in support of Ralph, writing to the Honorable Elijah Cummings, chair of the Congressional Black Caucus in 2004, "I am supporting Ralph Nader's candidacy because I believe he is the best candidate, and not only because his political positions express our interests. The fact that he is running as an independent and that his candidacy galvanizes a progressive independent political movement that is an alternative to weak-kneed conscienceless Democrats, makes him the best hope for creating something of value for black people in this election."[69] (In 2008, though, Fulani went out of her way to criticize Ralph and became an Obama booster, while the Independence Party supported John McCain.) We were constantly vilified for having anything to do with them. Indeed, Peter Camejo, Ralph's running mate, refused to appear on their ballot line in New York in 2004. The big tent was getting messier.

Peace and Freedom Party

What do convicted felon and Native American activist Leonard Peltier's and the Maharishi Mahesh Yogi's followers have in common? Well, they both had ballot access in California in the 2004 presidential election. And we did not—even though they weren't really running, and we were. The Natural Law Party (NLP), which emphasized transcendental meditation and was for peace, had decided to get out of the national party business, but a few states still had lines left over from the NLP's vigilant fight to create those lines. Peltier was running in California on the Peace and Freedom Party line to keep his name in the papers for attention to his ongoing legal and public relations campaign, supported by people around the world, to vindicate himself through a new trial. And so I was on the phone with their representatives from May to August to see if either of them would charitably give their line to Ralph Nader and Peter Camejo, who actually were campaigning for office. This conversation continued right up until five minutes before the close of the Secretary of State's Office in California on August 26, 2004, the deadline for submitting party nominees for the general election.

To seek Peltier's ballot line, I spent hours and hours on the phone with his Boston lawyer, who was completely devoted to trying to get his client out of jail. Ralph had gone in person to the Peace and Freedom

Party convention in Los Angeles at the beginning of August 2004 to seek their ballot line. According to one person traveling with him, the Peace and Freedom Party's convention consisted of approximately thirteen people, five of whom were related. They heard Ralph out and asked him questions. They concluded that Ralph was popular in the United States, but Leonard was an "international figure." And they were going to stick with him—even though he was in Leavenworth doing two consecutive life terms for killing FBI agents in 1975, a charge he and others vigorously dispute.

Here we were with an American icon and Peter Miguel Camejo, who was barred as a candidate in his home state of California even though he won more than 75 percent of the votes in the Green primary in that state. Did any of this make sense? The last hope was the "peace and yoga crowd."

Natural Law Party

My first encounter with the Natural Law Party was, unfortunately, unpleasant. Some of its members had infiltrated the Green Party's convention in Seattle in April 2000, by paying a $10 per-person fee, and overtook the Green Party's vote to gain the Washington Green Party's nomination. I didn't like this hostile action against another third party, and I really didn't know who to blame at first—the Greens, for naively giving anyone who paid $10 to get into their convention the right to vote on the spot, or the NLP, for exploiting another third party's process. On the heels of the blue-green 1999 Seattle protest against the World Trade Organization, I had wanted to use Seattle as a major symbolic forum, and here was the NLP taking the nomination from Ralph just a month or so after he had announced. We didn't play this way.

In 2000, the NLP and John Hagelin, their Harvard-trained nuclear physicist presidential candidate, were going around the country understandably trying to be the alternative to Pat Buchanan and to gain the Reform Party nomination (and the $12,613,452 that came with it as a consequence of Perot's showing in 1996) as well as the NLP nomination. Hagelin was the foil to Buchanan that many in the Reform Party had wanted Ralph to be in 2000. Ralph had declined. Hagelin wanted Ralph to engage in third-party debates and was therefore annoyed when Ralph's general policy in 2000 was not to debate other third parties but to try to break into the "big-boy" debates and not be marginalized to third-party debates.

Both camps had some bruised feelings from 2000. But we did agree on the larger issues of discrimination against third parties. I had had several pleasant discussions on this subject with Kingsley Brooks, the NLP 2000 campaign manager, and there was our joint lawsuit against the Commission on Presidential Debates, discussed in Chapter 8. There were also major substantive areas of overlap between the Greens and the NLP. The Greens didn't emphasize transcendental meditation, but their platforms agreed on renewable energy production and conservation, on health care to prevent disease and promote health, and on sustainable agricultural practices that did not involve genetically engineered food.

The NLP was founded in April 1992 by a dozen meditators who had spent substantial resources on getting ballot access nationwide. In 1996 they had run 400 candidates on the ballots in forty-eight states, which was quite an accomplishment for a new party.[70] I didn't think they would want to just throw away the legacy of those ballot lines. Robert Roth, their press secretary, wrote a book in which he estimated that 75 percent of Brooks's time and the NLP's money was spent on gaining ballot access.[71] Knowing all the blood, sweat, and tears that go into getting on the ballot, it is unthinkable to leave them fallow.

I called Brooks twice in May 2004 and asked him about NLP ballot lines and what they were planning to do with them since they had dissolved the national electoral party to focus on peace and they were not running a presidential candidate. Brooks said that it was up to the various state parties to decide what to do with their lines and gave me the numbers of the co-chairs in California, Iris Adam and Judy Barath-Black. He also suggested calling John Hagelin, which I did immediately. Numerous conversations could not move the California co-chairs past their fear of reelecting Bush—in California. I said that there was no chance in hell that Bush was going to win California and that it wouldn't even be close.

Ralph sent Hagelin a note in mid-August, stating,

> The Nader/Camejo campaign is standing for the rights of all Third Parties and independent candidates to access ballot lines without levels of statutory obstructions unheard of in other western countries. We have tried and exhausted all other petitioning avenues to make the California

> ballot in a state which all pundits and pollsters give to John Kerry. The only remaining opportunity is the Natural Law Party. With your approval and the support of some members of the Party in California, there is a good chance that the remaining skeptics will change their mind and see many of our common objectives widely highlighted in that state.[72]

After days of trying to reach Hagelin, on the morning of the California deadline Hagelin sent a note suggesting that he had heard from Barath-Black and maybe there was room for agreement somewhere. All day I went back and forth on the phone. How wonderful, I thought, until the final minutes before the California deadline, when at the last moment they emailed to say it would not be possible after all.

Having spent dozens of hours talking with Adam and Barath-Black, no amount of meditation was going to help me at this point. In retrospect, it seemed to me to be cat-and-mouse third-party politics, but the Michigan NLP graciously nominated Ralph Nader and Matt Gonzalez in 2008. The NLP, whose main issue was peace, let its line go to waste rather than give it to the only major antiwar candidate, because it irrationally thought California would be "close." The Peace and Freedom Party did its thing with Peltier. The Greens got David Cobb, even though Peter Camejo had won the vast majority of the votes in the California Green primary. And we paid a petitioning firm that couldn't deliver the requisite 150,000-plus signatures. Ralph and Peter, who had spent days and days campaigning in California, and for the issues many Californians cared about, were not going to be on the ballot in 2004 in the largest state, no matter what we did. We couldn't beg, borrow, earn, or buy a ballot line in California. What kind of system is this? And the lack of that one state's line seriously jeopardized Ralph's mathematical viability in the Electoral College, which is a key component of making the case for being allowed into the presidential debates.

The Juggling Act

At the end of August 2004, I was near despair, a mood I almost never allow myself to visit. How could the most-recognized, highest-vote-getting, progressive third-party candidate in the last eighty years in America not get on the ballot in its largest state? The process was perverse. In no other civilized democracy would this happen. I kept thinking of François Duc de La Rochefoucauld's maxim about people too much taken up with little things usually become incapable of big ones. It was one thing to get the runaround from the Democrats, but it was quite another to have to suffer it from other third parties, who should know better. How could we be mired in this minutiae of ballot access nationwide and not be allowed to put forth an alternative platform, the big things we should have been able to focus on? This was not a problem primarily among third parties and independents. This was a systemic, state-created problem that resulted in legitimate third parties or independent candidates being denied a chance to run.

There were of course other parties seeking Ralph to be on their ballot. One of the most memorable was called the "Personal Choice Party of Utah." Its logo was a smiley face. When representatives contacted us, they needed to know by noon the next day whether Ralph would be their candidate in Utah. We said, "No." We were also being contacted by the communications director for the Being Human Party. They had a U.S. Senate candidate, but he was running under the Personal Choice Party because it was so flexible and had a ballot line.[73]

Finally, there were the stalwart Libertarians, the Constitution Party, the Socialist Workers Party, and the Socialist Party. At every turn, they were helpful and cordial. We sued together and glued together when necessary to overcome our common barriers. No matter where you go on the third-party political spectrum, you will find upstanding people who want to make this country a better place, who care about the future, who are dedicated to ideals beyond themselves. Their adherents embody what is truly great about this country, no matter how different any one party, platform, or candidate may be.

Even so, for us as a campaign the big tent was starting to sound like a perfect storm for electoral disaster. As I had seen too clearly, even organized third parties with rules and requirements could be dysfunctional. Sometimes I would just howl in peals of laughter, often to avoid crying. I wondered if Karl Rove or Donna Brazile or Mary Beth Cahill had the kinds of issues in the two major parties that I faced almost every day. I thought about this again in mid-August when the Reform Party in Texas suggested we might want to stack the Reform Party convention with our supporters just to make sure that no one "overturned" the Nader nomination! Omigod. At the eleventh hour, the Reform Party was telling me it might not be a sure thing because anyone could do something wacky. As much as I believe third parties represent the possibility of political hope and America at its finest, I just wanted to curl up into a ball.

To keep everyone on the same page in 2004 and in the communications loop, I tried to recruit at least a few people from each party to help us and have key roles in certain states. Just as we had hired dozens of Greens in 2000 to promote the party and peace with the campaign, I wanted to make sure we had loyal party members inside the tent so that they would be on the weekly field calls and have a clear understanding of the nationwide scope of the campaign. Otherwise, some party people have a tendency to view everything through their state or local party lens, which is understandable but not compatible with a campaign that faces the complexity of fifty-one minicampaigns in every state across the country, with competing interests and limited resources. Moreover, I had become familiar with the key Greens and their procedures, but I knew virtually nothing about these other parties and how they operated: each one provided the potential benefits of experienced third-party workers and thinkers; but each also was a potential land mine of personalities, procedures, and old grudges, as I was to find out imminently.

Third-party development is extremely hard. It is usually two steps forward, one-and-a-half backward, as the parties lose ballot access and constantly lose competent, dedicated people who get burned out from the intense process of trying to maintain a third party in the face of the systemic adversity described in this book and with few spoils or even highlights of victory. With little exposure or media attention for what they are trying to achieve, and with no resulting patronage jobs or West Wing offices to hand out, there is little to galvanize third parties—except, of course, the failure of the two major parties and the third-party adherents' intense belief in offering alternative political choices to the American voter.

In some states, independents account for a significant percentage of the electorate. In New Hampshire, third parties and independents constitute more than 40 percent of the electorate. In addition to New Hampshire—the "Live Free or Die" state—Arizona, California, Nevada, New Mexico, Florida, and Maryland have all had fast growth in the shift away from major-party affiliation.[74]

But others take a contrary view: that the two parties have never been stronger! In a November 2006 op-ed in the *New York Times*, David W.

Rohde, a professor of political science at Duke, argued, "The 2006 election results confirm (with less ticket splitting and voting correlating to party identification) that the parties have been growing stronger, not weaker. The current political environment, in which two parties with sharply divergent views vie for power in closely contested elections seems likely to persist. As long as it does, powerful, centralized parties will dominate the landscape."[75] Unity08, a bipartisan effort designed to appeal to young voters, emerged in 2006 to elect a bipartisan ticket to the White House in 2008. They didn't have a platform or a slate, just a concept trying to celebrate the middle with an annoying clutch to "bipartisanship" and a possible candidate in Michael Bloomberg or Chuck Hagel. Ultimately, neither Bloomberg nor Hagel decided to throw his hat in with Unity08 or as an independent, and the party in early 2008 had to fold for lack of money after an unfavorable Federal Election Commission (FEC) decision that limited their contributions.[76]

In many ways, our experiment with being the unparty/multiparty independent candidacy left many bruised feelings and confusion. It looked unprincipled; it left many party loyalists within the Greens, Reform, and others furious that theirs was not the only party being advanced; and it had little ongoing effect after the race. Except for small efforts such as the Coalition for Free and Open Elections (COFOE), there is little sustained third-party and independent coalition building.

A party has to bring together people of similar opinion, seek to exercise power by running in elections, and use legitimate means to pursue more than a single-interest end.[77] Trying to bring together people of very different political platforms and opinions, who primarily share a common distaste for how the U.S. political system has been limited by the two-major-party rules, is a daunting challenge that routinely faces a collective action problem—what's in it for any third party or independent trying to breach that divide? It is a lot of work. It is a thankless task. It is almost impossible. It is also one motivation for this book—to help identify the many barriers that stand in the way of any group of people outside the two parties who seek to contest elections and to influence power and decision making. The initial commonality—in breaking down those barriers so that later competition for public approval of a series of ideas can take place—needs to override the political programmatic and strategic differences if third parties and independents want to forge a political place in our electoral spectrum by winning the hearts and minds of American voters.

Chapter 3

Suffer or Sue: Searching for a Level Playing Field

On March 1, 2004, I turned forty. The campaign had been under way for just one week, but after several months of exploratory committee limbo, I was already mired in the campaign fog of too little sleep, too much Chinese food, and feeling as if something that had happened only yesterday had taken place three weeks ago. That day, the *Legal Times* ran a piece saying that the Democrats "are tapping thousands of volunteer lawyers in hotly contested states. . . . And some of these lawyers could be called upon if Democrats decide to challenge Nader's efforts to get on the ballot in key states. . . . 'People are very, very concerned about Nader because they expect the race to be very tight,' says a well-connected (and unidentified) Democratic lawyer in Washington, D.C.'"[1] Similar reports were coming in from the field, but nothing prepared me for the lawsuit hell ahead.

Ironically, it was John Kerry himself who really warned us—in mid-May 2004 at the only face-to-face meeting between Kerry and Nader during the campaign. The news media was there for the entrance. The stakeout was so intense that I still remember driving and entering the building from some remote parking lot, feeling as though I were in some modern-day spy novella. We had agreed with the Kerry campaign not to do a joint press appearance so the television B-roll all night would be a picture of us walking into the Kerry offices with Nader and Kerry shaking hands.

After the meeting, Ralph told a *New York Times* reporter that Kerry was "very presidential," which I thought was a kind comment about an electoral opponent. Kerry, for his part also classy, said that he would try to appeal to Nader voters but never said Ralph should "drop out." These two have been in Washington, DC a long time. Ralph has more of a record to show for it. But Kerry looked like he had been running for president his whole life—and thus by many accounts was considered by the power structure "electable," regardless of what the Democratic blogosphere wanted.

Six people were in the conference room at Kerry's headquarters: Nader and Kerry; Kevin Zeese, our campaign spokesperson; Mary Beth Cahill, Kerry's campaign manager; Steve Elmendorf, a Dick Gephardt former aide then with Kerry; and me. We came with an agenda, as did they, though ours was written. I was the only one taking notes. I wanted to remember this.

Kerry stressed how much better a president he would be than Bush, with the underlying assumption that nearly everyone takes for granted—that presidential politics is a zero-sum situation between the two major parties. Ralph focused on the fact that he was opening a second front against Bush, saying things Kerry might not say, putting issues—like getting out of the Iraq war—on the table. Ralph suggested that the two of them should emphasize common ground, maybe even do a joint press release on corporate crime, raising the living wage, and health care for all. Ralph was also focused on setting a time to withdraw from Iraq, the topic on which the meeting began but from which Kerry redirected the conversation.

The Kerry people later denied to the press that the war ever came up. They wanted to avoid Iraq at all costs. Kerry had voted for the war, and his position throughout the 2004 campaign was that he was going to out-Fallujah Bush and "hunt down and kill the terrorists." Kerry would be "reporting for duty" the whole campaign, so he didn't want any ink on discussing troop withdrawal with the major candidate for peace. Outside of Representative Dennis Kucinich and former Vermont Governor Howard Dean, the Democratic Party was doing a "see no evil, hear no evil" on the war.

A Kerry supporter who knew Ralph well called me the next day, urging me not to make an issue out of whether there was an Iraq discussion and saying that he was proud of Ralph for calling Kerry "presidential." I told him that I was not making an issue out of it; the press was making it an issue on their own. But how would we not raise the number-one issue of the day—the fact that we were in a war we should not have been in—with the next possible president? Iraq was, after all, one of our campaign's main issues, and it was at the top of our agenda.

For most of the meeting, beneath all his politesse and good-natured engagement, Kerry was essentially saying "drop out" between the lines. He implied that he would use all means at his disposal, and said he would do "everything within the law" to win. And then Kerry said he had 2,000 lawyers lined up to help him, all around the country. Ralph took this to mean that the Democrats were not going to repeat their legal mistakes of Florida 2000. I took this to mean that they were going to try to squash us like a bug to keep us off the ballot. Both interpretations turned out to be accurate. But mine was the more imminent.

In 2004 third-party and independent candidates for federal or state offices were involved in at least fifty-one lawsuits to get on the ballot in a record number of states.[2] Thirty-nine of these cases involved our campaign; twenty-five were brought against us or our interests by the Democrats or parties in interest aligned with them in eighteen states, including one instigated by the Democratic secretary of state in West Virginia. As a result of our experiences during 2004, our campaign filed fourteen challenges proactively (during the elections and after) in an effort to assert our rights to be candidates in the political process and to ensure better access for third-party or independent candidates. Ralph filed three lawsuits and one FEC complaint after the election to address the harassment of his candidacy.[3]

From May 10, 2004 until 2009 as I finish writing this book, we faced a level of litigation not faced by any other candidate or party in the history of the United States of America.[4] The campaign to remove Ralph Nader from the ballot was a deliberate tactic of the Kerry campaign, the Democratic National Committee (DNC), and specific Democratic state parties, in coordination with the unreported and, in some cases, illegal actions of some Section 527 groups (political committees named after a section of the tax code regulating them). If you have ever been a litigant in even one lawsuit, you can only begin to imagine the amount of paper and number of depositions and hearings we endured.

Many of these lawsuits were prefaced by some sort of administrative hearing by the state, declaring the validity or invalidity of our signatures, and then proceeded through two or three more levels of state courts and sometimes federal courts. At the end of August, I found myself talking to lawyers about proceedings against us in five different states on the very same day. This was political death served up by lawyers with thousands of pages of motions. This was the Democratic Party's articulated idea: to keep our meager campaign resources tied up mentally, emotionally, and financially in courtroom after courtroom across the country.

On September 22, Chad Clinton, Kerry's spokesman, told the *Washington Post* about the lawsuits: "There are rules on the books that have been there for a long time, and we're just making sure that those rules are followed."[5] This was an interesting admission, since Kerry's official position privately on the phone was to keep denying to Ralph, over the summer and even after the campaign, that he was trying to get us off state ballots or that he knew anything about this assault. Ralph repeatedly called on Kerry, publicly and privately—to no avail—to call off the dogs, going as far as to warn him that this could be his "mini-Watergate."[6]

This chapter and the next briefly chronicle the intense effort we undertook to get on the state ballots, as well as the historically unprecedented effort made to keep us off the ballot. It reveals a concerted campaign to curtail the rights of citizens that in any context but the political would be deemed intolerable by a majority of Americans.

We began the campaign trying in earnest to get on the ballot in all fifty states and the District of Columbia. We knew that some of these were nearly impossible, as the requirements are ridiculously difficult: Georgia, Oklahoma, North Carolina, and Indiana were all in this unlikely category, but we recruited people in each state anyway to try to make it happen and to build interest in an independent campaign across the country. Ralph believes in showing up to campaign in all the states if you want to be president, not just the two-party major "battlegrounds" or the states that are going to be fund-raising spigots to finance the battleground states.

If more candidates went to all fifty states, all the commercials wouldn't be in Ohio, Florida, Iowa, and New Hampshire, and some other states might actually get a chance to see the candidates for something other than fund-raisers. Candidates don't visit because of the way the Electoral College and the winner-take-all voting system distort presidential politics and create "battleground" and "safe" states. As I discuss in Chapter 9, if you live in a safe state like Kansas (Republican) or Rhode Island (Democratic), you may never see a candidate or a TV commercial, whereas if you live in a battleground state such as Florida or Pennsylvania, you will be deluged with commercials and visits.

In the end, we managed to get Nader and Camejo on thirty-four state ballots and the District of Columbia ballot, with a combined potential Electoral College vote of 278, which put us above a mathematically viable 270 necessary to win the election. In seventeen of these states, Ralph was on as an Independent. In eighteen of the states, he was on with a party identification, such as "Reform." He was also on with monikers such as "the Better Life Party" or the "Populist Party," either because party terminology was required by state laws or because it was easier to obtain ballot status through a party, and one was created by supporters in those states. By Election Day 2004, we were on the ballot in states representing 50.15 percent of the population. (In 2008, Nader and Matt Gonzalez got on forty-six state ballots, representing 85.2 percent of the population.)

Nader and Camejo were also certified as write-ins in an additional twelve states with a total of 222 electoral votes, including some of the most populous states such as Arizona, California, Illinois, Massachusetts, Texas, Pennsylvania, Virginia, Missouri, Oregon, Indiana, Georgia, and North Carolina. We received no counted votes in four states—three (Hawaii, Oklahoma, and Oregon) just because those states refused to allow for, or to count, write-in votes unless the candidate could potentially be victorious. As discussed in Chapter 5, unbelievably, the U.S. Supreme Court says that this refusal to count write-in votes is constitutional! (Oregon counts only in the aggregate—by lumping all the candidates into one big write-in vote.)

No independent or third-party candidate in 2008 got on all the ballots. The last time someone running as an independent got on all the ballots was 1992, and his name was Ross Perot. The beneficiary of his predecessors'—John Anderson and Eugene McCarthy—legal efforts to open up the ballot, he didn't have to file a single lawsuit.[7] But he did have to spend $18 million to get on the state ballots, even with no major party trying to keep him off. And he had to spend $72.9 million (mostly his own) for all the rest of the campaign—buying name recognition, personnel, and ads. Remember the charts![8] By contrast, the whole Nader 2004 campaign cost about $5 million, plus incalculable sweat equity.

Once in a while during the 2004 campaign, I would think about my great-grandmother Rosa Zaccagnini. She died when she was ninety-six, but for the last few years, in her Italian dialect, she would say periodically throughout the day: "Oh Dio, mo'me mort"—which means, "Oh God, now I am going to die." This is about how I felt during 2004. Oh God, I am going to die, fifty years prematurely! And then I would think about my Nonna Lucia whose favorite phrase was: "We do the best we can." She would tell Rosa that the house was on fire in order to get her to get up and move from one room to the next. Of course, it wasn't. But over the years, this was the only thing that would get Rosa to shuffle from one room to another. Sometimes I resorted to similar tactics in the campaign. Every other day, I or one of the national field coordinators would yell the equivalent of "fire" in one state or another. It was all we had left when mountains had to be moved.

Early Deadlines: Texas, Arizona, Illinois, and North Carolina

In the history of our country, many third-party candidates did not even start their campaigns until July of the election year—such as Fighting Bob La Follette and the Progressives. In some cases, candidates did not start until August of the election year. But now candidates are forced to file as early as May in some states and even earlier for the candidates of some new third parties.

In 1983, the Supreme Court ruled in *Anderson v. Celebrezze* that early petition deadlines set by the states for minor-party and independent candidates are unconstitutional.[9] Justice Stevens, writing for the Court, said that the standard to be used to determine whether a state-imposed barrier to the ballot was constitutional was first to determine the severity of burden of the right infringed, then to evaluate the "precise interests put forward by the State" for justifying the burden of its rule. From our perspective in 2004, it was the rare court that would enforce this standard of scrutiny. And even election scholars say that this landmark decision doesn't appear to have been followed much, even though it is still good law.[10]

By 1988, all the states except for Texas had moved their petition-gathering deadlines for third-party and independent candidates to constitutionally acceptable time frames in July, August, and September of the election year.[11] But since then, two more states—Arizona and Illinois—have pushed up their deadlines to a much earlier date.[12] After

Nader declared his candidacy at the end of February, we challenged the deadlines in all three states (we had challenged Illinois successfully in 2000), even as we tried valiantly to collect the requisite number of signatures in each of the three states. We ultimately failed in all three.[13]

Texas: Bush's Home State

In addition to having an unlawfully early second-Monday-in-May petition deadline, the Texas requirements to get on the ballot are outrageously high for independent candidates.[14] Independents are required to obtain more signatures than new or third parties, and in less time, creating a discriminatory squeeze that most court cases rule illegal.[15]

Texas law requires independent candidates for president to collect 1 percent of the votes received in the previous presidential vote. New parties and other independent candidates for statewide office need only collect 1 percent of the votes received in the prior *gubernatorial* election, which is invariably less because of the diminished voter turnout in nonpresidential years. Independent candidates are allowed only sixty days to collect the requisite signatures. New parties or third parties have seventy-five days. In 2004, independent presidential candidates needed to submit 64,076 valid signatures collected in the sixty days beginning March 10 and ending May 10—and only from people who did not vote in the primary. Third or new parties had to submit "only" 45,540 signatures.[16]

In the 2004 election, nobody disputed that the Democrats would lose the state of Texas. It was not even going to be close. But we wanted to be on the ballot in Texas because it was symbolically important for our campaign. First, it was the earliest deadline, and the media would be sizing us up. Second, Ralph had received record levels of votes in Austin in 2000. Third, it was Bush's home state. If we got on the ballot, we were planning to open an office in Crawford to protest Bush's war and his reactionary record of corporatism.

To meet Texas's burdensome requirements, we had to spend money like water: flying circulators in, setting up signature-validity-testing stations, and paying circulators to collect signatures, which is legal and generally customary around the country when large numbers of signatures are required.[17] We had teams on the streets of Austin, Houston,

Dallas, San Antonio, and elsewhere. Even so, we knew we couldn't possibly reach the signature requirement by May 10, but we continued on past the deadline, collecting until the third-party deadline, believing that all major legal precedent was on our side to challenge Texas's discriminatory numbers and the deadlines themselves.[18]

One of our best national organizers was in charge of getting this job done, and yet it became clear to me that we were probably going to fall short, even with the longer deadline, in part because of a record amount of rain, mostly on the weekends, in key places including Houston. Yes, presidential politics (especially voter turnout) can depend on the weather. And our petitioners were getting thrown out of public places left and right, having to question and educate police and officials just to be able to stand their First Amendment ground to petition.

The Libertarians in Texas faced a similar situation. They said they were being thrown off the sidewalks of government property—taxpayer property—in Austin, Lubbock, Dallas, and Beaumont. According to the state volunteer coordinator of the Libertarian Party of Texas Ballot Access Committee, to compensate, the Libertarians "hired a telemarketer experienced at obtaining access for petitioning outside of large stores throughout Texas. She is accustomed to obtaining 2 locations per hour. However, here in Texas in 8 hours [she could] only obtain permission for 3 locations and they were for one or 2 day durations only."[19]

The First Amendment to the U.S. Constitution permits a petitioner to stand in front of government property on a public, taxpayer-funded sidewalk, with certain caveats about not blocking access and maintaining some decorum. This is not true for private property or, now, post offices, an issue still being challenged.[20] So given local officials' hostility to petitioners on government property, third parties are now reduced to hiring telemarketers to call corporate America to beg for permission to stand on their private sidewalks and parking lots! I could not believe the reports I was getting from the field. Initially, it sounded like "the dog ate my homework" kind of excuses: "I got kicked off the sidewalk."

And without a statewide corporate telemarketer to land locations to stand on public or private property, Nader petitioners were being threatened with arrest for exercising their right to petition. One petitioner who came from Arizona to help the Texas effort described the effect of an encounter with police at a public university: "As a petitioner, it is very stressful getting harassed when you are trying to do this and it really not only breaks your signing streaks, it shakes you up. I was very, very upset that evening. . . . I was shaken by the entire process."[21] On May 24, despite all the difficulty, we submitted 80,044 signatures. In 2000, we had needed a two-to-one ratio of signatures collected to valid signatures to make the 37,381 requirement, so I suspected that the 80,044 signatures collected in 2004 would not be "good enough" to attain 64,000-plus valid ones we needed this time.

In the meantime, the Texas Dems were taking no chances; even knowing that John Kerry had no more hope of winning Texas than Ralph Nader, they did not want Nader on the ballot. Their pitch in an email dated Friday, May 7, 2004, titled "The Political Week in Review from the Texas Democratic Party," read: "Ralph Nader's chances of getting on the ballot in Texas do not look good. . . . [A] vote for Nader is a vote for Bush. . . . We need to make sure he is nowhere near a ballot in Texas."[22] They didn't have to worry. The secretary of state in Texas used a sampling method to determine validity and concluded that only between 56,215 and 63,374 signatures were valid. So they denied us ballot access.[23] With the help of the only lawyer on record in Texas for winning this kind of case—ever—we challenged the early deadline.[24] We sued in federal court on the same day as the first deadline, May 10, in an effort to make the news cycle with a story about the injustice of these discriminatory laws. We even brought in livestock—a longhorn—to try to get the media to pay attention to discrimination toward independent candidates.[25]

At a pretrial conference on May 20, the judge, the Honorable Lee Yeakel, a Republican appointee, set a nonjury trial date months later (July 22) but promised he would have a decision by the first week in August or earlier so that the losing side would have time to ask the Fifth Circuit for an emergency stay or appeal of his decision. The Texas ballots were not going to be certified for printing until September 8, 2004, so theoretically this should have been adequate. Except the judge didn't keep his promise.

When he did finally rule, on September 1, 2004, we lost on everything despite all relevant legal precedent in our favor; the late date prejudiced our time to appeal. The judge concluded that the "challenged signature and date requirements are reasonable, nondiscriminatory restrictions on the rights of voters" and then went on to conclude that because the burdens were not *severe*, the state "need not present narrowly-tailored regulations to advance a compelling state interest, but only must show that the restrictions serve important state interests."[26] He didn't mention anything about the discriminatory process that required an independent presidential candidate to collect 41 percent more signatures than any other statewide candidate.[27] We filed an immediate appeal. Two days after the hearing, the appeals court affirmed the lower court ruling without issuing any written decision or correction of the lower court's factual errors.[28] Given the multitude of uncontradicted precedents nationally in our favor, we viewed this as a terrible abdication of judicial responsibility.

We went to the U.S. Supreme Court. It denied us a hearing, as it does most litigants. The federal courts were turning a blind eye to the very same factual predicates found in the landmark decision of John Anderson's litigation two decades before in *Anderson v. Celebrezze*.

First Blood: Arizona

I used to think of Arizona affectionately because I had fond memories of going there as a junior high student with my paternal grandmother Teresa. We traveled with a small Pekinese we called Marco Polo to visit my Aunt Rosetta. She wasn't really my aunt, but she was somehow related and had a bellowing, infectious laugh. Better still, for a kid, she owned one of those old-fashioned ice-cream parlors where they made the ice cream in a big vat in the window, in hot, hot Tucson. During 2004, those confectionary memories were replaced.

Arizona loomed next for the Nader campaign with the second-earliest deadline in the country. We were already broke after Texas, and we had to hire a professional firm to get ballot access in Arizona done by June 9. Our first state coordinator fell ill; the next one was hired with just three weeks to go and discovered that the first coordinator didn't have the face of the petition right. So we started from scratch and paid a firm to collect 20,000 signatures instead of relying on volunteers.

The firm's principal, a woman named Jennifer Breslin, seemed savvy and told me her philosophy was that everyone deserved a chance to get on the ballot. She had worked across the political spectrum for everybody from the Association of Community Organizations for Reform Now (ACORN) and the California teachers' union to antigay initiatives, something we did not support. She said that if one of her circulators had a problem with the content of the petition, or with circulating for us, they didn't have to do it, but it was her philosophy that they were for hire to get signatures for candidates who wanted to be on the ballot. This was the can-do spirit we needed. Many firms would not have been up to the hostile challenges that our petitioners were routinely facing. She also told me that she was very proud of her record of getting the job done. I liked her pluck and pride in her work. She didn't do email. She was no-nonsense and called me personally to report in on a regular basis, a measure of communication and accountability that is generally hard to find in field people of any sort, as many view "the people in Washington" as totally out of touch with their daily reality. (They are often right, but a campaign headquarters cannot operate without constant feedback from the field.)

True to her word, Breslin got the job done. I was impressed. She collected more than 14,000 signatures in Arizona drop-dead heat at the beginning of June. But turning in the signatures was a nightmare. On the day to turn in, our national volunteer coordinator got an email from a supporter in California who said that he used to work in the Arizona secretary of state's office and that a friend there was mocking the Nader effort because we hadn't turned in a particular piece of paper for designating electors, so none of the petitions to be turned in would count at all. Despite having two people on the ground full-time in constant contact with the secretary of state's office and trying to ferret out every last requirement, this was the first time our campaign was hearing of this requirement. We moved at lightning speed to see whether this was true and how we could overcome it.[29]

We had a signed form from each elector, a signed form from the vice-presidential candidate, and a signed letter from Nader designating his vice-presidential stand-in candidate, Jan Pierce, and each of his electors. But on the day of turn-in we were told—despite months of prior inquiries—that there had to be yet another, original document with Ralph's signature. Unable to fly it there in time (you should have seen the contortions we entertained for getting an original copy from DC to Arizona before 5:00 P.M.), we had to fax it, electronically send it with a public encryption key, and email it, and then hope we could fall back on the argument that the court accepts these forms of filings and so should the secretary of state's office, especially given their apparent complicity in the lack of clarity on the requirements.

On June 23, the Democratic Party of Arizona filed suit (behind two individuals named Dorothy Schultz and Elizabeth Hughes) against the campaign. The Democratic Party put out an official release claiming that of the 21,512 signatures filed by the Nader campaign, a whopping 15,467 were invalid. They claimed that because Ralph had nominated Peter Camejo to be vice president just two days before, the stand-in candidate on the petition was invalid and could not be substituted, thereby voiding all the signatures—this despite the fact that Arizona does not even print the vice president on its November ballots. They also claimed that because an ex-felon had collected signatures and had failed to have his voting rights fully restored, some 3,839 signatures were also not eligible, since Arizona requires all circulators to be residents and eligible to vote, which ex-felons may not do in Arizona unless rehabilitated by the state. The lawsuit and objection to our petition were 650 pages long, and the supporting documents filled fourteen boxes.

Since the state law was silent and thus ambiguous about substitution of the vice-presidential candidate, we were going to be sued on this anyway. But the Democrats went beyond this and actually challenged the state's own provided forms. They took issue with electors who put the word *Independent* in front of the word *Party* because that is how the form is constructed, with a blank before the word *Party*. The Dems challenged the fact that the vice-presidential candidate and the electors were supposed to submit a consent to the state to be the vice president and the electors, even though there is no mention of any special designation or consent procedure in the state-provided *Handbook for Candidates & Political Committees*. The Dems said that Camejo was a Green and therefore could not be an independent. They challenged the fact that some of the circulators lived at homeless shelters. They challenged 816 names for being illegible and said that 9,890 people were not properly registered to vote at the time they signed the petition. They even challenged Ralph's signature and wanted ten samples to confirm it! The Dems hired a handwriting forensic document examiner to determine whether each circulator signed the petitions. In short, the Democrats' strategy was to put everything plus the kitchen sink in the complaint in the hope that one of these issues, even if there were no case law on any of them, would find favor with a judge to keep us off the ballot.

It cost the campaign a $25,000 up-front fee to hire one of the best election lawyers in the state. It had cost us $30,000 to collect the signatures, and it was now the lawyers' projection that it was going to cost double that amount to defend their validity. This, of course, was going to be the pattern that the aligned Democratic Party forces would shamelessly use again and again over the course of 2004 to drain the Nader campaign of its resources.

As it turned out, we fell below the 14,694 necessary by about 550 signatures (not the 8,000 or more the Democrats claimed in their press releases.)[30] Apparently, one circulator was an ex-felon who had a valid voter registration card from the state and had done jury duty but had not paid a $450 state rehabilitative fee, so all his signatures were discounted, as he was not considered "totally rehabilitated" until the fee was paid. Another 1,349 signatures were discounted because the circulator failed to put the name of the county on the circulator's affidavit, even though there is no state instruction saying that listing the county is mandatory.[31]

In a painful, wee-hour decision in early July, we decided to drop our defense against the Democratic Party's state lawsuit to pursue instead a federal one arguing the unconstitutionality of the early deadline and of limiting petition circulation to only those who live in the state, a case we would ultimately win, but not until a wonderful Ninth Circuit decision in July 2008![32] Arizona in 2004 was our first defeat at the hands of the Democratic Party. The Democratic state chairman, Jim Pederson, told *Time Magazine*, "Our first objective is to keep him off the ballot. . . . This vote is about George Bush and John Kerry, and we think it distorts the entire electoral process to have his name on the ballot."[33] Our Arizona supporters were angry. I was apoplectic. Two states, Texas and Arizona, where we had been on the ballot in 2000 were now down the drain, along with hundreds of thousands of dollars.[34] And Pederson claimed *we* were distorting the electoral process.

During the Arizona litigation, two important developments occurred. First, the Democrats began to circulate rumors that the Republicans were paying for our signatures. This was news to us, as we had paid for each and every one. I signed the contracts and the checks. We paid $1.00 to $1.50 for each signature, a fair market rate. We ended up paying JSM, Inc., Breslin's company, more than $30,000 in Arizona. But this was the start of the Democratic Big Lie to try to smear Ralph's name, and they repeated it at every opportunity. The Democrats had apparently hired the services of Democratic pollster Stanley Greenberg to test what worked best against Ralph, and they concluded that saying that Ralph was taking money from the Republicans would tarnish him. Welcome to politics!

Second, on the day the Democrats filed suit in Arizona, Ralph and I called Terry McAuliffe, head of the Democratic National Committee, to tell him to cease fire. A most interesting conversation took place. I took notes.

McAuliffe is a talented fund-raiser by all accounts. As an *über*-Clintonista, he helped Democratic triangulation by raising money from the same corporate interests from which Republicans raised money. When you are in his presence, he is effervescent—literally brimming with bubbles and rosy forecasts, quick to throw an arm around you and declare you his best pal. I've seen him speak in person. Like Bill Clinton, he sucks up the oxygen in a room, and like any good fund-raiser, he is a political cheerleader. He is missing only the pom-poms.

On the phone, McAuliffe was very different—calculating and shrewd, alternating his bonhomie with velveteen threats. Ralph had talked to him and an assistant in his office several times in late 2003, after sending both parties an opus of ideas about the future course of the nation, seeking theirs. The Republicans said they wouldn't be replying. McAuliffe said he would read it and reply. Later his office called to say that they needed another copy because he had left the document on a train.

When they did have a substantive conversation in 2003, Ralph had told McAuliffe that if he ran, his campaign would be focused against Bush, as Bush was the incumbent. When Ralph got on the phone in 2004 to ask McAuliffe why they were challenging us in Arizona, McAuliffe said in his chummy voice, as if he were on speaker or talking to others in his presence: "Ralph, I would love for you to be running for President in 31 states; the issue is these 19 states" where "a vote for you is a vote for Bush." McAuliffe then lowered his voice and offered that "if you stay out of my 19 states I will help with resources in 31 states." But what started as a seeming financial proposition being put on the table changed into a directive with each repetition of "stay out of 19 states." He then went on to list the actual states he said he thought would cost the Democrats the election, including Oregon, Wisconsin,

Arizona, New Mexico, Washington, and Nevada. McAuliffe added, "Keep out of the South."

Ralph told McAuliffe that it was ridiculous to challenge us in places such as Georgia or Texas or North Carolina, which were "the South," but where the Democrats had no hope of winning. McAuliffe at some point in the conversation made a show of calling out to their publicity person, Jano Cabrera, who must have been within earshot, to ask about the challenges to the ballot, as if McAuliffe knew nothing about them. McAuliffe then said that the DNC was not financing them but "supported them," a statement Cabrera would make again in August to the *New York Times*.[35] This would later be contradicted—under oath, in cross-examination—by the testimony of the Maine Democratic Party state chair, as set forth in the next chapter.

What country are we in where the titular head of a major party committee can dictate the terms of how anyone else could run for office? The whole call was making me very uncomfortable. McAuliffe alternated between dictating to Ralph the terms and cajoling him, saying to Ralph, "You'd be a frickin' hero." He went on about how Dean and Kucinich were going to "actively go out there" to turn people against Ralph, and the Left was going to vote Democratic. He said there was a visceral hatred of Bush and that the Left and the independent swing voters were going to vote for the Democrats, not Ralph. Here he was telling us where we could campaign, apparently bribing us to stay in only thirty-one states with unspecified "resources" and indicating there would be more challenges in any of the nineteen he deemed to be "our"—as in "Democratic Party"—states.

I got my back up and felt like a lioness wanting to protect Ralph and political competition in general. I broke into the call, something I rarely did, and said that if these were going to be the terms—that Ralph couldn't run for office in nineteen states or else we would be challenged off the ballot—I was determined that the campaign would need to "park" in all nineteen states just to preserve political competition. The more McAuliffe presumed to put restrictions on Ralph, the more infuriated I became. I wrote "park" in my notes. McAuliffe was so positive that the Democrats were going to win. Right then and there, I felt the entire decay of the Democratic Party in the United States. They were going to win by bullying to make sure no third party or independent could run against them or no voter could have any other choice. I was ashamed for them. Saddened.

One reason McAuliffe was so desperate was that he was operating in a winner-take-all voting system. This does not excuse McAuliffe, but as a public interest lawyer, I have learned to look at how institutional processes affect behavior and engender bad behavior. Chapter 9 shows how winner-take-all corrodes our choices, but, first, let's go back to the early deadlines, in my home state of Illinois.

Illinois

I love Illinois. I was born at Loretto Hospital just off the Eisenhower Expressway in Chicago, where you can be stuck in "rush hour" traffic any time of the day. The state is filled with sensible, middle-class midwesterners who don't honk if you take three seconds too long to go at a light. I breathe better in the City of the "Onion Smell," the name's derivation from a nearly extinct Native American language.

Despite this little ode to Illinois, the sad fact is that we are also known as a smelly political cesspool. Illinoisans know it, practically from birth. By the time you are old enough to read a headline or watch someone on the South Side slip some bills to a police officer to "watch the car" during a White Sox game, you know exactly how the state "works." I grew up hearing stories about the "tip boxes" that used to be in downtown Chicago public offices. Now-pardoned Illinoisan Dan Rostenkowski went to the federal slammer and lost his Ways and Means chairmanship for the kinds of infractions that would not make Illinoisans blink an eye.

If you weren't born yesterday, you know that, in this state, petition signatures are political sport. There is a cottage industry of lawyers set up for it. Barack Obama, for example, knocked all four of his competitors (including his mentor, Alice Palmer) off the ballot in his 1996 state senate race to get his first seat in office by running unopposed in the Democratic primary.[36]

The way it works is that the state sets the official requirement for signatures. Whatever a candidate turns in is presumed valid, even if the facial requirements are not met, until "someone" makes a challenge to the petition with the clerk's office. I was once told that if no one makes a challenge, the clerk's office "rounds up someone" to make the challenge to prevent insufficient petitions from appearing on the ballot. If the clerk's office fails to round up a challenger, the petition can be considered valid, even if it has only *one* signature or is clearly facially invalid![37] At the other extreme, even if you have turned in thousands more than necessary, just one little objection filed by anybody can throw you into "signature defense hell" for weeks.

In our case, there would be no shortage of Democrats lined up to make the challenge, even though Democrats were undoubtedly going to win Illinois (which was not even on the McAuliffe list of the nineteen battleground states we were told to avoid). The Illinois Dems just wanted to harangue us to drain more of our resources early on, apparently as part of the national strategy to bankrupt the campaign.

In 2000, in Illinois, Ralph came in third out of eight candidates, pulling 2.19 percent of the vote total, or 103,759 votes. In 2004, by the time we turned in our petitions at the end of June, only the Libertarian and Democrat candidates were on the ballot. President Bush was waiting for a special dispensation—from the Democrats. Even though Illinois requires all nominations to be filed by September 1, the Democratic-controlled Illinois state legislature was going to allow Bush to submit his name *after* his nomination, which was to be on September 2. No one had objected to the Libertarian petitions even though they had filed approximately the same number of signatures as we had. So they were automatically on. But we were, in a state where the Democrats were making special allowances of the law for the Republican incumbent president, put through the wringer for trying to get on the ballot the legal way.[38]

Illinois required 25,000 valid signatures collected in ninety days, by June 21, 2004.[39] The combination of the early deadline, the high number of signatures, and the short time frame in which to collect them was going to make success difficult. We managed to turn in more than 32,000. This surplus margin should have been enough, but I was worried. I knew Illinois and the Democrats were planning to mess with us. A 7,500 surplus would not be enough to withstand scrutiny. A particular feature of the effort in Illinois would be the use of Democratic state employees to lead the charge against us.

Sure enough, within a week, an objection was filed by one John F. Tully Jr. of Chicago.[40] Tully was represented by Michael Kreloff and Michael Kasper, two prominent Illinois election lawyers.[41]

We hired a Democratic attorney, Dan Johnson-Weinberger, and Christina Tobin, a Libertarian who had done the line-by-line challenges before for the Libertarians; she was familiar with all the dirty tricks of Illinois petition challenges and knew how to mount an aggressive defense of signatures. In 2000, with the assistance of lawyers at the Brennan Center for Justice at NYU Law School, the Nader campaign had sued Illinois about its early deadline and its requirement that circulators be registered voters. This was an unconstitutional requirement that prompted the federal court to say we should have been able to turn in more signatures. The court permitted the campaign to submit signatures it had collected and notarized by August 7 and thus avoided the question of the constitutionality of the early deadline, because in the interim we had continued to collect signatures, and by turning in another 8,000, we had more than the requisite number to get on the ballot.[42]

This would have to be our strategy once again, though I suspected an extra layer of Democratic hanky-panky was in play. In July 2004, Tobin had identified approximately ten state employees who had signed in to visit the Cook County Clerk's Office between June 22 and June 28, when the objection to our signatures was created. We had the time sheets, their signatures, and a copy of the directory, which identified a number of them as coming from the House Democratic staff. That means that they worked for Illinois Speaker of the House Michael Madigan, who is also the chairman of the Democratic Party in Illinois.

Two state employees signed in after 5:00 P.M. The others signed in during work hours, begging the question of whether the taxpayer was paying for them to do election work, which would not be legal. One visitor signed a form requesting to examine the voter registration records regarding Ralph Nader.[43] He produced an employee ID and signed in at about the same time as the other state workers.[44] This man was listed in the Illinois State telephone directory as working for the House Democratic Staff, the House of Representatives, in the Chicago office. Three other helpers were interns from the Speaker's Office. And the lawyer for the Democrats, Michael Kreloff, is logged in on the same time sheet.

To get the time and vacation sheets of the state people, I asked Tobin to file Freedom of Information Act (FOIA) requests with Madigan's office. On July 20, Tobin received a letter from Madigan's chief clerk denying the request, claiming that the sign-in sheets of staff "to the extent they exist" "comprise the [employees'] personnel files," thereby making them exempt from FOIA requests.[45] This response is an attempt to insulate the sheets from disclosure because personnel records are exempt. But Illinois had already passed an ethics law saying time sheets should go to a fiscal officer, thereby placing them elsewhere, where, theoretically, they should be available for public inspection. Indeed, in 1998, the *Chicago Tribune*, using FOIA requests for time sheets, caught then–Secretary of State George Ryan (later governor and hero to the anti–death penalty movement, now indicted, convicted, and jailed for other reasons) and the Republicans using state employees on state time to remove Libertarian candidates from the ballot. Political hanky-panky in Illinois is a "bipartisan" affair.

IllinoisLeader.com, a conservative web magazine, compared the payroll for the Speaker's Office for June 2004 with the sign-in sheets for the Chicago Board of Elections and the Cook County Clerk's Office. It reported finding twelve full-time employees doing political work and eight others, who were not full-time but were on contract with the state, looking into our signatures. Some worked multiple days. All but one was paid the same amount for the first half of June and the second, while they were apparently checking our signatures instead of doing whatever the taxpayers paid them to do at Speaker Madigan's office.[46] Madigan's spokesperson denied the charge and told *Copley News Service*, among others, that political work was not done on state time.[47] In a separate attempt to obtain the documents, a court ruled the time sheets were exempt from disclosure, thus undercutting the ethics "reform."

We hired another lawyer, Andrew B. Spiegel, the Libertarian Party's general counsel in Illinois, who filed an objection for violations of the Elections Interference Act, which states: "No public funds shall be used to urge any elector to vote for or against any candidate or proposition or be appropriated for political or campaign purposes to any candidate or political organization."[48]

We also contested both the number of signatures required as well as the unconstitutional earliness of the June 21 deadline, which made Illinois the third earliest in the country. (The Democrats argued that the deadline in Illinois was "as late in the process as it could possibly be without endangering the county clerk's ability to prepare the ballot for the November election."[49] So do forty-seven other states and DC have particularly fast clerks, or is there something particularly slow about Illinois clerks that they have to have so many more weeks than virtually every other state to get the ballot prepared?)

The Democrats argued that the federal court should not even hear our case because it was *too early*, as the matter was "not ripe for adjudication" yet.[50] This proved to be an ironic argument because the Seventh Circuit would later rule—in favor of the Democrats—that instead of being *too early*, we were instead *too late* to get heard by the court even though most of the country at this point did not even require signatures to be turned in yet.

On August 30, the State Board of Elections ruled against us. Ralph and Peter would not be on the ballot in my home state. And the state employee issue was never resolved by any court or investigation. I was frosted. With the help of the Libertarian Party's counsel Spiegel, we appealed, and *Ballot Access News* publisher Richard Winger helped set the context for the deadline challenge in an affidavit: When the original government-printed ballot law was passed in Illinois—in 1891—it provided that new party candidate petitions were due just thirty days before the general election.

> In 1929 this deadline was moved to 50 days before the general election. In 1931 it was moved to 60 days before the general election. In 1947 it was moved to 78 days before the general election. In 1967, it was moved to 92 days before the general election, where it remained unchanged until 1999. In 1999, the legislature moved the filing deadline to 134 days before the general election. Thus, on five different occasions, the deadline was moved to an earlier date, even though the State of Illinois had never failed to have the ballots ready under the older deadlines or even claimed that the State ever had difficulty certifying presidential candidates in time for the ballot.[51]

Winger also noted in his affidavit that after being founded on July 6, 1854, the Republican Party had elected more members to the U.S. House that fall than any other party. But in Illinois it would *not* have been able to get on the ballot because of the early deadline. He also told the court that Theodore Roosevelt founded the Progressive (Bull Moose) Party in August 1912, after he lost the Republican nomination to William H. Taft. The Progressive Party got on the ballot in forty-seven of the forty-eight states then, starting in August! But it too would not have made Illinois's current deadline if it were then in place.[52] Finally, Winger noted that U.S. Senator Robert La Follette did not decide to run as an Independent Progressive for president until July 4, 1924, because he expected the Dems that year to run a progressive, William Gibbs McAdoo, but they did not. La Follette also managed to get on the ballot in forty-seven of the forty-eight states, but he too would not have made Illinois's early deadline, had it been in place in 1924.[53]

Spiegel argued that the June 21 deadline imposed a severe burden on the national presidential election and was well before either the Democrats or the Republicans would be hosting their conventions to choose a nominee. What was the narrowly tailored state interest here? Vacations in August? Finally, Spiegel argued that the state, which was supposed to certify the ballot by August 27, seemed to have no trouble accommodating George Bush's nomination as late as September 3, after the Republican Convention.

Spiegel's explanation seemed uncontestable: "Illinois has essentially turned a process that is supposed to filter out frivolous candidates into a process that bars candidates who cannot afford to pay circulators to gather signatures at a time when the campaign finds it most difficult to raise money."[54] I couldn't have said it better. Huzzah for the Libertarians who came to our aid in Illinois and elsewhere.

The Seventh Circuit, in *Nader v. Keith*, seemed somewhat sympathetic to our complaint about the unwarranted earliness of the deadline, stating that the time accorded to the state to process petitions "seems awfully long."[55] But the court then decided that we had filed the lawsuit too late, that we should have filed *before* we were thrown off or when Ralph had declared, even though we were filing *in July* and even though the U.S. Supreme Court had placed many candidates on the ballots in suits filed later than ours.[56] From our perspective, the Seventh Circuit just decided to duck this issue.

The same early deadline arguments apply to Indiana as well as to Illinois. Neither state has a justifiable or rational deadline. They should both be sued until these early deadlines are abolished.[57]

North Carolina

Pat Buchanan once told us ballot access for North Carolina alone cost his campaign on the order of $250,000![58] That's because North Carolina also falls into that unconstitutionally early boat; in 2004, the state required 2 percent of the state's registered voters as of January 4,

2004, or 100,532 signatures, making it the second-highest signature requirement in the country for an independent or "unaffiliated" candidate.[59] But it required 58,842 signatures, or 2 percent of registered voters who voted in the last election for governor, in order to form a new party.[60] North Carolina recently amended its law to fix the discriminatory signature requirements. In 2008, the signature requirement was 69,734 for both party and independent candidates.[61]

In 2004, we had our hopes pinned on a lawsuit named *Delaney v. Bartlett*.[62] Paul Delaney, an independent candidate for the U.S. Senate, had challenged the number of signatures required for a statewide independent candidate, compared to the number needed for a new party in North Carolina.[63] We sent our North Carolina coordinator to a hearing in March 2004; the judge said he would "have a decision within six months." Well, six months would be too late! Ralph wrote a letter to the judge, respectfully advising the court of the potential impact of its pending decision in *Delaney* on his candidacy and urged a timely decision. Ralph pointed out that the 100,000 signatures and the timeline required by North Carolina were unreasonable and unduly burdensome, especially compared to its neighbors, such as South Carolina, which required only 10,000 signatures by July 15; or Virginia, which required 10,000 signatures by August 20.[64]

On July 26, 2004, Judge Bullock struck down North Carolina's law as unconstitutional, holding that "[t]he statute's standards are unconstitutionally vague, and the law substantially disadvantages unaffiliated candidates without justification."[65] Outstanding!

Citing the *Delaney* decision, on August 11 we asked the North Carolina State Board of Elections to place Ralph Nader on the regular 2004 North Carolina general election ballot as an independent or unaffiliated candidate for the office of president of the United States. With the law struck down, the test for placement on the ballot was a question of equity,[66] balancing whether there was a "modicum" of community support for Nader against the "state's legitimate interest in preventing 'laundry list' ballots that discourage voter participation and confuse and frustrate those who do participate."[67] There was no question that Ralph met the test for a "modicum" of support in that he was the only candidate outside the two major-party candidates who was regularly polled and had received nationwide recognition.[68]

The campaign was advised that the letter would be addressed at the meeting of the North Carolina Board of Elections on September 3,

2004, the date that triggered the printing of the ballot. At their September 3 meeting, the board indefinitely tabled our request. Dean Rutledge, who was a lawyer for Eugene McCarthy's legendary ballot access litigations in 1976, graciously represented us in North Carolina. In a supplemental memorandum, we filed more than a dozen letters and emails demonstrating widespread support for Ralph to be placed on the ballot.

North Carolina, home state to 2004 Democratic vice-presidential candidate John Edwards, argued in response that voters could still vote for Nader as a write-in, so they weren't being harmed, stating that "there is no way, then, that any registered, qualified voter who desires to vote for plaintiffs Nader and Camejo will be denied the right to do so."[69] The state argued that the candidates could still campaign in North Carolina and that the harm from being a write-in versus on the ballot was "slight." This is laughable, as any write-in candidate knows. Prior to Ralph Nader in 2000, no write-in presidential candidate had ever received even 1 percent of the vote *in any* state! Just ask President Taft, who as an incumbent president couldn't even get one half of one percent in 1912 in California, which had nominated Teddy Roosevelt instead of him.

North Carolina then argued that we waited too long to ask the state to place Nader and Camejo on the ballot and to file the lawsuit, contending that by the time the court hears the motion on September 14, the state will have already started to print the ballots and absentee balloting will have begun, because North Carolina law requires the ballots to be available for distribution to absentee voters fifty days before the general election, which in 2004 was on September 13. Therefore, according to North Carolina, it was our fault for waiting so long to bring the lawsuit, even though the state set the date for determining our placement as September 3 and then did not act on it, intentionally, after we had sought relief a month earlier—on August 11.

For good measure, North Carolina also argued in the alternative that by filing for an injunction on September 2 to stop ballots without Nader's name on them from being printed, we had not allowed the state time to rule on our request at the September 3 board meeting. Their argument was that we were both too early and too late—simultaneously. This is the state-sanctioned flimflam to which third-party and independent candidates are subject. We were at the mercy of the State Board to hear us out, on their schedule, after *their* unconstitutional law was invalidated by a federal court, and then they argue that it was the candidate's fault for being late!

At a hearing on September 14, the federal court for the Middle District of North Carolina punted the case by ruling that the lawsuit should have been filed in the Eastern District because that is where the State Board of Elections was located, in Raleigh, the state capital. We refiled on that very day, but the Eastern District court ruled on September 24 that the case was filed too late even though we won four lawsuits in late September.[70] More judicial avoidance to get involved.

Fighting Back: Maryland and Oregon

Maryland and Oregon are representative of two states where we had to go to court to fight state determinations that our ticket couldn't be on the ballot for failure to meet unjustifiable state procedures. We won in Maryland and lost in Oregon in their respective state supreme courts. Here is what happened, including eyewitness accounts.

Maryland

In Maryland, we turned in 14,991 signatures by August 2, 2004, but the Maryland State Board of Elections told us that only 9,464 signatures were valid, and we needed 10,000.[71] It appeared that the counties in Maryland applied different standards to the signatures in determining whether to validate them, so a stellar team of volunteers went into motion. In just a few days of review, by cross-checking the state's voter registration base we found at least 445 clerical errors by the counties.

On August 27 we filed a complaint to restore at least 542 signatures invalidated by the board that should have been counted and certified.[72] The central issue in our complaint was that some voters signed on the wrong county sheet under the "wrong" county of residence but were qualified to vote in the state and should have been counted as valid for a statewide election.

This can happen easily. As Jason Kafoury, who organized a team of about twelve staffers to carpool and petition on Saturday and Sunday at the Artscape Music Fest in Baltimore, wrote in his post-campaign memorandum to Ralph and me: "Anyone can circulate in Maryland, but you have to divide each signature by county. The trickiest part of petitioning in Baltimore, especially at a festival of young people, is that nobody knows whether they are registered in Baltimore City or Baltimore County. . . . This led to many people signing the wrong sheet."

The Director of Election Management for the Maryland State Board of Elections testified to the court that the state does not verify the signatures but farms them out to the counties. Remarkably, the statewide registry of voters was *not* available to the local election boards—even though we were able to buy it from the state for $50. The twenty-four different Maryland counties were doing a county-by-county review with their own county registries, instead of using the statewide, comprehensive registry, a problem that HAVA should have fixed, had it been timely implemented. As a result, if a county had a valid registered voter but that voter was from another county in Maryland, the voter was stricken from our petition.[73]

The judge heard all of this testimony but concluded that the burden was on us and Maryland's Populist Party, the party line on which Ralph was running, to show that there is no rational basis for the state's restrictions.[74] In so ruling, the court concluded that the election law did not violate any state constitutional provision or our rights. The judge seemed to blame the plaintiffs for not filing early enough to cure the state's own defects.[75]

We appealed. The state of Maryland maintained that its procedure requiring a petition for party certification to be signed by voters registered in a specific county rather than in any county in Maryland was not unreasonable, even though there was a readily available alternative procedure—using the state's database instead of each county's—that would have allowed voters to vote for the candidate of their choice on the ballot.

Eyewitness Doug McNeil describes the argument of our Virginia lawyer Steve Scavuzzo at the Maryland high court:

> On Sept. 20 at 10:00 am, Steve got up and began his presentation to the high court. "Mr. Chief Justice, Justices, may it please the Court," he began. Then the chief judge John Bell unexpectedly interrupted him. "Mr. Scavuzzo," he said, "*there is no justice in this court.*"
>
> Steve just stood there totally shocked, not knowing what to say to a comment like that. So Bell went on to explain that in Maryland, they're all called judges, even on the state's highest court. So there is no Justice here, sir, only Judges. It was a joke, which he must have been

> saving for some time, waiting for the appropriate moment to use it. It kind of broke the ice. . . .
>
> After the oral arguments, Steve, Virginia [Rodino, the campaign's dynamic state coordinator] and I went to the Clerk's office, and we were told that the Court was meeting at that moment, and might reach its decision this afternoon. So we went to the cafeteria and had lunch, thinking that maybe it would be ready when we were done. The tension was almost too much to bear. . . . [A]fter we ate, we went back to the Clerk's office, and we were told that the court's *per curiam* order had been issued. "Would you like a copy?" she asked. Yes, we would. . . . [S]he sauntered slowly into the next room, and returned with a copy for each of us.
>
> We won the whole thing.[76]

By lunchtime on September 20, the highest court in Maryland had ruled in our favor, overturning the lower court and directing the state to put Ralph on the ballot and pay for the whole proceeding.[77] In a later thirty-page opinion, the court said: "An individual who signs a party's petition, regardless of whether the signature was on the correct 'county' sheet, enjoys the same protections of his or her right to suffrage under the Maryland Constitution as any voter casting a ballot on election day."[78] The clerk's office had already changed its procedure to be in compliance with the 2004 order. Our campaign and its dedicated volunteers broke down another state barrier, but the problem remains in many other states, all requiring challenges.

Oregon

The Nader 2000 campaign did well in Oregon, in large part because of the team of Greg Kafoury and Mark McDougal, two lawyers with big hearts, and Kafoury junior, Jason, a natural organizer. Oregon was the scene of our first superrally in August 2000 because the team had personally guaranteed its success by sheer persistence and lots of sweat equity. Though Oregon was labeled in 2004 as a Tier One state, difficult to get on the ballot, I figured the squad there could make it happen. I was wrong.

There are two ways for an independent to get on the ballot in Oregon. A candidate can either hold an "assembly" and get 1,000 signatures from registered voters on the same night in the same venue,[79] or a candidate can petition to get on the ballot, which requires 1 percent of the votes cast in the last presidential election (in this case, 15,306 signatures).[80] The signatures have to be collected 70 days before the election, and the candidates as well as the electors must not be members of a party for 180 days prior to filing.[81] Oregon also required that the petitions be filed with Secretary of State Bill Bradbury (a Democrat), after they are first reviewed by the counties and verified there.

We tried the convention route first. The Kafoury/McDougal team, trying to work within Ralph's rigid schedule, slated the convention on a Monday night, which was the same night as the National Collegiate Athletic Association (NCAA) finals. It fell short. We tried another convention on June 27, a Saturday night. It too failed, by less than 50 signatures. They got more than 1,000 people in the room. The only problem was it was stuffed with Democrats who, at the urging of party operatives, showed up to take up the seats in a limited hall, then refused to sign the petition, thus causing us to fall below the required number.

It was a public relations failure for the campaign. The Democrats, in full assault, got an early win in Oregon. The Democrats took to the airwaves and the Internet, claiming that the Republicans were making calls to turn people out to sign for us, which was to become their favorite campaign smear, sneer, slogan, and overall mobilizer of the masses: "The Republicans are coming . . . to help Nader!" We approved of none of these shenanigans.

There were even more issues about who had or could be nominated then and whether our legal notice of the assembly was sufficient. I couldn't believe we weren't going to be able to get 1,000 signatures in a room. The greater scrutiny of the statutory requirements led to even more questions that the secretary of state's office could not answer about its own rules. Indeed, our campaign prompted Oregon's secretary of state's office into emergency rule making because our ballot access liaison, Mike Richardson, who identified some of these problems as early as April, had called them to the attention of the director of the secretary of state's Election Division, but they still were not fixed.

Richardson was successful in getting Oregon to change some of its rules, such as the one requiring *nine* pieces of additional paper to be attached to each petition, but the state would not budge on its requirement for the petition process that the vice-presidential candidate be registered as an independent. If we were going to be stuck petitioning, we would have to get approval of a petition that included someone other than Peter Camejo as vice president.[82]

Even so, by July, the petition drive was looking easier than the rest of all this nonsense. We just didn't know how it too would present a nightmare. The Kafourys wanted to hire John Slevin, who had done the Pennsylvania collection, to help augment the thousands of signatures gathered by volunteers and local petitioners.

Our petitioners were accosted at every level. Verbal abuse on the street was just the beginning. Margaret S. Olney, an attorney from Smith, Diamond & Olney in Portland, sent our petitioners a letter stating that her law firm "is currently investigating concerns about a large number of invalid voter signatures that appear on nominating petitions filed with Multnomah County in support of Ralph Nader for President. We are looking into whether fraudulent signature-gathering techniques were used in the circulation of those petitions." And then she reminded our circulators that "[f]alsely signing the petition may result in conviction of a felony with a fine of up to $100,000 or prison for up to five years."[83] She invited our circulators to talk to her about the petitions they circulated.

I wrote a cease-and-desist letter stating that her letter "constitutes a blatant attempt to intimidate campaign workers, to disrupt and interfere with the Nader campaign, and may constitute a violation of Oregon statutes[84] and federal election law."[85] We sent a copy to lodge as a complaint with the director of the Elections Division (which was rejected).

Petitioners were also being visited at night, in their homes, by people claiming that they were "doing an investigation." One grandmother of two, with a heart condition, called to say that two people came to her home and gave her a letter from a lawyer, saying that she could go to prison if any of the people who signed her petitions were not qualified voters. She was frightened and explained to them she simply asked people if they were registered voters and, if so, would they like to sign to put Ralph Nader on the ballot. The "investigators" asked whom she worked for and exactly what instructions she had been given. They asked where she petitioned and who had hired her—they were "apparently looking for something they could use against me." She asked if they were saying she had done something wrong. They responded that they "really couldn't talk about it." According to the woman, the "whole thing was more frightening and intimidating than I could describe."[86]

More than thirty of our petitioners quit after this kind of "home visit." This was, of course, the point. The petition deadline was still twelve days away. The Service Employees International Union (SEIU), who had retained Ms. Olney, apparently was using union harassment methods to scare off our petitioners. I was disgusted. Here we were, trying to use union printers, sticking up for labor law reform and fair trade and the repeal of Taft-Hartley, only to have this union harass our petitioners at their homes. And was the SEIU making any demands on pro-NAFTA (North American Free Trade Agreement), pro-war Kerry? No.

Of course, the Democratic secretary of state's office did nothing to halt these tactics. I considered them to be affronts to the Constitution. Instead, we were told that additional complaints were being made against us, claiming possible violations of Oregon election law regarding the "date signed" by circulators and the lack of sequential petition numbering. What is more egregious behavior to the secretary of state's office in Oregon? Page numbering? Or visits to your petition circulators in the night, by self-appointed "investigators" who threaten people that they may go to jail or face $100,000 fines?

Yes, page numbering!

The problem was that—at the instruction of the secretary of state—the campaign had submitted more than 28,000 signatures to the counties. The secretary of state's office itself told the campaign to submit unnumbered pages so these sheets could be inserted later to restore consecutive numbering, where other sheets had been removed at the direction of the secretary. The counties had reviewed and verified more than 18,100 signatures, confirming that each of these signers was registered to vote. Nonetheless, on September 2, 2004, a compliance specialist from the secretary of state's office sent a letter to Ralph, stating, "The total number of qualified signatures needed to gain ballot access for President of the United States is 15,306. We have determined that the total number of qualified signatures you submitted is 15,088. Consequently, there are not sufficient qualified signatures for you to gain ballot access for this office."[87]

Dan Meek, our lawyer, wrote a piece, later published by *CounterPunch*, that explained how these unwritten rules operated to disqualify valid voter signatures "all of which had already been verified by county elections officers, who themselves signed and dated every sheet with an affidavit of authenticity (often with a county seal as well). This subtraction left Nader 218 short of the 15,306 needed":

> One "unwritten rule" Bradbury used to toss away over 400 county-verified voter signatures was that circulator signatures could not "appear to be initials." This appears in no statute and no rule on nominating petitions. When the rejected circulators came forward with affidavits, showing their same signatures on important documents (including drivers licenses, social security cards, and past tax filings), Bradbury refused to consider the documents.
>
> Another "unwritten rule" was that every circulator signature be "legible," even though the circulator's printed name is right below her signature on every sheet. Many people have signatures that are not "legible," such as Norm Frink, a Multnomah County Deputy District Attorney, whose signature did not seem to spell out "Norm Frink." Bradbury rejected all the Frink sheets (and hundreds of sheets of other circulators) with no notice to him or to the Nader campaign and then refused to consider the affidavits Mr. Frink and the others provided, vouching for their signatures and showing those same signatures on past important documents.
>
> Another "unwritten rule" rejected any sheet having any correction whatever [sic] of the date on the circulator's signature. If the circulator made any slip of the pen in writing the date, Bradbury threw out all of the county-verified voter signatures on that sheet. If a circulator began to write a "7" for the day of the month, realizing the error, crossed it out and wrote an "8," the entire sheet was discarded, and Bradbury allowed absolutely no way for the circulator to correct such a slip of the pen. Banks accept checks with such "dating errors," but not Bradbury, even though there exists no statute or rule requiring that the date on a circulator's signature be the result of a pristine flow of ink on paper.[88]

When all was said and done, Bradbury threw away 2,354 of the 18,186 county-verified voter signatures submitted to him as valid by his own local officials for lack of sequential page numbering. According to Meek, "Employees of the Secretary of State could provide no instance of this ever being applied to reject nominating petitions."

Meek's article laid out the larger problems. But the details are even worse. The unpublished order for the secretary of state was in the form of a "Hi Everyone" memo dated August 4, 2004, from the director of the Elections Division to the county elections people. Even after some of the counties followed this memo, we had sufficient signatures—the counties returned 18,186 signatures, until the secretary of state's office purged some more to drop the number to 218 fewer than the 15,306 required. This is what passes for due process in Oregon.

The next day, our vice-presidential candidate in Oregon, Sandra Kucera, various electors, and Greg Kafoury, co-chair of Oregon for the 2004 campaign, filed an appeal of the secretary's action and a petition for review of the administrative decision. The Honorable Paul J. Lipscomb of the Marion County Circuit Court found that the secretary's office had used inconsistent "unwritten rules" that didn't comport with the law, the prior policy of the Elections Division, or the written rules in the State's "Candidate Manual," concluding: "There appears to be no statutory or administrative rule authority for that novel action by the Secretary."[89]

Presiding Judge Lipscomb of the lower court ordered Nader and Kucera back on the ballot, and predictably the secretary of state's office appealed directly to the Oregon Supreme Court.

The Oregon Supreme Court, ruling against us, would later attempt in a footnote to charitably explain that although the "Hi Everyone" memo was written for "signature sheets for the Nader for President petition," there was "no evidence that any campaign other than the Nader campaign was employing the nomination procedure" at that time. The court generously said: "We assume that the written instructions are applicable generally to all elections procedures to which the Secretary of State has addressed them, not just to a single candidate or campaign, until the Secretary of State withdraws, modifies or supercedes [*sic*] them."[90]

Within one week of kicking us off the ballot, and before the secretary of state prevailed in the Oregon Supreme Court, "Friends of Bill Bradbury, Bradbury for Oregon" sent out a fund-raising letter, signed by Bradbury, that began: "Dear Friend: As you probably know, last week I upheld Oregon law and rejected Ralph Nader's petition to be on Oregon's ballot. This week a judge ruled that Nader should appear on the ballot. We will appeal this ruling, but let me be clear: I will never apologize for upholding the law, and I will never apologize for preventing fraud in our election system."

So here we went from merely submitting unnumbered sheets to "preventing fraud" as a fund-raising device. Quite a stretch. When people complained, Chief of Communications for the Secretary of State Anne Martens wrote in response: "While we understand your concerns about the Democratic Party, please understand that party and partisan consideration did not play a role in our application of the law to Nader." She then told people: "The Oregon State Supreme Court and U.S. Supreme Court agreed: Nader didn't follow the rules, and so he isn't on the ballot."[91] Of course, if you read either the state supreme court decision or the U.S. Supreme Court order, which is only about six lines, they say no such thing.

The Oregon Supreme Court unanimously concluded that this case was all about the authority of the secretary of state to make up rules. It acknowledged that the secretary of state's actions were the result of its unwritten rules. It said: "It is true that the review procedures that Lindback [the director of Elections] described were not themselves written, but that does not render them unlawful."[92] Yet the Oregon Supreme Court could not cite a single statute or published rule containing any of these *ex post facto* "unwritten rules" that knocked us off the ballot.

Indeed, the Oregon Supreme Court concluded that it could generally dismiss the rest of our complaints as well, merely shrugging off all of our constitutional claims.[93] According to the court, if the secretary of state makes up unwritten rules, which he or she is now entitled to do, and these novel rules then result in thousands of signatures being disqualified after the fact—after the clerks of the counties already certified them—that is okay, because your constitutional rights as a voter or candidate are not impacted. All you have to do is follow the law—as unwritten and *ex post facto* as it may be.

The campaign immediately appealed to the U.S. Supreme Court for a stay of the Oregon Supreme Court decision. On September 28, 2004, with Justice Breyer the lone justice to dissent, the Court again declined to intervene.[94] Later in 2004, our lawyers filed a full petition for a *writ of certiorari*, seeking to get the record set straight after the election, to prevent the secretary of state from imposing *unwritten* rules.

We asked the U.S. Supreme Court to weigh in on whether the rights of free speech, association, due process, and equal protection of qualified voters who wish to cast votes for independent candidates for office are adversely affected, particularly in a state that doesn't even allow for the counting of write-in votes except in extraordinary circumstances. Our petition noted that the Oregon Supreme Court simply failed to address the constitutional burdens placed on us by retroactively applying unwritten rules and upholding the sequential sheet numbering requirement. If the state allows state officials to retroactively apply unwritten rules to already turned-in signatures, "there is no practical way for independent candidates to run for federal office."[95] In 2005, the U.S. Supreme Court once again declined to grant *certiorari* in our case, but at least one justice, Justice Stephen Breyer, was willing to hear it.

In mid-August 2004, a blogger and anarchist activist named William Gillis who worked at America Coming Together, whose offices were shared by SEIU's election campaign, wrote that:

> For days now, most of the ACT staff had been aware of, if not complicit in, a scheme against the Nader Campaign.
>
> . . . A few of my fellow canvassers who were likely to be in the vicinity of the Nader campaign told me they had been asked to "mistakenly" invalidate petition papers. Misspelling names or information was a classical attack, but the SEIU had figured a better method.
>
> . . . If asked to sign the Nader petition, our canvassers were encouraged to accidentally sign their name in that section [where circulators attested to their collection of signatures] instead. Upon realizing their mistake, these innocent canvassers would scribble it out, thus invalidating an entire sheet of signatures.

The blogger, to his credit, went on to say that "malicious attacks and counter-attacks like this are simply not acceptable."[96]

At the same time SEIU was apparently defacing our petitions, SEIU was releasing press releases titled: "Widespread Forgery Shown on Nader for President Petitions." In this release (on the same date as the blogger's) Alice Dale, vice president of SEIU, represented by Margaret Olney, claimed: "Based on our experience fighting signature fraud in the past, we believe the problem originates from the circulators themselves. . . . This fraud is too pervasive to have been committed without at least the complicity of the signature gatherers. Furthermore, looking at the sheets for any length of time raises the question of whether campaign officials knew or at the very least should have known about the false signatures."[97]

The press release's lead line: "Evidence of overwhelming and systemic fraud in the Ralph Nader for President petitions was released today by the Service Employees International Union. An analysis of the petition sheets and a direct survey of people whose names appear on the petition suggests at least two-thirds of all signatures turned in by the Nader campaign to date are fraudulent."[98]

It must be nice to smear with impunity by press release. Not a single court or the secretary of state's office ever said there was any fraud on our part in any of our petitions in Oregon. But the SEIU broadcast this loudly—after it had apparently manufactured the deceit itself—and then this was in turn picked up by Kari Chisholm of BlueOregon ("a place for progressive Oregonians"), who claimed he had broken "the news of the SEIU fraud and forgery investigation into Nader's petition for the Oregon ballot."[99]

Secretary of State Bradbury was an open supporter of John Kerry. John Lindback, the director of elections, had worked for the former Democratic lieutenant governor of Alaska. The executive director of the Oregon State Democratic Party, Neel Pender, told the *Statesman Journal* after the state court ruling, "The Ralph Nader campaign misled voters and committed voter fraud," even though there was no such ruling in court and we had initially won. The Democrats' goal was tarnish by press release and innuendo.[100]

The *Albany Democrat-Herald* editorialized:

> At the state level, Bradbury's Elections Division disqualified 3,082 signatures that had been validated by elections officials because of the numbering problems. If they had been improperly numbered or not numbered at all, one might have thought that county clerks would have pointed this out. But instead, they validated the signatures.
>
> If you're a petition passer and you get the all-clear from county officials to whom you have submitted your efforts, you don't expect the state then to reject them. If it does so anyway, knowing how fervently the chief office holder does not want you to succeed, it's hard to avoid the suspicion that dark motives have been at work.
>
> All this could be avoided if the Elections Division was put under an official elected in a nonpartisan way. A law or constitutional change to that effect ought to be put on the ballot in 2006.[101]

Bravo. The *Democrat-Herald* proposed the right solution. The Oregon secretary of state's office is "Exhibit A" for why we need nonpartisan administration of our elections.

By the end of the campaign, we had filed at least thirteen affirmative lawsuits to try to even the playing field for third parties and independents with one more to follow in Ohio afterward. We filed affirmative suits to test state laws or procedures including Hawaii (two), Idaho, and Ohio (two)—one to be a write-in candidate and one after the election to remove unconstitutional restrictions on petition circulators (see www.amatomain.com). As we challenged these laws, we had no idea that within the next twelve weeks we were going to be sued or have to defend the sufficiency of our signatures at least twenty-four more times in seventeen more states. Oregon was just the tip of the iceberg.

Chapter 4

Democrats Fighting the Last War

"We're not going to let him do it again. We'll do whatever it takes within the law."

—Toby Moffett, quoted by Janice D'Arcy, "Anti-Nader Forces Coordinate Strategy"[1]

Against the historical and hysterical backdrop that was Florida 2000, from the beginning of the 2004 election, if Nader's issues were going to get attention, he had to be on that state's ballot again. I assigned this state to myself. If there were no Florida ballot access, there would be no specter of a repeat, no buzz, no coverage, no chance to raise the overlooked issues, no money, no chance to bring in new people to the political process, and no campaign. It was that simple. For Garibaldi, it was Roma o Morte! For me, it was Florida or Fuggedaboudit.

In Florida, to be an independent candidate for president was onerous, requiring the collection of signatures of 1 percent of the registered electors in the state by July 15, 2004.[2] There was no way we were going to obtain the required 93,024 valid signatures, certified by county, one sheet per county, with a fee of 10¢ a signature![3] We eliminated this possibility early on, in favor of an alternate route: namely, nomination by a minor party. To get on the ballot as a party's nominee, a minor party affiliated with a national party holding a national convention to nominate the candidates may simply submit its nominees and elector names before September 1 of the election year.[4]

Several parties in Florida have historically qualified for this party access method to the ballot, including the Green Party, the Reform Party, the Socialist Party, the Workers World Party, the Libertarian

Party, and the Constitution Party, which was formerly the U.S. Taxpayers Party. Indeed, some of these parties were on the ballot in the state of Florida only because of the relative ease with which they could get on the ballot as a party nominee. And there was no discernible abuse of this process even though some of these parties barely held a convention. In 2004, there were twenty-three registered political parties in Florida. Only six minor parties submitted names to the secretary of state to have their candidates placed on the ballot.[5]

To be sure we understood every curlicue of Florida's law, we went over every statutory provision with the secretary of state's office. And when it became clear we were going to be the Reform Party nominee, I started communicating directly with Florida Reform Party chairs Janice Miller and Ruben Hernandez to make sure I was getting accurate information. Miller and Hernandez were pros. They had lined up thirty-three electors, had all the paperwork covered, and were up to date on filing their reports with Florida; and there was no question that they were affiliated with the national Reform Party USA. The affiliation agreement had been in place and on file with the FEC since 1997—because it was part of the Reform Party's application for "national party committee" status, which the FEC had granted.

There was also no question that the Reform Party was a national party: it had run national candidates in the last two elections, it had FEC status, and it was the fourth-largest minor party in the country, with at least 63,000 registered voters. I asked our national volunteer coordinator to work with the state party chairs to double- and triple-check every single Reform Party elector's voter registration with the state. We weren't taking chances.

I still was worried and so told the Reform Party that because its members held their convention by phone, it would be best to hold another in-person convention to remove any doubt that a national convention had been held. Members had already come to this conclusion on their own and thus planned a national Reform Party convention in Irving, Texas, for the end of August. Ralph was there to accept the Reform Party's nomination and endorsement. C-SPAN and the local press covered it. The convention was attended by sixty-five delegates from several states. While there, I talked by phone to Hernandez, who was in Florida making sure everything comported with Florida law.

Everything was set. Hernandez submitted our names and electors on August 31, one day before the September 1 deadline.

The Democrats were lying in wait. On September 2, a small posse, including Scott Maddox as chairman of the Florida Democratic Party and the party itself, filed suit against Secretary of State Glenda Hood, Governor Jeb Bush, the Reform Party of Florida, the Reform Party of the United States, and Ralph Nader and Peter Camejo.

We got a fax on Sunday, September 5, of Labor Day weekend, saying that there was a hearing/status conference scheduled, that counsel could attend by phone, for Tuesday, September 7, at 3:00 P.M. in front of the Honorable P. Kevin Davey in the Circuit Court of the Second Judicial Circuit in and for Leon County Florida, Tallahassee.[6] This was an ambush. We had not been served with anything at this point. We didn't get any other papers for at least twenty-four hours. When we did get the Democrats' papers, they began with:

> This is an extraordinary proceeding. In their most recent stop on a nationwide crusade that evidently places its ideological and political agenda above the imperative of complying with the election process and dealing honestly and candidly with the electorate, Ralph Nader and Peter Camejo, as erstwhile candidates of the Reform Party, broke the laws applicable to *all* political candidates and parties in Florida by filing sham nominating papers with Defendant Glenda Hood, Secretary of State of the State of Florida. With those filings, Nader, Camejo, the RP-F, and the RP-A mock Florida's election laws and threaten to taint the entire Florida November 2004 general election for President and Vice President of the United States of America.[7]

You can get away with libel if you put it in a lawsuit. No level of flamboyance escaped these Miami lawyers. Based on the paper, I thought they would be wearing blue capes and red leotards to court. A second lawsuit, funded by the Ballot Project, Inc., former Democratic Representatives Toby Moffett and Elizabeth Holtzman's 527 group, was also filed by another posse of plaintiffs.[8] No legal papers arrived from them.

Meanwhile, Hurricane Frances hit Florida. We couldn't get information from the courthouse, and the notice of the hearing went from Tuesday, September 7, to Wednesday, September 8. The new notice said that this was a "case management conference and hearing, with or without notice for preliminary injunction," even though neither Nader nor Camejo nor the Reform Party had been served.

I got on the phone at 3:00 Wednesday afternoon to explain to the judge that we had just been served in the morning and had not yet secured counsel, that neither Camejo nor the national Reform Party had been served. Judge P. Kevin Davey said he was concerned about due process and the Nader/Camejo interest but that he was going to go forward anyway and hold an injunction hearing right then—with me on the phone—because of the time pressures on the secretary of state. What? The judge said he would hear from us by telephone, that he would give us a chance to get counsel, and that he would hold off on the declaratory part of the proceedings until the next day. The judge kept saying that the injunction was "only with respect to the secretary of state." I kept saying that we were the real party in interest and if he enjoined the secretary from putting us on the ballot, he was thereby changing the presumption of whether we were on the ballot, completely affecting our rights as the real parties in interest. He essentially admitted this, but nonetheless he launched into a seven-and-a-half-hour hearing with neither of the candidates represented by counsel. Periodically the judge would ask if I "wanted to say anything" . . . "to be fair."[9]

At every turn, I protested that this was not due process, that our rights were being violated. I felt like a hostage to the whole proceeding, unable to leave the phone.

While on the phone, I sent emails to the American Civil Liberties Union (ACLU) in Florida; to our in-house lawyer, whose full-time job was to coordinate all the lawsuit paper coming in; to our treasurer and our attorney; to attorneys I knew in DC and Florida; and to anyone I could think of to help us get a lawyer into that courtroom in Tallahassee. By 6:00 P.M.—three hours into the proceeding—a man named Andrew Byrne walked into Judge Davey's courtroom, saying that he represented the Reform Party. Since I could not get off the phone, as I had to listen to the Democrats' case against us in this hearing, I had no idea if we had really hired this person or where he came from. At 9:50 P.M., the court asked me if there was anything more I would like to say:[10] I said that Ralph and Peter, no one else, would be irreparably harmed by the court's removal of their names from the ballot.[11] I tried one last time: "Your Honor, it is almost 10:00 o'clock at night. I don't understand why we are not able to go and get counsel to appear before

Your Honor tomorrow." The court said: "You can. But not on the injunction. I will grant the temporary restraining order. And I don't do it lightly."[12] This steamrolled injunction prohibited the secretary from certifying Ralph and Peter's names to be on the ballot in Florida.

The court then scheduled a status conference for 12:30 P.M. the next day to set up the rest of the hearing. My understanding of Florida law was that if the secretary of state appealed, something I was not sure Hood would do, there could be an automatic stay to the judge's order, thus keeping the presumption that we were on the ballot. The Democrats were going to come back the next day to argue against a stay of the ruling's effect.

Between the minute I got off the phone and my flight the next morning at 6:05 A.M. to Tallahassee, I called Andrew Byrne to figure out who he was and whether he knew any lawyers we could hire. I also woke up Reform Party officials Shawn O'Hara in Mississippi, Beverly Kennedy in Texas, and John Blare in California and urged them all to get to Tallahassee, with all deliberate speed, to defend the existence of the Reform Party. At nearly 3:00 A.M., I sent an email message to Randall Marshall at the ACLU in Florida, as well as to others at the national ACLU, pleading for help.

I asked Marcia Jansen, my assistant, to get a list of lawyers from Martindale Hubbell. I got home in time to pack, shower, and get back to the airport. When I got on the plane, we still had no lawyer to represent us in Florida. My "plan" was to arrive in Tallahassee at about 10:00 A.M. and to just start calling down the list of lawyers. John Anderson had tried the day before to find us a lawyer, to no avail. Jamin Raskin from American University, the same. No one would represent us. We were the political untouchables: a caste generally reserved for Communists and known terrorists. Indeed, alleged terrorists were then getting more legal help from the many nonprofits set up to defend constitutional rights than we were.[13]

When I hit the runway in Florida, less than twenty-four hours post Hurricane Frances, I whipped out my cell phone and started dialing my list, hoping that someone who knew something about election law was in his or her office even though gusts of wind were violently blowing palm trees, like out of some Hitchcock movie. Everyone I called was either conflicted or understandably not there. I went to Byrne's office. It was small and humming efficiently, but my instinct was that we were badly outgunned. I finally reached a man named Ken Sukhia, who was genteel, firm, and—bonus!—the former U.S. attorney in Tallahassee!

Sukhia showed up at Judge Davey's court in jeans and a tweed jacket; the whole place was in hurricane mode. He took a shrewd look around at the players. There was a battalion of lawyers in that courtroom. He took me into the hall and explained he could start immediately, but he wouldn't start going to work for less than a $10,000 retainer up front.[14] The secretary of state had her lawyers from the Office of the Attorney General and seemed to be hiring even more by the hour as the proceedings went on. Also lurking in the courtroom was an attorney representing the GOP. We were the only ones not represented. It was apparent that these players were all familiar with the drill in some weird 2000 imbroglio redux. We were just the ping-pong ball.

Judge Davey on *day one* had thrown Ralph Nader, Peter Camejo, and the sixth-largest political party in the United States off the ballot—for not being a political party. In the meantime, parties like the Socialists, with 428 members registered nationwide, and the Socialist Workers Party, with 161 members registered nationwide, were going to be certified and appear on the Florida ballot.[15] Ralph told the *Tallahassee Democrat*, "I've never seen, in 40 years, a more pell-mell kangaroo court procedure involving any of our third-party activities. . . . this is nothing more than a judge responding to the political imperatives of a nervous and corrupt Democratic Party."[16]

This lawsuit was not about the law; it was about the hysteria. What were the legal arguments of those determined to force Ralph off the ballot?

Their arguments were these:

1. The Reform Party of Florida did not nominate Nader and Camejo through a national convention.
2. The Reform Party of Florida is not affiliated with a national party because the putative affiliate, the Reform Party USA, is "a gutted shell" that no longer operates as a "national party."
3. The Reform Party of Florida is not a "minor party" under Florida law because it is no longer active in federal elections.
4. The Reform Party of Florida's executive committee did not file a certified copy of a resolution recommending its electors.[17]

In support of these propositions, the Democrats relied heavily on comparisons of the Reform Party of Ross Perot with the Reform Party of today, usually with incomplete assertions. They claimed that Buchanan in 2000 was only on the ballot in thirty-six states as the Reform Party, even though he was on the ballot in forty-nine states and DC, if not always listed as of the Reform Party. They contrasted the 1996 and 2000 conventions, with hundreds of delegates voting in person, to the telephonic convention on May 11, 2004. They claimed the attendance in Texas in August for the nomination meant that no nomination actually occurred then. The plaintiffs stooped to using the *Merriam-Webster Online Dictionary* to come up with a definition of the statutory use of the word *convention*. They claimed that it required hundreds of people in multiday affairs and that this was "universally understood."[18]

The Dems also claimed that the Reform Party was not a "national party," this time relying on *Webster's Third New International Dictionary* (1986) to define *national*, stating that it required activities "of, affecting, or involving *a nation as a whole*, as distinguished from subordinate areas."[19] The Democrats made a big deal of the fact that the former treasurer of the Reform Party, who was removed from his position by the party, had tried to terminate the old committee at the FEC, leaving only $18.18 in the national bank account.[20]

The Democrats also noted that the Reform Party, in reports filed with the FEC, had only raised approximately $6,000 in contributions for the entire 2003–2004 election cycle.[21] They also proffered that the headquarters was in the home of the chairman. In essence, the party did not have enough money, according to the Democrats, to be a party; nor did it exist in enough places to be a national party.

The Democrats then devolved into an obfuscation about what triggers national candidacy reporting—the raising or spending of more than $5,000—with what constitutes a national political party. They also asserted that a party could not be a *national* party unless the candidate received at least 5 percent of the vote nationwide and was eligible for general election public funding—a hurdle that is so high virtually no party in U.S. history would have initially met this test![22] Finally, they claimed that the filing in Florida did not contain a "certified resolution as required by Florida Statutes Section 103.121 (2)."[23]

The judge issued his preliminary injunction order on September 9, without having the benefit of any paper filed on our behalf or hearing from any witnesses on our behalf. For example, before he issued his order, Judge Davey didn't hear any of the following:

- Florida used to have one of the most restrictive statutes in terms of ballot access in the country; the people of Florida had passed, by referendum, Constitutional Revision 11, adopted in 1998 to open up ballot access for candidates.[24]
- The FEC had never terminated the Reform Party; all of its filings were timely filed; and the Reform Party of Florida had been affiliated since 1997, without termination, with all of its filings up to date in Florida as well.
- The Reform Party had lapsed in membership and strength because of the brutal battle between Buchanan and Hagelin in 2000, but the intent of the remaining members was to rebound.
- The Libertarian Party and the Green Party have never received general election public funding, and yet the status of each had not been questioned as a minor party. The Reform Party amended its nomination procedures precisely to avoid having a convention like the one in 2000, with various factions attempting to stack or take over the party; six candidates competed for its nomination, with Ralph winning a two-thirds majority on the third ballot after hours of speeches.

Finally, Judge Davey didn't hear that if the Reform Party's certification was defective under Florida Statutes Section 103.121 (2), so too was the Democrats' because they had submitted nearly identical forms of "certifications." Indeed, the Democrats willingly dropped that fourth argument so as not to risk having the whole procedure throw John Kerry and John Edwards off the Florida ballot too.

After about three hours of wrangling on the wording of the order, on September 9, Judge Davey issued his ten-page order granting a preliminary injunction. The order began with the exigent circumstances, the hurricane, the secretary's time frame for mailing the absentee ballots by September 18, and the need to appeal everything.[25]

The court went on to find that the Reform Party of the United States was not a "national party" and fails in almost "every conceivable criteria" except that its presidential candidate is a well-known and -respected individual. The court found irreparable harm not to the Democrats but to the supervisor of elections in that there would be a "disaster" for the election process if an erroneous candidate for president were to appear on the ballot. The court never mentioned the disenfranchisement of the voters of Florida in its calculation of public interest. And the judge gave short shrift to the candidates—Nader and Camejo. Judge Davey recognized this as he told the *Tallahassee Democrat*, on Friday, September 10, "Their best point of appeal is that they didn't get a fair shot."[26] The judge denied the request to stay his own order.

Even though we requested an immediate hearing—starting the next day—as now for us time was of the essence because the presumption of whether we were on the ballot was reversed, the judge said he had a trip to California, so he couldn't schedule a final hearing on the merits for a permanent injunction until September 15! At this point, the wrangling was all about whether a higher court would stay the order, pending appeal. We all went home, only to rendezvous later in the month.

The Florida secretary of state's office filed an appeal and in so doing preserved the presumption that we were on the ballot, even though the secretary knew she would be mercilessly blamed for playing politics. Indeed, the *New York Times* editorialized against Secretary Glenda Hood, claiming she was a Katherine Harris redux.[27] The liberal bias of the *New York Times* editorial board, which had reduced itself to a Gore/Kerry propaganda machine, hammered Hood. A new hurricane, Ivan, was now threatening Florida, and there was no guarantee that any other court was going to hear anything pending the hurricane, thereby putting the supervisors of the election in an untenable spot. The secretary of state did what she thought was best for the voters—both when she sped up the hearing, ensuring that we wouldn't be represented and working against our interests, and when her office reps tried to speed up the resolution by appealing, when their "hurry up" tactics worked in our favor. Their behavior was consistent and rational despite the *New York Times*'s tar and feathers.

The judge, in the meantime, was being quoted by every paper who could find him that he was "quite confident in the ruling": "There's at least 15 reasons as to why they won't qualify, at least 15 that I counted up,' Davey said during a status hearing."[28] The Ballot Project, Inc., the 527 group devoted to knocking us off the ballot across the country, had hired lawyer Ed Stafman, who was telling the press, "At the convention, they didn't even have balloons"—as if this were the requisite indication of what constitutes a political party.[29]

By the time everyone reconvened for the September 15 hearing, the Reform Party had filed an affirmative count against the Democrats to have them removed from the ballot for certification failures akin to those the Dems had alleged against the Reform Party. Nader/Camejo did not, keeping with our stand of not preventing access to anyone for the ballot. The Greens also pointed out that George Bush had not timely filed his certificates. At this point I wondered if this lawsuit was going to knock everyone off the ballot in Florida, creating a scenario even weirder than 2000.

This didn't happen. All pistols were withdrawn. The Democrats quietly withdrew their objection to the Reform Party on the flawed certification ground. The very same Democratic Party chairman, Scott Maddox, also told the *St. Petersburg Times* that even though he knew that Bush's certificate of nomination didn't reach the secretary of state's office until September 2, a day after the deadline, he was not going to challenge Bush's papers because "to keep an incumbent president off the ballot in a swing state the size of Florida because of a technicality, I just don't think would be right."[30] Got that? The Democrats had no problem with George Bush being on the Florida ballot. But Ralph Nader? No way.

In the meantime, when the trial court judge returned to the jurisdiction, he immediately vacated the secretary of state's automatic stay, meaning we were back off the ballot. He then conducted a full day's hearing. At this hearing, I took the stand and explained both nominating processes, why we sought the Reform Party's nomination, and the status of the party. Shawn O'Hara, Beverly Kennedy, Janice Miller, and John Blare all testified about the state of the Reform Party, who did what, the national scope, and the processes.

Brian Moore, a registered Democrat in Florida, took the stand and testified about the health of the Reform Party in Florida; he testified that while he was currently running for office as a Democrat, he also had run on the Reform Party platform.

An expert named Dr. Gillespie, a longtime Democrat, testified that the Reform Party USA "very much is a national party today." Unlike Professor Allan Lichtman, who was being paid $250 an hour for his appearance for the Ballot Project,[31] and who would later seek the Democratic nomination for the Senate from Maryland, Gillespie was unpaid. Gillespie said that the Reform Party was a national party in that it was in more than one state and more than one region of the country. He testified that no matter how defined, the Reform Party qualified as a national minor party.

Richard Winger, also an expert in minor parties, also unpaid, and who had at that time published *Ballot Access News* for more than nineteen years, testified: "The Reform Party of the United States is definitely a national minor political party. It's one of the five most important nationally-organized minor parties in the United States based on hard statistical data."

The hearing went on all day. Nothing the judge heard changed his mind. (How could it after he spent the prior week telling the newspapers how right his prior decision was in so many ways?) He threw Nader/Camejo off the ballot.

By the end of the day, the Florida Supreme Court had reversed in part Judge Davey's order to preserve the status quo and prevented the secretary of state from sending out any ballot, pending the review of the Florida Supreme Court, which would be less than twenty-four hours later, at 8:00 A.M. on Friday, September 17. We had to file Florida Supreme Court briefs and get ready for oral arguments—and thirteen of those twenty-four hours had been spent in Judge Davey's court on the final hearing.[32]

What a roller coaster. In less than a week, we were on, off, on, off, and again on the Florida ballot and now were on our way to the Florida Supreme Court. My head was spinning, not just with Florida's but with the whole country's litigation. It was really too much. And of course this was the point. Death by a thousand motions filed across the country. Ralph and Peter were now opening their speeches by accepting service of summons—waiving thick packets of lawsuits in the air, saying, "This is what democracy looks like"—to the roar of the crowds.

On the morning of September 17, a battalion of lawyers, press, and interested parties descended on the Florida Supreme Court, an imposing building akin to the U.S. Supreme Court. I was exhausted.

As I entered that great hall of the Florida Supreme Court, I chose to sit alone in the front pew. George Meros argued for the secretary of state. He was superb, an obviously experienced appellate litigator. Larry Tribe parachuted in from Cambridge for the Democrats to reprise his role in 2000. Andrew Byrne, the Reform Party lawyer, went up to him before the argument and told him that he had studied his book on constitutional law, when he [Byrne] was in law school at Vanderbilt. According to Byrne, Tribe told him that he hoped he "had not read it too closely," then agreed to autograph Byrne's docket sheet. Ken

Sukhia skillfully represented our interests, in conjunction with Byrne for the Reform Party. They noted that the only term the Florida statute defined was the term *minor party* and that the other terms of *national party* and *national convention* had to be taken in terms of a minor party—not comparing the multiday, multi-balloon, multimillion-dollar shows of the major parties with a minor-party convention. They noted that *minor party* was defined by the statute as "any group of citizens organized for the general purposes of electing to office qualified persons and determining public issues under the Democratic processes of the United States" who has "filed with the department a certificate showing the name of the organization, the names of its current officers, including the members of its executive committee, and a copy of its constitution or bylaws."[33] That's it. There was no means test, no number of balloons or conventioneers required.

To the Florida Supreme Court, our side's lawyers posited:

> How can it be argued that the Reform Party is not a national party when in the last decade it has nominated and run for president, three figures of national importance (Ross Perot, Pat Buchanan, Ralph Nader), it stands as the fourth largest independent party in the United States based on its membership nationwide, it is the only minor party in the United States which has qualified for matching funds in the primary and [public financing in the] general election campaigns, it is identified by the Federal Elections Commission as having a "national political committee," it was identified by the Elections Commission as a national political party in a court filing only three weeks ago in federal court in the Northern District of Florida, and its presidential candidate ran on the ballot in 50 states [*sic* 49] and had undeniable national significance in the presidential race in 2000.[34]

The much-esteemed Mr. Tribe was remarkably unimpressive. He argued that if a party is not organized in *all* fifty states, it is not a national party. This would, by definition, virtually exclude every minor party in the United States, with the possible exception of the Libertarians. All other embryonic parties and minor parties, no matter how vigorous, would not qualify under Tribe's definition. I couldn't believe the intellectual dishonesty of this position.

Two weeks later, the *Harvard Law Record* wrote that Tribe defended his involvement, pointing out that "Nader's participation went against the very ideals which Nader had trumpeted for his entire career."[35] He went on to say: "For Nader to use the ballot box in states like Florida as a pulpit for his views, however progressive and enlightened some of those views may be, seems to me an inexcusable indulgence and a grave abuse of the electoral process." He claimed, "It is an abuse that Ralph Nader is perpetrating at incalculable human and ecological cost, and one that, among its many tragic consequences, risks fully erasing the great legacy that Nader would otherwise have left in his wake."[36] For Tribe, this was not about the Florida statute; it was about whether Ralph was entitled to run at all. The *Record* claimed Tribe alleged that "Nader's decision to run is based more on ego than on a desire to improve the country."[37] I told the *Record* that Tribe's involvement in the Florida case was "shameful" and "an example of the lengths the Democrats will go to get Ralph Nader off the ballot."[38] At bottom, Tribe's argument was about denying American voters the choice of a Nader candidacy.

I thought the Florida argument went very well for us. So did Randall Marshall from the ACLU, who had watched it remotely from Miami. I had asked Marcia Jansen to email him and see if he would reconsider representing us if the case went further. He said, based on his viewing of the argument, he would be very surprised if the Florida Supreme Court did not overturn the lower court. I flew back to DC, and by 6:00 P.M. that very night, the Florida Supreme Court ruled for us, 6 to 1.[39] I was so happy, I cried. I got on the office PA and told everyone at headquarters. There was a deafening cheer. You would have thought we won the election. But in this campaign we were now defining winning as keeping democracy alive on the ballot.

To fully understand what happened in Florida, you have to understand the lengths to which the Democrats went around the country to try to keep Ralph and Peter off the ballot in every battleground state where our campaign turned in sufficient signatures to qualify.

Litigation Hell: Democrat Style

In the 2000 presidential election, the following sixteen states were decided by five or fewer percentage points: Arkansas, Florida, Iowa, Maine, Michigan, Minnesota, Missouri, Nevada, New Hampshire, New Mexico, Ohio, Oregon, Pennsylvania, Tennessee, Washington, and Wisconsin. Arizona and West Virginia were within six percentage points.[40] In 2004 we submitted signatures in all of these closely decided states and were therefore challenged by the Democratic Party and their allies in each and every one of them (with the exceptions of Missouri, where the state did not certify sufficient signatures, and Minnesota, where there was no challenge), often on the most frivolous, gratuitous, and mind-boggling grounds. In a span of twelve weeks, the Democratic Party and its partisan allies, both in the government and in the state parties, challenged our interests with twenty-five different complaints in eighteen states. Amazingly, despite the concentrated effort to remove Ralph's candidacy, we survived in all but four of the battleground states: Arizona, Ohio, Oregon, and Pennsylvania. We also lost in nonbattleground Illinois.

We survived in Colorado and New Jersey, two other states the *New York Times* mentioned on October 26, 2004, in "Neck and Neck Around the Country."[41] Of the *New York Times*'s identified top twelve states, we would be on the ballot in ten.[42] This is a tribute to the effort that went into withstanding the historically unprecedented litigation onslaught that the Nader 2004 campaign faced by defying Terry McAuliffe, John Kerry, Howard Dean, and the Democratic Party, by daring to put issues—including the Iraq War—on the table. Defending against baseless lawsuits brought on trumped-up technicalities is quite different from initiating constitutionally based challenges to the law. In the latter, we were removing barriers to entry for third parties and independents that could be considered unconstitutional or were already declared unconstitutional elsewhere, including at the U.S. Supreme Court. Standing to bring these cases typically vests during elections with live candidates attempting to secure ballot placement. These affirmative challenges, where the candidate controls the venue, the timing, and the nature of the challenge, are quite different than defending against aggressive, breakneck-paced litigation designed to remove a candidacy after signature petitions have been submitted and before ballots are printed. The Nader campaign was doing both, simultaneously.

Defiance cost us dearly in terms of our ability to wage a robust, get-out-the-vote general election campaign. But our decision to go this route reflected our heartfelt rejection of forced harmonization,[43] the political equivalent of price fixing: colluding with the Democratic Party to limit Americans' choices on the ballot. Most liberals or "progressives," including the national Green Party, capitulated to the imperative of removing George W. Bush by swallowing whatever the Democrats offered. We did not. We opened a second front. This chapter provides a summary of some of the lawsuits filed against us by the Democratic Party and its allies simply because Ralph Nader dared to run for president in all the states. The massive litigation campaign was not about giving Americans free and fair elections. It was about conspiring behind the scenes to muzzle a particular candidate because he and his antiwar platform might actually appeal to a statistically significant part of the population.

I went through some forty boxes of legal briefs and opinions to digest and document for history this abuse of judicial process in the battleground states where Nader/Camejo submitted signatures to be on the ballot. The Democratic Party, its state parties, its lawyers, and its supporters did whatever they could to remove Ralph and Peter from the ballot; and the whole story of their endless, baseless litigation—and how they exploited loopholes and ambiguities in the law and the depths to which they sank—is really another book's worth of material. Here I offer spartan summaries of a few of them simply to re-create the mood. The rest can be found on my Web site at www.amatomain.com.

To defend against this litigation hell, our campaign was forced to keep litigation schedules akin to those of a major trial firm. Florida was just one case. On September 16, 2004, for example, this is the litigation schedule of court dates and hearings I had in my notes:

—9/17—Colorado (8:30 A.M.)

—9/17—Florida Supreme Court (9:00 A.M.)

—9/17—New Mexico (10:00 A.M.)

—9/17—Arkansas (1:30 P.M.)

—9/20—Maryland (11:00 A.M.)

—9/21—Ohio (9:30 A.M.)

—9/21—Wisconsin (time not set)

—9/24—Maine (2:00 P.M.)

—9/24—New Hampshire (time not set)

—10/4 (week of)—Texas (time not set)

The campaign employed one full-time young lawyer, a veteran of the 2000 campaign, just to manage the document flow. To combat the barrage of litigation, we retained lawyers of all stripes who believed in ballot access. Wherever we had Republican lawyers, the press would seize on this information and heap abuse on us for hiring a Republican. But with three dozen lawsuits pending, we were not going to have a political litmus test for lawyers. By the end, anybody with a law degree and a pulse who believed in electoral fairness and knew something about election law qualified.

In addition to Florida, the Democrats challenged three[44] other Reform Party ballot access lines—Colorado, Mississippi, and Michigan—in large part to try to obtain a nonbinding precedent to which they could point to undermine the validity of the Florida ballot line. Each of these states presents a colorful tale relegated to the notes published on my Web site, but perhaps the most revealing plot turn was to be found in the revelation under oath of the Democratic Party chairwoman of Maine.

Maine

Maine had a 4,000 valid signatures requirement, and the maximum a candidate could turn in was 6,000,[45] so we had to be extra careful about how many we collected and submitted there. The signatures had to be turned in—twice—once by August 8 to the registrar of the municipality where they were collected, and then picked up and refiled with the secretary of state by August 15, 2004.[46] Maine also required that all the electors named on the petition (four for four electoral votes) had to be registered as independents as of March 1, 2004. On August 16, the next day, the state had determined that we had filed 4,128 valid signatures. Two challenges followed. One was by Dorothy Melanson, "an individual" who just happened to be the head of the Democratic Party in Maine.[47] The state set a hearing for August 30.[48]

The reasons for the challenge? Allegedly, we had "defects that invalidate the petition forms in their entirety." These consisted of: first, the "use of a fictitious presidential elector," because John Noble Snowdeal, one of our electors, was registered as J. Noble Snowdeal, and his actual name is Joseph and not John; second, a "failure to file consent forms"; third, that Peter M. Camejo had not unenrolled from the

Greens by March 1, 2004, and therefore any petition with his name on it had to be struck; fourth, that the electors did not have their unenrollment certified by a registrar on the face of the petition; and finally, that circulators made false affirmations by affirming signatures that were not collected in their presence. Melanson, represented by the law firm Preti, Flaherty, Beliveau, Pachios & Haley, LLC, was trying in any fashion possible to get 128 signatures taken off the petitions. But then she went a little too far—by picking on the state employees. Melanson claimed that the municipal clerks had made mistakes, including accepting incorrect or missing address information on the petitions, certifying names where the signer was not registered to vote, and accepting names that were illegible.[49]

Our eloquent supporters gave testimony at the hearing; but it was Democratic Chair Dorothy Melanson who had the most interesting testimony: She testified at the hearing under oath before the secretary of state that the state and national Democratic Party was funding the effort nationally to stop Nader and to decertify his ballots. Indeed, they had funded two of the largest law firms in Maine to bring the challenges there.

This is the relevant part of the cross-examination of Melanson, which was conducted by Harold Burbank II, our lawyer in Maine:

> DM: We had heard from several people who felt that they were somewhat tricked into signing these petitions. We also were alerted to problems in other states—many other states. As I'm sure you're aware . . .
>
> HB: No, I am not aware, but . . .
>
> DM: So we started looking into the petitions themselves; we started looking into the electors, and just to make sure everything was okay. This is a nationwide process that many states are going through the exact same thing with the exact same problems.
>
> HB: When you say it's a nationwide process, is it being coordinated from any central location?
>
> DM: Um . . . the Democratic Party. The national Party is certainly looking at it. There's also an organization called stopnader.com.
>
> HB: Okay. Are you affiliated with stopnader.com?
>
> DM: I am not at all.

HB: Are you affiliated with the Democratic Party?

DM: I most certainly am.

HB: In what capacity is that?

DM: I . . . am the Chair of the Maine Democratic Party.

. . . .

HB: Did you make the assumption that your Party would support your work in this regard?

DM: My Party has supported that work.

HB: It is acting in concert to help you?

DM: My state party . . .

HB: The state party or the national party—either level.

DM: Members of my party—state and national—support this work.

HB: And do they support you?

DM: Well they certainly have.

HB: Do they contact you personally?

DM: Great many members.

HB: Do they send you funds?

DM: (Silence) Uhh—we get funds from state and national—from our members and from the national party.

. . . .

HB: Okay. Did they send you a separate fund to bring this challenge? Did they send you specified monies to pay attorneys to bring this challenge?

DM: There has been an arrangement, but it is not with me. I believe that come under client [*sic*].

HB: I'm asking you if the Democratic Party has contacted you personally and said we will support with money with other supports that as you need them to bring a challenge against the petitions of Ralph

Nader and Miguel Camejo [*sic*] in the state of Maine. Has the Democratic Party contacted you personally and asked you to do this?

DM: Yes.

HB: And have they said they will help you pay for it?

DM: They said they would help in many ways.

HB: Did they say they would help . . .

DM: Financially.

HB: Did they say they would help you pay for it?

DM: Yes.

HB: Did they tell you how much money they would give you?

DM: No.

HB: Did you ask them?

DM: No.

HB: Are they paying for your attorneys?

DM: They are.

HB: Do they expect that you should make a response to them in your capacity as state Democratic Chair once these hearings are concluded and decisions rendered by the Secretary of State's office?

DM: Are they expecting to hear what the decision is?

HB: From you personally?

DM: Yes.

HB: Was this part of the agreement that you made with them, I mean, I characterize what I've heard so far as an agreement between them and you to perform certain deeds for funds and to make a response as part of this agreement. Is that correct? In other words, they're expecting a report?

DM: There are members of the Democratic National Committee who certainly want to hear what the outcome of this. [*Sic*]

HB: They're expecting to hear this from you and from no other person?

DM: Or from my attorneys.

HB: Well, do you expect that they will call you and ask you to provide this information? Once these hearings are concluded . . .

DM: I'm expecting that I'll probably call them first.[50]

The Maine hearing officer issued her report on September 2. She recounted the testimony of how J. Noble Snowdeal actually went in to sign his consent form in the office of the Jonesboro town clerk and was a real person whose real middle and last name were on the petition. It was unlikely that anyone would be misled by the discrepancy of "John" instead of "J."[51]

On the matter of the lack of "consent" filings, the hearing officer noted: "The Secretary of State's Office has consistently interpreted these sections of law to mean that it is the presidential electors, and not the persons whose names are listed as President and Vice President, who are the nominees, and thus the candidates who are subject to the candidate consent and unenrollment requirements. In fact, the Elections Division has not provided in the past, and did not provide during 2004, the candidate consent and unenrollment forms to any persons whose names would appear on the ballot under the Office of President and Vice President." In a footnote, the hearing officer said that no other minor- or major-party candidates for president or vice president were required to file such forms.[52]

The hearing officer also said that the electors, not Camejo, had to be unenrolled. She went on to say that Rosemary Whitaker, another elector challenged in the second complaint, offered proof that she had been unenrolled for the last thirty-eight years of her life; the Democrats withdrew that challenge. The hearing officer also rejected the claim that the electors' unenrollment had to be on the face of the petition and said this was not true as long as they were unenrolled before March 1, 2004.

With respect to the validity of the signatures on the petitions, the challengers presented two town clerks whose testimony supported the Nader campaign, not the challengers. The challengers also failed to offer any evidence to support allegations of duplicate signatures or people not residing where they had indicated on the petition.

Finally, the hearing officer determined that no one was coerced into signing, and some who complained about being misled either did not sign or did not ask to see for what or for whom they were signing. The officer dismissed these claims as well and recommended that the secretary of state determine that the challenge to the petition was not valid.[53]

On September 8, 2004, the secretary of state, a Democrat, Dan A. Gwadosky, adopted the "Report and Recommendation of the Hearing Officer." Under the statute, challengers had five days to appeal by commencing an action in the superior court.[54] Unbelievably, after losing every single count they had raised, trivial as they were, the Democratic Party–financed Melanson appealed. This was not about the law.

Thankfully, the court made quick work in denying this flimsy challenge. On September 27, Justice S. Kirk Studstrup of the Maine Superior Court issued a decision stating that Melanson "has failed to sustain her burden to show errors of law, abuse of discretion, or facts unsupported by the record as to any of the four counts in her petition."

The court also noted that other arguments listed in the petition but not made at oral argument were considered abandoned.[55] Despite having lost all the counts in both the administrative hearing and the court, the law firm and Melanson again appealed. On October 6, the Maine Supreme Court heard oral arguments and issued two days later a decision, *per curiam*, affirming the superior court and concluding that the secretary of state did not err in placing Ralph Nader and Peter Camejo on the ballot.[56] Admission of the national Democratic Party's financing of these challenges had been smoked out on cross-examination, contradicting Terry McAuliffe's earlier statement that the party was "supporting" but not paying for these challenges.

West Virginia

On May 1, we lost the Mountain Party's nomination by a vote of 20 to 35. Even though supposedly independent, it would be supporting Kerry. So in West Virginia the campaign needed to collect 12,962 signatures, or 2 percent of the votes in the last presidential election, by August 2, 2004.[57] A candidate also has to pay a "certificate of announcement" fee—which amounts to $2,500!—to get on the ballot.[58] There was also some confusion over the face of the petition. The

West Virginia statutes on the book still had requirements that were declared unconstitutional by a court.[59] The state laws still required that the face of the petition contain language informing voters that their signature on a candidate's petition would *forfeit their right to vote* in the state's primary! We initially followed the state statutes and put this unconstitutional language on our original petitions. The West Virginia secretary of state wanted to make sure that we weren't going to sue over this snafu; we wanted to make sure that the secretary of state's office was not going to claim this against us, since we were following their out-of-date statutes.

We hired a professional company, turning to Jenny Breslin at JSM, who said she had an operation that could be in West Virginia. The problems began the moment Breslin's company set foot there. West Virginia statutes require that a circulator must obtain credentials from the county being worked in and file a copy of the petition with the county clerk.[60] Breslin got all of her circulators credentialed and filed copies of petitions in any county in which they were working.

When she arrived in the state, she went straight to the secretary of state's office and spent two hours there talking to Cindy Smith and Dan Kimble of the Elections Division. Breslin asked multiple questions about the credentials and was told "that in each county that the circulator would work in he or she must be credentialed in that specific county, but they could take signatures from any county as long as the voter came into the county the circulator was credentialed in." Breslin was told that "if anybody asked to see the credentials that the voter had a right to see them, so always keep them on your person or keep them with you."[61] Each circulator had multiple sets of credentials for a number of counties. Indeed, Breslin's people collected in fifty-four of West Virginia's fifty-five counties. Just imagine the paperwork simply to be "credentialed."

On July 18, the West Virginia papers ran a story saying that the Kanawha County prosecutor's office was "investigating" the Nader campaign's circulators. What? The county wanted to make sure they were circulating legally. When Breslin read this, she went through the roof—she had spent all week making sure that every law was being followed. She called me about the newspaper reports: she was marching into that county prosecutor's office the next morning.

She asked prosecutor Mike Clifford why he seemed to be advertising in the newspaper for complaints against the campaign and her company. He claimed that he had received several complaints from people that the circulators had failed to display the official credentials. She explained to him that the secretary of state's office did not instruct them to do this and that they explicitly always said that "a voter has the right to ask to see the credentials. It's best to have them with you" (that is, they could be in a circulator's pocket). The prosecutor said, no, they had to be exhibited, as the statute said. Indeed, the statute does say the credentials should be exhibited, but after repeated questioning, that is not what the secretary of state's office said. The two governmental divisions were in a dispute about their own law, with us in their crossfire.[62] Clearly, this wasn't some law being regularly enforced, but seemed like another way to harass us.

Breslin left the prosecutor's office and went straight back to the secretary of state's office and told Jan Casto, the senior assistant secretary of state, that they were giving people the wrong information, even though the office once again affirmed that they, not the prosecutor, were correct about the credentials. Indeed, they called Cindy Smith and Dan Kimble and got them out of a meeting in New Orleans to talk on the phone; they got out the office handbook and compared it to what the prosecutor was telling Breslin. Breslin had to tell the secretary of state's office that they had incorrect rules according to the face of the statute and that they were instructing people incorrectly. According to Breslin, "[N]ot one county registrar's office, but every single county registrar's office [said], 'no, if somebody asks to see them, they have got the right to see them. If they ask, show them.' "

At that point, taking no chances, Breslin went out and laminated and hole-punched every circulator's credentials and told them to wear the credentials around their necks or put them on a table in plain view if they were seated. She informed the secretary of state's office that this is what her circulators were doing to correct the erroneous instructions they had received from the secretary of state. They told her that this was fine. This is the sort of absurdity the campaign faced. Everyone, though, from the secretary of state's office to the prosecutor's office to the attorney general's office, who were all present at a subsequent meeting on July 23, were in agreement that this was now cleared up.

The prosecutor received no more "complaints." Indeed, it turned out that he was initially asked to investigate by a Democratic delegate to the state legislature (a state legislator), Carrie Webster (D-Kanawha), who we would find out later in the court case testimony, recruited a plaintiff and the attorney general's office to file a complaint against the campaign.

At one point, the secretary of state's office said it was going to put out a press release about all of the confusion surrounding the Nader campaign's petitions. As they read me their draft, I complained bitterly. It turns out that the secretary of state's office was particularly upset about an erroneous *Charleston Gazette* editorial that further clouded the issue about whether people lost their right to vote in the primary by signing a petition, and the secretary of state's office was trying to "clear this up." I told them that if they sent this release out, with language that corrected their problem but also read like an invitation for people to call up and take their names off all our petitions, I would be on the next plane to sue them for interfering in the elections. They deleted the offensive language and sent out a rather innocuous "notice."

On top of this, Breslin's circulators were facing all kinds of hostility on the street. Democrats outregister Republicans two to one in West Virginia, but Bush still beat Gore there in 2000 by 52 to 46 percent, with Nader earning less than 2 percent. People circled our petitioners in a threatening manner, and one petitioner was met with a shotgun. Breslin was so concerned for the safety of a team of eight or nine African American petitioners that she sent them away and canceled her trip to see her husband for their thirty-third wedding anniversary.[63] She testified in her deposition: "I became concerned for their safety. And they were frightened." After someone called the news cameras on JSM petitioners, some petitioners just ran away, not wanting any kind of publicity. Of course, this created all kinds of adverse publicity for our campaign—petitioners captured on camera running away from the press. Given the hostile climate, those petitioners did not want to be harassed for just showing up to do their job.

The *Charleston Gazette* seemed to be on a one-paper media campaign to discredit the Nader campaign, including big front-page stories and salacious headlines: "Nader Camp Admits Hiring Controversial Firm"—as if we, rather than the newspaper, thought the firm was controversial.[64] The *Gazette* editorial actually said, "Meanwhile we remain convinced that the Nader petitions are partly a Republican ploy to put his name on the November ballot to draw Democratic presidential votes away from John Kerry and give West Virginia's electoral votes once again to Republican George W. Bush."[65] They went out of their way to malign our campaign at every turn. Somebody from the *Columbia Journalism Review* should investigate their "coverage."

On July 29, we submitted 23,249 signatures. The secretary of state confirmed that more than 15,000 signatures were valid, and then they stopped counting. On August 16, 2004, Jason E. Huber, a lawyer from Forman & Huber, filed a petition on behalf of five petitioners[66] claiming that they were entitled to get access to the Nader petitions under the West Virginia Freedom of Information Act and that the secretary of state had failed in his duties to initiate an investigation of Nader's campaign or to refer this matter to the attorney general's office. Huh? Huber attached affidavits from a handful of people who claimed that they were not told who the petition was for or that it was for a "minority candidate" and newspaper articles claiming problems with the Nader ballot access campaign in West Virginia. Huber then wrote, "The issues discussed above are not limited to West Virginia but rather represent a pattern of unlawful and fraudulent behavior on behalf of Mr. Nader nationwide."[67] Sound familiar?

To put this in context, Joe Manchin, the secretary of state, was running for governor as a Democrat. To his initial credit, he said as of August 3, 2004, that no complaints had been filed against the Nader/Camejo campaign except by four people who did not actually sign the petition, so he had "nothing to stand on now" to investigate.[68] But within days of this statement and subsequent to the filing of the Huber suit against him, he did the politically expedient thing: he punted the problem to the attorney general's office so they could challenge the ballot status by using a little-known process called "quo warranto."[69] Manchin claimed that he was "following the recommendation of an investigating committee that has officially determined" that "there is doubt as to the legitimacy and the validity of the petitions in support" of Nader's nomination.[70]

I received the attorney general's complaint against Ralph on August 24.[71] The complaint stated that the affidavits of various people approached by Nader circulators complained of the following: (1) circulators failed to display credentials; (2) circulators failed to inform signers of the purpose of the petition; (3) circulators displayed the petition in a manner that failed to reveal it was for Nader; and (4) circulators evaded answering who the petition was for or (5) made misleading statements about the purpose, including that it was to raise the minimum wage, give everyone a chance to vote, get a minority candidate on the ballot, allow independent candidates on the ballot, allow a third party on the ballot, or allow anyone to run for president.[72] We were supposed to defend ourselves in court on August 30.

On August 27, I was still looking through Martindale Hubbell for an attorney in West Virginia. I even called the firm who had lawyers who would be testifying against us, as I didn't know who all was arrayed against us as of that date![73]

On the date of the hearing, I landed in Charleston, West Virginia, hoping to meet Harry Kresky from New York, who had agreed to represent us on the fly. The whole thing was surreal. The airport has no cabs. When I called one to show up, I noticed there was a big smiley face sign on the cab's window saying, "Smile, you are on candid camera." Sure enough, there was a camera in the cab, attached to the rearview mirror. What was this? I asked if the camera was recording me and our conversation, and the bleached-blond, seventy-year-old-plus female driver said yes. And then she went on about how much she hated it and that the company claimed it was there to protect the drivers against crime from passengers; but she felt it was being used to spy on the drivers. She couldn't blow her nose unless it was recorded for corporate headquarters. She once got in trouble and was "written up" for covering up the camera. She said the company had a monopoly. So even though the drivers hated it, there was no where else to go to work driving cabs. I, for the record, railed on right into the camera about abusive corporations and privacy intrusions. I was already hopping mad, and I wasn't even at the courthouse yet.

In a postmortem write-up of his litigation experiences with the campaign dated October 27, 2005, Kresky described his arrival as "right out of *My Cousin Vinnie* (Theresa and I, a Jew from New York, and an Italian from Chicago)." As he recounts: "It became apparent very quickly that the case against the Nader petition was completely frivolous. It consisted of 20 or so witnesses who testified as to alleged irregularities with regard to the one signature that they gave or the two or three signatures that they observed."

Kresky noted that:

> a substantial percentage of the witnesses were affiliated with the state itself or the local Democratic Party organization. A particularly egregious line of testimony came from an attorney who worked in the Consumer Fraud Division of the AG's office. She said that her office

had been solicited to look into the Nader petition drive by a Democratic State Delegate [legislator] and to provide an affidavit of complaint. She and a colleague went out to observe the petitioning operation, and she took particular note of the fact that some of the gatherers were poor and black. On cross-examination I asked her what was the problem. Were such persons not allowed to gather signatures? They were, she agreed, but claimed that such persons were likely to be misled and duped into doing something they didn't understand. I then asked her if the signers were told who the candidate was. She said yes and the Consumer Protection Division did not open an investigation. . . .

About midway through the Attorney General's case, the Judge called the lawyers up to the bench and asked the Assistant Attorney General prosecuting the case:

Q. Now is it true that the SOS validated the petition with more than 23,000 signatures?

A. Yes, your honor.

Q. Do you mean to say that you want this Court to invalidate a petition signed by 23,000 West Virginia citizens (and disenfranchise them) on the basis of anecdotal testimony by a handful of witnesses, including fact witnesses from the Attorney General's office itself?

The judge was particularly distressed that the Attorney General was calling fact witnesses from its own office. I gripped Theresa's arm as this colloquy occurred. The judge got it. The case was a farce.

The hearing ended at about 4:30 p.m. The Judge called us into chambers for a brief conference and asked the Assistant Attorney General "what is the statutory basis for the proceeding," and was told a "quo warranto." He then asked if the statute had ever been used before to attempt to invalidate a nominating petition. The Assistant Attorney General said, "no."[74]

Judge Kaufman ruled that "there are no West Virginia cases supporting the relief the Attorney General has requested herein." He noted that there is no requirement that petitioners in West Virginia had to begin their conversation with potential signers by stating the name of the candidate and that the circulators justifiably relied on instructions given by the representatives of the secretary of state. He said by way of example that the secretary of state's office testified that it was orally correcting erroneous instructions on its own Web site. The judge concluded that "the testimony of a half dozen citizens does not constitute the showing that would be required to invalidate these petitions as a matter of law." He said, "Whatever weight is assigned to the state's interest in the lack of display of credentials for a proven fraction of the petition effort, those state interests do not outweigh the harm that would occur from removing these candidates from the ballot."[75]

Kresky summed it up: "I was impressed with Judge Kaufman because he saw right through the nonsense and the state's ginned-up proceedings and pretty much called the AG on it." The next day the attorney general's office took an appeal to the West Virginia State Supreme Court. Their Petition for Injunction contained this language in its recitation of the "facts": "An unsupervised cadre of 38 people, paid on a per-signature basis, was released on unsuspecting West Virginians, without any restraints imposed upon their conduct, none of whom could be found by the State to appear for the hearing, and none of whom were produced by Mr. Nader's campaign. Thus, the easiest means of rebutting the State's evidence—calling the canvassers themselves—was a telling omission in Mr. Nader's evidentiary presentation."[76]

On September 9, the West Virginia Supreme Court, minus the justice who was related to the attorney general, denied the appeal unanimously in a one-page order two days after we had responded to the attorney general's brief.[77] Even the *Wall Street Journal*'s editorial board, no fans of Ralph Nader, wrote an editorial saying that the "fishiest situation involves West Virginia, where a state judge recently slapped down an unprecedented case brought by the state itself (rather than outside Democratic lawyers) to keep Mr. Nader off the ballot. . . . What was curious was that those objecting were the very state officials charged with instituting fair elections." The *Journal* concluded, "We don't buy Mr. Nader's argument that a two-party system is by nature corrupt. But these Democratic tactics are only bolstering Mr. Nader's complaint—not to mention giving him more incentive to campaign not just against the incumbent Mr. Bush, but also against Mr. Kerry."[78]

In defensive litigation, in addition to the Reform Party lines of Florida, Mississippi and Colorado, we also won all the complaints brought in Iowa, Nevada, New Hampshire, New Mexico, Washington

State, Wisconsin, and Arkansas. These state court victories follow the pattern of Maine and West Virginia—trivial complaints, usually over ambiguous statutory provisions, designed to find something on which a court could strike the validity of the signatures, and these cases are synopsized on my Web site at www.amatomain.com. There are only four battleground states where we lost to Democratic challenges after having submitted sufficient signatures. They are Arizona, Ohio, Oregon, and Pennsylvania. The Ohio facts on my Web site describe how the unconstitutional laws there were finally ruled to be unconstitutional by the unanimous federal appellate court in October 2008 (in a case we initiated in 2006), with a decision that states Ralph was improperly removed from the Ohio ballot in 2004. The circus maximus of Pennsylvania follows.

Pennsylvania

I was holding my breath. At 5:00 P.M. on August 2, Jason Kafoury was not responding to any of my urgent intercom pages. Why?

He was holding his breath. John Slevin, a hired petition firm principal, our eastern and western Pennsylvania state coordinators, and a Slevin deputy were in a mad dash for the secretary of state's office, with more than $100,000 worth of signatures totaling more than 51,000 citizens of Pennsylvania.[79] For reasons that will be explained, Slevin had spent the better part of the last two days combing through the petitions, striking out anything that on its face looked fabricated or forged by the signers while trying to save the good ones. This was a time-consuming endeavor, and they hadn't finished copying the petition before turning it in, a requirement we had of all circulators.

So now Kafoury was actually "MapQuesting" them from Washington, DC through the streets of Harrisburg at 4:45 P.M. They slipped in the door a few minutes before 5:00, and their cell phones went dead. Nothing in Pennsylvania went well.

It is not as if we weren't warned. One of the first emails I got after Ralph declared in February was from a man in Allentown, Pennsylvania saying, "PA is not simply a swing state but one of the dirtiest political whorehouses in America. If we are to succeed in ballot access we need to start now and move aggressively. Ed Rendell will destroy any lesser effort." Indeed, even Governor Ed Rendell, in a 1997 interview with the *Wall Street Journal*'s editorial board, admitted that Philadelphia judges had "a rich history of corruption."[80] That was a warning.

Pennsylvania had at least six obsolete, court-declared unconstitutional election laws on their books. For example, they had to send out hard copies of consent decrees dated *from 1984* to our statute coordinator as proof of their actual filing dates because the laws on their books were so outrageously out of date.

I also had to write to the secretary of the commonwealth because their legislature hadn't corrected the statutory requirements requiring circulators to be registered voters, a provision that had been struck down in Colorado as unconstitutional in 1999 by the U.S. Supreme Court in *Buckley v. American Constitutional Law Foundation, Inc.* The secretary wrote back, attaching another agreement to abide by the Pennsylvania court's decision in a case called *Morrill v. Weaver*. In that case, brought by the NYU Brennan Center for Justice, the secretary agreed to abide by a circulator definition of "an individual who at the time that individual signs the affidavit on the nomination papers is at least 18 years of age, has been a citizen of the United States for at least thirty days, and has resided in the Commonwealth of Pennsylvania for at least thirty days."[81] So all of our circulators had to meet a thirty-day residency requirement to be considered a qualified elector in order to be eligible to circulate. This meant that we could not send in a road crew but had to hire Pennsylvania residents.

This thirty-day residency requirement is what led us to hire Slevin, who had worked for the Libertarians and who had personally done a ballot drive in Pennsylvania in 1984. I told him I wanted a 75 percent validity rate. For myriad unpleasant reasons, I let Kafoury do all the communication with him.

By June 7, I made a note to myself that our first local state coordinator had only managed to recruit the twenty-one required electors and 1,912 signatures. We then hired a Reform Party devotee, Dan Martino, who made up in energy what he lacked in experience, and a second coordinator for the western part of the state. At that point, mindful of our limited budget, the drain of Texas, and the lawsuits that had begun, I had not hired more than two people in any state—indeed, mostly one or none. We were a campaign of volunteers. But we needed an army for Pennsylvania.

So Slevin was brought in to open up offices and recruit circulators and pay them by the signature to get the job done. He moved with great speed and did a nearly impossible job, for which I was grateful. But almost on arrival his office got overrun by Democratic Party operatives, and homeless people who were demanding pay for turning in obviously fraudulent signatures. With camera crews in tow. This was not going to happen.

Pennsylvania required the signatures of 2 percent of the highest vote recipient in the last statewide election, or 25,697 valid signatures, to be turned in by August 2, 2004.[82] The names of twenty-one electors had to appear on the nomination papers, and they had to be "independent" or "disaffiliated" before their selection and the commencement of petitioning.[83] The Democrats and Republicans each have to file only 2,000 signatures. And this passes as fair.

After we turned in Ralph and Peter's petitions, House Democratic Leader H. William ("Bill") DeWeese told the *Post Gazette*, "Working with the AFL-CIO, we will do everything humanly possible to fight this supreme egotist, who has lost his way."[84] On November 5, three days after the election—after Kerry lost (but won Pennsylvania)—the very same DeWeese would still be boasting that "our efforts to strike his [Nader's] name from the ballot proved successful for John Kerry in Pennsylvania."[85] Kerry beat Bush by only 144,248 votes—in a state of 9,273,421 eligible voters, half a million more registered Democrats than Republicans, and where his wife, Teresa Heinz, gives out tons of money through her foundation.[86]

The secretary of state's office knocked out about 5,000 of the 51,000-plus signatures Slevin had turned in, but seeing that we had far more than the 25,697 required, the secretary certified us for the ballot on August 9. The success was short-lived. Very.

On the same day, lying in wait, eight Pennsylvania registered voters moved to set aside our nomination papers through an armada of counsel, including Gregory Harvey of Montgomery, McCracken, Walker & Rhoads, LLP;[87] Daniel I. Booker and Efrem M. Grail and at least fifteen other lawyers[88] at Reed Smith, LLP (one of the fifteen largest law firms in the world); and Brian A. Gordon of the Law Offices of Brian A. Gordon, P.C.[89] Indeed, one state Democratic Party leader apparently told United Press International (UPI) that "we're ready to go to war."[90]

The law firm armada challenged approximately 37,000 of the signatures filed. They also claimed that Peter Camejo had filed a false affidavit saying he was "unenrolled" or not affiliated with a party when he was clearly a Green Party member and that alone prohibited him from appearing on the ballot. And they claimed that neither Nader nor Camejo could be on the ballot as Independents because they were Reform Party nominees in Michigan, so they couldn't be Independents in Pennsylvania.[91]

On August 19, 2004, Katharine Q. Seelye of the *New York Times*, one of the few reporters to even write about the breadth of the challenge against us, provided an insight into the scope of this legal campaign. In Pennsylvania, she wrote, "Mr. Booker [Dan Booker from Reed Smith] said that 8 to 10 lawyers in his firm were working pro bono on the case, 80 hours each a week for two weeks, and could end up working six more weeks. The firm also took on more than 100 volunteers. Working with Reed Smith was a Philadelphia lawyer, Gregory M. Harvey, an elections specialist who has been detached from his firm [Montgomery, McCracken, Walker & Rhoads] while he organized 70 volunteers at his end of the state."[92]

Meanwhile, Seelye wrote, "In Pittsburgh, software programmers and data-entry volunteers occupied three conference rooms at Reed Smith, where they created a database of the 47,000 names that were checked against the state's list of registered voters."[93] This is the kind of effort that was spent—and no expense spared from the corporate law firm world—to remove us from the Pennsylvania ballot. In the same article, Charles E. Cook Jr., a veteran nonpartisan political analyst, noted, "The Democrats are making this as difficult and as debilitating for him [Nader] as possible, making him expend blood, sweat and tears for every inch."[94]

Cook was right about the blood and sweat. But this just made me mad as hell. We were going to fight this all the way—through three trips to the Pennsylvania Supreme Court and two refused cert petitions to the U.S. Supreme Court. This is what happened.

We began the long legal haul to refute all this cooked-up effort by the Democrats, beginning with the charges in a hearing before the three-judge Commonwealth Court on August 27, 2004, at which the Honorable James Gardner Colins, Doris A. Smith-Ribner, and Charles P. Mirarchi presided. Within three days, the Commonwealth Court removed us for the first time from the ballot, stating that endorsements from other parties outside of Pennsylvania triggered the state's "sore loser" law. The court said that because Nader and Camejo were on the Reform ballot elsewhere in the country, this law meant that neither could appear on the ballot as Independents in Pennsylvania and that Peter had knowingly filed a false affidavit claiming to be an independent when he was a registered Green.[95] We appealed the next day to the Pennsylvania Supreme Court.[96]

Our argument to the Pennsylvania Supreme Court began by noting that the Commonwealth Court had erred in claiming that the Pennsylvania statutes barred the candidates from the ballot because they were not running as independents in other states. Not only did the Commonwealth Court's ruling contradict the plain language of the statute; it contradicted the last fifty-six years, during which the history and practice of the state was to include numerous candidates who ran as independents in Pennsylvania but were on different party ballots in other states.

We gave the example that in 2004 President Bush was running on the Conservative Party ticket in New York, a fusion state that permits candidates to appear on the ballot of more than one party, but that he was running as a Republican in Pennsylvania. Did that bar him from being on the ballot in Pennsylvania? We also noted that Michael Peroutka was being allowed in 2004 as a member of the Constitution Party in Pennsylvania but was also running as an American Independent in California; indeed, we pointed out that in 2000 Pat Buchanan and Ralph Nader both were on the Pennsylvania ballot even though each was running as a member of another party in other states. The same was true of Ross Perot in 1992; of Lenora Fulani in 1992; of Eugene McCarthy and Lenora Fulani in 1988; of John Anderson, Ed Clark, and Barry Commoner in 1980; of Lyndon LaRouche in 1976; of George Wallace in 1968; and of Henry Wallace in 1948!

We also argued to the Pennsylvania Supreme Court (and it noted in its decision) that Camejo did not file a false affidavit or intend to do so. To the contrary, we had gone over each and every word of that form with the secretary of the commonwealth's office and had filed it based on their interpretation that those statements requiring unenrollment or disaffiliation *only applied to the twenty-one Pennsylvania electors*, not to the candidates themselves.

In very simple terms, we argued to the Pennsylvania Supreme Court that the history of Pennsylvania and the interpretation of its code by the secretary of the commonwealth were correct and that the Democratic challengers and the Commonwealth Court's decision below had to be in error, as the U.S. Constitution would tolerate no other outcome.

While we were up there in the Pennsylvania Supreme Court, and in anticipation of winning and having to go through a painstaking review of the signatures, we also argued that Pennsylvania's hypertechnical standards on reviewing signatures unconstitutionally burdened ballot access and should be overruled. We pointed out that until 1995 Pennsylvania had allowed petitioners to add information in their own hand to the petition to supplement signer's omissions of dates, address, and occupation, which happens when you are moving quickly from one signer to another or as signers are eager to move on. After onerous decisions in *In re Nomination Petition of Flaherty* and *In re Nomination Petition of Silcox*, the petition-gathering process became much more burdensome in Pennsylvania, as these cases require the elector to personally write in everything.[97] This *Flaherty-Silcox* standard, we contended, was an unconstitutional burden on the process—that these decisions had turned nominating petitions into "political sport" in Pennsylvania. We said that "to run for office in Pennsylvania now, not only does one need political support, but now an election lawyer is a prime requirement."[98] Little did we know at this point that we really were going to need a dozen election lawyers and that we would be putting our candidates at risk of losing tens of thousands of dollars.

We also argued that people who had registered after they signed, or who were registered at a different address than where they signed, should be counted. We said that to strike these signatures was unconstitutionally burdensome in that the state's interest was not more compelling than the burden it placed on signature gathering. These were valid electors—they were qualified to vote, no matter what address they signed at, or whether they were registered five minutes or five days before or after they signed, as long as everyone was *eligible* to be a registered voter. Finally, we argued that there was no adequate time or procedure in the Pennsylvania statute to contest the secretary's action of striking signatures and that this violated the due process of the candidates.

The Pennsylvania Supreme Court reversed the Commonwealth Court's order.[99] We had won round one. In part.

The court majority agreed that Nader and Camejo could run as Independents in Pennsylvania and that Camejo had done nothing wrong in following the secretary of state's counsel. But the court rejected our claims that the registrations of people whose application was delivered or postmarked after the day they signed the petition should still count as if they were voters. The court also upheld its very stringent signature requirements in *Silcox* and *Flaherty*, holding that electors who sign nomination petitions also had to personally write their occupation, place of residence, and the date on the petition, as well as have signed their names precisely matching their names on the voter registration cards, even if they were validly registered to vote. In petitioning time terms, you might as well require voters to write a novel while they are signing!

The court casually dismissed our arguments that these standards were burdensome and unconstitutional by stating that these standards "do not concern the right of an individual to vote. Rather, they explain the steps that a candidate must take in order to be properly placed on the ballot."[100] As if there were no connection to burdening the ability of a candidate to get on the ballot and limiting voter choice! The high court remanded the case to the apparently none-too-happy Commonwealth Court to hold an expedited hearing on the validation of the signatures. The Commonwealth Court issued an order an hour or so later, ordering the campaign to appear in forty-eight counties and thirteen courtrooms to go over the signatures.[101] Counsel was supposed to be available from 8:30 A.M. until 10:30 P.M., including weekends! If we didn't have counsel, lack of representation would not prevent the review. Even the other side complained about the holding of simultaneous hearings in multiple courts with outrageous hours. Gregory M. Harvey, the Pennsylvania election law expert retained for the Democrats, told the Associated Press that the court's plan to hold multiple hearings is "without any precedent since the time the Commonwealth Court was organized in 1969."[102]

The campaign filed a motion stating that we simply did not have enough people to staff forty-eight voter services offices for voter registration review, nor did we have the attorneys to staff thirteen courtrooms for the sixteen hours a day contemplated by the Commonwealth Court's order. We argued that this shifted the burden unreasonably and unconstitutionally to us—because Pennsylvania has no rational administrative method for checking signatures—and here was the court implying that our failure to comply would allow us to remain on the ballot through "delay." Moreover, voter services was ordered by the court to help the objectors free of charge, but the court would then go on to assess all the court costs against the losers! The Commonwealth Court denied our motion.[103]

In the meantime, we had replaced Sam Stretton, a maverick Democratic lawyer whom we had hired initially, with Basil Culyba, a Pennsylvania native and topflight DC antitrust litigator who volunteered to take charge of the case. Culyba was not only supremely smart—he could actually litigate. We also flew out Ross A. Dreyer, a lawyer from California, who volunteered to help the campaign. And from time to time we sent in our master of logistics, a Princeton grad named Rob Cirincione—who could do just about anything short of turning straw into gold. I was hiring lawyers to show up for a day here, a day there, but couldn't possibly staff all the courtrooms all the time.

While all this was going on, we had additional nonsense to handle: On August 13, 2004, Louis Agre, a Democratic Party ward leader and lawyer, filed a class-action lawsuit against the campaign on behalf of Ralph Dade and all similarly situated employees. Dade claimed that homeless plaintiffs, numbering somewhere between fifty and one hundred, "were not paid wages for signatures collected" while employed by the campaign. There being absolutely no merit to this case, the Democrats ended up voluntarily dismissing the case with prejudice, after the election, but in the meantime, we got wind of why it was filed.

One of our campaign volunteers, because of his Nader bumper stickers on his car in a public parking lot, was approached by a homeless circulator and told the ruse was this: the campaign was a chump because we were paying $1.00 per signature when they (the homeless) were being paid $2.00 a signature to send in forged ones.

What was he talking about? The idea of the two-lawsuit front was concocted allegedly to get us to "confess" that the signatures were invalid for the purpose of avoiding liability in the bogus class action but valid for the purpose of qualifying for the petition. Allegedly this was supposed to trip us up and explain the one-two lawsuit punch.[104] Stunned by the information, unfortunately our volunteer did not have the presence of mind to get the informant's name or details but did immediately call us. We searched for this homeless person to substantiate the allegation, but ultimately we could not find him or confirm this scheme. To this day, I am hoping someone with information will step forward. Certainly such organized sabotage would explain some of the story that unfolded in this state and it wouldn't be the first time "walking-around money" was used in Philadelphia.[105]

Ultimately, the Commonwealth of Pennsylvania determined that we had submitted a total of 1,183 pages of nomination papers containing 52,398 signatures. Of these 1,183 pages, 38 with 2,457 signatures contained defects in the affidavit of the circulator, and 6 pages with 336 signatures contained defects in the preamble of the petition. After eliminating those pages and signatures totaling 4,936 signatures, the commonwealth counted more than 25,697 signatures that appeared facially valid and then stopped counting, determining that we had met the requirements of the code. This is the standard practice of Pennsylvania's election review applied to all candidates.[106]

In the meantime, Pittsburgh lawyer Ronald L. Hicks, of Meyer, Unkovic & Scott, LLP, filed a motion to intervene to challenge the court's holdings that to be a valid signatory to the nomination papers one had to be a registered voter. The intervenors argued to no avail that requiring signatories to the nomination papers to be registered voters rested on an incorrect understanding of Pennsylvania's election statutes and instead claimed that qualified electors included registered and nonregistered voters alike who signed the candidates' nomination papers.[107]

On October 12, Culyba called me to say there would be an order by 5:00 P.M. the next day. When all the tedious reviewing was said and done, this is how the numbers broke down: 18,818 signatures were accepted as valid; 32,455 were stricken for the following reasons:

- 7,506 were thrown out because eligible electors had not yet registered to vote
- 6,411 were registered voters but their current address did not match their registered address
- 7,851 were registered voters but had some information written in the hand of another, such as the date
- 1,470 were registered voters after the date they signed but still registered in time to vote
- 1,869 had omitted information, such as the date
- 1,855 had some affidavit problems—for example, they filled in the county of the circulator rather than the county of the signers
- 8 had printed their signatures
- 166 had illegible signatures
- 687 were considered forged signatures, which we had failed to find and strike out of the thousands we had struck and the more than 52,000 total filed

- 32 only put their nicknames or initials and not their name as registered
- 1,087 were duplicate signatures—they had signed our petitions twice
- 3,513—the rest—were miscellaneous other problems such as people who didn't correctly list their city or township

The final order of the Commonwealth Court removed Ralph Nader and Peter Miguel Camejo from the ballot.[108] I couldn't believe that we had such a low validity rate, even by Pennsylvania standards. But what was most troubling was the Commonwealth Court's language. It turns out that apparently this was the first time they ever had to sit and review so many signatures—prior to us, the most they had reviewed was on the order of 3,000 signatures. Well, we did not bring this challenge on the courts; the Democrats did. But the vitriol just dripped off the order.

The court accused us at every turn of ignoring their warnings and doing "as little as possible prior to the hearings," as if we were supposed to spend untold additional resources to fight a challenge we did not bring or have the burden of proof on, and after we had just spent months paying more than $100,000 to collect more than 51,000 signatures under their unconstitutional laws! Gratuitously, Judge Colins, a Democrat, wrote, "I am compelled to emphasize that this signature gathering process was the most deceitful and fraudulent exercise ever perpetrated upon this Court."[109] What?

Well, excuse us for running for office. The court's language really bothered me. It was as if they were striving to provide a media sound bite. At first I thought the court's hostility was because the judge didn't seem to like Sam Stretton. But he was gone, and Basil Culyba was a true gentleman type of lawyer. What was it that we had done that deserved this kind of inflammatory exaggerated statement? Despite our best efforts to strike the homeless circulators' phony signature ploy, the court found 687 signatures forged by signers, or 1.3 percent of the 52,000 we submitted in a flurry of signatures we had to gather to meet their impossible standards, surrounded by saboteurs at every turn!

One person suggested that this treatment could have been explained by Judge Colins's close association with the governor. According to a piece written by Darcy G. Richardson at the end of August 2004: "Judge Colins and Governor Ed Rendell are old friends and have known each other for more than twenty-five years. 'Fast Eddie,' as he is commonly known in Philadelphia political circles, is the popular ex-mayor of Philadelphia and former chairman of the Democratic National Committee, who is now serving as Governor of Pennsylvania."[110]

Culyba headed to the Pennsylvania Supreme Court in Harrisburg. To obtain the 25,697 valid signatures, we were going to need the supreme court to budge and include validly registered voters at some other address or those whose information got filled in by the petitioner. In response to our appeal, we were ordered by the Pennsylvania Supreme Court to file our briefs by 2:00 P.M. the following day. This was another Florida.

We argued four major points. First, we said that the Commonwealth Court erred as a matter of law in construing the term *qualified elector* to mean only a registered voter registered to vote at his or her address at or before the time he or she signed our nominating papers. This factor alone had excluded 15,387 otherwise perfectly valid signatures, even though we argued it was unconstitutional and unwarranted, given the Pennsylvania statutory requirement that the signatories be qualified electors—that is, just eligible to vote—rather than already registered voters.

Gaining ballot access was going to turn on the interpretation of Section 951 of the Pennsylvania Election Code.[111] This section provides, in relevant part, the terms under which independents, as opposed to major political parties, are to get on the ballot, including the number of signatures required, who is qualified to sign, and how they shall sign. In each and every paragraph of the relevant sections, the term used is *qualified elector of the State*. For example, "Each person signing a nomination paper shall declare therein that he is a qualified elector of the State or district."[112]

We argued that under the Pennsylvania Election Code a "qualified elector" is a defined term that "*shall* mean any person who shall possess all of the qualifications for voting now or hereafter prescribed by the Constitution of this Commonwealth, or who, being otherwise qualified by continued residence in his election district, *shall obtain such qualification before the next ensuing election*."[113] By definition, a qualified elector did not require someone to *already* be registered to vote, just to be able to be registered to vote. A federal court in Pennsylvania had already ruled this.[114] Under the Pennsylvania Voter Registration Act, individuals had until October 4, 2004, to register to vote for the

November 2, 2004, general election, but their names were being thrown out as petition signers in August![115]

Second, we argued that the lack of uniformity in procedures used by the courts below and the election officials resulted in a shifting of the burden to the petitioners, resulting in a violation of our due process rights and equal protection of the law under both the state constitution and the U.S. Constitution.

Third, we argued that by basing its ruling on hearsay and factual findings that ran afoul of basic evidentiary procedures regarding an elector's registration status, the Commonwealth Court also erred in striking our signatures. This is worth explaining because it helps to understand how so many signatures could get struck even when we were out there asking every petitioner whether he or she was registered.

The court relied on the testimony of election officials who did not bring any evidence—like voter signature cards—but rather stated that they had reviewed the SURE system—the Statewide Uniform Registry of Electors—except in Philadelphia, where nearly 70 percent of our challenges were heard. Philadelphia's system is not part of the SURE system and does not reference voters with the same identification number. As a consequence, someone who is properly registered elsewhere could show up as defective in Philadelphia just because his or her ID is no longer valid there.[116]

The director of the Allegheny County Elections Division testified in court that he didn't have the staff capacity to review all 9,800 of our signatures being challenged from his county, so he asked the Commonwealth Court to excuse his office from conducting a review of the paper voter registration records that were in his office and the electronic voter registration records that were on the SURE system. Instead, Allegheny County used an off-line copy of registration data that they had purposely extracted from the SURE system, which Allegheny County has no responsibility for keeping up to date. As a consequence, the Allegheny County database didn't include critical information—such as the receipt or postmarked dates of the voter registration applications that had been received but were not processed until weeks later! As of September 15, 2004, Allegheny County had some 40,000 registered voter applications, and there was at least a four- to six-week delay in processing these applications into the SURE system—all while the judges were reviewing our petitions. The Allegheny County office had all the paper registrations, but *none* of these were checked for the purpose of review of our petitions, only the out-of-date system.[117] Got that?

Our brief in the Pennsylvania Supreme Court noted that Mark Wolosik readily testified on cross-examination that he didn't agree with some of the voter registration determinations made by his own staff. But even he, when confronted with the record that there was only one voter in all of Allegheny County registered under a particular name, opined that that voter was not properly registered to vote because in Allegheny County's dubiously maintained off-line database his address was listed incorrectly, whereas he signed our nominating papers with his proper address which varied from their database by two digits.[118] These were not isolated incidences. The state's own "January 30, 2004 Final Report of the In-Process Quality Assurance Review Report of the SURE system . . . contained several notable problems as to the accuracy, reliability, trustworthiness and completeness of that computer database system, including without limitation that '[t]he SURE system lacks data quality and uniformity standards' which makes it 'slow at best and error prone at worst.' "[119] This is what passed for due process in Pennsylvania in checking our petition signatures.

Finally, we argued that the court below erred in striking the signatures of those who would be valid voters and allowed to vote because their addresses were not consistent with their registered addresses when they signed our petitions. In other words, it is not a crime to change your address between elections, and sign our petitions, as long as you are still able to vote. But the Pennsylvania Supreme Court was not prepared to overturn their prior ruling on this point in *Flaherty*.

On October 19, Culyba called me to say that the Pennsylvania Supreme Court had affirmed the lower court's decision to keep us off the ballot but that Justice Saylor was writing a dissent to follow.

The court's opinion, in its entirety, read: "ORDER, PER CURIAM, decided: October 19, 2004, AND NOW, this 19th day of October, 2004, the Order of the Commonwealth Court dated October 13, 2004 is affirmed. The Application For Supersedeas is denied. The Application For Intervention is dismissed as moot. Mr. Justice Saylor dissents. Dissenting Statement to Follow."

That's it. Fewer than than fifty words. I couldn't believe it. All those signatures, all those hours, all those volunteers, all the staff, all the lawyers. Tens of thousands of dollars down the drain, on top of the $100,000-plus we had paid for the signatures. I had to tell Ralph. We both shook our heads in complete disbelief that this was the process candidates—or just our candidacy—had to go through to have a chance to be presented to the voters in Pennsylvania.

When Justice Saylor's dissent arrived, we felt marginally better. At least one justice got it. Justice Saylor wrote that he believed that "the Commonwealth Court misconstrued relevant statutory authority, thereby assessing the candidates' submissions according to a standard that was more stringent than that which has been prescribed by the Pennsylvania General Assembly. Specifically, it is my position that the Commonwealth Court incorrectly construed the term 'qualified elector' as used in the Pennsylvania Election Code, to subsume a requirement of actual voter registration."[120] He took great pains to demonstrate how differing terms were used throughout the election code, as it recognized distinctions between a qualified elector and a registered voter throughout.[121]

Justice Saylor also noted that if his interpretation regarding the distinction between a qualified elector and a registered voter were the standard in place, the court below would have had to count not only the 1,470 signatures struck because the signer registered after they signed the petition but also the 7,506 signatures that had been invalidated solely because of a lack of registration at a particular address. Thus, 18,818 valid signatures and the 8,976 Justice Saylor would have added would have safely put the campaign over the 25,697 signatures needed. Justice Saylor would have ordered us to be on the ballot.[122]

Perhaps as important to us was Justice Saylor's footnote 13. The media kept repeating to great effect Judge Colins's view about deceit and fraud, but Justice Saylor calmly pointed out the following:

> A review of the tables and exhibits attached to the order, however, suggest that the problem was of a more limited scale (for example, 687 signatures out of 51,273 reviewed—or approximately 1.3% of the signatures—were rejected on the basis of having been forged). Moreover the Commonwealth Court cited no evidence that the candidates were specifically aware of fraud or misrepresentation at the time of their submissions, and the candidates note—and the objectors do not dispute—that when they became aware of any fraudulent conduct connected with specific signatures, they voluntarily withdrew those signatures from consideration. Finally, the Commonwealth Court's disposition is expressly predicated on a tallying of signatures as to which the objectors were

unable to meet their burden of proof (i.e. valid signatures), which is also the subject of my assessment here.[123]

Mark Brown, a professor at Capital University and a counsel for us in Ohio, wrote a law review article in 2006 detailing how the disqualification of signatures varied wildly from judge to judge, with Judge Colins responsible for invalidating 70 percent of the 10,794 signatures he reviewed and the other two judges, who had been initially reversed by the Pennsylvania Supreme Court, coming in with 73 percent disqualified (Judge Smith-Ribner) and 93 percent disqualified (Judge Mirarchi). No other judge had an invalidation rate more than 54 percent, and one judge found that 79 percent of those he reviewed were valid.[124] What was most curious was that the three-judge panel that had been overturned by the Pennsylvania Supreme Court, among the eleven judges sitting in review, managed to disqualify two-thirds of the signatures we submitted.

We had been looking into write-in procedures for Pennsylvania in case this happened. Early in October, Mike Richardson emailed to me that Pennsylvania "has the most archaic write-in law in the nation (except for Oklahoma). To cast a write-in vote for RN it will be necessary to write in the names of 21 electors!"

This was too ridiculous. According to Pennsylvania, our voters were going to have to write in twenty-one electors, in a small space on the ballot, to be able to vote Nader/Camejo. Nonsense. But the press person in Pennsylvania's Department of Elections had been telling reporters this, so there were a ton of Pennsylvania news stories saying that if Nader were off the ballot, people couldn't just write him in; they had to write in *all* twenty-one presidential electors and not misspell the names of any of them! This was laughable, but I was not laughing.

Richard Winger disabused the state's election person of this by sending him proof that in the past (November 1996, for example) the Pennsylvania Department of Elections did count various spellings of *Nader* as a write-in. The man was "surprised," but then, after checking with the Department of Elections, he said they would do the same this year. Less than a week before the election, the Department of State of the Commonwealth of Pennsylvania issued a two-page memorandum explaining how to treat votes for Ralph, Peter, or any of the twenty-one presidential electors, making it somewhat clear that the votes would be counted—but as a vote for a presidential elector, not really for president of the United States.[125]

We filed an emergency petition for *certiorari* with the U.S. Supreme Court on October 23, all to no avail. The Court denied us yet again, with no opinion or reasons given, as is typical at the Supreme Court.[126]

To add insult to injury, the Commonwealth Court ruled on January 14, 2005, that Ralph and Peter had to pay all the costs for the court stenographer appearances and transcript preparations, amounting to $81,102.19. We appealed this too in January 2005, and the litigation remains ongoing as this book goes to press.

To now assess costs against the candidates for doing nothing more than defending ballot access was unprecedented in the country and an unconstitutional penalty against our exercise of political speech. Can you imagine a more chilling effect on your right to petition than being liable for $80,000-plus in costs? People in Pennsylvania were going to have to mortgage their homes to run for office. If this was not an unconstitutional burden on candidates' rights under *Anderson v. Celebrezze*, what is? Still the Pennsylvania Supreme Court did not budge.

Instead, in a split decision, the court affirmed the lower court, holding that the Pennsylvania Election Code gives the trial court "discretion" to order candidates to pay and that the trial court did not abuse its discretion. The Pennsylvania Supreme Court treated this as a case of ordinary cost-shifting, rather than one in which constitutional rights were at stake. Indeed, they found "no evidence" that the penalty burdened our rights and that instead it was "rationally related" to the state's interest.[127] The objectors' counsel, Reed Smith, sent Ralph a new letter after the decision, demanding payment by November 3, 2006, for $89,821.23, representing the penalty plus "statutory interest." We told them to go "pound sand," and that we were taking this issue as well to the U.S. Supreme Court.

So on November 16, 2006, we filed yet another petition to the U.S. Supreme Court, seeking *certiorari* on the constitutionality of allowing a state to penalize candidates who submit nomination papers for public office by ordering them to pay $81,102.19 in litigation costs to opponents (not, mind you, a reimbursement to the court). We knew it was a long shot, especially because the Court had already turned us down on the underlying case, but this was truly unique in federal ballot access. In 2006 it was repeated. Pennsylvania decided to assess costs against another federal candidate, Green Party candidate Carl Romanelli, who had the audacity to run in the hotly contested 2006 Senate race between Rick Santorum (R) and Bob Casey (D). The Democrats didn't want Romanelli in that race because of their hopes of taking over the U.S. Senate, and so they pulled the Nader treatment on him too—and he was assessed $89,668.16 in costs and fees in an opinion that relied heavily on the flawed Nader court decision.

We argued that the largest election litigation in the history of the state of Pennsylvania, our case, was a direct result of the Democratic Party's strategy nationwide to "bankrupt the Nader campaign."[128] Ralph, after all, obtained ballot access in 2000 without controversy. Now, the politically motivated litigation campaign against us caused us to be hauled in to defend signatures that were being set aside—not because of any finding that we had done anything wrong but because of a legitimate question of statutory construction of the Pennsylvania code and because of the shoddy state of its database, stressed by unusually high registrations and a very contested political contest. At least fifteen of the twenty lawsuits filed by the Democratic parties in other states had already been dismissed.[129]

We argued that the decision would vest in trial courts an unlimited amount of discretion to penalize candidates for engaging in protected First Amendment activity. We argued that we were engaged in the lawful pursuit of achieving political ends to get on the ballot—these are classic First Amendment rights of speech, assembly, and petitioning, which should also be guaranteed for minor parties and independents. The assessment of costs was neither narrowly drawn nor serving any legitimate state interest. Indeed, we said that it was directly contradictory to the Supreme Court decision in *Bullock v. Carter*, which prohibits states from forcing "candidates to shoulder the costs of conducting . . . elections."[130] Pennsylvania had outsourced to us and its courts the job of verifying petitions.

The Supreme Court refused to hear the case. We couldn't believe that after the outrage of all this orchestrated venom that we would have to pay the attackers on top of it all. Ralph refused. After much wrangling, and unwilling to leave Ralph holding the bag, Peter gave the Reed Smith law firm $20,000 to get out of the lawsuit and so not face personal attachment of his business property. Reed Smith turned that over to the Western Pennsylvania League of Women Voters, and Philly-based "Committee of 70" since Reed Smith claimed they were doing this case "pro bono."[131] We believed that they had already been paid—by others—and that these were not their fees to collect in the first instance, an argument we made in a subsequent lawsuit, which remains pending.

Ralph went on the offense by writing to the partners of Reed Smith, a behemoth law firm, and to John Kerry personally. Kerry, in his ostrich routine, denied any knowledge. We are, as this book goes to publication, still fighting the Pennsylvania outcome in a lawsuit filed to challenge the Democrats' nationwide conspiratorial effort. In late 2007, we got more evidence. It turns out that the attorney general's office of Pennsylvania was investigating emails allegedly showing political activity occurring inside the Pennsylvania state capital offices and bonuses allegedly paid for, among other things, the "Nader effort."[132] On July 10, 2008, Pennsylvania Attorney General Tom Corbett released a 75-page Grand Jury presentment charging twelve current or former members and employees of the Pennsylvania House Democratic Caucus with criminal conspiracy, theft, and conflict of interest, including for their work on the "Nader effort"—allegedly on taxpayer time, using taxpayer resources. "Bonusgate" as the media calls it (because the state employees allegedly received $188,000 in bonus money for their political work in 2004, and even more in 2005 and 2006), may have additional fallout as Nader attorneys are pursuing these revelations in a Federal Election Commission complaint, along with pleadings to get the Pennsylvania courts to vacate their order to force Ralph Nader to pay costs for ballot access defense, both because of alleged judicial conflicts among members of the Pennsylvania Supreme Court and those seeking to remove Nader from the ballot, as well as the pending indictments.[133]

Dirty Deeds

Meanwhile, on September 22, 2004, the campaign got a call from a DNC whistle-blower. He said that the DNC was actually writing scripts that they gave to people on how to go after all the signers on Nader petitions and that these were being sent from www.dnc.org email addresses. He also said that he had to stay anonymous but that he would love to tell us who he was. He sent us a copy of an email from a principal assistant of Jack Corrigan, with a Word file attached. Corrigan, John Kerry's liaison to the DNC Convention in Boston, practices law at Corrigan & Levy, LLP, in Massachusetts.

The attached file had the following script—which apparently had been created as early as June 15, 2004—with this content:

SCRIPT FOR NADER PETITION SIGNERS (fill out for each signer)

Name on Petition: ____________ Address ____________________

Locality________

1. Hello, is this {Name on petition}. This is {Caller} I'm calling to check whether or not you signed a petition for Ralph Nader.

   Record a. yes

   a. no

   b. Signed something, didn't know it was for Nader

IF "YES", THANK YOU, JUST CHECKING, AND HANG UP.
IF "NO", OR "SIGNED, BUT DIDN'T KNOW IT WAS FOR NADER, PROBE AS FOLLOWS:

2. Your name is listed on a petition submitted by the Nader campaign. Do you recall signing any kind of petition? Record response:

   Yes

   No

   Don't know/remember

   a. If yes, what were you told you were signing? RECORD RESPONSE VERBATIM: ______________________________

   b. Can you describe the person who asked you to sign? (male, female, young. Old, beard, etc.) RECORD VERBATIM.

   ____

3. Would you be willing to meet with one of our volunteers to give a statement?

   Yes No

   If yes, thanks. I'll have someone get in touch with you right away. Do you have a cell phone as well, in case you're out?

   ____

Imagine the kind of effort that went into taking us off the ballot—calling up everyone who signed our petitions! Of course they could always find someone among the hundreds of thousands of signers who couldn't remember signing or came up with colorful imaginings of what they thought they were signing, and then the DNC through state parties and allies would use these few responses in court briefs to discredit the entire campaign. Individuals who are called, not knowing what is going on, might say, "Oh, I thought I was signing to affirm my voter registration," because now they are worried that someone is calling to check on them for exercising their First Amendment rights to sign a petition—and then this kind of reaction would get into a lawsuit complaint as we "deceived" people.

After Pennsylvania and Ohio, by late October 2004, the Nader/Camejo candidacy was barely mathematically viable. Unless the U.S. Supreme Court would reverse the state courts in Ohio or Pennsylvania, despite all of the time, money, and effort, we were going to be on the ballot in states with 50.15 percent of the population. This was not, and could not be, the standard for getting on the ballot in the United States of America.

Ten days before the election, I asked myself how this could be justice in the United States. We had won almost all of the big ones, but these two really bothered me: neither state procedure could be considered a test of whether you had a modicum of support among the electorate to be on the ballot. These "ballot challenges" were nothing more than hazing rituals by teams of highly paid, often Republican law firms, for hire to rich Democrats. Is this what someone has to go through to be a citizen candidate for president? I was so angry. I didn't care if I was considered a bitter harridan at this point. I vowed in my speech on election night to hold people accountable, which I have been doing in my own way ever since. I was also wounded by my fellow public interest lawyers. With a few notable exceptions, the public interest bar had sat on their hands as this denial of voter choice went down.

There is a verse in Eugenio Montale's *Cuttlefish Bones* that begins (in translation), "Often, I have met what is wrong in this life."[134] By the end of the campaign, I felt this mix of anger for the prior year and despair that was completely foreign to my personality. I felt run over. And that our longtime friends and allies had just left us in the street for dead. Worse, some of them thought we deserved it all, not even knowing a fraction of the battle details and the nonsense that went on to undermine our campaign.

Ralph would look at my facial expression every day we were in the office together, and he knew the score. We had fought like hell just to be on the ballot. We held press conferences encouraging reporters to investigate these anti-democratic activities. We tried to turn it all into lemonade by making the right to compete against the tyranny of the duopoly a central campaign issue.

What other democracy in the world would subject its citizens to this rigmarole? The answer is: none do. In my mind, the ginned-up ballot access litigation against our candidates constituted crimes of the highest order against the Constitution. At minimum, it reflected an abuse of judicial process and tortious interference into a federal election to suppress political dissent and remove political competition. Was there no law or legal process to stop this behavior?

The litigation had a number of results: First, the assault drained our campaign's time and resources, precisely as the Democrats designed it to do. It is no big secret that unless you are self-financed like Ross Perot or Michael Bloomberg, a third-party and independent campaign starts with the disadvantage of having to raise big dollars up front to get on the ballot, just to gain the privilege to compete. Millions of dollars get spent on ballot access, even before the legal fees. And if a party is trying to remove you, then you have to hire, as we did, even more people and buy more "insurance" signatures—double or triple the number of signatures required, because we knew every paper clip would be challenged.

Moreover, as the campaign manager and in-house lawyer, I wasn't just running the campaign. I had to run a law firm, too. I had lawyers sending me papers for review, affidavits to sign for me or Ralph or Peter, and places where I was required to show up to testify, be deposed, or felt compelled to go just to keep us afloat. The campaign was in constant lawyer recruitment mode, and the campaign became, as it was since day one, a fierce battle against a rigged duopoly just to be able to have the right to run.

Second, our campaign couldn't claim that Ralph and Peter had at least 270 electoral vote possibilities and that therefore we were a viable ticket, because the math wasn't certain until late in September. As a consequence, our demand to be in the debates was muted because we were electorally dubious.

Third, all this litigation was confusing for our supporters or would-be supporters and to voters generally. Our Web site ballot access map had to be coded as follows, with updates virtually every day, depending on the legal docket. We had Web codes that corresponded to colors for each state:

Codes

1. On Ballot
2. On Ballot—In Court
3. Petition Pending
4. Off Ballot—In Court
5. Off Ballot—Write-In
6. No Ballot Access

It is hard to say "Vote for me" when your ballot status changes from day to day and week to week.

Fourth, given the potential for bad precedent to be made around the country, I had urged the ACLU to get involved nationally. I put together a memo for the press and all concerned about what had become nationwide harassment. The response, with the exception of a few conflicted affiliates which politely declined, was silence.[135] We begged the national press corps to investigate.

There were a few minor references and scattered national survey articles in August from Katharine Seelye at the *New York Times* and Jonathan Finer and Brian Faler at the *Washington Post*.[136] But there was no investigative reporting whatsoever of the dedicated machine operating in the DNC to block Ralph from getting on the ballot. One local reporter, Eric M. Appleman of Democracy in Action, published a good road map to some of the major anti-Nader groups in 2004. He chronicled some of the efforts officially "outside" the Democratic Party. According to Appleman, they too were using the Democrats' poll-tested message of claiming that Ralph is "the recipient of financial and political support from right-wing campaign donors."[137] As far as I can tell, only two political action committees (PACs) were properly filed with the Federal Election Commission as a PAC spending money, trying to influence the election, though the FEC was in some part to blame for this having failed to set clear guidelines on who had to register.

The first was the Progressive Unity Voter Fund.[138] The second was the similarly titled United Progressives for Victory.[139] But United Progressives for Victory also set up a 527 companion group called "Uniting People for Victory" to "use resources for issue campaigns."[140] Their main activity appeared to be paying some people for flyering and others for "consulting," including some of the same people on another 527, the National Progress Fund's report.[141]

Alumni of Draft Clark 2004 set up a political action committee and Web site called StopNader.com, which was referenced by Dorothy Melanson's testimony, and were starting "scathing" television ads against us.[142] Different Draft Wesley Clark alumni, including David Jones, started "The NaderFactor.com," a website run by the National Progress Fund, which was never registered with the FEC, instead filing IRS statements.[143]

On June 2, 2004, Focus on Ballot Qualification, Inc., which shared the same tax identification number as "The Ballot Project," was also formed as a 527. Its purpose was ostensibly to "assess and prepare legal challenges to the ballot qualification of candidates seeking public office as well as measures, referenda, initiatives and ballot questions posed for public vote and engage in other non-federal activity lawful under section 527."[144]

Some of these various Democratic groups apparently paid Clinton pollster Stanley Greenberg[145] to do polling and apparently come up with the best smear tactics that would stick against us, and they settled on the line that we were being "bankrolled by the Republicans" or were "in bed with the Republicans." According to Katharine Q. Seelye in the *New York Times* on August 2, 2004, Greenberg's polling provided "two early clues": "[W]hen Nader supporters learned that Mr. Nader had accepted help and money from Republicans to get on the ballots in various states, they dropped away. And one of the few public figures who has credibility with Nader backers is former President Jimmy Carter, who is perceived as not compromised by or profiting from the political system. So some of the group's officials say they have discussed redeploying Mr. Carter, who they say has indicated a willingness to help."[146]

In late August, this smear of Republican bankrolling was rebutted by the *Washington Post*, which reported that the Center for Responsive Politics had found that only 4 percent of the total we raised, amounting to less than $55,000, came from donors to Bush. These donations were totally unsolicited, apart from a few friends of Ralph who happen to be Republicans. This amount of money in a national presidential campaign is of course *de minimis* and, at any rate, far less than the millions Kerry and other Democrats regularly raise from self-identified Republicans.[147] But this is the focus group–tested line that Dems used to tarnish Ralph. Ballot Project President Moffett was interviewed by *Seattle Times* chief political reporter David Postman:

" 'We were worried about attacking Ralph,' Moffett said, but no more. The polling found that Nader support drops precipitously when supporters are told 'he is in bed with Republicans,' a reference to the GOP helping to get Nader on the ballot in some states."[148]

As of October 4, 2004, the Center for Responsive Politics undertook a study at our request that found that Kerry and the Democrats had received more than $10 million from 50,000 large Republican contributions, compared with $111,700 received from 700 Republican-identified contributors to the Nader campaign. We had to ask the center to do the research since the Democrats kept repeating the big lie, and journalists, complicit as they seem to be in the illusion regarding the two parties, did no homework. This should have put an end to the smear, but it was—and still is—being repeated all over the country. But the numbers don't lie. If anyone was getting bankrolled by Republicans, it was John Kerry, not Ralph Nader.

Meanwhile, the state Democratic parties were also bragging with every challenge or lawsuit filed. On July 6, 2004, Ralph called John Kerry to congratulate him on his choice of John Edwards as vice president. My notes of the conversation reflect that Kerry said, "Well, you recommended him. He is a good man and is going to help." Ralph then raised the ballot access attacks in Oregon and Arizona, saying that he knows that Kerry was for fair play. Kerry responded that he was "not aware of any of these things." He then went on to say that he had to be candid "as a friend," saying, "You take votes away from me. Don't pretend you're helping me. I'm going to beat Bush. That's my goal." Kerry agreed that "dirty tricks have no place" in the election. Ralph told him that the head of the DNC told us that the DNC supported these ballot challenges. Ralph reminded Kerry that as the nominee Kerry was the head of the DNC. Kerry said that that "does not represent my view. Some groups we control and some we don't." Ralph said, "Well, this party under you is using this line," and then he warned Kerry, "You might have a mini-Watergate here." Kerry promised that he would have Mary Beth Cahill get back to us. And he said he'd stay in touch. Ralph asked him to get on it right away. For the next ten weeks, as another two dozen lawsuits unfolded, the Kerry campaign ignored our two dozen calls.

Then there was Vermont's former governor, Howard Dean. In early January 2004, we made a pilgrimage to New Hampshire in our exploratory phase and dropped in, unannounced, on the Dean campaign to say a friendly hello. It was a very late Sunday night, and tellingly, the other campaign shops in bitter-cold New Hampshire were all dark. Not Howard Dean's. The place was humming with activity. Karen Hicks, his gracious state director, gave us a tour, and young volunteers (some I recognized from our campaign in 2000!) were hard at work for the antiwar Howard Dean.

Of course, then there was Iowa—the ads, the scream—and Dean was toast. Except Howard Dean was assigned a new role that he started literally two minutes before he went on stage to drop out of the presidential race. He was on his cell phone with us just moments before he gave his own pullout speech. He was assigned to be the attack dog and to get us out of the race. Having said sayonara to Joe Trippi, who had put him on the Internet map with the grass roots, Dean appointed Roy Neel, a staid telecom lobbyist and aide to Al Gore in 2000.

Howard "the outsider" was fast becoming Howard "the insider." "Howard the II," as Ralph liked to say, was now "washing the Democrats' laundry." All, apparently, to become the new DNC chair. But in the meantime, he was meeting with us and I took notes.

Dean, Neel, Ralph, Kevin Zeese, and I all got together in a conference room in downtown DC. The conversation was wide-ranging, from our mutual support of IRV to raising the minimum wage, getting out of Iraq, and agreeing that the Democrats needed to show up in all fifty states, not just the battleground ones. Ralph talked about the common interest in getting the House of Representatives back and the need to think outside the box. He said that he had known Kerry since Vietnam and that he didn't trust the timid Democrats to beat Bush by themselves. Ralph indicated that our campaign was opening up a window into Bush's record and taking positions that the Democrats would avoid.

Ralph asked Dean about how he was going to deal with the defense budget, at which point Dean, who was antiwar, said he was *not* for cutting the defense budget—just "reallocating it" for pay, special ops, troops, and so on. Ralph tried to talk to him about unneeded F-22s costing tens of millions per plane and then went on to public works programs and a living wage. Ralph went on about the high crimes and misdemeanors of the Bush administration with Vice President Dick Cheney's mendacity. He told Dean that the Democrats need to call the Republicans to account and that he was helping by opening this second front, which was clearly missing in the Kerry camp. Of course, the Democrats finally came around closer to some of Ralph's positions. But in 2004, it was heresy to talk this way. Ralph talked about the Centers for Disease Control (CDC), and Dean said that it was a "disaster under Bush because he hates science." They then went on about money being the infection of the two parties.

Dean said he was an incrementalist, and Ralph volleyed back that he didn't think so. Neel interceded with his pitch at this point to say that if "a person accepts they are not going to win, it was good to advance a message in the next administration." This was his not-so-veiled attempt to say that Ralph could instead have an influence on the presidency of John Kerry. He went on about how if the goal is to beat Bush, and you are not the person to do this, then the idea is to drop out and be on good terms with the one who is. Ralph shot back again that he didn't trust the Democrats to beat Bush alone. He said after looking at OSHA (Occupational Safety and Health Administration), FDA (Food and Drug Administration), NHTSA (National Highway Traffic Safety Administration), and you name it, that he didn't "trust their words or that they can deliver." Ralph was on a roll. He said he was fed up with the two parties and that 95 percent of the House seats weren't even competitive. He said that dozens of legislators don't even have an opponent. "We have to have a new political system," he practically pled. Dean tried to say something about the environment to get back to their "drop-out" mission, and then Ralph just launched into more of his case against the Democrats. He talked about how they all voted 98–0 for Justice Antonin Scalia; eleven Democratic senators helped confirm Justice Clarence Thomas to the high court in a 52–48 vote. Then he moved to the uninsured without health care, then the minimum wage not going up. Ralph talked about the lack of fire in the belly of the Democrats. Dean should have cottoned to all of this, but he was not going to budge from his mission paper.

At this point Neel, exasperated, said, "Why should any Democrat vote for you? . . . It is one less vote to get rid of Bush." Dean jumped on with, "In the end when you run on principle, poor people suffer." He said that "the perfect is the enemy of the good" and that Kerry is a better candidate. Ralph talked about two fronts, how some voters would stay home, and he, Ralph, would take some Bush voters. I intervened at this point to ask Dean if he believed in third parties in principle. He said yes—but "not this year, not 2004." At the end, Ralph said, "Look, I want to defeat George Bush more than you do." Dean said,

"That's impossible." Ralph said, "Kerry is not going to do it." In retrospect, no truer words were spoken.

We left Dean and Neel agreeing that we had a difference in strategies. Ralph was right about a two-front strategy and that Kerry wouldn't cut it. What would Howard Dean say now? Privately he had to know that Ralph made sense, since Dean would later relaunch the DNC as a fifty-state campaign to go after 2006 House seats and build toward 2008.

At the end of the day, it was the DNC that we believed to be the central coordinator of the assault on our campaign. Despite the denial that they had anything to do with it, we believe they had a shop inside. Of course, the DNC and the 527s claim they did not coordinate with each other, as did the Kerry campaign, with Kerry still saying that he had nothing to do with it. But, then, what shall we make of the following?

At the Democratic National Convention at the end of July 2004, guess who were availing themselves of the opportunities to coordinate together? Ballot Project's Toby Moffett spent his time coordinating "six or eight anti-Nader groups" during the DNC's party.[149] "Calling themselves United Progressives for Victory" and raising money through a 527, the group included Neel from Gore's and then Dean's shop.[150] Moffett reaffirmed to the *New York Times* at this point that he and former Representative Elizabeth Holtzman were trying to "drain [Nader] of resources and force him to spend his time and money."[151]

At the time, Janice D'Arcy reported for the *Hartford Current* that the anti-Nader forces were coordinating strategy in the "second-floor ballroom of The Four Seasons hotel."[152] D'Arcy reported that Moffett said, "[W]e're not going to let him do it again. . . . We'll do whatever it takes within the law." When I read those words initially, it reminded me of the *exact* words John Kerry used, for he too was "going to do whatever it takes within the law." They were all on the same script. D'Arcy reported that Robert Brandon coordinated the Four Seasons session, and that Moffett, Greenberg, Holtzman, Neel, and even Arianna Huffington, who cleverly shows up just about anywhere there is likely to be press, were all there. The reporter wrote that "behind closed doors for more than an hour, they shared their research and strategies to undermine Nader."[153]

They also put the Democratic state parties on the case. For example, the *New Mexican* reported in late July 2004: "Toby Moffett, a former

Connecticut congressman and former Nader ally, told New Mexico delegates to the Democratic National Convention on Wednesday that the state party should appoint someone specifically to spearhead efforts to keep Nader off the ballot."[154] The reporter went on to write that Moffett also said, "We're going to make him spend time, money, resources."[155]

On December 7, 2004, Julian Borger quoted Moffett in retrospect in the *Guardian* in an article titled "Fasten Your Seatbelts": " 'I talk about it [spearheading the ballot access campaign against Ralph] without any glee because we lost the greater battle. It's a ridiculous little asterisk of history. But I think we had a role in the ballot challenges. We distracted him and drained him of resources,' Moffett claims, but adds: 'I'd be less than honest if I said it was all about the law. It was all about stopping Bush from getting elected.' "[156]

All the serious public interest institutional players were in absentia. I tried them all, plaintively: the American Civil Liberties Union, the National Voting Rights Institute, the Brennan Center for Justice at NYU School of Law, the Public Citizen Litigation Group, the Center for Constitutional Rights, and the all-too-few election law clinics at some law schools. They were either too busy, too resource strapped, too unwilling to be seen as involved politically, even if objectively, for ballot access issues. Almost all of these groups also depend on Democratic donors or liberal-leaning foundations for their funding. One exception, the John McCain–founded Reform Institute, sympathetically understood because of McCain's own ballot access battles in 2000, but they too did almost no litigation. They put out a press release on the ballot access issue, for which we thanked them and may have been willing to file an amicus brief if we had to go to the U.S. Supreme Court. Otherwise, the silence was deafening.

By early September we were trolling the Internet for lawyers. There was abundant goodwill from a number of individual lawyers, but the problem was that we needed experienced election law people who could come in, grasp the issues, know the case law, and appear in court, all usually within forty-eight hours of being sued. Election law moves at a breakneck pace on timetables of a day or two or five. There was no time to move a lot of people around the country in a training program in election law. And there was no way to totally anticipate people placement either, because in some states we weren't sure we were going to make it on the ballot or face a challenge. When you have to triage very scarce resources in an underfunded, understaffed campaign, you really don't have the luxury of having people standing by and on advance retainer.

In the entire United States, there was not a single organization dedicated to fighting ballot access injustice through litigation. There is, however, a small coalition of election advocates called COFOE that helps sponsor litigation of this sort. So when a young law school graduate named Oliver Hall approached us after the election, saying he would like to start a nonprofit organization, a Center for Competitive Democracy, I volunteered to help him. This organization too is still in its fledgling stages but deserves support. It is hard to believe that no major entity in the United States is devoted to checking government power and litigating to bring disturbing trends in ballot access law to the courts, to make sure that access to the ballot—one of our most fundamental democratic protocols—remains attainable for candidates of every stripe.

And the courts? Well, when invoked by us, they were MIA—missing in action.

Chapter 5

The Courts and Third Parties: "Delphic," Hostile, and MIA

> There is, of course, no reason why two parties should retain a permanent monopoly on the right to have people vote for or against them. Competition in ideas and governmental policies is at the core of our electoral process and of the First Amendment freedoms.
>
> —Warren Court, *Williams v. Rhodes* (1968)

> [T]he state's interest permits them to enact reasonable election regulations that may, in practice, favor the traditional two-party system, and that temper the destabilizing effects of party-splintering and excessive factionalism.
>
> —Rehnquist Court, *Timmons v. Twin Cities* (1997)

I am a lawyer. Two decades ago, thanks to John Sexton, Wayne R. Hannah Jr., and NYU School of Law, I went to law school on a public interest scholarship called a Root-Tilden. It made all the difference in helping me to understand how the law can be used to advance justice. After graduation, I had the privilege of being selected to "clerk," or work inside a judge's chambers. I clerked for a terrific Republican federal judge, the Honorable Robert W. Sweet (appointed by President Carter) in Manhattan, and interned the summer after my first year of law school for a renowned Democratic federal judge, the Honorable Nicholas J. Bua, in Chicago. I loved working with both Judge Sweet and Judge Bua and admired their willingness to do the right thing, no matter the political pressures.

As a public interest lawyer, I have also appeared before or written briefs for state and federal courts at all levels. My tremendous respect for the federal judiciary comes from having seen it from both the inside and outside. My experience is that judges work extremely hard to get cases right and to deliver justice, mainly insulated from partisan political concerns. This is tough because there are usually strong competing interests at play, and, of course, you get to be a judge by playing your political cards right—either being appointed or elected. In my experience, federally confirmed, Article III judges are more insulated because they are appointed for life, whereas in state courthouses the politics are much more palpable and even acknowledged.

In my home state of Illinois, some state judges have to get elected and therefore raise cash in the form of campaign contributions from the people who appear before them. This is true in other states as well. Once a state judge properly told me that he was going to recuse himself from hearing my client's case because he was facing reelection, and he was dependent on the support of the defendants and those seeking to intervene against us. I was extremely impressed with the judge's honesty about the political constraints he faced. The judge who replaced him was not facing reelection, and he went on to rule in our favor, striking down the law as unconstitutional. Another state judge told me that he thought it was terrible (and so do I) that he could go to a cocktail party fund-raiser, raise $75,000, and then go to court the next day with the same people who had given him cash the night before appearing on one side, or both, without anyone having to say anything about the prior night. External political pressures exist, yet most judges I have met are intent on "doing the right thing."

But as the Illinois Courts' Web site says now: *Audi alteram partem*—"Hear the other side." Had I not had such a personal affinity for the judiciary, I can only imagine how I would have felt during the 2004 Nader/Camejo campaign. Some of the legal proceedings were brutal. Some of the judges seemed openly hostile. Some of the statements made in opponents' briefs were gratuitous, patently false, played-to-the-media lies. Apart from the New Mexico and Hawaii federal courts and the Ninth Circuit and Sixth Circuit appellate courts—which would rule four *years* later in our favor regarding the Arizona and Ohio petition circulator requirements—no other federal court would provide us with relief. And only the New Mexico federal court provided us with timely relief of all of the cases where we had brought affirmative litigation. It was as if the fallout from Florida 2000 meant that no court wanted to entertain our First Amendment right to have a chance to get on the ballot.

At the end of the day, though, we did win the overwhelming majority of cases in which the Democrats or their allies tried to challenge us off the ballot, especially in the state supreme courts. But we could not get the U.S. Supreme Court to take up any of our cases, including the three outcomes I found most unjust: Pennsylvania, Ohio, and Oregon. Where were the federal courts? They were missing in action, no matter where we tried to engage them.

Richard Winger has written at least two articles detailing how hostile the federal courts were to the Nader 2004 ballot access claims. In "An Analysis of the 2004 Nader Ballot Access Federal Court Cases," Winger writes: "[I]n 2004 Ralph Nader failed to get injunctive relief from any federal court in his eight federal ballot access or vote-counting cases, which were filed against certain election officials in Arizona, Hawaii, Illinois, North Carolina (two cases), Ohio (two cases) and Texas."[1] He concludes that the "federal courts which heard these cases defied precedent, and made errors of fact and law when they denied relief to voters who wished to vote for Nader."[2]

Similarly, Capital University law professor Mark R. Brown has written a law review article about the Nader 2004 cases. He argues that major parties should not be allowed standing to sue or participate in ballot qualifications, concluding: "The lesson to be drawn from the 2004 presidential race is that neither major party can be trusted to police a general election ballot. Major party interests naturally lean more toward rigging and sabotaging than insuring fair and competitive fights. If America is interested in a truly competitive electoral arena, the major parties cannot be allowed a formal role in the qualification process."[3]

Despite a concerted multistate effort by the state Democratic parties, the DNC, unregistered 527 groups, and the Kerry/Edwards campaign to remove Nader and Camejo from the ballot and thereby interfere with the outcome of a federal election, the Supreme Court failed to take up any of the six (Texas, Oregon [2], Ohio, Pennsylvania [2]) petitions we brought.[4] With all due respect—and I have to tread carefully, as I am a practicing lawyer—the Supreme Court appears to be downright indifferent if not hostile to the problems faced by minor-party and independent candidates.

Darcy G. Richardson, author of the four-volume history *Others* about third parties, pointed out in a response to my inquiry that there have been a few famous minor-party justices: Justice David Davis (Independent); Justice John McLean (Anti-Masonic, Free Soil, and Know-Nothing); and Chief Justice Salmon P. Chase (Free Soil and Liberal Republican), who managed to run for president in 1872 while sitting on the bench. Of course, all of these were nineteenth-century jurists, before the government was even involved in printing the ballot, much less controlling access to it.

If some of the currently seated justices had attempted to qualify for the ballot as third-party or independent candidates, they would have instantly seen how both their ballot access jurisprudence and their avoidance of cases, in particular, are very hostile in practice and operate to serve as incumbent protection for the tyranny of the two major parties. Since the Warren and Burger Court landmark cases of *Williams v. Rhodes* (1968) and *Anderson v. Celebrezze* (1983), respectively, the Supreme Court has repeatedly turned a blind eye to the plight of third parties and independent candidates. According to Dmitri Evseev, a practicing lawyer at a big firm in DC, his study of Supreme Court ballot access cases showed that "the Supreme Court's jurisprudence has been consistent in its hostility to election-law challenges by minor political parties."[5] Lately, it seems as if someone has been giving them two-party Kool-Aid.

Lest you think this is my personal ax to grind, I am not saying that the Supreme Court is indifferent or hostile to the plight of third parties just because it refused all the Nader petitions for *certiorari* in ballot access cases. Oh no. The whole jurisprudence is a mess for *any* independent or third-party candidate trying to navigate his or her rights. And I am not the first or the only one to notice this. Supreme Court scholars who have far greater experience watching the Court than I have said this too, albeit usually more politely. "Delphic" is the term constitutional scholar Laurence H. Tribe has politely used to characterize the Supreme Court's jurisprudence in ballot access law.[6] Others have called it "a paradigm of confusion" and "random."[7]

In the *Stanford Law Review*, NYU School of Law professors Samuel Issacharoff and Richard Pildes sum it up best: "The Court's electoral jurisprudence lacks any underlying vision of democratic politics that is normatively robust or realistically sophisticated about actual political practices. Together with our co-author Pam Karlan, we increasingly see the images of democratic politics that underlie the Court's decisions as simply ad hoc—different views of the point of politics emerge almost at random as the Court confronts questions that range from patronage to redistricting to restructurings of the political process through voter initiatives."[8]

Lately, the Supreme Court has been unsympathetic to minor-party and independent claims under either the First Amendment or the Fourteenth Amendment's equal protection clause.[9] And it is not that they don't have time to intervene. Their docket is now down to about eighty cases a year, half of what it was twenty years ago. The new chief justice, John Roberts, explained to the *Washington Post* in early 2007 that the shrinking docket corresponded to "the relative lack of major legislation in recent years."[10] Well, I have a respectful suggestion: How about taking some election law cases and fixing the discriminatory electoral system in the downtime? Though given their recent rulings, I would have to retract that request.

If states pass laws that infringe on First Amendment rights, these laws are subject to judicial scrutiny, but ascertaining the appropriate level of scrutiny is complicated. If regulations cause "severe burdens" on plaintiffs' rights, then the state action must be narrowly tailored and advance a compelling state interest.[11] If the state actions impose lesser or "minor" burdens, then the state must still show important regulatory interests that justify "reasonable and nondiscriminatory restrictions."[12] Famously, the Supreme Court never really makes the states—whose laws are the product of two-party legislatures—produce any evidence in these cases to back up their assertions that they have state interests, such as "preventing ballot overcrowding" or "voter confusion" that might be impeded in some measure by letting candidates on the ballot.

How has this played out? Recently, the Supreme Court has repeatedly put its imprimatur on the "two-party" system, buying into a political science theory that reached its height in the 1950s, during the Cold War, that two parties promote political stability, that they gravitate to the political center, that they protect against factionalism, and that they provide "cues" for the voters who are too busy to figure out who they might want to vote for, given a range of choices beyond two.[13]

The Court's rulings sometimes come down to whether the state legislature intends to discriminate against third parties, which would be unconstitutional, or whether they just intend to promote and shore up two parties or have some other "benign" interest, with the outcome that third parties are discriminated against in the process, which is okay, according to the Court. If you understand this distinction with no difference in outcome, kudos to you. I think this is an unsustainable prism of analysis that will eventually fall, just as the idea of "motivation" in race-based discrimination cases has been discounted in constitutional (albeit not statutory) cases. It should matter if the net effect is routinely discriminatory. Democracy in America in the twenty-first century cannot mean that we live in a country where your right to vote for the candidate of your choice is not fundamental enough to prohibit against repeatedly skewed political outcomes that entrench two major parties to the exclusion of all others. This is especially true when the cartel that makes the rules benefits repeatedly, to the detriment of all third parties and independents.

The few decisions to the contrary, generally where the Court threw some rhetorical bones to democracy, are of little value. In Evseev's 2005 *Boston University Law Review* article, he states: "A close examination of the language in ballot-access cases demonstrates that the Court has consistently watered down the relevant constitutional inquiries when addressing claims by minor political parties because it sees these groups as a threat to orderly elections and to the stability of the major parties. The Court also underestimates the value of third parties because it tends to view elections as horse races in which it only matters who wins, and which otherwise serve no expressive function either for the individual voter or for the political parties involved."[14] Evseev notes that "[s]everal scholars have made similar observations and have rightfully criticized the Court's approach as inconsistent with contemporary understandings of the role played by minor political parties in our electoral system."[15] Law professor Richard Hasen took it one step further in his earlier discussion of the 1997 *Timmons* case: The "Supreme Court imprimatur of the two-party system is unjustifiable and dangerous. . . . When First Amendment interests are involved, a state seeking to shield Democrats and Republicans from competition should have a better reason than protection of the two-party system."[16]

The current debate in legal scholarship is over whether third-party and independent rights should attach as individual rights, like First and Fourteenth Amendment freedoms, or whether they are structural or marketplace rights—where the courts should intervene to level the playing field. Some scholars have suggested hybrid or alternative methods as a prism through which to evaluate cases.[17]

No matter which theory is used, though there is the potential for significant disparities in results, there must be a way to put a stop to the advantages routinely enjoyed and upheld by the two-party dominance of the electoral system. Here are my candidates for some of the worst decisions issued by the Supreme Court, from a third-party or independent perspective, that should be overturned. They are set forth here in chronological order and not order of importance because, frankly, it would be hard to parse which are more horrible than the rest. I am partial to First Amendment analyses, as I believe running for office and voting for candidates implicate core First Amendment rights that should rarely be outweighed by state interests (especially unsubstantiated ones). But whatever combination of legal theories the election rights community uses, the test litigation must be brought, repeatedly, to revisit and overturn these laws to render a more just outcome for voters and candidates of third parties and independents.

Just as the civil rights and women's rights movements strategically assaulted the decisions that upheld racial and sexual discrimination, so too must the electoral reform movement and third parties and independents chisel away at these bigoted decisions until the electoral equivalents of second class or "noncitizenship" and "separate and unequal" are removed from the electoral lexicon for independents, third parties, and all the voters. The Supreme Court has repeatedly recognized that voter rights and candidate rights are the flip sides of the same questions.[18] Yet third-party and independent candidates and their voters are not going to make progress until some of the following precedents are overturned.

Nine Supreme Court Cases

Jenness v. Fortson (1971)

Just three years after the Court in *Williams v. Rhodes* said there is "no reason why two parties should retain a permanent monopoly on the right to have people vote for or against them," the Supreme Court upheld the state of Georgia's requirement that independent candidates needed signatures amounting to 5 percent of the total number of *registered* voters in the last election for that office—a requirement that could be, and was, unreasonable if it represented a very high number of eligible voters such that it would keep out new parties.[19] In *Jenness*, Socialist Workers Party candidate Linda Jenness was required to collect some 85,000 valid signatures, not to mention a measure of insurance signatures. The two major parties, simply by virtue of prior electoral performance, *didn't have to collect any*. The result of this discriminatory treatment, as discussed in Chapter 1, has been that since 1943 when this requirement was first passed in Georgia, there has not been a single third-party candidate on the Georgia ballot for the U.S. House of Representatives.[20] No one on the Court at the time dissented from *Jenness*, because compared to the outrageously burdensome procedures that were struck down in Ohio three years earlier in the Court's decision in *Williams v. Rhodes* (1968), Georgia's lack of other restrictions looked relatively reasonable, even though the Court noted that the 5 percent standard was "apparently somewhat higher than the percentage of support required to be shown in many States as a condition for ballot position."[21] The Court's blessing to treat minor parties to such discriminatory procedures for getting on the ballot in Georgia has been the bane of ballot access challengers across the country.

Gaffney v. Cummings (1973)

In a challenge to the state of Connecticut's "bipartisan gerrymander," Justice White, writing for the Court, upheld a redistricting plan that the state claimed assured "political fairness" because it "aimed at a rough scheme of proportional representation of the two major political parties" by drawing districts that deviated both from the voting population and from the existing geographical subdivisions in order to represent the proportionate number of Democratic and Republican seats in the last three statewide elections.[22] The Court said nothing in so doing about diluting the voting power of independents or other parties and instead could see nothing in the plan that violated the equal protection clause of the Fourteenth Amendment. Apart from the dissent by Justice Brennan, with whom Justices Douglas and Marshall joined, where they said the focus should be on "ascertaining whether there has been any discrimination against certain of the State's citizens which constitutes an impermissible impairment of their constitutionally protected right to vote,"[23] the Court seemed oblivious to the fact that by cementing the political boundaries of those in power, in "recognizing" the strength of those parties, that it was foreclosing the development of other parties or the number of swing districts where there could have been actual competition.

Storer v. Brown (1974)

Justice White, writing for the Supreme Court, upheld the state of California's law making independent candidates ineligible for the ballot if at any point within the seventeen months before the general election they had voted in a primary for a party or if they were previously registered as a party member. As a consequence, if a candidate decides his or her party has gone off the deep end and wants to offer an independent candidacy, the Supreme Court says a state could keep the candidate off the ballot if he or she undertook any party-affiliated activities any time in the prior year. In this decision the Court backed off its heightened scrutiny standard in *Rhodes* to uphold what have become known as "sore loser laws," meaning that if you run in a party primary and lose, you cannot go on to the general election as an independent. Worse, the Court seemed to fault independent candidates who didn't make "early plans to leave a party." Indeed, the Court simply equated these independent candidacies with "pique" or a "short-range political goal."[24]

The Court also noted that most state election laws would withstand scrutiny under the Court's rulings and that applications of the standard of review to individual laws are "a matter of degree," thus engendering the infamously ad hoc, case-by-case jurisprudence we now have.[25] Justice Brennan, with whom Justices Douglas and Marshall concurred in dissent, noted the slippage and tried to reassert the standard by stating that "the test of the validity of state legislation regulating candidate access to the ballot is whether we can conclude that the legislation, strictly scrutinized, is necessary to further compelling state interests" because "such state laws place burdens on two different, although overlapping, kinds of rights—the right of individuals to associate for the advancement of political beliefs, and the right of qualified voters, regardless of their political persuasion, to cast their votes effectively."

The dissent noted that it was not enough for the governmental action to be rational; it could only withstand constitutional scrutiny "upon a clear showing that the burden imposed is necessary to protect a compelling and substantial governmental interest."[26] Justice Brennan wrote that "not even the casual observer of American politics can fail to realize that often a wholly unanticipated event will in only a matter of months dramatically alter political fortunes and influence the voters' assessment of vital issues. By requiring potential independent candidates to anticipate, and crystallize their political responses to, these changes and events 17 months prior to the general election [] clearly is out of step with 'the potential fluidity of American political life,' [quoting and citing *Jenness*], operating as it does to discourage independent candidacies and freeze the political *status quo*."[27]

American Party of Texas v. White (1974)

Here Justice White, writing for the Court, said that it did not find anything invidious about a host of regulations imposed on minor parties and independent candidates, including the state of Texas's 1 percent petition signature requirement of only those who had not voted in the primaries, collected within fifty-five days after the primaries, and a signature notarization requirement, because "the foregoing limitations, whether considered alone or in combination, are constitutionally valid measures, reasonably taken in pursuit of vital state objectives that cannot be served equally well in significantly less burdensome ways."[28] The Court did invalidate the state's supposed long-standing practice of not printing, on absentee ballots, any candidate except for those of the two major parties. Justice Douglas dissented from the entire ruling, except for the absentee ballot portion, noting that the "totality of the requirements imposed upon minority parties works an invidious and unconstitutional discrimination."[29]

Munro v. Socialist Workers Party (1986)

Justice White, writing for the Court, upheld the state of Washington's decision to remove Socialist Workers Party candidate Dean Peoples from the general election ballot because he did not succeed in getting a state-required minimum of 1 percent of the vote in the blanket primary election for statewide office, when the ballot offered thirty-two other major- and minor-party candidates. The Ninth Circuit appellate court had declared the law unconstitutional, noting that the 1 percent requirement had resulted in only one of twelve minor parties ever making it to the general election ballot in the decade before the case, but the Supreme Court reversed, saying that the state was justified in removing him from the general ballot, asserting the potential for confusion in the winnowed field.[30] The state asserted that to let him on would crowd the general election ballot, but the court of appeals put that one to rest by noting that the state had not produced any evidence of "voter confusion from ballot overcrowding."

The Supreme Court said the state doesn't have to proffer evidence! The Court would just take the state's word that the challenged provision would thwart a state interest, as it had done in prior cases. Indeed, the states have not been required to put forth any evidence *at all* backing up their alleged "interests" in claiming a right to kick off candidates to "prevent voter confusion" or to run "orderly elections." Richard Winger has pointed out that there hasn't exactly been an avalanche of presidential candidates on the ballot; at the most and in only the rarest of cases does any state get fourteen.[31] If states, including mine, can handle dozens and dozens of judicial candidates, can't we use a standard that renders a choice of more than two when voting for our nation's president? And shouldn't the state have to make some record as to how its interests are impinged by permitting more candidates to have ballot access and voters to have more choices?

Justice Marshall, writing for himself and Justice Brennan in dissent, noted that the Court did not articulate the level of scrutiny it was applying in holding that the restriction on ballot access was constitutional. Justice Marshall noted the importance of requiring states to demonstrate their interest because "major parties, which by definition are ordinarily in control of legislative institutions, may seek to perpetuate themselves at the expense of developing minor parties."[32] He went one step further to explain the contribution of minor parties to political discourse, noting that their "contribution cannot be realized if they are unable to participate meaningfully in the phase of the electoral process in which policy choices are most seriously considered [that is, the general election]. A statutory scheme that excludes minor parties entirely from this phase places an excessive burden on the constitutionally protected associational rights of those parties and their adherents."[33] Justices Marshall and Brennan got it.

Burdick v. Takushi (1992)

Justice White, again writing for the (6–3) Court less than a decade after *Anderson v. Celebrezze*, said it was permissible—no violation of the First or Fourteenth Amendments—for the state of Hawaii to enact a *total ban* on write-in votes on its ballot. The Court viewed this provision as a "very limited one," saying that just because a state law "creates barriers" that "limit the field of candidates from which voters must choose . . . does not of itself compel close strict scrutiny."[34] The Court, again retreating from *Anderson*'s heightened scrutiny standard, meant that it does not now compel the states to have "narrowly tailored" their laws in election administration to achieve the ends of the state's interest. With this case, the Court effectively allowed any state that allows a candidate some other mechanism for getting on the ballot to prevent the voter from writing in candidates and having that write-in count as a vote.

The Court said that a First Amendment right doesn't attach to the voter's expression on the ballot because "[a]ttributing to elections a more generalized expressive function would undermine the ability of States to operate elections fairly and efficiently."[35] But the Court took it one step further and, dripping with disdain for "protest votes," wrote: "[T]he objection to the specific ban on write-in voting amounts to nothing more than the insistence that the State record, count, and publish individual protests against the election system or the choices presented on the ballot through the efforts of those who actively participate in the system."[36] Clearly the Court wasn't contemplating that some candidates may have tried unsuccessfully to get on the Hawaii ballot and thus lumped all their supporters in with "protest votes" and those not actively seeking participation.

Justice Kennedy, joined by Justices Blackmun and Stevens, dissented, noting that the record demonstrated how a voter could not vote for his preferred candidate, a "recurring, frequent phenomenon in Hawaii because of the State's ballot access rules and the circumstance that one party, the Democratic Party, is predominant. It is critical to understand that the petitioner's case is not an isolated example of a restriction on the free choice of candidates. The very ballot access rules the Court cites as mitigating his injury in fact compound it systemwide."[37] Justice Kennedy even wrote that "[t]he majority's approval of Hawaii's ban is ironic at a time when the new democracies in foreign countries strive to emerge from an era of sham elections in which the name of the ruling party candidate was the only one on the ballot. Hawaii does not impose as severe a restriction on the right to vote, but it imposes a restriction that has a haunting similarity in its tendency to exact severe penalties for one who does anything but vote the dominant party ballot."[38] Bravo, Justice Kennedy.

The *Burdick* Court is saying that your right as a voter to express yourself in elections depends on the candidates' having sought—and successfully obtained—ballot access in another way—a way that does not leave you with having to write them in. You would think that if this is going to be the Court's position, they would be especially sensitive to taking ballot access cases, as that is the only way voters are going to be able to express themselves during an election in some states. As of today, Hawaii, Oklahoma, South Dakota, Louisiana, and Nevada do not permit voters to write in their votes. And Oregon doesn't even total those votes unless the candidate has received *enough* write-ins to have a chance to win. The Court views these restrictions as "politically neutral"—totally ignoring that they fall, almost always, on third parties and independents, as the two major parties always have ballot access.

Timmons v. Twin Cities Area New Party (1997)

The "New Party" (which is now the Working Families Party), co-founded by Joel Rogers and Daniel Cantor, was hoping for fusion laws to support their new third party. They sought to defeat state antifusion laws. The antifusion ban stemmed initially from the states' desire to squash the power of the People's Party back in 1896.[39] The historians who submitted the amicus brief in the Supreme Court said antifusion laws were a tool to ensconce the two parties, because fusion is one tactic a third party can use, in the absence of proportional representation, to deliver a block of votes to a major party that chooses to appear on the third party's ballot line; this helps to keep the major party accountable to the minor party if the minor party delivers a significant block of votes. The Independent Party and the Working Families Party do this in New York, one of the few states to still have fusion. But after the New Party challenged Minnesota's law and met with success at the lower court, the Eighth Circuit appellate court ruled for the state. In another terrible decision for third parties, the Supreme Court affirmed the state.

Justice Rehnquist, writing for the (6–3) Court, said, "The Constitution permits the Minnesota Legislature to decide that political stability is best served through a healthy two-party system. And while an interest in securing the perceived benefits of a stable two-party system will not justify unreasonably exclusionary restrictions, States need not remove all of the many hurdles third parties face in the American political arena today."[40] In less than two decades, the Court went from imposing a heightened inquiry over restrictions that impinge on the "fundamental" right of voters to choose the candidate of their choice for office to just making sure that state restrictions were not "unreasonably exclusionary." How's that for your right to vote for the candidate of your choice? Too bad for you if your state decides—without evidence—to be "somewhat exclusionary." The Supreme Court will look the other way while states ensure a two-party monopoly in the name of stability.

It should be noted that Justice Stevens, joined by Justice Ginsburg, wrote: "In most States, perhaps in all, there are two and only two major political parties. It is not surprising, therefore, that most States have enacted election laws that impose burdens on the development and growth of third parties. The law at issue in this case is undeniably such a law. The fact that the law was both intended to disadvantage minor parties and has had that effect is a matter that should weigh against, rather than in favor of, its constitutionality."[41] Amen. Justice Souter also dissented, but he was unwilling to reject categorically the majority's "preservation of the two party system" rationale as the Stevens dissent did. He argued that states "have a strong interest in the stability of their political systems" and "if it could be shown that the disappearance of the two party system would undermine that interest . . . there might well be a sufficient predicate for recognizing the constitutionality of the state action presented by this case."[42] He left that question open for another day.

Arkansas Educational Television Commission v. Forbes (1998)

Here Justice Kennedy, writing for the (6–3) majority Court, said it was okay for the *state-owned* public network television station to exclude from its televised debate Ralph Forbes, a ballot-qualified independent candidate for Congress in 1992, whom the Court described as "a perennial candidate who had sought, without success, a number of elected offices in Arkansas."[43] The director of the state's television commission offered only that the station had "made a bona fide journalistic judgement that our viewers would be best served by limiting the debate" to the candidates already invited, that is, the Republican and Democratic candidates.[44] Forbes tried to get the federal courts to issue an injunction, to no avail until the Eighth Circuit, *en banc*, looked at his First Amendment issue because a state actor was involved. The appellate court asked whether the state television station's view of Forbes's views impermissibly motivated its ban on his participation. The lower court had said no, but the appellate court said that the state's assessment of Forbes's "political viability" could not dictate whether he could debate, once the state had opened a political forum. The U.S. Supreme Court disagreed.

Justice Kennedy wrote that "the First Amendment of its own force does not compel a public broadcaster to allow third parties access to their programming." And then, after waxing eloquently about the importance of televised debates to the American political process, the Court ruled against Forbes, even as it noted how "a majority of the population cites television as its primary source of election information, and debates are regarded as the 'only occasion during a campaign when the attention of a large portion of the American public is focused on the election, as well as the only campaign information format which potentially offers sufficient time to explore issues and policies in depth in a neutral forum.'"[45] The Court agreed with the television agency, concluding that the debate, despite state sponsorship and despite its purpose, was "a nonpublic forum" where the state could "exclude Forbes [or one out of the three ballot-qualified candidates] in the reasonable, viewpoint-neutral exercise of its journalistic discretion."[46] The Supreme Court bent over backwards for this one, noting that the state's exclusion was justified because the station said Forbes was not "a serious candidate" and because he "had generated no appreciable public interest"—before the public was allowed to see him in the debate, where he might have gained that interest. (This standard would have nixed Jesse Ventura from becoming governor of Minnesota, as well as Ross Perot from obtaining 19 percent of the 1992 vote for president.)

Notably, Justice Stevens, writing in dissent along with Justices Ginsburg and Souter, said that Forbes had been a serious contender for the Republican nomination for lieutenant governor twice, in 1986 and 1990, and that in the most recent election prior to this debate exclusion he had received 46.88 percent of the vote in a three-way statewide race as well as the majority of votes in fifteen of the sixteen counties in the congressional district for which he was seeking to be elected.[47] The dissent related how the state's television station had determined *two months before* he was a ballot-qualified candidate that Forbes was "not a serious candidate as determined by the voters of Arkansas," rather than set any objective, written criteria prior to the debate!

Clingman v. Beaver (2005)

In this case the Libertarian Party of Oklahoma tried to invite all of Oklahoma's voters into its primary. The state refused; the party could only conduct a semiclosed primary and invite registered Libertarians and independents. The Court in *Clingman* upheld the semiclosed primary as not violative of the First Amendment right to freedom of association, even though the Court in *Tashjian v. Republican Party of Connecticut* (1986) struck down a completely closed primary system that did not allow parties to invite independents into their primaries. The Court was able to reach its conclusion by claiming that it is fine for parties to go after independent voters in their party primaries but not members of other parties unless those members reregister as independents or Libertarians. By concluding that the Oklahoma law was a "minor" burden on associational rights, whereas in *Tashjian* it was a "severe" burden, the Court didn't have to apply a strict scrutiny standard. Justice Thomas, writing for the majority, said that the state had an interest here in avoiding "primary election outcomes which would tend to confuse or mislead the general voting population to the extent [it] relies on party labels as representative of certain ideologies."[48]

In 2004, Oklahoma was the only state where no voter could cast a vote for anyone except John Kerry or George Bush. No other party was able to overcome the state's unreasonable ballot access laws, and Oklahoma is one of the five states that doesn't allow write-in votes. To make matters worse, if you are registered for a party in Oklahoma, and then your party does not keep or regain ballot access within three years, your registration is automatically turned from whatever you registered as into "independent" whether or not you want to be registered or called an independent! Unfortunately, the aggregate burden of Oklahoma's laws was not properly an issue before the Court. Had it been, Justice O'Connor, who sided with the majority but was soon to retire, suggested that the case may have gone otherwise.

O'Connor wrote in her concurrence, in part, that "a realistic assessment of regulatory burdens on associational rights would, in an appropriate case, require examination of the cumulative effects of the State's overall scheme governing primary elections."[49] O'Connor also noted, "Although the State has a legitimate—and indeed critical—role to play in regulating elections, it must be recognized that it is not a wholly independent or neutral arbiter. Rather the State is itself controlled by the political party or parties in power, which presumably have an incentive to shape the rule of the electoral game to their own benefit."[50] She even said that as the restrictions become "more severe, however, and particularly where they have discriminatory effects, there is increasing cause for concern that those in power may be using electoral rules to erect barriers to electoral competition."[51] Are we not already there?

Justice Stevens, writing in dissent for himself and Justices Ginsburg and Souter, who for the most part have recently become the only minor-party champions of note, wrote: "If states were able to protect the incumbent parties in the name of protecting the stability of the two-party system in general, we might still have the Federalists, the Antifederalists, or the Whigs. . . . In any event, we would not have the evolution of thought or policies that are occasioned through the change of political parties. While no such change has occurred in recent memory, that is no reason to ossify the status quo."[52] Bravo. Stevens, with Ginsburg joining, wrote, "Decisions that give undue deference to the interests of preserving the two-party system, like decisions that encourage partisan gerrymandering, enhance the likelihood that so-called 'safe districts' will play an increasingly predominant role in the electoral process. Primary elections are already replacing general elections as the most common method of actually determining the composition of our legislative bodies."[53]

How to Level the Playing Field

These are the top nine cases that should be overturned to help level the playing field for third parties and independents. There are others, of course, though their focus is not so pointed toward third parties and independent candidacies and their voters: for example, *Clements v. Fashing* (1982),[54] in which the Court ruled that "candidacy" is not a fundamental right, or the recent *New York State Board of Elections et al. v. Lopez Torres et al.* (2008),[55] which gives the disfavored candidates of the two parties some of the treatment minor parties are used to getting. I am not out on a limb here in recounting the judicial hostility, though I have lived through it firsthand more than most.

Constitutional scholars Samuel Issacharoff, Pamela S. Karlan, and Richard H. Pildes have published a casebook titled *The Law of Democracy: Legal Structure of the Political Process* in which they have surveyed the state ballot access cases and concluded that "the trend in lower federal courts is to uphold most state ballot access restrictions."[56] Instead of protecting the rights of minor parties and independent candidacies, the Supreme Court has engaged in a trend toward promoting the "two-party" system through hostile ballot access rulings and debate decisions that tolerate invidious discrimination. "In fact," according to Richard L. Hasen in his book *The Supreme Court and Election Law*, "the Court shows considerable deference to barely defended or defensible state interests."[57] Regarding ballot access cases, Jamin B. Raskin writes in *Overruling Democracy* that "the Court has made itself part of the assault on democracy rather than its champion."[58] Simply put, the courts have failed, repeatedly, to protect freedom of speech and association for third parties and independent candidates.

Finally, for those speculating that wealth or political centrality may be the answer to overcome the hostility, it is not. All the money in the world does not mean a candidate can buy his or her way around ballot access. In New York State, which has infamously difficult laws for party-disfavored candidates, Steve Forbes didn't even try to get on the 1996 Republican presidential primary ballot. In 2000 Pat Buchanan couldn't buy his way around the Reform Party split and the Michigan secretary of state's position that it had no duty to put anyone on the ballot if it couldn't figure out who the party's nominee was unless he had anticipated all the chaos and did an independent ballot drive instead. Ralph Nader turned in, and the county certified, sufficient signatures in Oregon, only to have the secretary of state make up new rules after his employees had certified Nader, to take him off. At the end of the day, if partisan officials or the two parties want you off, they will take you off, and if the courts don't intervene, off is where you will forever remain.

This is why it is so important for candidates, third parties, and third-party and independent voters to keep bringing their properly constituted challenges to higher-level courts and for the Supreme Court to turn its act around. A number of test cases should be brought, including a challenge to the aggregate burden of these ballot access rules at a national level, akin to Justice O'Connor's thinking in her concurrence in *Clingman*. I keep reminding myself that five decades ago, in 1959, the U.S. Supreme Court was upholding literacy tests as barriers to the vote.[59] Third parties and independents and their voters—democracy builders of every kind—will have to keep knocking on those hallowed courtroom doors.

Whither the federal government?

Congress is not powerless to intervene in these electoral messes, though it likes to hide behind states' rights to avoid the discussion. It just doesn't want to get involved. The federal government has not stepped into ballot access at all, preferring to leave the administration of elections up to the states. Just about every GAO report on "Elections" states something prefatory akin to:

> All levels of government share responsibility in the U.S. election process. At the federal level, Congress has authority under the Constitution to regulate presidential and congressional elections and to enforce prohibitions against specific discriminatory practices in all federal, state, and local elections. . . . At the state level, individual states are responsible for the administration of both federal elections and their own elections. States regulate the election process, including, for example, . . . ballot access, registration procedures . . . and certification of the vote. In total, the U.S. election process can be seen as an assemblage of 55 distinct elections systems—those of the 50 states, the District of Columbia, and the 4 U.S. territories [sic].[60]

It is this traditional role of the states in ballot access, combined with the natural instincts of legislators to protect their own incumbency and the parties to protect their supremacy, that has led to this hodgepodge of burdensome rules for minor parties and independents. In 1999, reacting to the "restrictive and complex ballot access laws" of states that "make it extremely difficult for non-major party candidates to secure a spot on the general election ballot," the *Harvard Journal on Legislation* proposed a model, rational, state-based ballot access law.[61] If adopted by any state, it could do much to alleviate the discrimination against federal minor-party and independent candidates.[62] To be truly effective, however, it would have to be adopted by all fifty states, whereas to date it has not been adopted by even one. Since 1985, either Representative John Conyers (D-MI), Representative Tim Penny (I-MN), or Representative Ron Paul (R-TX) has introduced federal legislation in nearly all of the congressional sessions to provide for uniform federal ballot access standards for candidates for Congress and, in Conyers's bills, for presidential elections.[63] These bills have gone nowhere.

If there were any political will, I would propose three reasons why—instead of waiting for the courts to wake up and assume their role as protectors of the First and Fourteenth Amendments, or for the bipartisan members of state legislatures to act against their self-interests to adopt a model ballot access statute—Congress should step in to regulate ballot access and help restore candidates' rights and voter choice.

First, Congress has the power to administer elections. The federal government stepped in to create a mechanism to determine the electors of the Electoral College in the Electoral Count Act of 1887; officials did so again to ensure political equality through the Voter Rights Act of 1965, which was renewed in 2006; to register voters, they have told states through the National Voter Registration Act of 1993 (Motor Voter law) how to enable more comprehensive voter registration;[64] they told the states to allow eighteen-year-olds to vote in federal elections.[65] Most recently, they have stepped in to pass campaign finance regulation (Bipartisan Campaign Reform Act [BCRA]), which has (mainly) survived constitutional challenge, and they have passed the Help America Vote Act of 2002 (HAVA), which requires states, among other things, to have statewide databases and to provide for provisional ballots.[66] The federal government has even hauled out the Department of Justice to enforce HAVA. Thus, though there is limited express authority, there is abundant precedent for the federal government's power to act when it comes to overseeing the administration of elections, both for congressional and for presidential elections.[67] But there has been no congressional action to date on ballot access to ease the outrageous burden on federal candidates, especially presidential ones.[68] Might the cause of this inaction be rooted in a Congress stuffed with Democrats and Republicans?

Second, the state legislatures have failed in their duty to assure fair and open elections, and now it is time for the federal government to step in to right the discriminatory effects, as it has historically done when voting injustices prevail. Alexander Keyssar, a history and social policy scholar at Harvard's Kennedy School of Government, notes: "Throughout our history, the claim that voting was a state matter, rather than a federal one, has invariably been deployed by those who wanted to restrict any expansion of the franchise. 'States' rights' was the cry of opponents of the 15th Amendment, the 19th Amendment and the Voting Rights Act of 1965."[69] I would argue the same for minor parties and ballot access. The articulated state interests in maintaining some of the most restrictive ballot access laws in the world, devoid of any evidence or requirement to produce any by the courts, are negligible. The Supreme Court has repeatedly required states to comply with Fourteenth Amendment protections of voting rights for racial minorities. Why not political minorities?

Third, the failure to undertake this federal reform of the ballot access laws, as long as we have a Supreme Court dedicated to "stability" instead of to the First Amendment or equal protection under the law, may make it virtually impossible, absent great wealth, for third parties to get on the ballot in succeeding years, especially after a series of incredibly close elections. The extensive litigation against the Nader campaign in 2004 demonstrates this result. Our campaign essentially got the 1948 Henry Wallace Treatment, just with far more vigor.[70] The next third-party candidate of any substantial profile and following may well find himself or herself receiving the 2004 Ralph Nader Treatment.

What would a model federal ballot access statute look like? I have several proposals, informed by the prior chapters' detailed inanities and set forth in the Conclusion. The pretenses and technicalities used by political opponents to exploit the ambiguities in poorly written state ballot access laws in order to force a campaign to defend its ballot access should not be tolerated. I welcome the help of others interested in preserving political competition, and I implore the assistance of academics and civil libertarians in drafting, sponsoring, and litigating a model federal ballot access statute—to stop hazing third-party and independent candidates seeking to compete in the political arena. But there is much more than just ballot access discrimination. Third parties and independents must face whole other discriminatory arenas, starting with the Federal Election Commission.

PART 2

HOW RIGGED IS OUR DEMOCRACY?

Chapter 6

Regulations, Regulations: Beware of the Code

> Weak by design, hobbled by congressional interference, slow and captive to the community it regulates, the FEC is an agency that cannot reasonably be expected to enforce and defend campaign finance laws.
>
> —Editorial, "Replace the FEC"[1]

"Stop. Don't even move." After I landed in Washington in March 2000, those were the words I used to the three people already working on the Nader 2000 campaign. The campaign then had no office, no phone, no clue. We did have a Web site and about 400 messages on voicemail. The first thing I needed to do? Read the entire chapter 11 of the Code of Federal Regulations—the Code—and meet with our election lawyer—all before any paper could be printed, any event scheduled, or any funds raised. Campaigns are simultaneously overregulated, underregulated, and ineffectually regulated. Supposedly the Code spells out many of these regulations. Except it doesn't. The rules are often ambiguous; worse, they are not written for third parties and independents but for the two major parties.

When Congress created the Federal Election Commission in 1974, the FEC was designed to be an independent regulatory agency and enforcement mechanism for campaign finance laws. Before 1974, there had been virtually no regulations. Indeed, people who worked at the agency in the mid-1970s recall devoting several hours a day just to writing regulations to fill in Congress's holes. Thirty-five years later, the law has devolved into something similar to a Da Vinci Code that very few people in the nation understand fully.

Today the FEC is considered a "small" agency, with a total budget in fiscal year (FY) 2007 of $54.8 million. About 70 percent of this is spent on personnel: 400 full-time employee positions.[2] The FEC is headed by six commissioners, no more than three of whom may be from any one party. The parties Congress evidently had in mind were limited to the Democrats and Republicans. So there are three of each and little political will to add any other party or independent commissioners. Informally, Congress recommends the commissioners, the president appoints them, and the Senate confirms them—sometimes in bitter battles. This appointment and confirmation tango serves to guarantee that the commissioners are only Democrats or Republicans.

In 2000, when I showed up for the first campaign, not knowing what we didn't know, all I knew was that Ralph Nader had a squeaky-clean reputation. Under my watch, we were not going to do anything to put "campaign finance violation" in the same sentence with "Ralph Nader." Mismanaging money is the easiest way to get in hot water. We held in-house seminars for the staff and field teams on what could and could not be done with money. For the 2004 campaign, when Al Sharpton's campaign spending was making the front page of the *New York Times*, I brought our superb finance team into my office, held up the newspaper, and said, "I never want to see our campaign in the paper in this way."

The laws are very complicated. If you are not a regular political fund-raiser or political consultant schooled in all the regulatory curlicues, mastering the finance laws is like having to learn a foreign language in a few days. Worse, you have to simultaneously do your other job—a 24/7 presidential campaign. As one FEC employee told me, "Even if you are a lawyer, if you are not versed in the regulations, [understanding the regulations] is like asking a general practitioner to do brain surgery."[3] If it is tough for lawyers, imagine having to ensure that every organizer new to presidential politics in each of fifty states has cleared the language on their flyers, the specific kind of community room they rent, and whose money they use to make photocopies, to do everything according to the Code.

I challenge anyone to read the Code without falling asleep 4,000 times. The Code tells you things such as what type point your disclaimers have to be in communications to 500 people or more.[4] It says that a disclaimer of "Nader for President 2004," for example, is supposed to be in a box *and* to be a specific font size, with a "reasonable color contrast."[5] The Code tells you how specific closed-captioning disclaimers must be used in television advertisements if you plan to get matching funds.[6] The Code tells you what "educational institution" venues are appropriate for giving speeches and where you may host fund-raising events.[7] The Code tells you how much money people can give, what triggers reporting requirements, and how many days you have to return a check, or to document that a foreigner has an American passport and is entitled to give money.[8] The Code also tells you that you have to use your "best efforts" to hunt down information about donors' employers and occupations within a certain number of days.[9]

In addition to the Code itself, you must master voluminous supplementary manuals, as a whole body of advisory opinions issued by the FEC each year—and a monthly bulletin update—fill in the many gaps in the law. An entire staff of the Information Division at the FEC is on call every business day to answer campaign finance regulatory questions. They are professionals, always courteous, always eager to be helpful, and they are experts in "the Code." Unfortunately, more often than not, for the complicated questions they don't have answers on which a campaign can rely. Worse, if you ask the same question to different FEC people, you may get different answers. I always made everyone who called the FEC on our behalf keep a log of their conversations. If you should ever be found in violation, though, conflicting FEC answers are not a defense. All of this hotline help is just "advisory," just as the advisory opinions issued by the FEC are not binding on whatever your facts happen to be.

It's not the information professionals' fault. They are really first-rate; the laws are simply ambiguous when applied to certain fact patterns. They don't even contemplate many fact patterns, especially those of third-party, new-party, and independent candidates. Indeed, one gentleman at the Information Division in January 2004 told me that "the FEC is not designed for a grassroots campaign."[10] Imagine that! If the FEC had been around then, Thomas Paine might have been fined for passing out "Common Sense" pamphlets in the wrong font size. Those riding the whistle-stop trains of Harry Truman would have had to worry about exactly who was paying the conductor.

Nader campaign people were always coming up with great grassroots ideas. I was always in the position of saying, "Let's see if it's legal first." This restriction was understandably annoying to people who just wanted to get the campaign's message out. I was annoyed with myself. Now, some campaigns, PACs, and 527s have a "Let's just do it and see if anyone complains" philosophy. Then they will pay whatever fine they are assessed as a cost of doing business—if they are caught—years after the fact when the harm cannot be undone. But our campaign was under a microscope, and our candidate's calling card is his integrity and his reputation for standing up for clean government, clean elections, and clean corporations. I was not about to sanction anything that might undermine the campaign's number-one asset. This made me Ogre Number One in the eyes of some people. Even Ralph was frustrated, dubbing me "Stickler in Chief."

When they don't know the answer, the FEC Information Division's stock response is: "The Code is silent." Callers are then advised to request an advisory opinion—a process often requiring months. Each opinion has to go through the General Counsel's office and then to the whole commission for a vote. This is not a realistic option for a time-sensitive question. And they all are. It also doesn't seem fair to burden third-party and independent candidates simply because Congress and the FEC failed to think of them when writing the statutes and regulations.

Let's take an ordinary example. In the 2000 campaign, our campaign had to ask the FEC through an advisory opinion the "date of ineligibility" for Ralph Nader and Winona LaDuke, nominees of the Green Party. The "date of ineligibility" is the date a campaign switches from the primary election cycle to the general election cycle—important in terms of campaign finance laws because it signals the end of eligibility to spend primary federal matching funds and the switch to general election public financing. For Democrats and Republicans, the date of ineligibility is the night they are nominated by their party conventions.

But for third-party and independent candidates, who often seek the nomination of several smaller parties or state parties simultaneously, the date of ineligibility is not clear. These candidates are typically not eligible for general election public financing unless they received 5 percent or more of the vote in the *last* general election (a rarity). But they are eligible for primary matching-fund federal money and to spend it, up to the date of ineligibility.

One facet of the problem we faced in June 2000 was that the Green Party was in the process of becoming FEC-recognized and thus was not yet an FEC-recognized national committee of a political party at the time. The question we asked the FEC was: "If you are the candidate of a nonrecognized party and are nominated in June, and expect to be nominated by or seek the nomination of other state parties as late as September, what is your date of ineligibility?" The FEC advisory opinion said if we are a minor party or independent still seeking the nomination of some state party after the date of ineligibility of the two major parties, our date of ineligibility is "the date of the last day of the last major parties' nomination." This is not exactly intuitive. It tags a third-party nominee's election cycle to the national convention date of another campaign—of a major party.

But that was the ruling. So given this opinion in 2000, four years later, I asked the FEC in the spring of 2004 to confirm, based on their prior opinion, that the 2004 Nader campaign's date of ineligibility would be September 2, 2004, the date President Bush was nominated by the Republican Convention, "the last major parties' nomination," about a month later than John Kerry's convention. It took the FEC *more than three months* to confirm our date.

I will never forget the phone call I got at about 8:00 A.M. from an FEC counsel on the morning of September 2, 2004. The lawyer said that she was "not certain that today is actually the date of ineligibility." She then said that since they couldn't find the original decision about the 2000 campaign in the file, did I have a copy I could fax to them?! My head was hurting. Not simply because the FEC—a federal government agency—didn't appear to have a copy of their own records. But because everything in a campaign changes when you move from primary to general—the source of all disbursements is supposed to shift. We had told everyone to get rid of all their primary merchandise by this date, to switch over to "paid for by the General Election Committee" letterhead. We had prepared to switch the Web site contents, account routings, and everything in the whole campaign, nationwide, to the General Election Committee at midnight. And the FEC was telling me on the morning of, after I had asked more than three months prior, that they still weren't sure "it is today."

These regulatory ambiguities are part of the hazards of being a third-party or independent campaign. Indeed, when I asked a senior FEC official about third parties and independents, he said that it is "extremely difficult for a third party on just about every level."[11] If you don't have 2,000 lawyers at your disposal, who can write these questions up four months in advance of when you need the answer, you are out of luck and must "proceed at your own peril." As a lawyer, I found this extremely disconcerting; Ralph, many of our staff and volunteers, and I are normally watchdogs, not professional political operatives or "regular campaign people." We knew we would be held to a higher standard, and we tried to comport with it, even though the regulatory minefield was almost impossible to navigate.

The mission of the FEC is "to prevent corruption in the federal campaign process by administering, enforcing and formulating policy with respect to federal campaign finance statutes."[12] They do this through requiring public disclosure of political committee reports detailing revenues and expenditures and compliance. In my experience, the FEC is generally superb at requiring public disclosure. In any election cycle you can find between "85,000 and 90,000 statutorily required campaign finance reports" from nearly 8,000 committees on their Web site.[13]

Though disclosure is what the FEC does best, disclosure for controversial candidates can be a problem, as it does deter people from giving, for fear of reprisals. I saw this firsthand when people asked me if they could give the maximum legal donation without it having to "show up" on our reports. No! But I understood why they asked. They didn't want spousal or community disapproval. They didn't want to have to explain themselves and get into political fights or risk adverse consequences at work. This is not new. The FEC has developed a method by which a third party can ask for an exemption from disclosure—because the Supreme Court in 1976 required them to in *Buckley v. Valeo*[14]—if the party could demonstrate "reasonable probability" that the givers would be subject to "threats, harassment, or reprisals."[15] The Socialist Workers Party, the Communist Party, the Socialist Action Party, and the Freedom Socialist Party have all availed themselves of this protocol. Despite my proclivity for disclosure, given the overall reprisals we faced in 2004, I wonder whether we too should have made nondisclosure possible. Giving to unpopular third-party or independent candidates (or being associated with their campaigns) can engender the same kinds of retaliation as being a member of an unpopular group, be it the Communists or the NAACP. The landmark *NAACP v. Alabama* Supreme Court case in 1958 allowed nonprofits to not disclose their donors because of the adverse consequences to the First Amendment right to associate.[16] The same problem exists for controversial candidates.

Trying to comply with FEC regulations can be a significant barrier for a small campaign. For instance, all of the reporting for presidential campaigns requires software that allows the public to see campaign revenues and expenses. When Nader ran in 2000, the FEC did not offer presidential compliance software. Compliance with the reporting rules alone—just the technical software capacity to file reports—cost the campaign approximately $5,000 a month, not a small sum for a start-up campaign. By 2004, the FEC had created presidential reporting software and provided it for free, eliminating one big barrier to entry for small campaigns.

The manual side of raising money and processing the checks is a whole other story. Dozens of rules govern when and how to solicit funds. There are at least sixteen items (no exaggeration) you have to look for when processing a donor check and all kinds of codes that are assigned to each factor. Then all of the information that is captured has to be data entered: the donor, the donor's address, the amount, the donor's occupation and employer, the date the campaign received the money, the date the money was deposited, and so on. The FEC has a thick manual just to regulate this process. It's called "PIGO." (I'm serious.) It is the manual for "Presentation In Good Order" that a campaign must follow if it wants matching funds.

You can see why most politicians want to have high or no limits on donations when they have to raise more than a quarter million a day just to be competitive for president; it is far more cost-efficient to process $4,000 or $4,600 than to process $10. Indeed, the cost of processing a very small donor check is almost the cost of the donation. By the time you pay for staff to get the mail, open the mail, copy the $10 check and file it for compliance records, follow up on procuring the necessary information about the donor, thank the donor, and data enter the date received, amount, and all donor information, you have nearly spent the $10. If your campaign is a grassroots one like ours, with 90 percent of the donors giving under $100, be prepared for a huge compliance effort. Internet fund-raising is more cost-efficient than direct mail, but all of those donors still have to be recorded and accounted for. I asked two senior FEC officials if there was anything that could be done to address this incredible burden on small-donation campaigns. Short of congressional action, neither could think of a thing.

The FEC also has an entire staff called the Reports Analysis Division. Each campaign is assigned an analyst to ensure that their reports are in compliance and to answer questions about how to report data. After reviewing your reports, these analysts will send the campaign a letter if they see something that needs to be fixed. Campaigns are expected to fix problems within a short and certain time frame, no extensions allowed.

As part of the compliance process, every presidential campaign that receives federal money also agrees to an audit to ensure that a candidate is not using taxpayer money to buy himself or herself a yacht. The presidential candidate also has to agree to limit his or her own contribution of personal funds to under $50,000 in the election cycle during which federal funds are received. These funds are currently provided via the voluntary checkoff on tax forms. The FEC determines which candidates are eligible to receive federal funds in the primaries, for party conventions, and for the general election.

To qualify for federal general election funding, your party's presidential candidate has to have received at least 5 percent of the national vote in the prior general election. This is what Ross Perot did for the Reform Party in 1996 and what Ralph Nader wanted to do for the Greens in 2000. Perot's performance in 1996 entitled Buchanan and the Reform Party to get federal funding in the 2000 general election. In 2000, Ralph fell short, with only 2.7 percent of the vote. In 1980, John Anderson got 6.6 percent of the vote (as an independent) but did not run again, and thus the federal financing to which he was entitled was never used. No other recent minor-party or independent candidate has qualified for federal funds in the general election. The FEC gives significant amounts of money—in 2008 approximately $85 million each—to the general election campaigns of Republicans and Democrats willing to cap their spending (as McCain did but Obama did not, easily able to exceed that amount), but a third party is almost never entitled to even a proportionate share.

Qualifying for primary, rather than general election, funds is a bit easier. Candidates have to raise $5,000 in increments of $250 or less from donors in at least twenty states to be eligible for federal matching funds for the primary. They also have to limit spending to, in 2008, $57 million. For a small campaign, the first part is harder than it appears. To raise money in twenty states, you have to have a very broad-based fund-raising campaign and can't just rely on a few big donor states like New York and California.

Once a presidential campaign committee accepts federal funds, an audit is automatic. However, Congress has conveniently made it maximally difficult for the audit division to audit *congressional* campaigns within the time frame that Congress allots.[17] If you think the campaigns are too long, take a look at the regulatory compliance process. For presidential campaigns, an FEC audit can take longer than the campaign. We had barely finished closing down the 2000 committees before the 2004 committees began. In large part the delay was because of a dispute about how to handle winding-down expenses for a third-party candidate. The FEC was not sure what to do with a candidate who went from the primary straight to the general election but did not receive general election funds, as the nominees of the two major-party candidates do. This is an example of the rules not being written with the minor parties in mind. Shortly after the 2004 election the FEC correctly estimated that it would take three to four years to finish those audits and compliance actions.[18]

Our FEC auditors liked to arrive at our office at 8:00 A.M. They were there until 4:00 P.M. every day. For a campaign that took only eight months and whose total raised was on the order of $4.5 million, we had anywhere from two to four auditors in our office every day for about eight weeks. A former IRS agent told me that if an IRS auditor took longer than eight hours on $4.5 million, "his supervisor would think he was dilly-dallying." But the FEC is camped at your office for a long time, checking for a gazillion things: Did you deposit the money within ten days of receipt? Did you reconcile your bank statements? Did you take illegal cash or contributions? Did you make best efforts to acquire the information you need to collect within the correct time period? Did the FEC give you the right amount of money or too much? (In which case, they want some of it back, and they need to figure that to the penny.)

Having the rules streamlined for campaigns that spend under a certain amount of dollars would take an act of Congress. The two major parties have ongoing committees dealing with audits in perpetuity. In Democratic or Republican circles, you can have a lifetime career doing this. Third parties usually have novices. This is in and of itself a barrier to entry to third parties or independents. Many third-party or independent candidates just do not have standing finance committees and a cottage industry of consultants familiar with the terrain or even available for hire.

Our auditors were competent and dedicated. But I have to wonder about the cost ratio of spending so much time auditing campaigns that have received so few federal dollars. The audit process can also prevent small-start candidates from accepting matching funds. Several third-party and independent candidates *have* figured out how to comply with all this, including Leonora Fulani and now the Greens. The Libertarian Party and the Constitution Party say they do not take federal money on principle. The late Harry Browne qualified for matching funds in both 1996 and 2000, but he wrote in *The Great Libertarian Offer* that he didn't want, as he put it, the "thirty pieces of silver."[19]

In practice, the FEC does not give anyone but the two major parties any money for operations. The candidates of the two major parties get the benefit of millions of dollars of federal convention money ($16.8 million in 2008); they can spend unlimited amounts on legal and accounting expenses; they have national, state, and local parties that can spend untold amounts on Get Out the Vote activities; and now they are likely to have 527s making unlimited "independent" expenditures.[20] What do impoverished third-party and independent candidates have? They get federal financing for the general election only after the fact—if, and only if, they break 5 percent of the national vote total. The uncertain possibility of getting money after the fact is just about useless to the candidate running in the current election who cannot count on it, though it may be helpful to the party next time around. As one book on third parties put it, the Federal Election Commission Act "is a major party protection act."[21]

Even citizens not directly working on a campaign can come within the regulatory trappings of the FEC. If a group now spends more than $1,000 to influence a federal election, it needs to start filing financial reports with the FEC—a ridiculously low amount to trigger onerous filing burdens. Just ask the NASCAR driver who put a decal for "Bush-Cheney '04" on his car! After a Democrat complained, but before the FEC settled on just issuing an admonishment, the FEC sent the driver a letter saying that his bumper sticker may have violated independent expenditure or corporate contribution limits. Or ask the four men who put a "Vote Republican" sign on their trailer on a highway and the FEC's investigation was not resolved for nearly eighteen months![22] Bradley Smith, a former FEC commissioner and the chairman in 2004, in a June 27, 2007, *Wall Street Journal* op-ed, gave these examples of how ordinary speech, if it is designed to say something to influence an election, comes into the web of campaign finance laws in a heartbeat.[23] Smith also wrote about lawyers, teachers, doctors, and retirees facing investigations and fines for their volunteer political activity, including one who said, "I will NEVER be involved with a political campaign again."[24] A certified public accountant (CPA) wrote, "No job I have ever undertaken caused me more stress than this one. I was frightened and concerned every day that I would do something wrong."[25] In 2008, retailers trying to give perks to voters also became aware of the election laws!

I feel their pain. It *is* worrisome. And I am in favor of campaign contributions being regulated! Unlike Smith, I think it would be a lot easier if we just publicly financed our elections, as we do our parks and streets and schools and other things we value as part of the civic fabric. If there were public financing, some of these rules could be eliminated.

If we can't publicly finance our elections, then someone with common sense should go through the regulations and get rid of the piddly rules that ensnare the innocent for *de minimis* political activity. The FEC, in April 2007, finally recommended to Congress that they step up the spending levels that have been used (without adjustment for inflation!) since the 1970s, thereby trapping individuals who spend slightly more than a few yard signs' worth ($250) to advocate the election or defeat of a federal candidate.[26]

In addition to overseeing campaign disclosure and compliance, the FEC is tasked with enforcement of the campaign finance rules. What happens if your campaign does violate an FEC regulation or someone just thinks you have? Anybody, anywhere, can file a complaint against your campaign if he or she believes you have violated FEC laws or are *about to* violate them. One good reason for a campaign to run novel things by the anonymous Information Division hotline is to make sure it doesn't unwittingly tell an FEC person during a nonanonymous call that it thinks it is about to violate the law, because the FEC can write you up! Of course, anonymity has its limits for third parties and independents: how many "hypothetical independent or minor-party candidates getting matching funds" were there in 2000 and 2004? Uh, one.[27] If there is only one candidate who fits the profile for the hypothetical, the anonymity does not do much good.

An FEC complainant needs only to provide his or her full name and address and present a signed, sworn, notarized complaint, which triggers a short time frame in which the respondent must answer. After looking at both the complaint and response, if four of the six commissioners vote to open an investigation, because they believe a violation *may have* occurred, the office of the general counsel (which has about one hundred people) or the Office of Alternative Dispute Resolution (ADR) will investigate the respondents. The commission then decides on whether there is an actual violation; in the meantime, you are labeled as believed to be a potential violator. If there is a violation, the commission tries to get a "conciliation agreement" with the violator. This can require the violators to pay a civil penalty or engage in a remedial action, such as taking an FEC course or amending their reports.

At least six complaints were filed against the Nader campaign in 2004—all by nongovernmental individuals. All of these were dismissed, with no penalties assessed against the campaign or other remedial actions required.

A Sample Complaint: Rented Office Space!

The Nader campaign received its first complaint about a matter with which I was involved, and it is emblematic of the complaints filed against us. Recall that I told the finance staff I never wanted to see us on the front page on an ethics or campaign finance question. But in June 2004, the *Washington Post* published a Sunday front-page story questioning why a nonprofit I had worked for had rented office space to the Nader exploratory committee.

The Nader presidential exploratory committee, one of among a half-dozen subtenants, had paid fair market value pursuant to a standard rate and sublease approved by the landlord who owned the building. We had even inquired in advance with a lawyer and the FEC to make sure that there is nothing impermissible about a nonprofit renting space to a political campaign, much less to an exploratory committee where no one is running for office, as long as the rental is for a fair market value in an open transaction.[28]

But in late May, a reporter from the *Post*, James Grimaldi, showed up unannounced at the office on the same topic. Ralph told the *Post* reporter that he could look high and low and find no impropriety, that he "had no story," and that I "was a stickler for compliance." Yet the *Post* still ran a piece—the only page-one story the *Post* had written about our campaign since Ralph's announcement—filled with innuendo and suppositions, to raise the question of whether the office space rental breached either tax or campaign finance laws.[29]

Citizens for Responsibility and Ethics in Washington (CREW), whose Web site indicated that "the overwhelming majority" of their "complaints and critiques" targeted opponents of the Democratic Party, used the *Post* piece as the basis for filing an FEC complaint.[30] We were required by the FEC to respond within fifteen days—in July, amidst all the ballot access deadlines and hurdles. Six days after its office space complaint, CREW then filed *another* complaint, alleging that Republicans were making phone calls on our behalf in Oregon. They claimed that *if* we were aware that the telephone calls were being made on the campaign's behalf, then the campaign had somehow improperly accepted an in-kind corporate contribution.[31] The whole state of Oregon knew about these calls! These were the kinds of flimsy charges brought against the Nader campaign: that we might have been guilty of a violation if we knew about some Republicans making telephone calls.

Unfortunately, once a complaint is filed, the FEC has to trigger its back-and-forth procedures even if the complainant were to withdraw it. And a campaign must respond or risk the FEC will open an investigation.

The campaign received *four* more such complaints—with fifteen days to respond to each and a petition to suspend our matching fund payments. Most followed the CREW model: filing a complaint based on a news report, giving rise to a "hypothetical scenario" in which someone could imagine how a violation could occur. The next complaint filed said that the Nader Committee "has accepted and welcomed" assistance from the Bush-Cheney campaign.[32] And this "acceptance" and "welcoming," according to the complainant, constituted illegal behavior because it proves that we coordinated with them. Coordinated what? The evidence for this complaint? In a news report, our Oregon state coordinator, lawyer Greg Kafoury, when asked about Republican voters supporting Nader, stated, "It's a free country."[33] We had a hard time taking it seriously.

But it was tiring. That was the point. Each new complaint was accompanied by another flurry of press coverage hinting that Ralph had violated ethics laws. Right. Ralph Nader was suddenly a "national scofflaw." And we had to spend time refuting the allegations and explaining why we were not engaged in any wrongdoing. This is how a major party can bog down any small third-party or independent campaign: file a boatload of complaints to the FEC because it is obliged to investigate! The process is an invitation to political skullduggery.

The FEC evaluates each complaint and response to determine whether it warrants the use of the commission's limited resources. Cases that meet the threshold criteria are assigned to attorneys as their caseloads permit, and cases that do not are then dismissed. The FEC uses unfortunate nomenclature to open an investigation, stating that "there is reason to believe a violation has occurred" or may be about to occur, even though sometimes all this means is that the FEC doesn't have enough information and has to pursue more investigation because of the inconclusiveness of the information the parties have submitted thus far, which happened in the last complaint filed against us right before Election Day.

Four affirmative votes of commissioners are required to go forward with any enforcement action. This can be why the commissioners' party affiliations have the potential to distort judgment. Imagine if there were two independents or another third party instead of three Republicans and three Democrats! If the commission decides there is "no reason to believe" a violation has occurred, or is about to occur, with respect to all of the allegations, the case is closed.

Throughout 2005, the FEC began dismissing all the complaints filed against the Nader campaign, starting in February 2005, when it issued its first certification that it had found no reason to believe any violation occurred by the nonprofit, me, or the campaign regarding the office space; then in June 2005, it certified the dismissal of the various complaints regarding Oregon (both of them), Michigan, and New Hampshire.[34] By April 2006, the FEC had dismissed the final complaint against the Nader campaign regarding Arizona, determining to take no action against us after we provided supplemental evidence that we had not engaged in any wrongdoing.[35] Two years after the alleged activities, thanks to our lawyer, Bruce Afran, we finally put to bed all of these efforts to tag us as violators. Six complaints. Six dismissals. But the hassles and time, especially during the campaign, are exactly the barriers few minor parties should be required to withstand.

"Feckless"

The problem with the FEC is not only what it does regulate—but what it fails to regulate. The *Washington Post*'s Jeffrey H. Birnbaum wrote, "If Merriam-Webster possessed some whimsy, its dictionary would picture the FEC seal next to the definition of feckless. Its weak-kneed rulings over the years have opened the way for the worst abuses of the election finance system, including loopholes that led to the infamous soft money of the 1980s and 1990s and, more recently, the free-spending 'independent groups' called 527s that cast a pall over the last presidential election."[36]

The most glaring problem in 2004 was the unbridled flow of millions and millions of dollars in large campaign contributions—$434 million in 2004 alone—to 527s. Many 527s did not even bother to register with the FEC, even if their clear purpose was to influence federal elections. According to the Center for Public Integrity, at least ninety-eight of the 527s, which were supposed to focus on "nonfederal" political activities, "targeted all or part of their message on federal campaigns."[37] Fifty-three of them "focused their activities largely or exclusively on the presidential election."[38]

It was the Wild West poker table of 527s, and all the gazillionaires—from George Soros and Peter Lewis to the Club for Growth and the Swift Boat Veterans for Truth gang—had their chips on the table. Despite all this money doing end runs in effect around the McCain-Feingold soft money ban, the FEC failed to regulate the 527s. While Rome burned, the FEC was looking at each one individually to determine if its "major purpose" was to influence federal campaigns.[39] The Honorable Emmet G. Sullivan, in the DC federal court, called the FEC's regulation on a case-by-case basis during the 2004 election a "total failure."[40]

Some of the biggest early violators—MoveOn.org's Voter Fund, the Swift Boat Veterans and POWs for Truth, and the League of Conservation Voters—paid *de minimis* fines totaling $630,000, compared with the $29 million in prohibited and excess funds that they spent on campaigns, and only years after the fact when the harm could not be undone.[41] Absent some heftier penalties, lawless spending will prevail. As Lawrence M. Noble, a former longtime general counsel of the FEC told the *Washington Post*, "Many campaign managers, faced with a choice between finding enough money to win an election and avoiding what could be an FEC fine, routinely decide to test the agency."[42] Well, not our campaign. But I could see how a campaign manager would be tempted to behave this way, given all the nonsense.

I had to talk to the FEC almost weekly to keep our campaign in compliance, and we weren't aiming for West Wing offices.

There have been open calls for the complete dismantling of the FEC. Indeed, the *Washington Post* once editorialized that it has become precisely the weak and ineffective agency that Congress intended it to be.[43] Scott E. Thomas, the former FEC chairman who was perhaps most in favor of strong enforcement, told the *Post*, "I would like us to be more tilted to interpreting the law rather than creating loopholes that undermine the effectiveness of the statutes passed by Congress."[44]

While the candidates and government spent more than $4 *billion* on the 2004 election, and $5 billion in 2008, the FEC is inadequately staffed and financed and is structurally set to punt when it comes to the hard calls. Donald J. Simon, who has spent twenty-five years studying the FEC, testified to the Carter-Baker Commission on Federal Election Reform in June 2005: "The FEC's decision-making has devolved into either a 3–3 partisan deadlock that meant the agency could not act at all, or a 'lowest common denominator' solution that served the interests of both parties in maximizing their fundraising opportunities, but failed to serve the public interest in law enforcement."[45] Its fines even for egregious violations are usually years late and essentially just a slap on the wrist, compared to the billions of dollars spent, millions spent illegally.[46]

The FEC is in clear need of reform. Simon suggests creating an independent agency akin to the FBI or the Federal Reserve Board, headed by a single, highly qualified person with a long tenure in the office, such as ten years, to get rid of the partisanship.[47] Another solution would be to add independent or minor-party commissioners. Other proposals for reform for particular regulations that impinge on third parties and independent candidates exist, but some have the potential to do even more harm—for example, by making it harder to obtain matching funds because the bill also requires candidates to raise $25,000 in *each* of twenty states or more.[48] Others, such as one from the Campaign Finance Institute, suggest a ballot access fund to level the playing field.[49] Ultimately, these are well-intentioned but ill-conceived bandages on the symptoms, not the cause. The FEC needs to be rethought completely, starting with nonpartisan election administration and public financing to take the issue of money out of our elections.

There has been much written about campaign finance laws, speech, and the regulatory process, so I won't rehash it here, but overall, money does matter. How much money a candidate has (or has access to) helps determine who gets to be on the political field. Spencer A. Overton, a professor at George Washington University Law School, points out in "The Donor Class," "Less than 2% of the U.S. population makes financial contributions over $200 to federal candidates. These larger contributions represent the vast majority of funds that candidates receive from individuals," and "approximately 85% of this money" comes from households with "incomes over $100,000 or more, 70 percent are male, and 96 percent are white."[50] Under current law, as Senator John McCain told the *New York Times*, any billionaire can form a 527 and "dive-bomb into your state or district."[51] According to Jeffrey Rosen, in the *New York Times Magazine*, "more than half the $500 million in soft money raised in 2000 came from only 800 donors, each contributing a minimum of $120,000. Fully 435 of them were corporations and unions, and the rest were among the wealthiest 1 percent of individual citizens."[52] McCain-Feingold has helped curb this. But in my experience, the money now gets rerouted to the 527s and the states where it is even harder to track because of widely varying laws and enforcement.[53]

And money matters in who gets elected. The powers that be tell us that we are all supposed to "be happy that great strides have been made" in the ninety-two years since Jeannette Rankin (R-MT) was elected to the U.S. Congress—*a total of 242 women* have been elected to Congress. And, yes, we now have a female Speaker of the House—but so do Turkmenistan and Gambia. We recently hit a record number of women in Congress: 16 in the Senate and 73 in the House, which puts us just shy of 17 percent—behind Rwanda and Costa Rica (but we are still ahead of Tuvalu). Only a *total* of 25 black women, 3 Asian women, and 7 Hispanics have *ever* served in the U.S. Congress. Just 1 black female, Carol Moseley Braun from Illinois, has *ever* been elected to the U.S. Senate. At this rate of progress, we might get to parity in 200 more years. Is this something to brag about? We need to come up with a better way to finance our public elections to open the playing field to those who may not have been born with, or accumulated, a donor base of millionaires. I haven't made the complete case here how the current money race hurts race and gender minorities, since I am focusing on third parties and independents, but others have.[54] And the numbers—well, they speak for themselves.

One other regulatory barrier is unique to third parties and independents: the provision of security. It turns out that the nominees of the two major parties virtually automatically get Secret Service protection. If you are a third-party or independent candidate, you are probably out of luck, even if you are a formidable election force facing violent threats. I know because of my firsthand investigation into this matter. This is what I learned when I found myself calling the FBI and going to visit the Department of Homeland Security in February 2004.

Homeland Security agents politely pointed me to Title 18, U.S.C. Section 3056, stating they had no power to do anything. This statute was the *only* proper way to request Secret Service protection. After initial consultation with agents at the department, and reading the statute, I understood that this was a discretionary decision. It gets made by the head of Homeland Security, then Tom Ridge, in consultation with an advisory committee composed of the Speaker of the House, the Senate Majority Leader, the Senate Minority Leader, and the House Minority Leader, as well as one additional member chosen by the committee.

So what are the criteria, which are discretionary, not statutory, for extending protection? The candidate must be a "major candidate," meaning he or she must:

- Be announced
- Be actively campaigning on a national basis
- Have national prominence, as shown by major media polls
- Maintain matching funds of at least $100,000
- Receive an additional $2 million in contributions
- Have 10 percent of the political party's delegates at the previous national convention

In other words, you must not only be already popular; but you have to be a *well-funded* candidate to get protection. What about breathtakingly unpopular or broke third-party or independent candidates? Too bad, Charlie. The United States routinely affords Secret Service to visiting dignitaries of even minor rank. But the two major parties in charge of the House, the Senate, and Homeland Security get to decide which candidates' lives are worth protecting—in a country with an ignoble history of eliminating some of its truth tellers.

Chapter 7

The Corporate Fourth Estate

> "You can rock the boat, but you can never say that the entire ocean is in trouble. . . . You cannot say: By the way, there's something wrong with our electoral system."
>
> —Keith Olbermann, quoted by Robert F. Kennedy Jr., "Was the 2004 Election Stolen?"[1]

In the late 1970s, when I was twelve or thirteen, my maternal grandfather Achilles, a tailor and a dead ringer for the late Marlon Brando, did something that I remember to this day. We were all on a rare restaurant outing (he disliked them) for Mother's Day. He was the father of four and the grandfather of sixteen by then. He stood up and in his Italian accent loudly told everyone in the room to "stop smoking." They were making him sick. If they wanted to be "chimneys or trains," they could go outside or go home; they just could not smoke where he was eating. He was ahead of his time. But I remember wanting to dive under the table, mortified like any preteen would be at the spectacle we had created in a large public room. This was his standard fare. He did not pander to anyone.

I thought of my grandfather during the 2004 campaign because that kind of refreshingly candid talk rarely comes out of a candidate's mouth. It's so rare, in 2000 it made Republican candidate John McCain an overnight sensation with his "Straight Talk Express." What media pundit Joe Klein calls Harry Truman "Turnip Day" talk—moments of unscripted reality—virtually does not exist anymore.[2] Every two-party candidate has been poll tested, prescripted, and message disciplined into a monotony unknown among human chatter. As the satiric *Onion* quipped, just about the only thing it is safe for them to say anymore is "thank you all for coming" and "God bless America."[3] The candidates don't dare step out of their three message points and bland platitudes, lest they complicate the political tango of what they are told the American public "wants" to hear. Al Gore talked on the margins of major issues, about "lockboxes" and prescription drugs, instead of economic inequality and lack of access to decent health care. And John Kerry failed to tell the Swift Boat veterans to put their tails between their legs and hang their heads in shame for their attacks. The Bush campaign, and in particular, Vice President Cheney, took this to a new level, by screening their audiences for loyalty. Now if candidates don't sound so hot, they can at least make sure that no one but the party faithful know.[4]

Joe Klein blames this phenomenon on the campaign consultants and the image makers. But I also blame it on the press. Yes, the press. They focus on the trivial. They play gotcha politics with a vengeance. They actually look for ways not to cover what a candidate says but which guy staged the flashiest prop, who planted a question, who sounded idiotic, who got the $400 haircut. In a well-documented example of how the Beltway press corps is "increasingly uninterested in substance and more concerned with stagecraft and personality" than actually covering issues, Eric Boehlert, writing on *Media Matters*, shows how the mainstream media managed to smear Nancy Pelosi, the Democratic Speaker of the House, all day long, just by repeating the phrase "*pre-emptive* allegations of ethical wrongdoing."[5] This, he wrote, "represented the latest, most glaring example of the at-times nonexistent standards by which Beltway newsrooms now function."[6] In a piece called "Electio ad Absurdum," Michael Kinsley noted that as "Election Day approaches, the campaign becomes increasingly about itself. . . . [A] candidate's offhand remark or offbeat facial expression can sustain the cable TV news channels for a couple of news cycles."[7] Howard Dean's 2004 Iowa "scream," which was more a microphone issue than a scream, was repeated endlessly, while virtually wiping off the news the fact that John Edwards had come in second in Iowa. An Annenberg study confirms that only one in four stories in the days before the 2000 election actually talked about issues.[8]

The media claim they want "the story behind the story" with all the palace intrigue. Maybe if for once they wrote that "the Democratic and Republican nominees said the same damned thing today for the 346th time, with no inflection," people might get the picture and demand a little more than the three-point speech out of the can. Howard Kurtz of the *Washington Post* complains, in writing a story about access to Hillary Clinton's 2008 campaign, that "campaigns often brush off national correspondents in favor of local journalists, who tend to be less critical."[9] Well, this might be true for the leading major-party candidates, but it also might be that the candidates are sick of the national press corps doing stagecraft stories instead of covering the details of their health-care plan.

I can't help but be annoyed. I had a candidate who wrote all his own speeches and talked about the issues, the reforms, the redirections required. He was like a jazz musician: once he was warmed up and into the groove, his words were rhythmic and mesmerizing. Oh, he too would give variations of the same speech over and over again, but it never contained just three points or came out in the same order. On any given day, in addition to corporate power run amok, Ralph might talk about our bloated Pentagon budget or how great "hemp" is or how Bill Clinton was a womanizing perjurer who rolled back *habeas corpus* and presided over massive prison building. I still remember Ralph talking in October 2000 about the 1872 Mining Act in a standing-room-only Madison Square Garden event—and, to my shock, nearly 20,000 people who had paid to attend, cheering wildly. There was no containing him. We did have a "Cuba" rule, though, and if he got to Fidelian lengths, the music had to stop, if only to make it to the next plane or event "semi on time."

But Nader did not pander. Ever. Ralph going to Detroit meant he would tell them they made lousy cars with outdated fuel-efficiency standards that they should be ashamed of allowing on the road. In corn country—Iowa in 2004 and Illinois in 2008—he said we should get rid of energy-wasteful ethanol. In Las Vegas, Ralph would heap criticism on the gambling industry. In college auditoriums, Ralph told young people to get rid of their silly hang-ups and trivial, text-messaged discourse about who is wearing what or gossiping about whomever and start being serious about how they were going to be productive in their twenties and thirties. He told the granola crowd to move out of their comfort zone of being "concerned" and actually get out there and do something. Once, to my enduring mortification, he sent out a press release criticizing Michael Moore (for health reasons) for being fat. I could do nothing to stop any of it. Ralph doesn't necessarily listen to his very inner circle much less consultants, focus groups, or polls. Maybe some of the major-party candidates should try the same technique. The political discourse would be a little livelier. The reporters would have something to write about. And not just whether Al Gore was paying a consultant to tell him to wear "earth tones." Listening to the canned major-party candidates after listening to the impassioned minor-party candidates reminds me of sixteenth-century comic poet Francesco Berni; he compared Michelangelo's late-in-life poetry to all other sixteenth-century Petrarch copycats by declaring, "Ei dice cose, e voi dite parole"—"He says things and you say words."[10]

I am a news media junkie. I once organized a picket, at the encouragement of the reporters who worked there, of a local newspaper being bought up by a corporate holding company. The reporters rightly feared their award-winning paper would be turned into a shopper's ad and happy-news rag announcing who made the high school honor roll. I have also helped countless journalists and investigators use the Freedom of Information Act to get information, both in my prior jobs and in my free time—for fun. I enjoy GAO reports as much as novels. And I can't throw away a delivered newspaper until I look at it, even if it takes me years.

But. For the most part, during my time as a presidential campaign manager in both 2000 and 2004, I could not abide how the media covered our campaign and others. I generally tried hard not to talk with most reporters for fear of telling them exactly what I really thought of their two-bit coverage of third parties and independents and our campaign in particular. Like my grandfather, I wanted to stand up and tell them that they made me sick to my stomach—even though I really like most reporters I have met as people.

My hitherto unqualified adoration for the *New York Times* changed markedly during the 2000 campaign, even though it did a glowing profile on me in its "Public Lives" section. Ditto for the *Washington Post* and just about every other newspaper. Once you are the subject of the news and are actually at the events that get covered or are a part of making them, the news purveyors take on a different hue. You start to wonder if they attended the same event you did. You cannot fathom what prompted some descriptions or total lack of coverage. You see gross biases that you would never have otherwise surmised. And then you start to think about how you believed all the rest of what you read in these "news reports."

As I read the *Charleston Gazette* during the West Virginia petitioning and lawsuit, I was reminded of a trip I had taken to Russia in 1996 to discuss Freedom of Information laws. The Russian reporters were out campaigning for Boris Yeltsin. Here we have media reporters and editorial boards campaigning for candidates too but claiming a patina of "noninvolvement and neutrality" when nothing could be further from the truth. At least the Russian reporters were honest about their biases. I'll never forget one who said, as I was *defending* the American press, "You Americans claim neutrality and are good writing technicians, but you don't know what you are writing for." He was proud to be writing "for" Yeltsin. The more I saw of presidential campaigns, the more I realized that some of our media just write for or against a candidate but don't acknowledge, much less disclose, their own biases, even as they or their staffers are making campaign contributions.

I now read newspapers and look at media, especially the corporate mainstream media, in a totally different way. First, I ask who owns it or is the publisher. And, sure, I still subscribe, but I look at who the reporter is, the sources quoted or not sought out, and the spin between the descriptions. Same for TV ads and talk shows. I have been in the green rooms with Ralph and on a chunk of these shows myself. From the now-defunct *Crossfire* to Chris Matthews's *Hardball* to Rush Limbaugh and Bill O'Reilly's compulsive spin, it often feels more like staged entertainment for corporate profits than serious discourse about the right direction for the country. (This is, of course, exactly what you should not write about the media if you want your book reviewed with any favor.)

Like most other people, and certainly all third-party media managers, I am immensely grateful for C-SPAN and the Internet.[11] C-SPAN doesn't filter through a reporter's lens or deploy talk show hosts who overtalk and play games with their guests. They actually let the subject making the news speak. This is rare in today's homogenized media air. I am also more tempted to look at outsider coverage of events. I listen to the BBC and read from the *Economist*, the *Guardian*, the *Financial Times*, and the right-wing and left-wing magazines and Web sites. I try to mix up sources to avoid the ideological cul-de-sacs that tend to doom the thinking of those who communicate only with people already predisposed to their views.

I first got the idea for broad media grazing as a college student in the early 1980s, when I went to pick up John Naisbett, the bestselling author of *Megatrends*, from the airport. Naisbett told me during our ride about how he read gazillions of local papers and other indicia to get a cumulative picture to declare his trends. It was all fascinating to a nineteen-year-old. I remember being even more impressed in retrospect, about fifteen years later, when many of his predictions that the world's political hot spots—such as the Berlin Wall and Northern Ireland (and not the Middle East)—would go away seemed to have come true. The Internet has now made everyone with access capable of doing the same Naisbettian grazing, and I would contend that this is even more necessary today, as the mainstream media become even more consolidated under corporate behemoths.

Apparently, I am not alone. According to *Washington Post* reporter Dana Milbank, citing facts from the Pew Research Center for the People and the Press, 45 percent of the public today, up from 16 percent two decades ago, "now say they can believe little or nothing of what they read in the papers." (That is, of the public still regularly reading the papers, since that too has fallen from 58 to 42 percent in a decade.)[12] Milbank points out that a reader perceives biases filtered through the prism of where he or she is standing politically. Fair enough. But that also goes for reporters and all of the media, despite what are noble efforts to divorce the editorial pages from the reporting pages. Leonard Downie Jr., the executive editor of the *Washington Post*, says that he actually goes so far as to deprive himself of the private right to make a political choice by not voting in order to try to maintain objectivity. He notes that despite the strict separation between news coverage and editorial, even so there are human emotions, but from what he sees, "the most common bias I find in our profession is the love of a good story."[13]

Candidate interaction with the media also depends on where the candidates stand. Some major-party candidates, inundated with coverage, are now refusing to appear on some of the shows.[14] Howard Kurtz, media critic for the *Post*, points out how candidates from both parties prefer to stay "on safe ground."[15] For third parties and independents the dynamic is the opposite. They often beg not to be excluded by the media. Kurtz himself has been quoted as asking, "Why should a network allow somebody with, say, zero chance of becoming president into these debates?"[16] In the same month, Bob Schieffer made a similar complaint. This was after former Arkansas Governor Mike Huckabee, winner of the Iowa Caucus, was bumping up from nowhere in the polls to register a blip. As Peter Hart of Fairness & Accuracy in Reporting (FAIR) points out in "Clear the Stage," "Often reporters and pundits act, when they're trying to winnow the field, as if they're only aiming to improve the democratic process."[17]

For the 2008 election cycle, it wasn't just Mike Gravel, former Democratic senator from Alaska, and Dennis Kucinich, Democratic representative from Ohio, who faced this media-winnowing music but also Ron Paul on the Right. Joe Klein declared him "history" after a Republican debate when Paul brought up some U.S. foreign policy before September 11 (echoing the 9/11 Commission) and Rudy Giuliani shot him down, to the press's approval.[18] Paul and his Internet crusaders went on to have the single-largest fund-raising haul at the time of any presidential candidate by bringing in more than $6 million on the anniversary of the Boston Tea Party in 2007. So much for the media's premature reports of his political demise. As Clarence Page of the *Chicago Tribune* wrote in an August 2007 column responding to why Paul doesn't get more coverage despite his ability, like Anderson, Buchanan, Perot, and Nader, to engage a "segment of the electorate that usually seems to lie dormant": "The short answer is the Catch-22 of winability. As news media allocate precious time and space, our attention gravitates toward those who have a prayer of winning. And, of course, without coverage, one's chances of winning are even worse."[19]

Witness the establishment media's contempt for the so-called second-tier candidates *inside* the major parties—the "windmill tilters" who try to broaden the stultifying three-point debate and put more issues, challenges, and reforms out there for discussion in two-party forums. According to Peter Hart, in May 2007, Howard Kurtz said that "news organizations are allowing ego-driven fringe candidates to muck up debates among those with an actual shot at the White House."[20] Now imagine how the media treat third-party and independent candidates. They drip with condescension and ridicule even before they touch their keyboards or call in their stories, even though staunch defenders of the two parties John Bibby and Sandy Maisel, authors of *Two Parties—or More?: The American Party System*, noted that "minor parties have raised issues not being addressed by the major parties, have affected the outcome of elections, and have helped precipitate major electoral realignment."[21] Would our current media critics have treated the antislavery or prowomen parties of the nineteenth century with the same contempt?

A full year before *anyone* has voted, members of the "first-tier" media tell America who has a chance to win. Jimmy Carter, Howard Dean, and Jesse Ventura would all be excluded from the national debate because members of the media—not the voters—deemed they were irrelevant.

Why is this? Colman McCarthy, a veteran journalist, peace activist, and longtime former syndicated columnist for the *Washington Post*, wrote in his column on October 1, 1996: "If the political views and reforms of today's allegedly minor candidates—so labeled over drinks at the National Press Club or faculty lounges—are seen as 'fringy,' perhaps it is because the two major parties, with their shared monopoly on what is safe, stale, and sterile, fear freshness."[22] Alan Keyes, the eloquent, conservative, two-time Republican presidential candidate, writes about the perceptions created by the media in much more cynical terms:

> Candidates spend the bulk of the money they raise on political advertising. We should see this as an obvious conflict of interest, *since it gives the media outlets good reason to promote the candidates with the most money to spend on their services*. Of course, we're supposed to believe that their editorial judgments are never corrupted by this self-interest. To encourage this belief, they promote the fiction that the so-called news media represents an independent source of political information.[23]

According to *New York Times* public editor Clark Hoyt, a 2007 study of the media's behavior in the coverage at that point of the 2008 campaign found that "news organizations—including newspapers, television stations and Web sites—long ago narrowed the field of eight Democrats and eight Republicans to only five presidential candidates who matter." That reflected the *Times*'s performance as well: the *Times*'s front-page newspaper articles that were about substance (46 percent of the time) vastly outdid the other papers in the study which were "just over 10 percent."[24] When the "paper of record" ignores the majority of the major-party candidates and fewer than half of its *front-page* stories are about substance, imagine how the rest of the media treat third parties and independents.

I knew I was not in Kansas anymore when on June 30, 2000, the *Times* editorialized (as they would four times that year) against Ralph's run. They said that he and Pat Buchanan should get out of the way so that the two major-party candidates could "compete on an uncluttered playing field."[25] So we were "cluttering" the field, according to the newspaper of record. But the *Times*—whose editorial board is a covert cheerleader for the Democratic Party—had been pleased as punch about John Anderson's run in 1980, when he bolted from the Republican Party to compete as an independent against Jimmy Carter and Ronald Reagan. Likewise, the *Wall Street Journal*'s editorial board is for the Republicans. The media show their biases, and people sense it. A Pew Research Center survey, cited in the *Washington Post* in 2004, for example, said that half the voters surveyed "say most newspaper and TV reporters want Kerry to win, and 58 percent say their [the reporters'] personal views color their coverage."[26] *Times* public editor Daniel Okrent acknowledged in 2004 that the *Times* is a liberal newspaper, stating that "the editorial page . . . [is] so thoroughly saturated in liberal theology that when it occasionally strays from that point of view the shocked yelps from the left overwhelm even the ceaseless rumble of disapproval from the right."[27]

From the same public editor's October 10, 2004, column: "Here's the question for a public editor: Is The Times systematically biased toward either candidate? No."[28] Well, nonsense. Let's just start with the formulation of his question and the fact that there were more than "either" of two candidates running in 2004. It would be okay to excuse the public editor of "the paper of record" for not noticing there are more than two candidates, given his paper's dearth of coverage of all other third-party and independent candidates, but shouldn't his examination of whether political bias exists in his paper, in a country whose voters are one-third registered independents, extend slightly beyond just how Bush versus Kerry was depicted in the *New York Times*?

As for the *Washington Post*, I wrote a letter to publisher Donald Graham back in October 2000. The *Post* had barely covered our campaign, from the moment Ralph announced—right across the street from their headquarters—to the end. I was fed up. This was a newspaper that referenced Bill Clinton's $200 Air Force One haircut in 1993 more than fifty times in fewer than fifty days.[29] Here we were, selling arena seats to 20,000 people in New York and 10,000 in my hometown of Chicago—on a Tuesday night—and we could not beg ink from the

Post. In rare third-party coverage, the *Chicago Tribune* put Ralph on the front page after the packed University of Illinois at Chicago (UIC) event. But the *Post*? No, they snored on about Al Gore's vacation somewhere. I asked Graham if his paper "could at least cover the history-making aspects of our campaign?" He wrote back courteously, and coverage picked up a little—but about the horse race, of course, not the issues.

The truth is that the corporate media think of minority candidates as freak shows—blips to be ignored unless it is a story about how they can affect the prospects of the major-party candidates. The Media Research Center provides an example by publishing the series of questions Jane Clayson, host of the *Early Show* on CBS, spewed in my direction in what passed for an interview.[30]

—"Ralph Nader can't win the White House himself, but perhaps is in a position now to decide who will, is that satisfying to him?"

—"Well, Mr. Nader doesn't want Governor Bush to win the White House, why doesn't he work with Al Gore for change within the Democratic Party?"

—"So he's not out here to hurt Al Gore in this election, because it appears he is at this point?"

—"Well, polls show that Ralph Nader has between 5 and 10 percent support in states like Oregon, Washington state, Michigan excuse me in Wisconsin. Let's listen to part of an ad that the Republican Leadership Council is running in those states. . . . The GOP believes that a vote for Nader is a vote for, for Bush, is that your goal here?"

—"But how do you feel about being used essentially by the Republicans to elect their candidate?"

—"Let me run this by you, Ms. Amato. *The New York Times*, an editorial in that newspaper called Mr. Nader's run a 'disservice' to the electorate and said that the country deserves a clear up and down vote between Mr. Bush and Mr. Gore. Calling Mr. Nader's wrecking ball candidacy a matter of principle, it says it looks like ego run amok. Is it?"

—"Well is there a lesser of two evils, now with the election just days away? Would he support, drop out of this race to support one of the candidates?"[31]

Well, thanks for asking about my feelings, Jane. If you are asking about how I would "feel" if my candidate got more votes, the answer is "just dandy." That is the point. That is why it's called an *election*! When was the last time the press asked a Republican how he or she would "feel" if that person "hurt" the rival Democrat's chances? Notice Clayson's reference to one of the *New York Times* editorials about how Ralph does a "disservice" to the electorate, who deserve "a clear up and down vote"! This is the U.S. media, quoting *itself*—as an authority—to tell a candidate to drop out. Bar the gates, American voters. The American media is telling you that you are being disserved by broader ballot choice!

What about coverage on the issues Ralph stood for or the Green Party platform? Dream on. There are notable exceptions, of course. Maria Recio (Knight Ridder/McClatchy), Tom Squitteri (then of *USA Today*), John Nichols of the *Capitol Times*, Amy Goodman of *Democracy Now!*, Jim Ridgeway of the *Village Voice* and now *Mother Jones*, Lewis Lapham at *Harper's*, and ABC's *The Note* provided fair and regular coverage. The *New York Times*'s Mike Janofsky once notably put Ralph's issues into one big article. But for the most part, after the one-story dispatch to sum up months of a candidacy, few reporters actually write about the content of minority candidates' campaigns. Do you remember any major media front-page substance stories on the Constitution Party's Michael Peroutka or the late Libertarian Harry Browne or the Natural Law Party's John Hagelin? Like Ralph Nader, they would put on press conferences and put out press releases galore. No luck. The Nader campaign actually had much more coverage than the average third-party candidate. Stephen J. Farnsworth and S. Robert Lichter said that the three network news stations provided *three minutes* of total candidate speaking time to Ralph in the 2000 general election, for an average of sixty seconds per network.[32] As the Natural Law Party's media manager Robert Roth noted in his book *A Reason to Vote*, in all of 1996, not a single third-party candidate, with the exception of the *über*-rich Ross Perot, appeared on any NBC, ABC, or CBS network news show.[33]

In a campaign, there is earned media (what the candidate says/does that gets coverage) and paid media (what the campaign purchases as advertisement). Both of these are terribly flawed processes. First, the overall earned media of elections has declined substantially. Substantive coverage of politics on the four network channels (ABC, NBC, CBS, and Fox) dropped 50 percent from 1992 to 1996.[34] It used to be that television network news would at least cover the conventions. As people no longer watched—the news or conventions—the networks cut back, but far more drastically than the decline in viewership. Professor Thomas E. Patterson, in *The Vanishing Voter*, notes that from 1976 to 2000, as cable stepped in to provide more coverage (and conventions became more like scripted coronations), "broadcast coverage was cut by more than 80 percent, from 60 hours to 10 hours per network."[35] According to Farnsworth and Lichter, "[T]he average candidate statement on network news during Campaign 2000 was about 80 percent below the 1968 level."[36] Candidates now have about "8 seconds or less" to make their case.[37]

Simultaneously the money paid to corporate broadcasters for political commercials during campaigns has gone way up. Anyone see a correlation here? Well, of course. The studies have been done. Just visit the Alliance for Better Campaigns, now a part of the Campaign Legal Center, or the Center for Media and Public Affairs, or the Annenberg Public Policy Center, or read the Pew Charitable Trusts reports. Is it any wonder that most of the American people can't name even one justice of the Supreme Court? The justices don't and can't buy ads; they barely get covered. In a political campaign it can work the same way. You are not getting covered until you "show a little leg." You need to pony up for the home team, put out the dollars for paid spots. By definition, if you don't have enough money to advertise, you are not worthy of coverage, unless you do something very extreme.

The paid media is a racket. In 2004, $1.6 billion was spent on political advertising, which was double what was spent in 2000.[38] In presidential years, $1 of every $4 (and up to $1 of every $2 in hotly contested elections) can be spent on media. Campaign media consultants routinely take 10 to 15 percent of an ad buy right off the top. They get very, very rich during campaigns, not based on efficacy—the ads are generally boring, vicious, or both—but on how much television they buy. In 2004, just one group of three of Kerry's consultants "walked away with a total of $5 million" of the $9 million the Kerry campaign spent on consultant fees, according to Christopher Drew's front-page story in the *Times*.[39] Bush's campaign spent $4.2 million on ten consultants.[40] These were not the ad buys themselves—these were the fees! When I negotiated our advertising contract in 2000, I knew Ralph would have none of that. We came up with a very different kind of contract, not based on TV buys but on overall success.[41]

In a December 2000 report, the Annenberg Public Policy Center found the following totals of "candidate-centered discourse"—that is, the story couldn't be about the horse race or the strategy behind something but about candidate discourse. This is a table from their study of the three major networks during the 2000 campaign:

Average Amount of Candidate-Centered Discourse (CCD) per Night—For All Candidates

CCD/night	*ABC*	*CBS*	*NBC*
Primary	39 seconds	42 seconds	28 seconds
General	39 seconds	58 seconds	97 seconds[42]

So we now measure substantive stories during our presidential elections in matters of seconds. These are not statistics about the coverage given to the mosquito abatement district elections. These are the totals of substantive discussion on network news for the race to be the leader of the United States. It is appalling. Third-party and independent candidates seem to be statistically more likely to get hit by lightning than to appear on network news.

Third-party media coverage is not only scant; it is frequently punitive. Steve Hill, in his book *Fixing Elections*, tells the story of Carol Miller, a veteran activist and Green Party member; she was punished by the press for daring to get 17 percent in her New Mexico special election congressional race in 1997, thereby, according to them, giving the election to the Republican candidate. The Democrats blamed her for their loss of the seat, and she was iced out of the local media thereafter—even by newspapers that had previously endorsed her run.[43]

The best summary I have seen on how this backward electoral media system works was written by former *Washington Post* reporter Paul Taylor, the former head of the Alliance for Better Campaigns, in a 2000 piece he wrote in *Mother Jones* about the vicious cycle:

> We the public give the broadcast industry our airwaves for free, in return for their commitment to serve the public interest. At election time, the industry turns around and sells airtime to candidates, fueling a money chase that saps public confidence in the political process and restricts the field of candidates to the wealthy and their friends. The

> money pays for ads that reduce political discourse to its least attractive elements: The spots tend to be synthetic, deceptive, inflammatory, and grating. As campaigns choke on money and ads, the public drifts away from politics in boredom or disgust. Ratings-sensitive broadcasters then scale back on substantive political coverage—forcing candidates to rely even more on paid ads as their sole means of getting a message out on television.[44]

In October 2002, the National Association of Broadcasters, fighting against the notion that they should be delivering free airtime to candidates as a condition of their free bandwith, released a self-serving poll that said, surprise, "By an overwhelming margin—71 percent to 27—registered voters oppose government-mandated free airtime for political candidates," claiming that, by a 2–1 margin, "voters believe that if political candidates were offered government-mandated free airtime they would use the time for ads attacking their opponents (64 percent) as opposed to informing the public on issues through speeches, forums, and debates (32 percent)."[45]

From 2000, I remember that a prime-time commercial in just one pricey media market on a popular show ran $25,000—for one minute. That would be someone's yearly salary in the public interest places I have worked. The Nader campaign raised our money, primarily in checks of $100 or less, from hardworking donors who thought it a stretch to give to a political campaign. What a travesty to spend it this way. (This is just about candidate advertising. Issue advertising is a whole other field, accounting for over $400 million in the 108th Congress alone. The ratio of corporate issue ad dollars to those for citizen causes or public interests? More than five to one.)[46]

Reforms to prevent the money flow to the broadcasters during our elections have been proposed, although they don't do much to help the non-major-two-party candidate. The most prominent reform currently proposed is for free media airtime for candidates on broadcast television. If it ever got passed, it would work like this: First, Congress would acknowledge that the public owns the airwaves—they are a commodity of the commonwealth, worth at least $100 billion. Second, Congress would appropriately charge big business media for the rights to use those airwaves. And third, in the negotiation for airwave bandwith, corporations would have to accord candidates free airtime each election cycle. The current Federal Communications Commission

(FCC) rules require broadcast TV to provide candidates with *equal* airtime beyond the news coverage, but there is no rule that they provide *any* airtime in the first place (or that they cover the news, either).

The premise of the free airtime bill is that "qualifying" federal candidates and national parties could receive up to $750 million worth of "broadcast vouchers" to use during political election cycles, split between parties ($100 million) and candidates for federal office ($650 million). Candidates for the House and Senate have to agree not to spend over a certain amount of their own money and raise at least $25,000 in increments of $250 or less; they would then receive $3 worth of vouchers for every $1 raised in this fashion, up to $375,000. Presidential candidates must qualify in the same way they do now for federal matching funds and would receive $1 of vouchers for every $1 raised for the primary and $0.50 of vouchers for every $1 raised for the general election. Minor parties qualify for a proportionate share of the voucher dollars available only if they field 5 U.S. Senate candidates and 18 House candidates. They would get the same as a major party, or a full share of the available vouchers, if they field at least 218 House candidates and 17 Senate candidates, a rarity among minor parties. Because minor parties rarely qualify for general election financing—and if then, only in the next electoral cycle—even the free airtime bill, should it get passed, would not really help overcome the media barriers for minor party candidates.[47]

Under the free airtime bill, the broadcast media would be required to provide at least two hours a week of mainly prime-time "candidate-centered programming" or "issue discussion" for at least six weeks before a primary or general election. The bill, formally known as the "Our Democracy, Our Airwaves Act," sponsored by Senators John McCain (R-AZ), Russell Feingold (D-WI), and Richard Durbin (D-IL) in 2003, was sent to the Committee on Commerce, Science, and Transportation, where it expired.

The bill applies only to broadcast companies, because cable companies don't license the public's scarce spectrum in the same way—they pay local governments for their privileges and should have public access channels on which candidates could get out their message. Back in 1994, I once had to sue a county seat for this access because the municipality actually had a written policy that said "no political speech" *at all* was allowed on the cable channels. This was constitutionally laughable. Now the cable airwaves are filled with politicians talking. But network news coverage is at its lowest. Congress doesn't make the broadcasters pay for the privilege of using the public airwaves, despite their record profit levels.

Ultimately, perhaps America will TiVo around media spending and move to the digital age of Internet information and YouTube-only ads. In the meantime, people still get their politics from TV,[48] and we may have to suffer through a few more election years of the fake discussions about health insurance at the kitchen table before campaign dollars are spent differently or become avoidable through Internet geniuses doing end runs on the political consultants' media-buy racket.

Finally, as Mark Crispin Miller pointed out in his article "None Dare Call It Stolen," "America's servile press" tends to close ranks quickly to dismiss "the strange details" about the 2004 election preferring "to ridicule all efforts to discuss them."[49] This is exactly the mainstream media's pack reaction to anything outside the electoral comfort zone. Question the evidence on weapons of mass destruction? Ask unasked questions about September 11? Query whether there is rampant fraud in our elections? Do so and candidates and commentators alike are all labeled "nutso" and laughed off.

This is the treatment for minor-party and independent candidates too, usually from the get-go, because their candidacy itself questions what passes as "mainstream" politics. Even Miller, a fierce critic of the voting system's failures, in his book *Fooled Again* buys right into the Democratic spin campaign to malign Nader as being "used . . . whenever possible" by the Republicans.[50] Minority candidates who question the norms and dare to participate are too inconvenient—even for the bloggers, the cutting-edge journalists, and normative news makers alike, who decide what the news and parameters, if not results, of elections "should be" according to their preferences.

Once in a while, a glimmer will come through the mainstream media, like Nicholas Kristof, a columnist for the *New York Times*, when he wrote on the op-ed page on November 20, 2004, "The U.S. electoral system looks increasingly dysfunctional, and those of us who used to mock the old Soviet or Iraqi 'elections' for lacking competition ought to be blushing."[51]

Chapter 8

"The Debate Commission Sucks"

"The Debate Commission sucks." This was Karl Rove talking at a dinner at Harvard's Institute of Politics in late February 2001.[1] Rove was complaining that the Commission on Presidential Debates (CPD) had set late dates for the 2000 debates, crammed them together, and used a very rigid format. He asked whether it was right to set the debates around the schedule for "the Olympics, Monday Night Football, and baseball and the sweeps."[2] These were valid issues. Ironically, the one question Rove believed that the CPD handled well was the "question of who gets to participate." He then added, "I know Theresa Amato is here and she doesn't agree."[3]

That was an understatement. The debates have a monumental role in presidential campaigns. Think Nixon/Kennedy in 1960. Think Ross Perot in 1992. Who gets to participate—and who doesn't—is a defining feature of candidate viability. Just ask Jesse Ventura, who, in fewer than ten weeks, went from being a wrestler with single-digit popular support to governor of Minnesota in large part because he was permitted to participate in the debates.

As a candidate, if you are not in the debates, you cannot really be running to win the votes of the American people. Historically, the American public tunes in to the presidential campaign right after Labor Day. That seems to be when Americans are ready to begin making up their minds about for whom they will cast their ballots. The free publicity, the opportunity to reach tens of millions of voters, and all the attendant press and spin that surround presidential debates are irreplaceable in terms of the strategic viability of national presidential campaigns.

When it was my turn to speak at the Harvard conference, I pointed out that the CPD is a private corporation, funded by corporate contributors, "around as long as the political players suffer it."[4] I said that there could be thresholds set for the debates in terms of who gets to participate, but if the CPD sets "three debates and all three of them exclude any voices except the Republican or Democratic candidates, then you've deprived the American people of the chance to hear alternative viewpoints."[5]

Under the law, an organization hosting the presidential debates is supposed to be a neutral arbiter or educator, so that the American people can hear about their choices in the presidential election without bias.[6] The CPD is neither. Rather, it is a private entity, controlled by the two major parties, funded by corporate interests, and it acts as the gatekeeper to the candidates for the millions of Americans who view each presidential campaign. The public is exposed (or not) to the important issues of the election based on which candidates the CPD deigns to invite to participate in the debates.

Many people think the CPD is a governmental entity, but it is not. Others think the League of Women Voters hosts the debates, because it once did. But it does not. The two major parties created the CPD, under the guise of being a nonprofit, so that they could control the presidential debate process. The former chairmen of the Democratic and Republican parties, Paul G. Kirk and Frank Fahrenkopf, lobbyists for pharmaceutical and gaming interests, respectively, have run the debates since 1987, when they engaged in a hostile takeover of the League of Women Voters' sponsorship, which had been ongoing since 1976. The League hosted the debates after the FEC allowed for televised presidential debates to be exempt from the 1934 Communications Act "equal-time requirement," as long as they were not sponsored by broadcast media. When the League ran the debates, John Anderson, a Republican running as an independent in the 1980 election, was allowed to participate, even though that meant that Jimmy Carter, the Democratic nominee, refused to show up for the first debate.

George Farah, in his book *No Debate*, documents the partisan origins and affiliation of virtually everyone involved in the CPD as either a Democrat or a Republican.[7] Indeed, many CPD members have made public comments about the virtues of "the two-party system" and have disparaged independent candidates.[8] On February 18, 1987, when the formation of the CPD was announced in a press release—sent out by the Democratic National Committee and the Republican National Committee—the second paragraph read: "The 10-member commission is a *bipartisan*, non-profit, tax-exempt organization formed to implement joint sponsorship of general election presidential and vice presidential debates, starting in 1988, by the national Republican and Democratic committees between their respective nominees."[9]

The very next paragraph read: "In launching this new initiative, the two party chairmen said, 'A major responsibility of both the Democratic and Republican parties is to inform the electorate on their philosophies and policies as well as those of their respective candidates. One of the most effective ways of accomplishing this is through debates between their nominees.'"[10] This is the raw motivation of the parties and the reason the League of Women Voters said it refused to lend its "trusted name to this charade."[11] Frank Fahrenkopf admitted to me and our lawyer, Jason Adkins, in a sworn deposition in December 2001: "In truth, at the very beginning, I think the commission was created and the recommendations were the two parties, that it should be a bipartisan rather than a nonpartisan entity. . . . It became very clear to us, however, when lawyers started getting involved to draft documents and so forth that you probably couldn't do it if you were a bipartisan entity and that we had to be nonpartisan."[12] When asked if the CPD was formally created as a bipartisan entity, Fahrenkopf responded, "Initially." When asked if it was "ever formally changed,"[13] Fahrenkopf said: "No, it wasn't changed. We just changed the way we operated. It was going to be a nonpartisan entity. We cut off any input, control by the parties over the Commission."[14]

In a penetrating chapter in *No Debate*, Farah shows how the two parties have dictated to the CPD precisely which candidates are included in the debates. In just one example, in 1992, the George H.W. Bush campaign demanded Perot's inclusion, calculating, erroneously, that Perot appealed to Bill Clinton voters more than Bush voters. In 1996, the Dole campaign was adamant that Perot not be included and thereby destroyed virtually all of their negotiating leverage against the Clinton team in terms of the format and schedule of the debate. The Clinton team, to obtain a negotiating advantage, was always prepared to threaten Perot's inclusion. They did this even though, according to George Stephanopoulos, they did not want Perot in either![15]

Amid all of this, the CPD pretended that it, rather than the two parties' negotiating teams, had an advisory committee that actually made the decision through "objective criteria." But the CPD acceded to what the two parties negotiated, no matter how it had to twist its own objective criteria to meet the parties' ending terms.

The degree to which the CPD would bend to accommodate the desires of the two parties was transparent with Ross Perot. When Perot had only 7 percent support in the polls in 1992, he was included in the debates and went on to earn 19 percent of the national vote. This performance, one would have thought, would virtually guarantee his inclusion in 1996, especially given that the taxpayers were then spending $29 million in federal funds on Perot's campaign. The CPD's advisory committee had set "receipt of federal matching funds" as an indicator of potential success and worthiness of inclusion in the debates; but when Perot was slated to get millions in federal funds, the very same committee turned this against his inclusion by saying that by accepting the federal funds Perot, who had millions of his own money, limited his own ability to spend infinite sums of money. They reasoned, absurdly, that this meant that Perot actually diminished his chances of success and thus his worthiness to be in the debates. The reality was that both parties wanted him out in 1996, and the CPD had to retrofit its rationale.

The CPD couldn't just use the standard objective terms to determine inclusion in the debates, like how many ballots a candidate is on and his or her mathematical eligibility, because that would have allowed the inclusion of Lenora Fulani of the New Alliance Party and Ron Paul of the Libertarian Party in 1988; and in 1996, Fulani again and Andre Marrou of the Libertarian Party would have had to have been included, as they all had near-universal ballot access status.[16]

The CPD could not use popular will, as more than three-fourths of the public wanted Perot included in 1992, and in one poll in 2000, 64 percent wanted both Nader and Buchanan included. Nor could the CPD use receipt of primary or general election funds as criteria for inclusion, because that too would have allowed in non-two-party candidates, such as Fulani, Buchanan, Perot, and Nader. Indeed, Buchanan, on *Larry King Live* in 2000, referring to his own candidacy, asked why "the American people are not permitted to hear a candidate whose campaign they are paying for, because a couple of political hacks are fronting for the establishment parties in Washington and freezing them out."[17]

The CPD had to come up with criteria for inclusion in the debates that appeared "objective" but could be manipulated. At first it asked a 1988 "advisory committee"—headed by academics and "civic leaders" who believed in the hegemony of the two parties—to issue criteria of "evidence of national organization," "signs of national newsworthiness and competitiveness," and "indicators of national enthusiasm or concern" as the test on whether to include a candidate. Then, threatened with lawsuits all around for these subjective criteria,[18] the CPD announced at the beginning of 2000 new, more "objective" criteria. It would require constitutional eligibility; evidence of ballot access in enough states to have a mathematical chance of securing an Electoral College victory (that is, on state ballots worth at least 270 electoral votes); and as an indicator of electoral support, 15 percent support in an average of five national polls by early September. This effectively created an Iron Curtain for third parties; with these criteria in place, neither Ventura, Perot, nor anyone other than John Anderson, who drew just barely 15 percent in the polls prior to the first debate in 1980, would have made it into any debates of the last thirty years. Indeed, only two minority candidates have ever polled above 15 percent since the presidential debates began. (The standard used for the granting of federal money in general elections is 5 percent of public support, so why is it 15 percent of poll support for the CPD?)

By the time the 2000 campaign rolled around, both of the major parties had learned that inclusion of third parties—or feigned desire to include them—could hurt their long-term interests in maintaining two-party hegemony. More important, the two parties could damage their negotiating position when it came to dictating the terms of the debates by pushing for the inclusion or exclusion of a third party. In 2000, the two parties behaved accordingly. Insisting on the rights of the Nader and Buchanan teams to participate would have been a path to "mutual assured destruction" for the two major parties, and therefore neither demanded third-party inclusion.[19]

It was against this historical backdrop that the Nader campaign set out in 2000 to get included in the debates. When Ralph announced his campaign in February 2000, our first goal was to get on the ballot everywhere, but by early April we started meeting weekly with a small group of academics and others familiar with the undue control of the CPD to strategize about how to open up the debates. I was amazed at how few people—even those in politics—understood that a coterie of people essentially control presidential political discourse in the United States of America. And the mainstream media has been complicit in this, though a number of reporters and editorial pages are exceptions, from David Broder and the *Washington Post* to the *PBS News Hour*'s Mark Shields, who apologized to Ralph Nader "for not demanding he be included in the presidential debates."[20]

One of our first concerns in 2000 was the use of the corporate media to conduct polls to determine who was entitled to participate. We wrote to the media, saying that they were now complicit in determining the CPD's lineup. They were no longer journalistic observers of campaign events. Now, depending on whom they polled, when, and what questions they asked, and which candidates they included, they were actual political players. And we had substantial concern about their parent companies. After all, according to the Center for Responsive Politics data, in the 2000 cycle, individuals and officials affiliated with Walt Disney (parent of ABC news) had given almost half a million dollars in soft money to both parties and $100,000 to the Democratic Convention; Time Warner's people had given more than $400,000 in soft money to both parties; General Electric (parent of NBC) gave more than $300,000 in soft money to both parties; Fox Entertainment (parent of FOX) had given more than $440,000 in soft money and PAC contributions to both parties and $100,000 to the Democratic Convention; Westinghouse (parent of CBS) had given more than $190,000 in soft money to both parties. So we had the media deciding who got coverage, then essentially using the amount of coverage, as translated into awareness and support of the candidates in responses to polls, to determine who was worthy of being in the presidential debates.

We also examined prior lawsuits brought by Fulani and Buchanan, and theories with lawyers Jamin B. Raskin of American University and Jason B. Adkins in Boston, to determine how to open the CPD's process. We decided to try a fresh approach: addressing the corporate funding of the debates. In our view, these were not debates but parallel interviews financed by beer and tobacco companies, who were doing an end run around the prohibition on corporate contributions to the candidates by channeling their support through corporate naming opportunities—such as the Anheuser-Busch beer tents and Ford Motor Company lanyards in the spin rooms pre- and postdebate—under the guise of "nonpartisan educational" debates that sponsored only two parties.

In June 2000, the Nader campaign, Ralph Nader, and the Green Party, along with eight individuals including Phil Donahue and Susan Sarandon, filed a complaint in the federal district court in Boston. Our position was that Congress had unambiguously barred corporate and union contributions in connection with federal elections but that the FEC had exceeded its authority when it adopted regulations that allowed corporations to fund the staging of the debates.[21]

The lower court ruled for the FEC, deferring to the FEC's own interpretation of its regulations under *Chevron U.S.A. Inc. v. Natural Resources Defense Council, Inc.*,[22] saying that Congress did not spell out clearly an intent to prohibit corporate funding of the debates.[23] The appellate court also found the statute ambiguous and said that the FEC was entitled to deference as its construction of the statute was "not unreasonable" nor "inconsistent with the statute."[24] The court noted that "Nader's interpretation of the FECA is also not unreasonable," but "Congress gave the choice as to the preferred reasonable interpretation to the FEC, not to Nader."[25] So the bipartisan FEC says it is reasonable to allow corporate funding of the bipartisan CPD, and the courts defer to this interpretation, referring to a Supreme Court case which the court quoted for the proposition that "the FEC is 'precisely the type of agency to which deference should be presumptively awarded' because its bipartisan composition makes it especially fit 'to decide issues charged with the dynamics of party politics.'"[26] The Supreme Court denied our effort to seek review.

When appeal to the courts of law failed, we turned to the court of public opinion. First we decided to spend our remaining primary money to create an ad designed to bump our numbers high enough to get Ralph into the debate. Then we adopted a daily rallying cry of "Let Ralph Debate"—a crowd favorite that resonated with a number of media outlets and sympathizers. At every opportunity, Ralph and I, along with our press people, our superrally participants, and anyone with a microphone, were going to raise public awareness by bringing attention to how the CPD was unfairly controlling the gateway for American presidential politics.

We also resolved early on that despite the well-intentioned entreaties of our colleagues in the other third parties, Ralph would not appear in third-party-only debates, though Ralph did one high-profile third-party debate with Pat Buchanan on *Larry King* to encourage other big media to host their own debates. Our issues were not with the other third parties but with the CPD's exclusionary tactics. This posture caused some bruised feelings among other third-party candidates in 2000, but we had to focus on the real culprits: the CPD and the two-party domination of the political landscape.

Priceless

In June 2000 we retained William Hillsman, a media guru with a penchant for supporting independents and populists. I knew nothing about television. Indeed, during the campaign, at age thirty-six, I had to go out and buy my first television set. Ralph doesn't watch much TV either, so poor Hillsman was at a serious disadvantage pitching us on the virtues of the medium. But Hillsman shared our distaste for spending such huge amounts of money on ads that primarily benefit avaricious TV companies that neither one of us liked. So we liked him. And we could all agree on the power of television and the right commercial in a political campaign.

Hillsman's idea that we liked best, for its "not-for-sale" anticorporate message, was a parody of the MasterCard ad campaign known as "priceless." Our ad said: "grilled tenderloin for fund-raiser: $1,000 a plate"; "campaign ads filled with half-truths: $10 million"; "promises to special interest groups: over $10 billion." At the end, it had an old picture of Ralph in his cluttered office, piled high with papers, with the tagline, "Finding out the truth: priceless . . . there are some things money can't buy." Then we said that Ralph should be allowed into the debates. The ad did not ask for any money.

The goal was to buy the ad in enough places across the country to be able to call it, barely, a "national ad buy." We then tried to leverage free media by appearing on C-SPAN and calling it a news event that a third party had enough money and savoir faire to actually make and run a national ad! This was going to be a "man bites dog" story: "Third party runs ad!"

We offered Tim Russert the first viewing on *Meet the Press* in early August, between the two major-party conventions. This was our way of keeping the campaign on the national radar screen while most third-party campaigns, by conventional wisdom, would be discarded by Labor Day. Ours was one of the few third party campaigns in history to surge coming out of the major-party conventions. When we learned C-SPAN was coming to our press conference the next day, where we were going to show the rest of the media the ad, Hillsman and I did an ad-lib hour-plus news conference cramming as much information as humanly possible about Ralph's stance on the issues and his reasons for running before actually showing the ad to the press. I think I went over our ballot access status in every state.

The next day our deputy press secretary told me that a *Wall Street Journal* reporter had called her to say that MasterCard was going to sue us if we didn't pull the ad. I couldn't believe it. It was our First Amendment right to run that ad, and hell would freeze over before we pulled it. There is a long-standing legal right to parody (or to create another original work from) an original work. This ad was a parody of the idea that corporate America, in the form of your credit card company, is going to protect what is free and priceless in this country—when our elections are for sale—and then sue the Nader campaign for saying so! It was too rich. There were, after all, dozens and dozens of "priceless" parodies in common jokes, in greeting cards for sale at the dime stores, and in parodies all over the Internet, even on porn sites—some of them exceedingly vulgar, including a *Saturday Night Live* parody involving cigars, Bill Clinton, and Yassir Arafat. (We later submitted more than seventy examples in court.)

We continued to run the ad, and sure enough, a senior vice president of MasterCard sent a letter saying that "it does not serve the public interest to create a situation where consumers could be misled or confused." Were these people humorless? Did they have a list of people who actually thought that somehow Ralph Nader's campaign was going into the credit card business or that MasterCard was endorsing us? It turned out that MasterCard's own evidence—some 452 emails to them about the commercial—showed only two people with any possible confusion. They later said that the ad enabled us to "take advantage of the famous reputation and goodwill enjoyed by MasterCard"! So somehow Ralph—a consumer advocate with nearly universal name recognition—was benefiting from *its* good name! When their vice president called me, I was polite but firm: we would not be pulling the ad.

Nor did we have any intention of running the ad much longer, as our budget for television was about to disappear: we had to do our ad buys and go into debt before the end of the day on August 17, 2000. For FEC purposes, in order to continue to remain eligible for matching funds after the end of the primaries, a campaign has to be in debt as of the end of the primary season, known in campaign jargon as the "date of ineligibility." In 2000, this date was August 17 for our campaign, just days after we received MasterCard's cease-and-desist letter. Since all of our television money had to be spent by the cutoff for the primary election, we had no ad buys for the MasterCard parody purchased for broadcast after August 17. But MasterCard went ahead and sued us anyway—on August 16—resulting in even more free airtime than the campaign could have or would have bought. We called the suit a case of corporate immolation.

We had tried to talk them out of it, but there was no way we were going to agree to a gag order, on principle. So the corporation came down heavy on us: MasterCard argued that they owned the word *priceless.* We got served with a nine-count complaint including trademark infringement and false designation of origin; infringement of a registered mark; dilution; copyright infringement; unfair competition; misappropriation; infringement of New York common-law trademark rights; state law dilution; and deceptive trade practices. The only thing we were really worried about when we were making the ad was accurately documenting how much special interest money was being taken in elections! But MasterCard stated that they were suing us for $5 million, plus $15 million in punitive damages, plus $15 million more in treble damages, plus fees! I chortled; we were a shoestring operation.

Of course, my second reaction after reading MasterCard's twenty-three-page complaint was to regret I had only taken "Trademarks and Copyrights" pass/fail at law school. Could there be any merit to any of this? Could it be enough to befuddle a jury or get us bogged down? My next thought was that even a meritless case could seriously derail our attention in the general election. Ralph talked to MasterCard's chief executive officer (CEO) Robert Selander to see if he was being hoodwinked by his corporate law department into pursuing this case. Selander didn't budge. This confirmed that the suit was coming from the top and not from some misguided in-house corporate counsel on a spending spree.

Lawyers I knew called to assure me that the case was ridiculous. People in the media guffawed. I felt better, but as a lawyer, you know you can't bank on anything. In 2000, we had been truly amazed that anyone had the chutzpah to sue us. Neither Ralph nor I had any real experience being a defendant. We were always the plaintiff. I asked our researcher to start looking into MasterCard's contributions and political affiliations. Was this some sort of political dirty trick to waste our time, or did they really think that they were being harmed by a parody?

MasterCard attempted to get a restraining order, prohibiting us from airing the ad for the rest of the campaign, still apparently clueless in September that we had never paid to broadcast it after August 17. Indeed, at this point the ad was being aired only by the news media because of the controversy MasterCard had created around it. Moreover, it was the most exciting commercial in a dull, dull field; it was getting critical acclaim from ad people and would go on to win many prestigious awards for Hillsman and the campaign from political media connoisseurs.

On September 12, 2000, the Honorable George B. Daniels of the Southern District of New York held a long hearing. He heard MasterCard's beef and basically said, "So what?" MasterCard whined that any negative impression made by our campaign would reflect badly on MasterCard—and "all that investment in time and money [on its priceless campaign] goes to waste." We said the campaign's political speech right "to express [our]selves in any manner trumps the rights of corporations not to be made fun of."[27]

Judge Daniels rightly refused to force us to drop the ad. The court concluded that MasterCard had not made a showing of irreparable harm, that the ad was a parody, and that there was "very little likelihood of confusion" that viewers would somehow start to think MasterCard was endorsing Ralph. After the election, we thought MasterCard would walk away. Instead, the company sent an insulting letter indicating it was planning to carry on the lawsuit and go to trial.

Ralph and I had to sit for depositions in the spring of 2001, but it was worth it—for the First Amendment. We waited in suspense for nearly three years for the court to rule on summary judgment motions and then the court gave us a great victory. We won on summary judgment on all nine counts: slam dunk. Judge Daniels issued a decision dismissing each of MasterCard's claims.[28] We issued a press release, in the form of a priceless MasterCard ad, ending with "victory over MasterCard: priceless." Oh, and it didn't sue us for the press release. We won an important round for the First Amendment and political speech.

Let Ralph Debate

Throughout the fall of 2000, the campaign used the rallying cry of "Let Ralph Debate" in all the superrallies. Thousands of people would holler this, incensed about the unfair debate process. It violated their idea of fair play to exclude a nationally known candidate like Ralph or even one of another stripe, Pat Buchanan. Our message was resonating.

At a superrally at the Fleet Center in Boston before the first debate in 2000, Ralph had stirred the crowd into a frenzy, declaring he would see them all there at the first presidential debate even though he would not be participating and had not even been offered a ticket to attend. We started advertising for a ticket on all media outlets. On *Meet the Press*, the Sunday before the first debate, Ralph again said he planned to be at the first debate and joked that he might "crawl up on the stage." In the green room after the show, I told him I thought this was a poor choice of words—because presidential candidates do not "crawl." But it was exactly this choice of words, political humor for Ralph, that would allegedly cause the CPD to "fear us" as a threat to its presentation of the debates.

By the morning of the first debate, October 3, 2000, several polls consistently showed that the public wanted Nader and Buchanan in the debates. A laundry list of prominent papers, including the *Washington Post*, the *Los Angeles Times*, and the *Christian Science Monitor*, editorialized in favor of letting Ralph in to at least one debate, as had many politicians, including former Governor Mario Cuomo, Senator Paul Wellstone, Senator Barbara Boxer, former Senator Howard Baker, and then Minnesota Governor Jesse Ventura, as well as commentators from Don Imus to William F. Buckley.

Representative Jesse L. Jackson Jr., a Democrat from Illinois, to his great credit, went the furthest by introducing a congressional resolution (H. Con. Res. 373) to open up the presidential debates for the 2000 election. He proposed that "all constitutionally and mathematically eligible presidential candidates" be allowed in the debates if "at least 5 percent of respondents in national public opinion polls of all eligible voters support the candidate's election as President; or a majority of respondents in these polls support the candidate's participation in the debates."[29]

On the night before the first debate, a University of Massachusetts student by the name of Todd Tavares let us know that he would be willing to give us his ticket to the debate. It was not even a ticket to the actual debate venue in the Clark Athletic Center but to an overflow space, Lipke Auditorium, elsewhere on the University of Massachusetts campus, where people would watch the live televised feed.

The campus consisted of six buildings in a compact area, but the CPD itself was to control entrance only to the Clark Center. Shuttle buses took people from the train station to the live debate as well as to other destinations on campus, including the Lipke Auditorium. When Ralph and Tarek Milleron, his nephew and traveling aide, were the last to remain on a shuttle bus that had already dropped off people for the live debates, they were told by the bus driver that the CPD wanted to see them, and a police sergeant signaled the driver to pull into a parking lot that was outside of the secure area controlled by the CPD.

The CPD did not have a list of people with tickets to Lipke Auditorium. These tickets, unlike the debate hall tickets, had been freely given out to university students, as the auditorium was not going to be filled. Tickets were also transferable, and there was no list to check against. Anyone in possession of a ticket was authorized to enter Lipke.

Ralph *had* a ticket to Lipke, but the CPD did not care. Indeed, the CPD, through its lawyer, had instructed its security agent to tell Ralph, even if he had a ticket, he was not invited. The CPD later claimed that it meant "not invited" to the Clark Center, the main debate hall, and the only place over which it had control—but it didn't even bother to check which ticket Ralph had. He held it up to show it to them—it was square; the ones to the Clark Center were rectangular. This seemed not to matter. If Ralph showed up, independently contracted security agent John Vezeris was to tell Ralph on behalf of the CPD that ticket or no ticket "he was not an invited guest," and then Sergeant McPhail of the Massachusetts State Police was to step in and threaten him with arrest if he didn't leave.

So when Ralph said he had a ticket, showed that ticket, and said, "What does this mean to you?" to Vezeris, Vezeris kept saying that he was not an invited guest whether or not he had a ticket in his possession. Ralph's traveling aide told Vezeris that it was not a ticket to the main debate and that the ticket was transferable. Vezeris kept repeating his one prearranged line and then said, "I ask you now to leave voluntarily and that's the position of the commission." At that point, Vezeris spoke to Sergeant McPhail, telling McPhail that Nader was an unwanted guest, leading McPhail to conclude that Nader should not be permitted onto the premises. Sergeant McPhail then told Ralph that he would be arrested for trespassing if he remained there! Faced with arrest or leaving, Ralph left. Ralph and I had already decided in advance that Ralph should not get arrested in this instance—or on any other occasion during the campaign—as he could do little as a presidential candidate in jail despite the headlines that would have been generated.

Later that night, Ralph went back to the campus to try to get to the Fox News interview that had been scheduled with him, but he was again greeted by Sergeant McPhail. Ralph told McPhail he had an invitation from one of the major television networks, but McPhail said that the CPD was not allowing him access to the grounds, once again asserting control over parts of the campus outside the CPD's mandate. Ralph tried to change the officer's mind, saying: "This is a political exclusion. I'm not a security risk. I'm not being disruptive. This is a political exclusion. You should not be misused. The authority of the state of Massachusetts should not be misused for a political exclusion of a presidential candidate who has a ticket to be in Kripke [*sic*] auditorium to watch the debate on remote television and who has an official invitation from Fox News."

A number of reporters saw this exchange, and it was widely reported and even caught on film. People started sending the CPD emails to complain. We later found out that on the morning of the debates CPD executives had met to discuss how to "handle" Ralph if he showed up to the debate with a ticket. They decided to talk again in the afternoon, after their lawyer got to Boston. Lewis Loss, their lawyer, had prepared a "face book" by pulling photos of the third-party candidates off the Internet; he testified in our lawsuit that he did this in the event that the CPD decided to bar all third-party candidates from entering.[30]

In a later deposition, Frank Fahrenkopf, a co-chair of the CPD, said that the decision indeed was to ban all third-party candidates, but then he changed his testimony and said the decision applied just to Ralph and Pat Buchanan and that "we didn't make a decision to exclude all third-party candidates. I mean, that's wrong."[31] However, Paul Kirk, his other co-chair, admitted that the decision may have applied to other third-party candidates, while Loss testified that they all did indeed decide that "Mr. Nader and third-party candidates more generally, even if they had a ticket to the debate would not be admitted into the debate hall" and that he handed out his face book, which included pictures of all the prominent third-party candidates running in 2000, to CPD volunteers checking tickets at the entrance to the Clark Center.[32]

It should be noted that no one from the publicly financed university said Ralph was unwelcome. Also, no one else with a ticket to Lipke was threatened with arrest for trying to attend. Ralph was singled out because of who he was and for his political beliefs—his political statements about the CPD.

On the date of the third presidential debate in St. Louis, Ralph was again denied entry, this time to Washington University in St. Louis, even though he had a valid pass and was scheduled to be interviewed by a student television station. The campaign was given three green passes called "host perimeter" passes by a representative of the WUTV station, a student named Dan Beckman. Beckman explained that as a member of the media he was entitled to bring any guest onto the campus for an interview. He called the CPD to confirm this and according to Beckman, a CPD official answered "Yes." He then said, "How about Nader?" He was told, "Anyone but Nader."[33]

This time when entering the university, we brought a crowd, including members of the press from the Associated Press (AP) and *U.S. News & World Report*. According to George Farah, who was there and thus inspired to write the *No Debate* book:

> Once Ralph Nader crossed the vaguely defined checkpoint (an unaligned series of portable fences), a blue uniformed police officer placed his body immediately in front of Ralph Nader and stated, "I cannot let you onto the premises." Ralph Nader told the officer that he had a host perimeter pass and showed the pass to the officer. The officer repeated his statement, brusquely grabbed Ralph Nader's arm and pulled Ralph Nader to the curb behind the fences. Reporters swarmed Ralph Nader and asked him a barrage of questions. The officer said that a "supervisor" would be arriving soon to meet with Ralph Nader.

Farah and Milleron then tested the viability of the green pass, noting that "officers simply glanced at our passes and let us in. They did not request any other form of identification; they did not cross-check the numbers on the back of the passes; they did not ask for our names. Clearly, the green 'host perimeter' passes were functional, sufficient credentials for any unarmed human being to enter the campus—except Ralph Nader."

When a senior officer did arrive, he volunteered to provide an escort to any other location and acknowledged that Ralph had not been disruptive. Ralph asked why he was prohibited from the premises. The officer "made every effort to avoid public acknowledgement of his orders to exclude Ralph Nader alone." A CPD official, who would not identify himself, then appeared on the scene to state Ralph Nader was not welcome and then "scampered away from the crowd, refusing to answer any questions."[34]

A few days later I spoke with Fred Volkmann, the vice chancellor for public affairs at Washington University in St. Louis. He claimed that WUTV 22 "did not have the authority to credential anyone at any time," and the credentials issued to them were only for them—the students working at the station—and not transferable to anyone else. Moreover, Volkmann insisted that "[t]he credentialing system was imposed by the authorities in charge of debate and candidate security."[35] The university was getting its story out early because on the same date as the incident in St. Louis, we filed suit against the CPD in federal court in Massachusetts regarding the October 3 exclusion.

We filed a civil rights lawsuit—not about participating in the debates, just about the constitutional right not to be treated differently and excluded from the Boston campus because of your political beliefs.[36] This was Soviet-style paranoia combined with police power. It was even more outrageous that the CPD planned to use police power to do this for *any* third-party candidate who had the audacity to show up. We argued that it was a violation of both Ralph's right to associate and his freedom of speech.

We spent two years defeating the CPD's motions to dismiss and its motion for summary judgment, taking depositions, and sitting for depositions, all to hold an unaccountable entity accountable. The CPD poses as a semiofficial body, but it is not, and it certainly does not have the authority to wield state power to deprive people of their constitutional rights. The state police may have been confused and misused.[37] But we were not.

On the eve of trial, we settled the case. Ralph's supporters would probably have preferred to put the CPD on trial, even if we were to lose. The problem was that in order to get to the CPD we first had to win against former Secret Service agent and CPD security agent John Vezeris, who would likely claim he was confused and did not intend to deny Ralph access to the other parts of the debate. Vezeris seemed to me to be the reluctant implementer of the CPD's bidding, so a jury may have found him not liable, but the judge was going to force us to start with him if we were even going to get a chance to put the CPD on trial. In the end, Ralph got what he had asked for: a public apology. The CPD and Vezeris also had to pay compensation to our lawyers.

Many candidates from across the third-party and independent spectrum have tried to break into the debates. In May 2000, Dr. Lenora B. Fulani's Committee for a Unified Independent Party, Inc., unsuccessfully brought litigation contending that the CPD was bipartisan, not nonpartisan, and discriminated against independents. Pat Buchanan had also filed a lawsuit challenging his exclusion from the debates, arguing that the CPD was bipartisan. He lost in large part because he lacked "contemporaneous evidence"—at the time of the suit—that the CPD was acting in a manner that was not nonpartisan.[38]

About a year after our own lawsuit had settled, John Hagelin, Ralph Nader, Pat Buchanan, Howard Phillips, Winona LaDuke, and the Natural Law, Green, and Constitution parties got together to file a complaint with the FEC.[39] In it we said that the structure and conduct of the CPD since its inception to date are bipartisan and distinctly controlled by Democratic and Republican officials to benefit the two parties. Our main argument was that the prohibition of all candidates from entering the 2000 debates as audience members, even if they had tickets, and the distribution of the "face book" to secure that result, patently provided the contemporary evidence Buchanan's suit had lacked—that the CPD not only was formed but was still acting as a bipartisan organization, not a nonpartisan one.

Our federal suit contended that the bipartisan conduct was evidenced by the CPD's decision to exclude *all* third-party candidates; we said that the CPD should return the millions of dollars in corporate contributions that had been made to it in 2000 and 2004. Our point was that a bipartisan entity no longer fell into the safe harbor for nonpartisan organizations in the FEC's regulations, and thus the CPD was not entitled to host the debates or collect corporate donations to do so.

In March 2004, the FEC dismissed our complaint.[40] So we took the complaint to court, where a federal district court judge in DC found the face book argument compelling, concluding, "The sole criteria CPD used to exclude people from the debate halls in 2000, even if they had tickets, was their status as third party presidential or vice presidential candidates . . . not their individual potential to disrupt the debates."[41]

Victory! It was the first time any court or petitioner had made a real chink in the CPD's "nonpartisan" armor, though appeals by the FEC meant there would be no relief for minor party candidates in time for the 2004 presidential debates. But we lost on appeal; the appellate court deferred to the FEC's conclusion that not even a face book designed to assist the CPD to physically exclude third-party and independent candidates (even a former Perot associate was listed!) from the premises of the debates showed the CPD's partisanship. At this point, the only two victories against the CPD have been the lower court victory in the *Hagelin* case and our litigation that resulted in settlement in Boston. But perhaps other third-party and independent candidates or their supporters will find another way to remove this major barrier to presidential political participation.

In 2004, I sent letters to the Democratic and Republican campaign managers, Mary Beth Cahill and Kenneth B. Mehlman, seeking their support for Ralph's inclusion in the debates. Neither responded. To their credit, in 2004, Michael Badnarik of the Libertarian Party and David Cobb of the Green Party got arrested for protesting their exclusion from the second debate at Washington University. Cobb said that "these are not debates, these are infomercials."[42]

As anyone who has litigated in the area of discrimination knows, discrimination can exist even if all the purported motivations are routinely touted as benign and "objective." If no women got into college and no African Americans got into housing in certain neighborhoods, ever, people would start to wonder about so-called objective criteria. Why is there no similar outcry with respect to our national discussion about who gets into the debates to ascertain who is worthy to run our country?

The CPD contends that because "so many" run for president, there must be some cutoff of those who can be on stage and debate. Okay, yes, but let's set that cutoff where there is a chance for third-party and independent candidates to make it in more than once every three or four decades. In 1988, only four people were mathematically eligible; in 1992, five; in 1996, six; in 2000, seven; in 2004, five. Not one of them (apart from Perot) was allowed in the debates because each did not meet whatever was set as the CPD's "criteria" du jour. The threat of too many presidential candidates on stage has not even reached in peak years more than the number of participants in the Democratic and Republican party debates during any primary season. The heavily favored major-party candidates get more time in the primary debates than the rest of the contenders, but at least the rest, with a few notable exceptions, get to participate in some, if not all, of the debates.[43]

Given the extreme difficulty in gaining ballot access, would it not be fair to allow all those mathematically eligible to participate in at least *one* presidential debate? And then see what happens in terms of polling and public desire from there? Are we saying that one group of candidates—third parties and independents—have to buy all their air-time rather than get any of it free, when the two major parties, who continue to grant our publicly owned bandwith for free, are rewarded with hours of exclusive airtime in the form of extended televised debates—infomercials permitted only to them throughout the campaign season?

If Perot's inclusion is any example, more people would watch more inclusive debates, and if more watched, perhaps more would vote.[44] The 1992 Perot debate was the all-time high in viewership, and the third debate with Bush/Gore in 2000 was the lowest ever.[45] It is sad commentary that sitcom television lately has been outdemocratizing the real presidential debates: Executive producer John Wells of the now-retired *West Wing* told the *Washington Post* in October 2005, " 'To even call our current presidential debates "debates" is stretching the term,' " so Wells was producing live debates on the *West Wing* with the goal of allowing the *fictional* candidates for president to "have a real exchange."[46]

As it is, more Americans tune into *American Idol* than to the presidential debates. *New York Times* reporter Alessandra Stanley posited that perhaps one reason for the popularity of *American Idol* is that, unlike our electoral system with its Electoral College, the people actually do have the final vote on *Idol*.[47] It is true that 63,400,000 votes were cast in the 2006 *Idol* finale, whereas only 62,028,719 voted in favor of President Bush in our 2004 election, but *Idol* fans can vote more than once.[48] Of course, given our current mess, maybe so can we. What is distressing is that a poll found, "Thirty-five percent of 'American Idol' voters believe that their vote counts 'as much as or more' than their vote for president."[49]

Columnist David Broder concluded in the *Washington Post* that "if the law allows (and in some ways encourages) both donors and grassroots activists to go outside the two-party system to participate in the campaign, then what is the logic of restricting the debates to those who have passed through the major-party primaries and conventions?"[50] More recently, Norman Ornstein, a resident scholar at the American Enterprise Institute, wrote in the *Wall Street Journal*, "[T]he debates are largely artificial exercises" with candidates' campaigns in "risk-avoidance mode." Even though he didn't seem to be able to imagine more than two-party or two-candidate debates, he did at least acknowledge that "[t]he current debate formats don't lend themselves to providing answers" to major policy questions, such as "how to respond to climate change" and "how to provide affordable health care to all Americans."[51]

Similarly, Marvin Kalb, writing in the *New York Times* in May 2007 as a former network correspondent, has proposed nine debates on nine Sundays with each of the nine major networks obliged to cover at least one, thereby forgoing the revenue from their ordinary Sunday programming. This proposition grew out of a meeting that he chaired of scholars, journalists, and politicians trying to improve the political process back in 1991. At the time, the media balked at losing high-viewership Sunday-evening revenues, and the candidates also "conspired in their own way to sidestep the challenge." According to Kalb, the "networks felt it was not their job to fix the political system."[52]

There are many worthy ideas to explore on how best to open up the debates. In 2004, despite the formation of a Citizens' Debate Commission, a truly nonpartisan group, there were no independently hosted all-inclusive presidential debates. How many more election cycles will the populace suffer the rigged charade of presidential debates and the CPD that purports to hold them?

Chapter 9

One Person, One Vote. Or Maybe None. Or Maybe Two.

> It's hard to believe that nearly six years after the disasters of Florida in 2000, states still haven't mastered the art of counting votes accurately. Yet there are growing signs that the country is moving into another presidential election cycle in disarray.
>
> —Editorial, "In Search of Accurate Vote Totals"[1]

In late November 2000, alternating between disbelief and tequila, I watched with anxiety as our punditry attempted to figure out who had been elected president. Since half the country was irrationally blaming the Nader campaign for the chaos, and I was past exhaustion from eight months of no sleep running a presidential campaign, I had decided to "get out of Dodge" for a week with the national field director, Todd Main, who I would later marry. Abroad in the tropical sun, wondering if we had a president yet, we would walk the main drag every day at about 4:00 P.M. to greet the arrival of the shipment of the *New York Times* at the bus depot. And then we would retreat to a crowded hut with a hundred different kinds of tequila on the wall to read about the vote-counting fiasco in Florida.

It was a reverse–Third World experience. Usually we read about "banana republics" not being able to count their votes. Here we were, in a banana republic, watching as citizens of the United States of America—world hegemon, beacon of democracy to the billions of huddled masses, richest country in the world—held up punch cards to the light, tried to distinguish between dimpled or hanging chad, and issued daily reports of lost, uncounted, and undecipherable votes.

Now, I was born in Chicago, where we routinely heard about the enthusiastic voting habits of the dead. But what about those accusations of keeping tens of thousands of the living off the voter rolls? This was a reverse graveyard strategy—don't let the living vote! Does this sort of thing still go on in the United States? And could it be true that people are given misinformation, misdirected, and blocked from exercising their franchise in our country at the dawn of the twenty-first century, after all the shame of poll taxes and Jim Crow laws?[2]

We watched with disbelief as our election administration officials openly admitted that the systems they have in place cannot accurately preserve, count, and report all the votes, so they just "pray to God" and hope that it won't be close enough for people to care. And then the U.S. Supreme Court said that Americans have no constitutional right to vote as they stopped the Florida Supreme Court's order to count the votes. This was insane.

Each day as we read about the Florida mess, I kept thinking back to my first unpleasant encounter with election officials. In 1993, just four years out of law school, I had returned to live in DuPage County, Illinois, where I had gone to high school. The state of Illinois is routinely ranked by good government groups as near or at the bottom of the fifty states in terms of campaign ethics and finance laws.[3] Every year judges, aldermen, mayors, inspector generals, or former governors go to jail after some sting operation. Illinoisans have seen it all—shoeboxes stuffed with cash, barbecued evidence, bribes for driver's licenses, and more.[4] In 2006, a *Chicago Tribune* op-ed calculated, "Of our seven prior governors, three now have been convicted."[5] Our most recent one was impeached. How many other states can claim this honor?

Yet back in 1994, my state (along with Mississippi) was fighting vehemently against the 1993 National Voter Registration Act, a federal law also known as NVRA or the "Motor Voter" law. The law made it easier for people to register to vote by allowing them to register when applying for or renewing their driver's licenses.[6] Why was the state of Illinois fighting against the imposition of a federal law that had already made it easier for more than 11 million people across the country to register to vote? For fear of "fraud."[7] Apparently, some people in my state thought that the problem we had here in Illinois was neither so many corrupt politicians filling the jails nor declining citizen participation in elections—with single-digit voter turnouts in odd-year school board or township contests. No. Here, in the Land of Lincoln, under the new federal law, it would be far too easy for the living to be able to register to vote!

So one day in 1994, I went into the local Clerk's Office in Elmhurst, a conservative bedroom community where I was living, about fourteen miles west of downtown Chicago. There was a large yellow sign with a pad of application forms that said how to register to vote. The local clerk explained that this sign came from the county election commission to register people to vote for federal office. The assumption for many was that if you wanted to vote for state *and* federal office, you had to drive to the county seat in Wheaton another fifteen miles west, whereas the local clerk could actually register you for local elections, but you had to ask.[8] This was the system imposed by the state of Illinois (not the city or county) as a way of responding to the Motor Voter law.

At first the governor, Jim Edgar (R), fought against implementation of the law, saying it was an unfunded federal mandate. The Republicans in power at the time in Illinois did not want a bunch of newly registered voters. New registrations could mean unpredictability in state elections—especially if there were an avalanche of newly registered Democrats. The Republicans could lose.[9] So they refused to implement the system. In January 1995, at least three lawsuits demanding that the federal law be followed were filed.[10] In June 1995, an appeals court told the Illinois governor that the law was constitutional, and he had to implement it. All the state's arguments about cost and fraud were rejected. So the state officials decided on their next nonacquiescent move. Having been told by two federal courts that the law was constitutional, Illinois would implement the federal law in its unique style. If Illinoisans wanted to register to vote in convenient places, like local public offices or at motor vehicle departments, fine—but only for federal elections unless the voter requested to register for all the offices.[11]

In Illinois, this difficult and confusing dual registration system became known for a brief time as the "two-tier" model, with approximately half of the people getting registered exclusively to vote for federal offices. We already have the most complicated ballots in the country because we have *6,000 more taxing bodies* than any other state. Now we were going to have two different kinds of ballots! It was embarrassing. We were producing "second-class voters." Plus the process was costly. Cook County alone estimated it would have to spend $2 million on mailing notices, printing "federal-only" ballots, and preparing two different sets of polling places.[12] Even Republican-leaning papers were starting to editorialize about the state's "deception" and only wanting "a certain *kind* of person voting."[13]

The state was registering 15,000 people a month[14] but with a disturbing pattern emerging: in 1995, "about 94 percent of Chicago residents who registered to vote at licensing facilities were registered for only federal elections, while about 50 percent of voters registered downstate were logged for all elections."[15] This was the idea, of course. Chicago was filled with African Americans, Hispanics, poor people, and Democrats. Downstaters and suburbanites—predominantly Caucasian and Republican—were being steered by the registrars to get registered to vote for all the offices.[16]

Finally, the League of Women Voters, the Illinois Federation of Labor, and the Cook County Clerk's Office sued again, this time in state court. They won in June 1996 at the lower court and in September of the same year in the appellate court. The appellate court wrote that the state's constitution would not "allow a system that makes it easier to register for some elections than for others."[17]

While all this was going on, I drove to the county seat in Wheaton, taking with me Charlene LaVoie, a community lawyer who happened to be visiting from the Office of the Community Lawyer/Advocate in Winsted, Connecticut. DuPage County, where I had gone to high school, was then considered the third-most-conservative county in the country. For decades, since World War II, all county-wide offices have been held by Republicans. So many of the Democrats run as Republicans, and many of the voters just register Republican to be able to vote in the primary for what is the real local election. In neighboring Cook County, which contains the city of Chicago, it is the opposite. If you don't vote for the right alderman, your garbage may not get picked up by the political machine. A *Chicago Tribune* investigation in 2006 found that Democratic campaign workers walked Chicago's wards with the Streets and Sanitation team behind them, "promptly" fulfilling requests for tree trimming, graffiti removal, and new garbage carts.[18]

The two counties' turfs are very well defined. You cross the county line, and you are in a new political world. Democrats do what they want in Chicago and suburban Cook County, where I now live. Republicans do as they please in DuPage County, where I used to live.[19] It wasn't always this way. For 110 years before 1980, there used to be cumulative voting and political minority representation. Not every state in the country, and certainly not historically, has had winner-take-all representative systems. But lately, as a nation, one-party rule at the local level, without any challengers, is becoming the norm, not the exception.

Now, Illinois, like many states, has a state board of elections, which covers 100 out of 101 non-home-rule counties. Only 1 county has its own board of elections.[20] Are you raising an eyebrow? Good. That would be Republican-dominated DuPage County. The DuPage County Election Commission has a "bipartisan" board. That day when Charlene LaVoie and I walked in, we talked to an employee named Jack. I asked Jack straight up: "Why is the county making it so hard for people to register to vote?"

Jack looked at me and Charlene and said sympathetically, "Have you ever seen how long it takes someone to vote? All those offices, judges . . ." His voice trailed off.

"Yes," I said, wondering where this was going.

"Well," explained Jack, "if everyone who was registered to vote in DuPage County, much less those eligible, actually turned out to vote, we wouldn't have enough time or machines to process their votes."

"What?"

"So, you see, if they only vote for federal offices, it takes less time, and we can keep it manageable," he went on to say.

"No, I don't see," I said. "I think that everyone should be able to vote for all of the offices."

He then looked at me as if I were some weirdo or troublemaker who just didn't get it. Charlene didn't say much, not wanting to interfere in my county's lunacy, but she was a witness to the whole thing. At the time, she couldn't believe that an election official felt comfortable saying this out loud. Jack's explanation, delivered with such bureaucratic conviction, was a cognitive disconnect with everything I had learned in school about democracy in America.[21]

Flash forward to 2000. As I was looking at the distraught and sleep-deprived Florida elections people, at the preppy Republican protesters allegedly on leave from their day jobs on Capitol Hill, I couldn't help thinking of my conversation with Jack. My guess at the time was that nearly every board of elections employee in America was probably watching the Florida mess and saying, "There but for the grace of God go I."

In 2000, Chicago, not Florida, actually took the prize for being "the site of the biggest single vote-counting error in the 2000 presidential election."[22] *After* spending $25 million to upgrade their machinery, Cook County alone had 122,914 ballots not registering a vote for president—more than twice the number it had in 1996.[23] What an improvement! I kept thinking at the time, "Why isn't every American outraged about this?" The country was in a stew over Florida. But what about Illinois and every other place in the nation that cannot manage to count its votes? Some 1.9 million ballots were not counted countrywide in 2000.[24] A Caltech-MIT study estimated that 4 to 6 million votes for the president were lost.[25]

How can a country lose *6 million* votes? According to the General Accounting Office, "the type of voting equipment" and "the demographic characteristics" of the jurisdiction—but, most telling, the actual state in which the votes are located—constitute the greatest determinants of lost presidential votes![26] By 2000, the Haitian elections were, in retrospect, not looking so primitive. Despite their many other troubles, a few days after their first free election, the Haitians knew who was elected.[27]

In February 2001, Ralph Nader and I went to the National Association of Secretaries of State (NASS) annual conference with a seventeen-point proposal on how to repair elections, including some proposals that responded to our observations of the manifest injustices from the 2000 campaign. Some points were very straightforward, such as "enforce the Voting Rights Act of 1965" and "establish the nonpartisan administration of elections."[28] Others were a bit more outside the box, including establish a standardized national ballot for federal elections to prevent defective "butterfly ballot" designs or the Duval County "caterpillar ballot."[29]

The secretaries of state listened politely, but the proposals were largely ignored. Congress formed a "bipartisan" commission to study the whole fiasco of the 2000 election. The co-chairmen were the thirty-eighth and thirty-ninth presidents—Gerald Ford and Jimmy Carter—as well as former U.S. Representative Robert H. Michel and former counsel to the president Lloyd N. Cutler. The commission's final report told the story of the then–chief election official Cathy Cox

(D-GA), who had testified in 2001. She said, "As the presidential election drama unfolded in Florida last November, one thought was foremost in my mind: there but for the Grace of God go I. Because the truth is, if the presidential margin had been razor thin in Georgia and if our election systems had undergone the same microscopic scrutiny Florida endured, we would have fared no better. In many respects, we might have fared even worse."[30]

The commission reported that it heard from "official after official who feels the same way."[31] And so, after holding four public hearings, the commission offered a report in August 2001 that had thirteen policy recommendations, some that overlapped with ours. Some were very basic, such as: "every state should adopt a system of statewide voter registration" and "the state and federal governments should take additional steps to assure the voting rights of all citizens and to enforce the principle of one person, one vote."[32] Other recommendations were attempts to be more inclusive: creating a national holiday to vote and restoring voting rights to ex-felons who have fully served their sentence.[33]

The commission concluded in August 2001 that in three to five years it could "envision a country where each state maintains accurate, computerized lists of who can vote," where "qualified voters in our mobile society would be able to vote throughout their state," and where "millions of military and other overseas voters would find it easier to get and return their ballots." The commission said that Election Day should be held on a national holiday, "freeing up more people to serve as poll workers and making polling places more accessible." Then it got really fancy by hoping "every *official* would obey the Voting Rights Act."[34] All of this you would think is fairly elementary for a democratic republic worthy of its name. The commission basically concluded that we should let the American people vote and have a functional system to count the votes. But Congress ignored most of its recommendations.

Finally, because Congress had to look as if it were responding to Florida 2000, and because the voting-machine-maker lobby was helping the members write the law that would eventually fill industry coffers, Congress did pass the Help America Vote Act of 2002 (HAVA). HAVA was supposed to help states create accurate statewide voter rolls, update state voting machinery, and provide for provisional ballots to make sure no one would leave a polling place without having a chance to vote, even if only provisionally. The title of the legislation alone should be indicative that we have a "democracy problem" in the United States.

When President Bush signed the bill, he said, "The vitality of America's democracy depends on the fairness and accuracy of America's elections."[35] He went on to say that we had to make the "fairness of all elections . . . a national priority."[36] Well, this all sounds good if you are willing to put aside how he got to be president, twice. But Bush was essentially saying we have to pass legislation to help ourselves vote because our system is so messed up that we can only "envision" a country where there are accurate voting systems.

Try to imagine the president of a banking commission who says, "We envision a banking system where the deposits are recorded correctly, and the withdrawals can also be recorded accurately." Would *anyone* have enough faith to bank in that system? If the automated teller machines (ATMs) couldn't dispense money accurately, we would have a revolution! (I'm thinking of starting one just based on their fees!) But when the same company that makes some of the ATMs makes some of the voting machines that can't count, and our democracy depends on it, and we can't get it right? Silence.

Election fiasco after election fiasco seems to have produced little palpable public outrage. HAVA was supposed to create a bipartisan U.S. Election Assistance Commission (EAC), with two Republicans and two Democrats, that would, among other things, assume responsibilities previously assigned to the FEC's Office of Election Administration. The first annual report the EAC sent to Congress correctly complained that the legislation establishing HAVA required the president to appoint the EAC by February 26, 2003, but that nobody bothered to appoint the commission until December 13, 2003.

The EAC remained so woefully underfunded—it had "no offices, equipment, or staff"—that it couldn't do its work.[37] Throughout most of 2004—a presidential election year—it had neither a general counsel nor an executive director. Was this a federal government serious about making election reform "a national priority"? The EAC, despite disbursing approximately $1.3 billion to forty-four states in FY 2004 alone, couldn't get the job done.[38]

The media had a field day with the lack of electoral reform and preparation for 2004 and 2008.[39] In the days leading up to the 2004 election, there were so many articles about the flaws in the electoral system and the "incompetent or malevolent election administrators," even a foreign observer was prompted to query in a letter to the *New York Times*: "How is it possible that a country that prides itself as being the beacon of democracy to the world and that likes to have frequent elections for so many offices seems to do elections so badly?"[40]

And sure enough, on Election Eve 2004, a *New York Times* poll reported that "only one-third of the American people said that they had a lot of confidence that their votes would be counted properly, and 29 percent said they were very or somewhat concerned that they would encounter problems at the polls."[41] Even after the election, according to a Pew Research Center survey, "a minority of Americans—only 48 percent—said they were very confident that the votes cast across the country were accurately counted."[42] Heather K. Gerken, who now teaches election law at Yale, told the *New York Times*, "'We dodged a bullet this time, but the problems remain. . . . We have problems with the machines, problems with the patchwork of regulations covering everything from recounts to provisional ballots, and problems with self-interested party officials deciding which votes count.'"[43]

After the 2004 election, there were so many complaints across the country that the ranking Democrat on the House Judiciary Committee, Representative John Conyers (D-MI), conducted an investigation into the irregularities. Conyers's report, focusing on Ohio, listed egregious problems, including unprecedented long lines, predominantly in minority districts; "improper purging and other registration errors by election officials that likely disenfranchised tens of thousands of voters statewide"; "numerous, significant unexplained irregularities in other counties throughout the state"; and "widespread instances of intimidation and misinformation in violation of the Voting Rights Act, the Civil Rights Act of 1968, Equal Protection, Due Process and the Ohio right to vote."[44]

A second commission, the Carter-Baker Commission, a private, *bipartisan* commission, after very limited public hearings, released a report echoing the prior commission: "The Commission *envisions* a system that makes Americans proud of themselves as citizens and of democracy in the United States."[45] After two fiasco presidential elections, this commission had become very good at writing "envisioning" statements. Though the commission's aim was "both to increase voter participation and to assure the integrity of the electoral system," the commission issued an impressive eighty-seven recommendations, primarily focused on election machinery mechanics, managing to say *absolutely nothing*, for example, about such fundamental aspects of our elections as the lack of political competition; the barriers to entry for political competitors, especially third parties, independents, or the nonfavored major-party candidates; the role of money in politics; the Electoral College and the lack of a direct vote for president; the lack of any alternative voting systems to winner-take-all, such as instant runoff voting or proportional representation; or the lack of a fundamental, explicit right to vote in our Constitution, placing us in the distinct minority of nations without such a provision.

Our current, deserved obsession with election mechanics has served to obscure many more fundamental problems. Just because the 2008 election margin was not razor-thin does not mean these problems have been fixed. Everything I came to witness or experience in the Nader campaigns in the 2000 and 2004 presidential elections says distinctly that our electoral system does not work for supporters of third parties and independents, but it also doesn't work well for voters of the two major parties, either. The mainstream media is talking about this at the most rudimentary level, highlighting our collective inability to count and record. But the problems are not limited to getting a better abacus. This may be hard to accept if you share, as I did, our collective bedrock belief that we live in the most advanced democracy on the planet.

Whether you can vote—and whether your vote counts—depends primarily on where you live. Whether candidates appear on your ballot, and in what order they appear, is conditioned on where you live. How much your vote counts compared to others also depends on where you live. Yes, your vote is *conditional. It is based on your location in your state and among states.* In Chapter 1 we discussed the as-yet-unfixed problems with voter registration rolls—purged and inaccurate as they are from state to state. Here, I set forth a brief look at additional factors—the Electoral College, the mechanics of vote counting, write-in votes, military and overseas voting, absentee ballots and early voting, provisional ballots, and recounts, because as a country we need to get to the point where we say that where you live in the United States should not affect whether and how your vote counts for president of the United States.

Though I encountered these issues in the context of whether a voter for a third-party or independent candidate could get his or her vote counted accurately, timely, and fairly, the problems, albeit to a lesser degree, exist also for two-party voters. All voters should demand more federalization to our federal elections to eliminate the arbitrariness of geography on the value of an individual's vote.

The Electoral College

There are 538 electors (the number of congressional representatives plus senators, plus three for DC). Unless you live in Maine or Nebraska, the only two states, since 1969 and 1992, respectively, that apportion electors among the candidates by the number of congressional districts won, you are going to be represented in the Electoral College by the electors of the party that wins your state elections. So if you are in a state that always elects Republicans for president, all of your state's electoral votes are always going to the Republicans—even if 49 percent of your state is made up of voters who are Democrats or Greens or Libertarians. This is how the two parties have implemented the winner-take-all system. The Constitution doesn't say how the states have to fork over their electors. The two major parties do. In the beginning, only three states allocated electors on a winner-take-all basis. The others just copied this bad idea. As Maine and Nebraska prove, there are different ways to award electors, without touching the Constitution, but that would require the two major parties to do something to change the status quo, which currently benefits them.

If you live, like the majority of the population, in one of the nine states (California, New York, Texas, Florida, Illinois, Pennsylvania, Ohio, Michigan, and Georgia) containing this numerical majority of voters in the country, your Electoral College vote is seriously undervalued, all the time, no matter for which party it gets cast in the Electoral College. If you live in one of the thirteen states (such as Wyoming, Rhode Island, Delaware, and Nevada) representing about 5 percent of the population, your vote is seriously overvalued. This is how it works: Each state, plus DC, gets the number of electors equal to its number of congressional districts, plus two Senate seats. So the seven states that have just one member of the House of Representatives have their voting power tripled because they get the two Senate votes as well.

The Senate seats are overweighted for low population states, and so too are the elector seats. Wyoming, with under half a million people (493,782—U.S. Census Bureau, 2000), is given the same number of Senate electors, two, as California, which has close to 34 million people (33,871,648—U.S. Census Bureau, 2000).

Even among the small states, the way the electors are allocated based on the House congressional districts is skewed compared to their population. For example, Idaho and Rhode Island both have four electoral votes (two Senate, two House). Their populations according to the U.S. Census Bureau in 2000 were 1,449,402 and 1,048,319, respectively. So with 450,000 more people, Idaho still has only the same number of electoral votes as Rhode Island. Compared to Rhode Island voters, the votes of Idahoans are undervalued.

If you believe that democracy means that each vote should count equally—one person, one vote—and most people in this country do, the Electoral College does not fulfill this value. And that is why people argue that the Electoral College is "undemocratic." The Electoral College distortion dictates how presidential campaigns are now run. The national candidates don't campaign in all the states for entirely different reasons than population—it's because they know they have, or could never have, at least 50.1 percent of the vote in that state and thus shouldn't waste time in a "safe"-for-the-opposition or "impossible"-to-win state. FairVote points out that in the last five weeks of the 2004 election, twenty-five states—comprising 51 percent of the entire population—were virtually ignored, with only three visits, total, from major-party presidential or vice-presidential candidates.[46] Candidates don't bother to show in unchallengeable states.

Strategic voters know that voting for a third party in a state that is always going to be safe for one of the two parties won't affect any Electoral College outcomes. But strategic voters in battleground states are wary of voting for a third party. This is why scholars report that 96 percent of those who support a two-party candidate will cast their vote for that candidate, but only about 70 percent "of those who favored third-party candidates—such as George Wallace, John Anderson and Ross Perot—voted for them."[47] Geography plays a role not just in Electoral College calculations and strategic voting but in vote order, voter registration, voter ID, vote machinery, provisional voting, recounts, and a host of other issues, all of which can have an impact on the voters and votes for third parties and independents.

Vote Counting Mechanics: "12345678"— Who Is the Threat to Security?

How does your state count votes? There are plenty of books and scholarly articles written about this subject. We now have people—scientists, academics, citizen advocates, and public officials—studying this all over America, from who owns the vote counting machinery and software to how they perform in any given test or election. And there is good reason why there is all this suspicion. The whole process is enmeshed in secrecy.

When I first moved back home to DuPage County in 1993, a number of people from all parts of the political spectrum told me that they were suspicious of the vote counting software in the county. Well, no wonder. The results were *always* for one party, and the vote counting software had been subcontracted, no bid, to the same vendor for more than twenty years. Mother Theresa could have been counting the votes, and there would still be suspicions under these circumstances.

In the now-classic Ronnie Dugger piece "Counting Votes," which the *New Yorker* published in 1988, Dugger began with the following, "During the past quarter of a century, with hardly anyone noticing, the inner workings of democracy have been computerized." He went on to write, "It appears that since 1980 errors and accidents have proliferated in computer-counted elections. Since 1984, the State of Illinois has tested local computerized systems by running many thousands of machine-punched mock ballots through them, rather than the few tens of test ballots that local election officials customarily use. As of the most recent tests this year, errors in the basic counting instructions in the computer programs had been found in almost a fifth of the examinations." Michael L. Harty, who was the director of voting systems and standards for Illinois, told Dugger, "At one point, we had tabulation errors in twenty-eight per cent of the systems tested, and nobody cared."[48]

In 1994, I tried to care. At age thirty, I tried to help an even younger person, Tim Ryan, a maverick, who had been the county's top Democratic vote-getter but lost in a heavily Republican county whose state's attorney was named Jim Ryan. Tim was trying to get access to the software through a Freedom of Information Act case. When I met him, he had already lost in the lower court and on his first appeal, so I tried to get a rehearing of the appellate court decision and then filed an appeal to the Illinois Supreme Court.[49] Neither court would hear the case. Everyone said it was "okay" to keep the vote counting software a secret—it was "proprietary" information that only the vendors could know, and therefore citizens couldn't see it under the open government laws. The Federal Election Commission was advising this response nationally! You didn't even have election officials understanding or knowing how votes were being tabulated, but, hey, this was confidential business information, like the recipe for Coca-Cola.

Except this is our democracy.

On November 3, 1994, I wrote a letter to the DuPage County Board of Elections to ask if I could at least be present to watch a vote count, as an observer from the democracy-building organization I had founded, the Citizen Advocacy Center. I got a really interesting response. The county claimed, "You, Ms. Amato, are a threat to security." I couldn't view the counting. According to the lawyer, no one could—we were all threats to security. At the time, I let it slide a little, thinking that "these people take themselves way too seriously." I found it pretty bizarre that I, a woman raised in Itasca, Illinois, a League of Women Voters member, and a registered lawyer in the DuPage County Bar Association, was considered "a threat to security." What harm would it have been for me to witness what was going on?

Apparently, plenty.

And this was true all over the United States. Ordinary citizens might have actually realized before Florida happened in 2000 what pure chaos was going on in our election commissions and boards and offices of secretaries of state across the country. The curtain would have been lifted for all to see that the wizard was a wee bit disorganized: our country didn't have standards; we didn't know how our machines and the software worked or whether they did; we didn't know who was registered; we didn't know who got purged; we didn't know how we verified votes, how we counted ballots, or how confused poll workers were. And all the while the FEC was telling states not to disclose their vote counting software,[50] even though the machines didn't work a substantial part of the time—and no one was prosecuted for electoral malfeasance against the people for depriving them of their votes.

We were—and still are—a national electoral mess!

The comptroller general and the Government Accountability Office say it more politely. They refer to everything as "challenges" with "varying" results across shocking numbers of "jurisdictions." The comptroller general's office has been putting out reports documenting the mess regularly since 2000. For example, in its June 2006 report to congressional committees, it "found that states *varied* in their progress in implementing their statewide voter registration lists and how they have implemented their voting systems."[51] It further found "that implementation of the identification provision for certain firsttime mail registrants *varied* . . . [and that] the states *varied* in their implementations of HAVA's requirement for provisional voting." The GAO noted that in the "states' reported plans and local jurisdictions' estimated plans for acquiring voting systems for future elections, the election technology environment *varied*."[52] These *variations* are *scary*.

Amazingly, as of 2001, *after Florida*, according to a GAO estimate, "32 percent of jurisdictions nationwide had no written instructions, either from the state or local jurisdiction, to interpret voter intent, such as marks on paper ballots or partially punched chads [*sic*] on punch card ballots."[53] Some states had very specific instructions, such as whether to count a chad with three corners attached.[54]

With the passage of HAVA, Congress finally put into place minimum voting systems standards for systems to be used in an election for federal office and created processes to test these systems. These standards would allow a voter to verify his or her vote and provide the voter with the opportunity to change or correct that vote before he or she cast a ballot.[55] HAVA also provides for the EAC to give "voluntary guidance" to the states on how to comply with the minimum requirements, but it left it up to the states to implement their own procedures.[56] As a consequence, some states are applying acceptable security system standards, but according to the GAO in 2006, "27 other states are requiring their jurisdictions to apply federal standards to their new voting systems that are outdated, unspecified, or entail multiple versions."[57] Two states "do not plan to require their voting systems to comply with any version of the voluntary standards," and three more had not decided yet.[58] And this passes as progress.

Moreover, local election jurisdictions use different ways to count the vote. Sometimes it is counted on-site at the precinct, sometimes at a central location, sometimes both. We all have heard stories of ballot stuffing, from Robert Caro's epic of how Lyndon Johnson won his Senate seat with Ballot Box 13 to the legend of Mayor Richard J. Daley delivering Illinois to John F. Kennedy in 1960 with help from "a few friends."

There are a number of problems that can occur with vote counting, from machine failure to human error. According to the GAO, in some of the election jurisdictions it visited to study vote counting, problems included "punch cards that stuck together and could not be read by the counting machines"; difficulty in reading punch cards produced by different vendors; "optical scan equipment that stopped working because it became clogged with paper dust" from the ballots; "incorrect marks by voters on optical scan ballots that could not be machine read"; and "programming errors in the software used to tally optical scan ballots."[59] According to the GAO, 88 percent of jurisdictions compare the number of ballots at the end of the day to the number of people who signed in to vote. Some 64 percent compare the number of ballots cast with the number they started with, accounting for spoilage and unused ballots.[60] Once again, there is no uniform procedure on how to protect the integrity of the machines, how to account for votes, or what to do if there is a discrepancy in the count.

Echoing Ronnie Dugger's 1988 *New Yorker* article, James Fallows pointed out in the *New York Times* after the 2004 election that the reason he asks for a paper ballot, not electronic, is because the electronic machines are all in "beta version," having had little opportunity to work out the kinks, as they are only used under stress a few days a year, if that.[61] And for good reason. In January 2006, I read a *Washington Post* article that made my hair stand on end. It began with the elected Leon County, Florida, supervisor of elections, Ion Sancho, who has held that position since 1989.[62] His job is to make sure the elections are free from fraud.[63] Sancho invited computer specialists to break into his Diebold system four times in 2005. Guess what? They did. All four times. They were able to change results "with what the specialists described as relatively unsophisticated hacking techniques."[64] According to the *Post*, more than 800 jurisdictions use this same technology.[65]

The *Post* reported later in March 2006 that none of the three state-approved vendors who sell voting equipment in Florida were willing to sell Sancho any machines for Leon County.[66] They didn't like his tests. Apparently, this may have been Sancho's punishment (and perhaps a message from the industry to state election employees) for pulling back the curtain to show how any marginal hacker or even your teenager could subvert the machines' memory card without detection. Whether your vote counts may depend on whether your state has a brave Mr. Sancho.[67] By December 2006, the most devastating condemnation about the machines had been issued. The National Institute of Standards and Technology (NIST) concluded that the paperless machines "cannot be made secure." The report even said that "a single programmer could 'rig' a major election."[68]

Then I read this in the pinstriped *American Banker*. On August 8, 2007, the *American Banker*, citing a California secretary of state report, quoted Techdirt Inc.'s president and chief executive Michael Masnick, saying the California Diebold machines used the "hard-coded" passwords "'diebold' and (I kid you not) '12345678'." You couldn't make up this farce if you tried.[69]

Prior to HAVA's passage in 2002, the United States did not have voting equipment standards at all. This too is hard to believe. But a GAO report in October 2001 spells it out: "No federal agency has been assigned explicit statutory responsibility for developing voting equipment standards; however, the Federal Election Commission assumed this role by developing *voluntary* standards in 1990 for computer-based systems."[70] The FEC's voluntary standards did not cover paper or lever methods, as they don't use computer technology, and it would be *nine* years before the FEC engaged in any updates of its standards.[71] The GAO concluded that the "FEC has not proactively maintained its voting equipment standards"[72] and suggested to Congress that it "may wish to consider assigning explicit federal authority, responsibility, and accountability for voting equipment standards, including proactive and continuous update and maintenance of the standards."[73] *May wish*? The lack of federal voting and equipment standards means that whether your vote is not lost, or counts, depends on the state in which you live.

Despite this standard-free existence, for the 2004 election the majority of states (twenty-nine plus DC) did not require *any* kind of vote audit.[74] Most states have no standing rules on checking the machines against paper. Many still do not even have paper trails. Of those that do audits, the sample of votes tested can vary widely—from 1 percent in Colorado or 3 percent in New York to 10 percent in Hawaii.[75] Reports of problems and flaws persisted through the 2006 and 2008 elections. In August 2007, Voter Action called for a congressional investigation of "whether U.S. voting systems companies have engaged in commercial fraud by knowingly marketing defective products to jurisdictions throughout the country."[76]

Voter ID

How long you have to wait in line to vote may also depend on which state you live in. The *New York Times* covered the release of a report by the Century Foundation, Common Cause, and the Leadership Conference on Civil Rights, saying that most states have vague standards, "if any," for voting machine distribution.[77] So if you live in Michigan, there might be one machine for every 600 voters. If you live in Wisconsin, you probably will have shorter lines, with a 1:200 ratio of machines to voters.[78]

And states have varying ID requirements, so which state you live in may determine whether you are allowed to vote based on your document portfolio. As of April 2007, twenty-four states requested or required IDs for all voters, but three of those allowed voters to vote on a provisional ballot if they didn't have one, and four allowed voters with affidavits to cast a ballot. Two more states require photo IDs for first-time voters only. The other states say that you can vote, but if you are a first-time voter who registered by mail, then you need to show up with a photo or nonphoto ID.[79] States are likely to add more ID requirements, as the Supreme Court, in a facial challenge to Indiana's ID law, upheld this voter requirement.[80]

In the United States, our problem isn't that we have too many people voting; our problem is that we have too few. (And on the rare occasion we break 60 percent of the eligible population showing up to vote, the system can barely handle it.) Nonetheless, to prevent what most studies reveal to be "nearly nonexistent fraud," Republicans have been pushing voter ID with statements such as, "You have to show ID for almost everything—to rent a Blockbuster movie" and similar adages.[81] The concept is not problematic. It *is* important to verify voters' identities against accurate registration lists or the national census, like Canada does. The problem lies in both the rationale and the implementation. First, the rationale for the voter IDs is that there is massive vote fraud. There has been almost no evidence of vote fraud with respect to people actually showing up to the polls acting as imposters. Election law experts and law enforcement people agree on this. A front-page *New York Times* story on this subject said that a "crackdown" of enforcement over the last five years of the Bush administration has resulted in just eighty-six convictions.[82] Michael Waldman and Justin Levitt of the Brennan Center for Justice at New York University School of Law declared in a March 29, 2007, op-ed in the *Washington Post* that the probe of the U.S. attorney firings for failure to find and prosecute voter fraud was akin to "firing a park ranger for failing to find Sasquatch"—because "evidence of actual fraud by individual voters is painfully skimpy."[83] Any problems tend to be because of misunderstandings regarding the rules or because of fraudulent registrations or state election officials' failure to maintain accuracy. For example, the *Wall Street Journal* editorialized about voter drives that have resulted in convictions in some states and investigations in others.[84]

Second, in the implementation, some of these laws have disenfranchised people for partisan political gain. Missouri, Georgia, Indiana, and Arizona have been restricting what is considered to be acceptable ID to be able to vote. No longer can you show your utility bill or bank statement. You now need a state-issued photo ID. If you don't drive, like some 12 to 18 percent of the population, well, then you have to get a state-issued photo ID—by showing up with a birth certificate and money to pay a fee. In Georgia, where this law was passed, and then stopped by a state court judge calling it unconstitutional,[85] "there was not a single office in Atlanta where the [voter ID] cards were for sale."[86] In Ohio, a federal judge halted the implementation of the ID law for absentee ballots because the state's eighty-eight counties were not applying it consistently.[87] No surprise there. In Florida, the NAACP and others have sued because a law wrongly barred people from voting at all in the 2006 election because their identification did not match faulty databases—with, say, a mistyped birth date in the database.[88]

Let's look at Arizona. The data there are that of 2.7 million registered Arizona voters, 238 in the last *ten* years were believed to be noncitizens; only 4 of them were believed to have voted, and none were "imposter" voters.[89] The state of Arizona did not dispute this data in a lawsuit, and it is similar to the lack of imposter voting evidence in Georgia, Indiana, and Missouri.[90] Nonetheless, the state has been requiring people to show up with state-issued photo IDs, such as a driver's license or a passport. In Maricopa County alone, according to the

Times, "election officials said that 35 percent of new registrations were rejected for insufficient proof of citizenship last year and that 17 percent had been rejected so far this year."[91] Whether you must show up with a voter ID and whether you get to vote depend on where you live.

Absentee and Early Voting

Whether you can vote early or obtain an absentee ballot also depends on where you live. All states and DC permit some type of early voting or absentee voting. But as of 2001, states did not "routinely collect and report absentee and early voting data."[92] In 2004, in twenty-one states (up from eighteen in 2000), you didn't have to provide an excuse, such as being overseas or sick or having a disability or being away at school, to gain a ballot. In other states an excuse is required. In some states, whether you could vote absentee depended on how fast the postal service got your ballot to you and back to the election jurisdiction. In one state, the election commission's telephone system crashed "numerous times leading up to Election Day" because so many voters were calling to see where their absentee ballots were.

Other jurisdictions had to hire extra people to process absentee ballot requests. The GAO estimates that in *55 percent* of the jurisdictions absentee ballot applications were received "too late to process," and in *77 percent* of the jurisdictions it surveyed there were problems because absentee ballots themselves were received "too late."[93] All kinds of factors could go into this—including late printing of ballots because of third-party candidacy challenges, a slow U.S. postal service, a convoluted student mailing system at a university, inexcusably short statutory time periods for turnaround, voter errors, and the shortage of personnel in general in election offices across the country at crunch time.

Whether you get to vote early also depends on your state. The trend is to institute early voting. In 2004, twenty-four states offered some kind of early voting, and some others have since implemented or will consider implementing it. In Oklahoma, you could only vote three days early. But if you lived in New Mexico, you could vote almost a month early, which might make some of those October surprises candidates face a little less valuable. The popularity of early voting clearly caught a lot of election jurisdictions by surprise too. They weren't prepared, and so the press reported on long lines, filled with children tagging along with their waiting parents, sometimes as long as three and a half hours—all for early voting![94] In 2008, record numbers of people voted early, some to avoid what turned out to be long lines for a historic election.

Military and Overseas Votes

Your vote may also be conditioned on whether you are voting from overseas or in the military. There is a law that is designed to assist uniformed and overseas voters. Enacted in 1986, it's called the Uniformed and Overseas Citizens Absentee Voting Act, or UOCAVA, and according to the GAO, it applies to approximately 6.5 million people, including 1.4 million military members, 1.3 million of their dependents of voting age, and 3.7 million overseas American citizens who don't work for the government.[95] An executive order designates the secretary of defense or his or her designee to distribute information about how to vote absentee, to design materials to register and vote as absentee, to work with state and local officials in charge of elections, and to report about the effectiveness of these activities.[96]

This is done through the Federal Voting Assistance Program (FVAP), an office that is under the direction of the U.S. undersecretary of defense for personnel and readiness. According to the GAO, the FVAP had in 2004 a full-time staff of thirteen and an annual budget of about $6 million.[97] An October 2007 Electionline.org briefing paper states that even with all this effort, data released by the EAC in September 2007 showed that "less than 48 percent of votes cast by overseas military voters were counted during the 2006 midterm elections, with similar numbers for overseas civilian and domestic military voters."[98]

The Pentagon is practically the new Department of Agriculture, where the common joke is that the ratio of civil servants to farmers is 1 to 1. According to the *New York Times*, "For every 100 soldiers, there is now a voting representative. Armed with absentee-ballot information for every state, the 'voting rep' must make two 'personal contacts' with each soldier."[99] According to the *Washington Post*, an FVAP survey shows "nearly 80 percent of people in the uniformed armed services voted or attempted to vote in the last presidential election."[100] But according to the *New York Times*, and confirmed by the GAO, the experts at the National Defense Committee and the Overseas Vote Foundation say that "anywhere from a quarter to half of overseas voters fail in their attempt to vote."[101] And, surprise: "Local election officials are also partly to blame for the confusion according to a draft report from the Government Accountability Office in April 2007. The report cited 18 states or territories that had inconsistent or misleading information instructing overseas voters how to cast their ballot." A November 2007 release from the AEI-Brookings Election Reform Project is even more damning.[102]

The FVAP publishes information through its Web site at www.fvap.gov, but it is primarily the responsibility of the overseas voter to undertake registration and voting activities. On its Web site, the FVAP states that it "provides U.S. citizens worldwide a broad range of nonpartisan information and assistance to facilitate their participation in the democratic process—regardless of where they work or live."[103]

When I started to research the federally funded FVAP in 2005, its Web site only had on it links to the Republican National Committee (RNC) and the Democratic National Committee (DNC), with this lame explanation: "Additional Political parties: Currently, there is no single location on the Internet to get information on other political parties operating in the United States. However, candidate information is available at the following sites"; and then the Web site provided links to the League of Women Voters and Project Vote Smart.[104] Presumably the national Web sites for the Libertarian, Green, Reform, Socialist, Natural Law, and Constitution parties—all available online to search—were not considered the equivalent to the RNC and DNC and were excluded from the Web site most of the military and overseas voters would be told how to access. Up until recently, there was no mention of any other parties in the United States or any other standard source of candidate information on this "nonpartisan" Web site, paid for by your tax dollars. Recently, though, someone with historical or minor-party sensibilities obviously did a review of the site. The FVAP now has become acutely aware of minor parties and offers links to many sites, claiming, "Today, America is a multi-party system. The *Democratic* Party and the *Republican* Party are the most powerful. Yet other parties, such as the *Reform*, *Libertarian*, *Socialist*, *Natural Law*,

Constitution and *Green* Parties can promote candidates in a presidential election."[105]

One very interesting aspect of the FVAP is that it has managed to develop a voter registration form and an absentee write-in ballot that is accepted by *all* states, DC, and the territories (except for American Samoa and Guam). This proves it is possible to administer registration and balloting at the federal level. A citizen overseas can fill out the online version of the federal post card application (FPCA), even though he or she is entitled to also receive the postage-paid cardstock FPCA for those using U.S. mails, such as APO/FPO (Army Post Office/Fleet Post Office). The government provides an online version for people to also mail and send in. If a citizen abroad or someone who is military personnel is absent from home (even if within the United States) and has timely requested but not timely received a ballot, he or she is allowed to use the Federal Write-in Absentee Ballot (FWAB SF-186), which permits the individual to write in a choice for each office.[106]

The GAO notes that there remain additional challenges to getting it right when it comes to providing the vote to military personnel and citizens overseas. Top among its recommendations are "simplifying and standardizing the time-consuming and multi-step absentee voting process, which includes different requirements and time frames for each state" (including DC and the territories).[107]

The FVAP has tried to make the voting process easier for citizens overseas by getting states to standardize and simplify their requirements. This impulse should prevail for citizens at home as well. But certain initiatives butt up against the ballot access deadline timetable. For example, the FVAP is trying to get all states to mail out absentee ballots forty to forty-five days before the election, and all but fourteen states have agreed to this initiative.[108] Of course, the problem then is that candidates have to get on the ballot by that time in order to be included in the military and overseas ballots.

As an indicator of how difficult and recalcitrant state elections officials can be, the GAO reports that the FVAP began its legislative initiatives to try to get states to agree to certain provisions to make absentee voting easier back in the 1980s. Two of these eleven initiatives, to get rid of restrictions on how early someone could request ballots during the calendar year and to accept one registration for all elections in a calendar year, became law, respectively, through HAVA and the National Defense Authorization Act for FY 2002.[109] But of the remaining nine initiatives to facilitate absentee voting, only five have been adopted by the majority of states.[110]

Write-In Votes

Whether you can write-in a vote for a candidate is also dependent on the state in which you live. Richard Winger, the publisher of *Ballot Access News*, has been on a thirty-year crusade to get legislatures to pass laws providing for an official tally for self-declared write-in candidates. When he started, "California was the only state that had such a law (California had passed it in 1951). Now, 35 states have such a law. Oregon and Washington are the only states that ever had it and then repealed it."[111] And five states don't permit it, as discussed in the *Burdick* case in Chapter 5. Winger points out, correctly, that some day if there is a question about whether a third-party or independent presidential candidate broke the 5 percent barrier to collect FEC general election funding, it could be crucial to know the precise write-in vote tally for the presidential candidate.[112]

Given how difficult it is to count the standard ballots, you can only imagine how lax some state standards are with respect to write-in votes. And yet they are important and can add up.[113] In 2004, in the twelve states where he wasn't on the ballot, Ralph Nader received 52,331 write-in votes.[114] But we will never know what he received in Ohio and Oregon in 2004. We missed the Ohio write-in deadline because we were presumptively on the ballot when it passed, and Oregon refuses to require its counties to tally write-ins for individual candidacies, just in the aggregate.

According to Michael Richardson, who reviewed the ballot access statutes for the Nader 2004 campaign, the write-in procedures for each state are even harder to discern than the petition requirements in terms of establishing eligibility of candidates to be counted as write-in candidates. Massachusetts and Pennsylvania, for example, according to Richardson, would permit stickers with the names preprinted on them but would require three different-sized stickers to match the various voting machines. In Massachusetts, paper ballots would need a 4×5/16-inch sticker with black ink. Scanner voting machines needed a 2¼×¼-inch sticker. Lever machines would vary from town to town. And so it goes.

To become a write-in candidate in Illinois, Ralph Nader and Peter Camejo *each* had to execute 110 affidavits to mail to each county or city election commission in Illinois; and for the vote to count, each had to be listed on the ballot, and the local official could determine whether or not to count the votes. The hassle was incredible. In California, for example, we had to ask the state to count as valid thirty-three different spellings of their names.[115] Texas, on the other hand, was considerate enough to put a list of the write-in candidates in its polling booths.

The complexities of the write-in process for each state were so numerous that we actually commissioned a "WriteinRalph.org" Web site to handle the twelve states for which we were going to have to run write-in campaigns. The difficulty stems from the multiple types of voting machines. You cannot just tell everyone in the state to do the write-in in a certain way. Oh no. In Virginia there were *eleven* different voting systems, so we had to have *eleven* ways to instruct people to undertake a write-in vote.

On the day after the election, we got reports from voters who said that in their voting precinct (for results in their county) they saw no Nader votes listed even though they knew they and others had cast such votes. On the morning of November 3, I had a message on my voicemail from voters in Schaumburg, Illinois, who were told that there was no list of approved write-in candidates, and it wouldn't make any difference if they wrote in a candidate because "it wouldn't count." Because some states and local officials view it as "optional" to count write-in votes, we sent a letter to all fourteen secretaries of state where we were write-in candidates, asking them to ensure that write-in ballots were counted.

In a number of states, we had to go and ask about peculiar returns, where it was implausible that there were "zero" votes for our ticket. One of our volunteers "found" about 1,000 votes for Ralph in North Carolina when several people contacted him to complain their votes for Nader had not been counted.[116] Similarly, Richard Winger "found" 499 votes for Ralph in San Bernardino County in late December 2004 when he called the county and was told they had 499 write-ins for Ralph, but the official state Web page of California did not show these votes.

We tried to get the write-in votes counted for Nader in Ohio by filing suit in federal court since the deadline in Ohio was in early

September, a time when we were presumptively on the ballot, and then had passed before we were taken off the ballot. The judge denied our suit, claiming it would be confusing to the voters.[117] There is no state interest in having a write-in deadline so early. In most states the deadline is two weeks before the election. But in Ohio—it's two months before the election. Other third-party candidates for president have also brought significant write-in litigation. For example, in November 2000, Howard Phillips, the 2000 Constitution Party presidential candidate, managed to get West Virginia to waive its fee (of $4,000!) to file as a write-in candidacy in *Phillips v. Hechler*.[118] Whether your write-in vote counts also depends on where you live.

Provisional Votes

Whether your provisional vote counts for a federal election depends on the state in which you live. Of the 19 million registered voters who did not vote in 2000, the U.S. Census Bureau estimated that "6.9 percent did not vote because of uncertainty regarding their registration."[119] The GAO, in a 2001 report, estimated "that 30 percent of jurisdictions considered dealing with unregistered voters at the polls to be a major problem."[120] It was such a problem in 2000 that HAVA required states that did not have same-day voter registration or had no voter registration (North Dakota) to have some kind of mechanism for collecting the votes of people who claimed they were properly registered to vote. Thus was born the "provisional ballot." Congress finally concluded that it was better to allow someone to vote provisionally than to just turn them away because of rampant registration issues. If a voter turned out to be registered after all, then the vote cast on the provisional ballot would be counted. Like much of HAVA, this provision is vague and lacks federal standards for application. As a result, provisional ballots were treated differently in the 2004 election from state to state and even within counties. Chaos ensued.

In 2004, according to the Century Foundation, of the more than 1.6 million provisional ballots cast, "nearly 1.1 million, or 68 percent, were counted. In twenty-eight states, a provisional ballot cast in the wrong precinct was not counted. In seventeen states, a ballot cast in the wrong precinct but correct registrar's jurisdiction (usually the county) was counted."[121] The GAO is less definitive. It says that somewhere "between 1.1 and 1.7 million provisional ballots were cast in the 2004 election." The reason it did not know for sure is "because of a very high level of missing data—an estimated 40 percent of the jurisdictions did not provide data on the number of provisional ballots counted."[122]

In some states, if you were not registered or not a resident of the jurisdiction, you may not have gotten a provisional ballot.[123] The GAO estimates that "12 percent of [state or local electoral] jurisdictions nationwide encountered poll worker performance problems related to their failure to follow procedures with provisional voting."[124] On the day before the 2008 election, my college roommate, now a public-interest lawyer, called me on her drive from New York City to Toledo, Ohio. She had rented a car to join at least *ninety* other lawyers in Toledo alone, to make sure people could vote. This is what democracy has come to in the United States. Lawyers are riding circuit to make sure that states can properly hand out the ballots. Whether you get a provisional ballot and whether it counts depend on where you live.[125]

Recounts: "Close Happens"

In general, we don't have many recounts in the United States.[126] We don't usually see hundreds of thousands of people marching in the streets, naked bicyclists, or singers singing "our beautiful nation will not stand for another fraud," all demanding a recount, as the Partido de la Revolución Democrática (PRD—Democratic Revolution Party) did in Mexico City on behalf of Andrés Manuel López Obrador, who in the "official" count of 41 million cast, came within 244,000 votes of victory.[127]

When I read Obrador's op-ed in the *New York Times* in August 2006, I thought, "wow," he is complaining pretty loudly about arithmetic mistakes and fraud at 12,000 polling places in twenty-six states—and he is disputing a differential of hundreds of thousands of votes.[128] As a nation, we are counting dimpled chads—and it was much, much closer—with just a few hundred votes separating the potential leaders of the free world, and nobody was in the streets at all. The citizenry just seems to grumble and watch Jesse Jackson Sr. do another press conference. I don't know anyone who wrote an op-ed in *El Diario* about Florida. Do you? Where is our outrage?

Maybe Mexicans vocalize theirs because at least they know where to go to complain: Mexico has a tribunal to police electoral fraud. There the ruling party's winner didn't want the tribunal involved—indeed, Felipe Calderón's legal team claimed the tribunal had no authority to annul a presidential election by ordering a blanket recount.[129] I found it interesting that commentators thought this decision to recount could jeopardize the stability of Mexico but that no one really says that here. We don't like our singers to sing songs critical of the incumbents. We ban them from Clear Channel. Just ask the Dixie Chicks. But whether you as a voter are going to get a recount in a close call also depends on where you live. And, as we know, close does happen.

In 2000, the margin of victory in the presidential race in Florida, Iowa, New Mexico, and Wisconsin was less than one-half of 1 percent of the votes cast in each of those states. "From 1948 through 2000, the winning margin in 31 presidential elections in 22 states has been less than 1 percent."[130] Now, after Florida 2000, it was pretty clear to most people that we had to come to a consensus as a people, if not election jurisdiction by election jurisdiction, as to what counts as a vote. Is a dimpled chad a vote? Or must it be pregnant? Does it have to hang by three corners or two? These are questions sure to provoke a debate on any first date. Even after Florida we still have big problems. In an exhaustive study of the knock-down, drag-out 2006 gubernatorial contest in Washington State, the closest in U.S. history for governor,[131] for example, the GAO politely concluded that "were any state's election processes subjected to the very close scrutiny that characterized the recount in Washington State, it is likely that imperfections would be revealed."[132]

Some states, like New Hampshire and Wisconsin, have lots of recounts, mainly local.[133] HAVA required states to implement uniform rules—within the state, not among the states—for counting votes by 2006, but it didn't say what rules states had to have. Not surprisingly, this meant that each state picked its own criteria. By November 2004, only thirty-nine states and DC had in place some guidance for what passes as a vote. Forty-five states and DC came up with rules governing "how and whether to count a machine-unreadable ballot."[134] These could vary widely. In Illinois, if the machine didn't read your punch mark, your vote would not be counted. In Washington, if your punch-card vote was unclear, it was sent to a canvassing board for review![135]

According to the GAO, forty-seven states and the District of Columbia have recount laws, some mandatory, most not.[136] But some states have no provision at all for a recount, and states have differing trigger points for mandatory ones. So, for example, in Michigan, a vote spread of 2,000 for statewide elections will automatically trigger a mandatory recount. In many states, a 0.5 percent spread will trigger a recount. In other states, a certain absolute number, like fewer than 100 or 150 votes' difference or 0.25 percent of total votes cast for the top two, will trigger a recount.[137]

Each state also determines who may trigger a recount if it is not automatic. In Florida in 2000, any candidate could call for a recount. In 2004, *no* candidate could call for a recount. Recounts would happen only triggered by a percentage of closeness, and they would be mandatory.[138] Some states only allow the second-place finisher to trigger the recount. Twenty-five states will allow any candidate to ask for the recount, no matter the margin of closeness.[139] Fourteen states will only let a candidate who loses by not more than a certain percentage or absolute number to request the recount.[140] Three states had no recount provisions, so who knows what would have happened in 2000 or 2004 if results were close in Hawaii, Mississippi, or Tennessee, Al Gore's home state.[141]

There are different provisions on who is to pay for the recount. Recounts can cost a bundle, and how close the election is may determine who should pay, depending on the state. Given some of the recent recount results, you have to question whether it is fair of any state to make a candidate pay when the state process can be ludicrously riddled and not at all the fault of the candidate.

Additionally, the type of systems in use can further complicate the potential for a recount. A state with multiple systems, Virginia, can require recounters to have to figure out a variety of systems. According to one lawyer who participated in a Virginia recount for state attorney general, Jan Baran, a lawyer at Wiley Rein & Fielding, LLP, and former general counsel to the RNC, told the *Washington Lawyer*, "'It would be a lot easier if it was all the same statewide, not only for election officials. It would presumably be easier for the voter.'"[142] Of course.

At the end of the 2004 campaign, we had questions about the vote for president based on the information that was pouring into our Nader campaign offices—allegations about improperly purged voter registration lists; lack of sufficient voting machines in certain precincts, thereby creating excessive waits; and problems with paperless electronic machines and optical scans. Bev Harris of BlackBoxVoting.org, a consumer group for elections, came to our office in November 2004 to meet with Ralph and me to explain her concerns. Lowell Finley, formerly of Voter Action, and now an official in the California elections division, also weighed in. Statisticians were concerned about the discrepancy between exit polls and the actual vote counts.

John Kerry conceding in Boston on November 3 said, "In America, it is vital that every vote count, and every vote be counted," but he didn't seem game for a legal fight. Indeed, he said, "I would not give up this fight if there was a chance that we would prevail."[143] But people were demanding a recount in Ohio. Within a few days after the election, boatloads of people were calling the 2004 Nader campaign to ask us to seek a recount first in New Hampshire. New Hampshire had the first deadline in the nation to call for a recount, by 5:00 P.M. on the Friday after the election. We received more than 2,000 faxes requesting us to seek a recount. The Nader campaign wanted the Kerry/Edwards campaign to make good on its promise to count the votes. As a consequence, Ralph was the first to speak up about Ohio, immediately after the election. We got on the phone and called Michael Badnarik, who was on the ballot in Ohio, to urge him and the Libertarians to call into question the narrow vote and to investigate the alleged improprieties, which he said he would do. And then we faxed a letter to New Hampshire Secretary of State William Gardner by late Friday afternoon, November 5, so that the Nader campaign became the first to call for a selective recount, to test vote results in New Hampshire.

We chose New Hampshire not only because of citizen concerns but also because of the state's election procedures. New Hampshire had a voter-verified paper trail for its machines; it had experience conducting recounts; and it had an amenable recount law and a seasoned secretary of state. The New Hampshire law required that candidates whose margin of loss is greater than 3 percent pay an initial fee of $2,000 and agree to pay for the actual state costs of the recount.[144] Therefore, because of the potential cost, and based on information we received from voting rights activists, we decided to test eleven selected wards that used the Diebold AccuVote optical scan machines, where the vote count favored President George W. Bush by 5 percent to 15 percent over the expected result based on exit polls and voting trends in New Hampshire.

Secretary of State William Gardner anticipated that our sample test would take one and a half to two days using twelve teams, and the cost would be about $12,000. We raised the money to send a $2,000 downpayment and assured the state we would pay the rest. I designated Kevin Zeese, the campaign spokesman, along with his partner Linda Schade, to head the team effort, as both are experts in voting machines and founders of TrueVote in Maryland. They led a team of staff and volunteer voting rights activists to oversee the recounting from 9:00 A.M. to 7:00 P.M. daily.[145]

After our initial eleven selected precincts were completed, we decided not to proceed with more testing. We found only very minor discrepancies between the optical scan machine counts and the recount, and we stated this publicly in a press release to provide assurance to voters across the country who had raised concerns about New Hampshire.[146] We thought we had provided a public service. Later we learned that, on the one hand, some voting rights activists were incensed we had stopped. On the other, the bipartisan New Hampshire House passed a bill (HB 365), known as the "Nader bill," that would increase the recount costs in the future precisely to prevent activists from even checking the count. The bill, another example of the two parties teaming up to even prevent third parties from trying to recount a vote, died in the Senate Internal Affairs Committee.[147] Similarly, Green candidate David Cobb and Libertarian Michael Badnarik applied for a New Mexico recount in 2004, which the state refused to conduct, and paid the deposit of $114,400. New Mexico then demanded $1.4 million, the full cost of the recount, up front! The recount didn't happen and the legislature increased the recount fee "by a factor of ten."[148]

By November 22, the National Voting Rights Institute (NVRI) had filed the recount case in Ohio on behalf of Libertarian candidate Badnarik, Green candidate Cobb (who was a write-in candidate there), seven individuals, and Common Cause of Ohio. They exposed flaws in the state's recount procedures, but could only get the recount to start on December 13, the day that the electors were already voting for President Bush.[149] But they did get some members of Congress to speak up this time around, as opposed to 2000.

Given the condition of our electoral process and the slow, ad hoc repairs, without significant change we can expect many more Floridas,

Ohios, and Washington states to come—witness the 2008 Minnesota Senate race. The minor trend toward standardization among the states is grossly incomplete. In the next chapter, I propose that we need to federalize our standards for national elections so that whether you can vote, how that vote is counted, and whether a third party or independent can even get on your ballot are not dependent on the vagaries of state geography and competence.

Conclusion

The instrument of all reform in America is the ballot.
—Woodrow Wilson, Seventh State
of the Union Address[1]

In my lifetime, dozens of countries have become democracies. This is exciting considering that the last big waves of democratization were in 1848 and 1918. Samuel Huntington wrote *The Third Wave*, a book in which he recounts how the current wave started with a Portuguese song—"Grândola, Vila Morena," by progressive folksinger Zeca Afonso. The radio played it as a broadcast signal in the wee hours of April 25, 1974, to start Portugal's "carnation revolution."[2] A friend, one of the participants in this bloodless coup, told me how overnight, but with much planning, the remnants of the by-then-deceased António de Oliveira Salazar's repressive regime were replaced by revolutionaries—a military wearing carnations, accompanied by student sit-ins.

I spent part of the early 1990s visiting Portugal, the former Eastern bloc countries, India, and others to share how our access to information, media, and privacy laws worked as they built their systems of transparency. Democracy in practice takes much more effort than a revolution. What is interesting to me is that not one of these thirty-plus countries in this new wave of democracies has chosen to adopt our two-party-dominated electoral system. New democracies may eat our hamburgers, download our songs, and watch our movies, but they do not adopt our electoral system. As others have noted, today almost all countries with free elections have five, six, or more parties which regularly field candidates.[3]

In his study of regime change between 1974 and 1990, Huntington looked at how, with a few exceptions, authoritarian rulers used three devices to attempt to preserve their power and stave off democratization: (1) they sponsored and affected the results of the elections by controlling the timing; (2) they rigged the elections by "establishing electoral systems highly favorable to the government, by harassing and intimidating the opposition, and by employing government resources in the campaign"; and (3) the conditions were such that opposition groups didn't know whether it was better to participate or boycott the elections.[4]

Now we do not live in an authoritarian regime of the kind Huntington studied, but the control of our electoral conditions is removed only by degree, not in kind, from the three devices Huntington talks about authoritarian regimes using. The two parties, through their incumbent legislation, control the timing of the primaries, the redistricting in most states, the ballot access laws, the presidential debates, and the airwaves. In contrast to countries with nonpartisan election administration, the two parties control the federal rules, the Federal Election Commission, the Election Assistance Commission, the Congress, and the government purse. The small opposition parties (and those that never got underway) and the 50 percent of the electorate who have dropped out[5] see a system so stacked with self-perpetuation of the two parties that they don't know if they can mount a challenge or whether it is worth their time to participate in a rubric so highly calibrated to work against their interests. Our elections have become so uncompetitive even for the two parties that there is almost no chance a third party or independent can succeed in the current system when often not even the other major party can survive in uncompetitive political subdivisions.[6]

At the presidential level, elections are uncompetitive in most states. FairVote, in their report "The Shrinking Battleground," provides the example of 1960 against 2004. In Kennedy/Nixon, twenty-four states were up in the air. By the time we got to Kerry/Bush, it was thirteen states and, arguably, even fewer—that is, Ohio and Florida.[7]

What about at the congressional level, even with 535 seats of members of Congress at stake and 435 of them every two years? Not a chance. In the most "representative" institution we have, electoral competition has been declining "for several decades."[8] It has become so bad, according to *The Marketplace of Democracy*, a book on electoral competition, that since 1988, incumbents in the House "have been reelected more than 98 percent of the time."[9] In 1998, 99 percent of the incumbents in the U.S. House of Representatives (95 of them without major-party opposition) won reelection. In 2000, it was 98 percent (with 64 of them running unopposed by a major party).[10] Almost half of the seats in the U.S. House of Representatives (215 of 435) were won by landslides of more than 20 percentage points, and some without any election were just "reinstated."[11] How rigged is our democracy? A *Washington Post* reporter gave the example of California where "all 101 incumbents" who ran for reelection over both 2002 and 2004 won! "All but two [clobbered] their opponents by 20 percentage points or more. The story is the same in most states."[12] In 2004, an Election Observation Mission (EOM) from Europe "took notice of the fact that only a small proportion of the elections" for congressional seats "were generally perceived to be competitive."[13] Even in 2006 and 2008, despite large Democratic sweeps, only a few dozen of the 435 seats in Congress were viewed to be competitive in the first place, including open seats.

At the state level, a study by David Lublin and Michael P. McDonald of the 2000 and 2004 elections in thirty-seven states at the state house level concluded that partisan gerrymandering often "has a dampening effect on competition."[14] In my home state, according to the *Illinois Assembly on Political Representation and Alternative Electoral Systems*: "Half of all races for the Illinois House of Representatives were uncontested in 2000. In one of every two races voters had no choice in either the primary or general election. They could vote for the incumbent or not vote at all. Among the remaining races, a large majority lacked meaningful competition; two candidates ran in opposition, but who would win was never in doubt."[15]

Can third parties break through this ossified system where even the other major party cannot compete? The numbers speak for themselves. The 110th Congress is at a highwater mark in the U.S. Senate with Senator Joe Lieberman of Connecticut, an Independent Democrat who is neither. Lieberman lost his Democratic primary to Ned Lamont and then ran as an independent so that he could win in the general election. The Senate also includes Senator Bernie Sanders, a longtime Socialist who uses the label "Independent" (but is counted as a Democrat for caucus purposes) who replaced Senator Jim Jeffords of Vermont (who was a Republican until he broke away in 2001 to caucus with the Democrats). Sanders is the only Socialist to hold a seat in the U.S. Senate; he was the only one in the U.S. House for about fifteen years. Since 1955, outside of Bernie Sanders, there has been one Conservative (James Buckley-NY) and a small handful of independents, including Dean Barkley, who held the late Democratic Senator Paul Wellstone's seat for just a few weeks before the elections.

In the U.S. House, outside of Sanders, you could count on two hands how many other independents have ever been elected to those 435 seats since 1955. Prior to 1955 in the twentieth century, there were Populists, Progressives, Independent Republicans, Socialists, Silver Republicans, and members of the Union and Prohibitionist, Union Labor, Farmer Labor, and American Labor parties. No member of the Green Party, Reform Party, Natural Law Party, Constitution Party, or Libertarian Party—not to mention all the small state or regional parties—has ever held 1 of the 535 seats in the U.S. Congress.[16] What does this say about our national trend in the last half century?

In *The Marketplace of Democracy*, McDonald and Samples say that in the 2004 election results show that of the 66 minor-party candidates for the Senate and the 319 minor-party candidates for the House of Representatives, the best showing was the Constitution Party's senatorial candidate, who got 4 percent in Pennsylvania, and two Libertarians, who got 20 percent in Arizona and Florida, while the median House Libertarian candidate received only 1.6 percent of the vote.[17] One reason might be that the average third-party candidate running for an open House seat raised on average $11,000 in 2000, whereas the major-party candidates raised in excess of $1 million.[18] The amounts raised by third-party challengers for an incumbent seat are even less than those raised for open seats. In 2002, a minor-party candidate challenging an incumbent raised on average $2,478.[19] It's hard to run on lunch money against a flush incumbent everyone knows is likely to win—like the other 98 percent of the entrenched House incumbents.

Similar dismal conditions prevail at the state level, despite the hundreds of thousands of political elections jobs available. Richard Winger lists in the December 2007 issue of *Ballot Access News* the whopping 37 instances in which a minor party nominee (who was not simultaneously a major party nominee) was elected to a state legislature.[20]

Can we reform this uncompetitive system? Other countries have reformed their systems after deciding that they were not working well. In the 1990s, New Zealand, also operating under commonwealth-imposed winner-take-all, said "enough" when it had back-to-back elections with the party getting the most votes *not* getting the seat of power.[21] Papua New Guinea did the same in 2003 when *the majority* of its parliamentary winners "polled less than 20 percent of the vote."[22]

Had John Kerry won Ohio and the Electoral College with another 60,000 votes in Ohio, and Bush had won the national popular vote by 3 million, we would have found ourselves, like New Zealand, with successive perverse outcomes. It will probably take this kind of electoral scandal, in a cycle not too removed from Florida 2000, to get the kind of changes and dialogue required.

What should motivated Americans do to prevent additional electoral crises? What would an improved electoral system look like? One task force at the state level, after surveying the work of scholars and practitioners who spend their days considering these matters, concluded that certain criteria should be considered for state legislatures. I have extrapolated, modified, and paraphrased from that list here for presidential election systems.[23]

I would ask the following: Does the proposed electoral system reform:

1. Encourage citizen participation in the electoral process—both as a voter and as a candidate?
2. Encourage competition and offer voters a meaningful choice?
3. Simplify voting and enhance voter understanding of how the vote counts and the candidacies?
4. Ensure that the partisan—as well as significant racial, ethnic, economic background, and gender—characteristics of the candidacies are not an obstacle to participation and that overall outcomes generally reflect the electorate?
5. Provide fair representation of the concerns of all the states and enhance the accountability to all the states' constituents?
6. Enhance the accountability of the elected to their constituents?
7. Provide for the electorate's vote to count and be counted accurately?

From my perspective, a level playing field with low barriers to entry and a roused and engaged citizenry is a fundamental starting point. If you apply the above criteria to current U.S. presidential elections, I think we fail on just about every score, some much more than others. So I would start over. Thomas Jefferson certainly suggested reexamination when stating that the founders considered "each generation a distinct nation, with a right, by the will of its majority, to bind themselves." He figured on having a constitutional convention every twenty years or so.[24] So among the proposed reforms that follow in this conclusion are a few for the Constitution, recognizing that they are "pie in the sky" at the moment, given the rigorous constitutional amendment procedure and given our current love of *not* touching our Constitution. If we can rearrange our national attitude and get out a new feather pen, I would start with the following.[25]

Eliminate the Electoral College

The first constitutional amendment would be to eliminate the Electoral College. As A. James Reichley has written, "The thing that has really kept this [two-party] system locked in place has been the institution of the electoral college for selecting presidents."[26] The arguments for[27] and against[28] the Electoral College have been set forth in many publications. I favor eliminating the Electoral College and having a direct one-person, one-vote system for the presidency. To enhance third-party and independent participation, and to remove the chance of a president who does not have majority support, we could build in an instant runoff voting method so that in one election (as opposed to having a "top-two only" runoff second election) we could elect a majority-backed president.

But the reality is that we are probably not going to get the Electoral College eliminated through Article V because the amending provision allows one-fourth of the states plus one (thirteen) to veto any constitutional amendment. All the overvalued voters of small states (about eighteen) can act in their own interest, if not the national interest, to prevent their own power from being diminished by just having thirteen of them refuse to get rid of the Electoral College. Unless we add some more states, and heavily populated ones at that, it is highly unlikely that we are getting rid of the Electoral College by constitutional amendment any time soon.

So if we can't eliminate it, what can be done to make it fairer for third parties and independents and even minority major parties who risk winning the popular vote only to lose the electoral vote, which has happened four times now in our history?[29] There are several ways to do an end run on the Electoral College. The first is to allocate votes based on congressional districts, like Maine and Nebraska currently do. Though this would be a step away from winner-take-all, this would just tie the presidential vote to the already excessively gerrymandered and unequal congressional districts. Until 2008 there had never been a single electoral vote changed because of this different allocation, though if larger states had it, undoubtedly there would be. I oppose it though if only for the increase in bloodshed that would accompany the already ferocious redistricting battles. This would just create a different set of battleground states where the states in play would be tied to the congressional districts in play; that is, it would be competitive between the two major parties only.

A second reform would be to allocate votes based on percentage of votes within the state—as opposed to nationwide—as the Republicans proposed in 2007 for California, or as the Democrats proposed in 2004 in Colorado, and in the abandoned 2007 proposition in North Carolina. Though these were singled-out initiatives, not nationwide proposals, this change in method would result in the electoral votes being distributed more equitably and more closely approximating the national vote, thus giving third parties and independents the best chance to win at least some electoral votes. For example, in Florida in 2000, based on the vote percentage, Bush and Gore each would have received 12 Electoral College votes, and Nader would have received 1, for his 97,488 votes. Nationwide, based on population and vote percentage within each state, Bush and Gore each would have received 262 electoral votes, making Ralph the potential power broker in 2000, had votes been allocated in this way, because Nader would have received a total of 13 electoral votes in 2000—California (2), Colorado (1), Florida (1), Illinois (1), Massachusetts (1), Michigan (1), New Jersey (1), New York (1), Ohio (1), Oregon (1), Texas (1), Wisconsin (1)—while 1 additional vote would have gone to other third parties based on their returns in California.[30]

Nationally, Gore, Bush, and Nader, as the top three candidates, would have all been eligible under the Constitution's Twelfth Amendment to be chosen by the House of Representatives, and that is where a 262–262–13–1 tie would have gone under the Electoral College. So if the states had chosen their electors proportionately rather than by winner-take-all, Ralph or any other similarly situated third-party candidate could have been viewed as a hero, throwing his or her votes to the candidate most responsive to his or her voters' issues, rather than tarnished as a "spoiler." We have an already spoiled Electoral College system about two centuries out of date. Nothing in the Constitution prohibits states from allocating their electors in this fashion. Of course, the way to prevent the situation of having a third-party candidate controlling this outcome would be to have a different voting method, like IRV, in place before any election was thrown into the House.

The state population–allocated electoral method could thus, but not always, give substantial power to a third party trying to break through. As FairVote points out, it could also throw a bunch of elections to the overly gerrymandered House of Representatives because no candidate would get the required 270 electoral votes, and the top three candidates would then go to the House, under the Twelfth Amendment. George Wallace could have brokered the 1968 outcome of Nixon/Humphrey by receiving a substantial chunk of electors, 78, under the population-allocated electoral method, because Nixon would have only had 235 votes to Humphrey's 225, and all three of them, falling short of 270, would have had to go to the House election.[31] But it could also have no effect, despite a close national vote. The example FairVote provides from 1960: the combined third-party vote would have been 6 electors, but they would have had no say on the 1960 outcome of Kennedy/Nixon, who would have had 270 and 261 electoral votes, respectively, with Kennedy squeaking in.[32]

A state population–allocated system would give third parties and independents far more power to broker outcomes or send presidential elections to the U.S. House. But if you are a fan of one person, one vote, there are two overwhelming flaws in this reform. First, do you want third parties to have the power to overturn the national popular vote or cause elections to go to Congress, whose members are congressional district winners, who are currently allocated under winner-take-all? Probably not. Once the election gets to the House, since each state gets only one vote, it is clear that third parties and independents are not going to control the statewide vote. Even if I would have wished for Nader to have that power in 2000, or would have thought the presidential election would at least have been decided more democratically in that branch than in the Rehnquist Supreme Court, I would not have wanted "segregation now, segregation forever" George Wallace wielding that kind of power back in 1968. The outcome by the House of Representatives is ultimately less democratic, even if the process would initially allow more third-party and independent participation.

The second reason to reject this system is that it doesn't actually nationalize the vote for federal office; it just replaces the current system of battleground states with a new slate. These new battleground states would be based on "rounding"—meaning that the current battleground states where the populations were fairly evenly broken out at 49/51 or 50/50 would be ignored by the presidential candidates, instead of excessively courted, as they are today. And the new battleground would be based on rounding breakpoints! FairVote's report titled "Fuzzy Math: Wrong Way Reforms for Allocating Electoral College Votes" explains how the "whole number proportional allocation" problem or the "rounding rule" problem arises: first, to divide the electoral votes among the candidates, you have to round the vote based on the percentage won in each state for each candidate. Then you have to allocate votes in a whole unit because you can't have a 0.4 percent elector. So "if a state has three electoral votes, a 60 percent popular vote share will translate into 1.8 electoral votes and a 75 percent share into 2.25 electoral votes."[33] The rub is that both shares are rounded to the nearest whole number—two electoral votes—even though the margin of difference of the vote could be huge.

A candidate who gets more than 50 percent of the vote in a three-electoral-vote state but less than 83.3 percent will still get only two electoral votes. So if you live in a state that goes overwhelmingly Democratic—say, by 84 percent—an electoral vote could be in play if the Republicans perceived that they could knock down the Democratic vote outcome to just under 83.3 percent, that is, to 83 percent. For skimming that 0.3 percent they would pick up a whole electoral vote. On the flipside, if you live in a three-electoral-vote state that always goes Republican by 65 percent, there is probably no chance it will be in play because the Democrats will figure that they can't lower the vote outcome to under 50 percent Republican. (Alternatively, if you abolish the Electoral College and the need for electors to be a whole person, under the Lodge Gossett Plan—which actually passed the Senate back in 1950—electoral votes could be allocated to presidential tickets directly proportional to the popular votes each ticket received in the state, without rounding to the whole unit number of electors.)[34]

The FairVote report rejects both the congressional allocation method and the whole number proportional method in favor of a third option, the National Popular Vote plan, the third potential reform to bypass the Electoral College. Under this plan, the states would have to agree to cast their electoral votes for the winner of the national popular vote. So if you live in a state that voted for Kerry, but

Bush won the popular vote nationally, as he did in 2004, your state's electoral votes are going to Bush. This is a state compact that doesn't kick in until states representing at least 270 electoral votes agree to do this, and there is a six-month "blackout" period from July 20 to January 20 to make sure no state engages in hanky-panky by voting to get out of the pact because it read the political tea leaves in advance. Four states have passed this plan as of November 2008.[35]

The real question is: Why do we still use winner-take-all at all? Why not use other methods of voting, which are more likely to present a truer position of the voters in any state and in the country as a whole? We haven't really even had a national conversation about proportional voting, preferred voting, cumulative voting, range voting, approval voting, or instant-runoff voting, though many have tried to start one. Professor Lani Guinier, FairVote's Rob Richie, author Steven Hill, mathematician Warren Smith, the Greens, and many others, to their enduring credit, have been trying to get people to pay attention to these important voting matters in the United States for years. Yet there is no mass outrage that we continue to use an antiquated voting system that fails to take into account and accurately represent the choices of the majority of voters in the United States.

Add an Affirmative Right to Vote

We should also have an affirmative right to vote in our Constitution. Once upon a time (in the nineteenth century) the Supreme Court and legal scholars could find a fundamental right to vote in the Constitution, but those halcyon days appear to be gone.[36] And as Illinois Democratic Congressman Jesse L. Jackson Jr., the original sponsor of the constitutional amendment to make the right explicit, proclaims on his Web site: "According to Harvard's Constitutional Law Professor Alexander Keyssar, 108 of the 119 nations in the world that elect their representatives to all levels of government in some democratic fashion explicitly guarantee their citizens the right to vote in their Constitution. Both Afghanistan's Constitution and Iraq's interim legal document contain a right to vote."[37] But ours does not.

After *Bush v. Gore*, it is clear that we really cannot leave it up to the states to determine whether their citizens have the right to choose electors depending on whether the state decides to have an election, like the rest of the civilized world. We need to have an affirmative right to vote in the Constitution. Congress should pass an amendment at least. Moreover, people who care about voting rights need to get with the program and realize the Constitution is not static and get busy putting some rights back in it. As Representative Jackson correctly notes, the Republicans have aggressively proposed constitutional amendments as part of a long-term wedge strategy. The Democrats and others are MIA.

Even if we never touch the Constitution, with political will, we could still make the electoral system more just for political competition. To do so we have to focus on our own currently made institutional barriers; these have been made not by some long-gone *über*-race of "framers" or "Founders" but by the very same Democrats and Republicans who are busy writing their incumbency protection acts in between every dollar they fund-raise for the next electoral go-round. Even John F. Bibby and L. Sandy Maisel, third-party scholars who are unabashed two-party supporters, recognize and have written in *Two Parties—or More?: The American Party System*: "Institutional arrangements impose major barriers to third parties and bolster the electoral dominance of the Republicans and the Democrats."[38]

Federalize Federal Elections

After the elections of 2000 and 2004, and all the suspicion leading up to 2008, I contend that it is well past time for the federal government to step in to preserve itself, à la Alexander Hamilton. The federal government, which is no model of efficiency, nevertheless needs to assume a much more proactive role in the administration and standardization of federal elections; it cannot just continue to dole out federal taxpayer money and leave the problem of administering the elections to the states.

Some states may have fine systems, and many individuals involved in administering elections are dedicated public servants. But as a whole, the group is not competent to do this very complicated deed. Worse, in my experience with partisan administration, allowing the states to administer elections has allowed them to discriminate against and exclude candidates, something the U.S. Supreme Court says they cannot do.[39] Not only have the locals made a complete mess recently—but arguably, they have never really done a good job. In 1934, Joseph Harris, an expert writing for the Brookings Institution, noted: "There is probably no other phase of public administration in the United States which is so badly managed as the conduct of elections. Every investigation or election contest brings to light glaring irregularities, errors, misconduct . . . disregard of election laws and instructions, slipshod practices, and downright frauds. . . . The truth of the matter is that the whole administration—organization, laws, methods and procedures, and records—are, for most states, quite obsolete."[40] Unfortunately, after seventy years and billions of dollars, new laws, new people, and new machines, the exact same statement could be made today. And the context has not been made easier.

We live in a highly mobile society. Some people have two or more homes in different states. Some have none at all. (Some don't know how many they have!) Some move within their state on average every year. To tie the administration of the vote in a federal election to geography is a losing proposition just on twenty-first-century mobility alone. Then there is the problem of all kinds of differing standards for whose vote should count and how, and who should get on the ballot and how. There are gross, constitutionally unsupportable discriminations going on, from whether a state allows you to vote to how it registers you, to how it counts your vote, to the candidates for whom it lets you vote. This is no way to run a nation, much less a world superpower that prides itself on spreading democracy worldwide. In the twenty-first century, where you live in the United States should not dictate whether or not your vote for president counts. For candidates for federal office, in particular for president, there is no sound reason why we don't have uniform federal standards for federal elections.

So if we are not going to have a Constitutional Convention to amend the Constitution, we could still pass federal laws to fix federal elections. Article II, read with the Twelfth Amendment, states that "Congress may determine the Time of chusing the Electors, and the Day on which they shall give their Votes." And it contemplates rules to settle contested presidential elections thrown into the House of Representatives. The Founding Fathers foresaw the convenience of localities to administer elections, but as Alexander Hamilton noted in *Federalist* 59, the national government should not subject its existence "to the pleasure of state governments." Indeed, he wrote, in all capital letters, that the defense of keeping the ultimate power in the federal government to regulate federal elections was "the evidence of this plain proposition, that *every government ought to contain in itself the means of its own preservation*."[41]

As we discussed in Chapter 5, Congress has the power to regulate federal elections. Congress knows how to take a federal role in governing our elections. Since Florida 2000, the good news is that Congress has been entertaining hundreds of laws (albeit not really seriously and many not even improvements—but at least they are on the docket), showing that Congress *knows how* to step in.[42] Congress could thus fix the lack of our federal standards on all aspects of voting as well as the patent discrimination against the First and Fourteenth Amendment rights of third-party and independent candidates and the disenfranchisement of their supporters and voters—indeed, all voters.

We need federal, nonpartisan standards for federal elections. The votes of those who live in more or less competent states are diluted at the federal level because the rest of the country doesn't have competent administration of elections. Moreover, we have two entrenched parties, slowly but surely over the last five decades seeking to bar all others by controlling all the levers of competition, at all levels, and manipulating them to serve two parties only: via the FEC, the financing, the media, the debates, redistricting, and the ballot access laws. Arguably, the shutout will become even worse as the major parties try to eliminate each other through redistricting or other unfair advantages so that we essentially have one-party rule at the congressional and state levels.

If there are any members of Congress left who value political competition and are so inclined, they should have the Congressional Research Service study and draft legislation for several reforms which affect third parties and independents, and may also serve two-party voters, described below.

Federal Administration and Financing

- Both the FEC and its supplemental HAVA-created counterpart, the Election Assistance Commission, are not inspiring much confidence.[43] If they are kept in current form, contrary to my recommendation for an overhaul in Chapter 6, they need third-party and independent administrators, regulations, and sensitivity training.

- There should be federal financing for federal elections. Raising the bar for federal financing to a level that few, if any, third-party or independent candidates can ever meet is not an appropriate solution because it restricts potential competition and fails to ensure a competitive democracy. Equally problematic is having a system so poorly funded that the major-party candidates find it unattractive and opt out if they can raise more money, as we have seen in 2008 with Obama raising some $750 million and thus backtracking on his pledge to take the public limit of $85 million in general election funding. Just as good tax policy looks not only at which behaviors should be discouraged and which should be encouraged, we need to rethink federal financing, as Michael J. Malbin has written, not just to avoid "corruption" and undue influence but to focus on behaviors we want to encourage—such as broader participation and competition, including third parties and independents.[44] Clean elections legislation or public financing is now working at least partially in five states. There should be greater experimentation with public financing because of the benefits both in reducing the influence of money in elections and in increasing candidate participation, including third-party and other less-well-financed candidacies.[45]
- The problem with private money in elections is that the small donor (who gives under $200) still represents in 2007, despite all the ballyhooed accessibility of Internet giving, only about 21 percent of the donations to the presidential heavies. (In 1999, it was 20 percent, and in 2003, it was 18 percent, according to a press release by the Campaign Finance Institute.)[46] Most of the money in the system, with certain candidacies the exception, is still coming from large donors, and, at minimum, the perception exists that those donors and their interests curry access and favor with which other constituents cannot compete. Worse, minor parties tend to have to rely on individuals while major party candidates also have party money and PACs.[47]
- We should shorten the campaigns, not elongate them, as the horrible front-loaded 2008 national primary schedule for the two parties has proven. There should be less time between the primary conclusions and the convention, as Harvard professor and voter participation expert Thomas Patterson suggests, to keep voters engaged and

interested.[48] Anyone who starts early should have financing penalties or lose free media time. Shorter campaigns may also encourage diverse candidacies from people who cannot afford to not earn income for months on end.

- In exchange for free bandwidth, we should require broadcasters to provide free media time so that all candidates, including third parties and independents who are mathematically viable or publicly highly supported, can get free coverage on network television to enable the American voter to hear and learn at least a little about each candidate.
- We should adopt the policy of other countries, such as Germany, which provides parties that receive 0.5 percent—not 5 percent—of the vote federal financing to help small but substantial political starts grow and provide additional voices in the political discourse. At the invitation of the Heinrich Böll Foundation, I learned about the German electoral system, from the conduct of campaigns to the development of the nascent Greens, to the functioning of the Bundestag and the executive branch. I met with trade union leaders and cabinet ministers. It was a great experience to see a country so determined to build a stable democracy for historical reasons and yet so welcoming of many party voices. If Germany, with its twentieth-century history, can afford to cultivate and financially support diversity in politics, why can't we?
- Another way to help level the money is to reward low-donor campaigns or PACs. Derek Cressman, formerly of TheRestofUs.org, put out a suggestion in April 2005 that PACs receiving donations limited to $100 could give candidates much more than the standard $5,000 contribution.[49] So if a PAC could give $50,000 from low donors bundled with other low donors, a low donor could have an impact comparable to the current high donors who just make $5,000 contributions directly to a PAC, which can then turn around and give it to a candidate, on top of the contribution already made by the donor directly to that candidate.
- In July 2006, Representatives Christopher Shays (R-CT) and Martin Meehan (D-MA), as well as Senator Russ Feingold (D-WI), introduced presidential public financing reforms (House JR 5905 and S 3740) that would, among other things, have rewarded with public financing in a four-to-one—rather than a one-to-one—ratio, donations up to $200 to presidential campaigns. This proposal would unfortunately cover only those candidates who could raise $25,000,

as opposed to the current $5,000, in each of twenty states, effectively barring most minor parties from qualifying. It also would have limited the soft money still spent on the lavish major-party conventions. The bills promptly went nowhere. There are numerous creative ways to level the playing field, rewarding broad, low-donor participation, and to do so fairly to minor parties and independents. The problem is not the shortage of ideas; it is the lack of political will to ensure that candidates who are not self-financed multimillionaires or the favored major-party nominees can also put their candidacies in front of the American people.

- We should open up the two-party system by adopting proportional representation at the federal level; but if not there, there are countless opportunities on the state and local levels to reestablish this markedly more participatory system, which could allow third parties and independents a greater role in governing. Municipalities across the nation—including New York City—used proportional representation systems for years before the major parties crushed it.
- We should make every vote count by allowing instant-runoff voting, preference voting, range voting, or another system that maximizes voter choice. Just about any of them is better than our current winner-take-all voting system. We should follow the lead of London, Ireland, and Australia by allowing voters to rank candidates; we can liberate citizens to choose their favorite candidate and ignore the idiotic cries of "wasted votes" and "spoilers." Australia manages to have proportional representation and instant-runoff voting, resulting in a robust "average of seven [candidates] from across the spectrum" per district.[50]
- We should adopt a binding none-of-the-above (NOTA) option. Voters should be able to reject the candidates put forth by choosing NOTA and, if NOTA wins, force a new election with new candidates. This may also help eliminate uncertainties with determining whether undervoting or machine failures are at issue.
- We should require the FEC to regulate 527s as the political action committees that they are and require 527s to report under the same terms as other political committees so that stealthy, well-funded entities deployed to eliminate alternative candidacies must disclose and get a chance to be audited.
- The Commission on Presidential Debates should be reconstituted as a nonpartisan governmental entity run by individuals with diverse

party (or no-party) affiliation. It is unacceptable to allow a private gatekeeper to control our presidential debates with an exclusive, bipartisan operation that purports to set "objective" criteria but actually operates to exclude all other competitors for our presidential elections. Fair standards for inclusion must be afforded to every mathematically viable presidential candidate to participate in at least one nationally televised debate.

- We should stop disenfranchising our citizens. Felons and ex-felons should be allowed to vote. In Europe, ballot boxes are brought into prisons. Here we keep people from voting for life, banning them from the polity long after they have done their time. This is in violation of the International Covenant on Civil and Political Rights, one of those treaties we actually ratified. Worse, because we disproportionately lock up racial minorities, we disproportionately disenfranchise them.[51] There has been a recent trend in sixteen state legislatures to loosen restrictions, but we are far from restoring full voting rights to more than 5 million ex-felons, much less those currently imprisoned.[52]
- We should require federal ballot access reform as a key component to ensuring a level playing field for all competitors in a competitive democracy, rather than a duopoly. The terms for ballot access for federal elections should not be controlled by the bipartisan legislatures of the fifty states. There should be one federal law for access to the ballot for federal elections, with *de minimis* requirements designed only to protect the sole legitimate interest states have in controlling that access—the integrity of the ballot. We should give serious thought to whether the collection of signatures in public forums has any correlation whatsoever with candidate support in a democracy in the twenty-first century. What state interests do these ballot petition laws serve now? As Bradley A. Smith, the former chairman of the FEC and now a professor says, "Surely no more than a few hundred, or at most few thousand, signatures are needed to address any concern the state has about ensuring orderly ballots."[53] No large state should require more than 5,000 signatures, and most small states should require only 1,000 or fewer, as Ron Paul has suggested in his legislation to minimize the restrictions for congressional ballot access.[54] We are a worldwide aberration on this score.
- We should design a uniform component for the federal portion of the state ballots and pre-test it with real voters. We are capable of

doing that now for military and overseas voters, so why not do it for all fifty states and make them use it for federal office so that we do not have another "butterfly" and "caterpillar" ballot national crisis? This could minimize the local design incompetence that adds to over- and undervoting. If Australians can prepare uniform ballots, so can we.

- We should move Election Day to the weekend. As the nonprofit organization Why Tuesday? points out, surveys find that it may convenience only one in six voters, but three of ten nonvoters might be more likely to vote if Election Day were moved.[55] We should also keep the polls open longer (and break up the election day for polling officials into two shifts), at least until 9:00 P.M. Think how grateful people with long commutes would be!
- We should remove administration of the federal elections from the partisan hands of secretaries of state, state election boards, or their subsidiaries. Legions of improprieties exist. Those who administer elections should not be running for office themselves or chairing another candidate's campaign at any level over which they have jurisdiction.
- The Voting Rights Act of 1965 should be enforced, and criminal penalties should be imposed for state officials who violate federal laws or interfere with the administration of federal elections. A nonpartisan prosecutor or inspector general should be appointed to pursue violations and be open to taking complaints, as an ombudsman, for both voting rights violations and election interference allegations of all kinds. Ditto for the National Voter Registration Act (Motor Voter) and HAVA.
- We should have a permanent, national registration of voters from which voters may opt out for any reason they choose, with all the requisite guarantees of privacy any national database of any sort should have.
- Every voter must have an ID to vote, but it should be reasonable and accessible to that voter. We should not have a national identity card; for lack of ID, voters should be given provisional ballots or affidavits to sign along with a regular ballot, not disenfranchised.
- The provisions of HAVA should be federally standardized, including database parameters, registration list accuracy tests, and federal standards on the counting of provisional ballots.

- Federal procurement for voting equipment and repair warranties should be open and monitored so that each election administration is not bargaining for the worst per-unit-cost of machines from private vendors who are wining and dining the state decision makers.
- Federal standards for recounts and vote auditing should be devised and implemented.

State-Level Reforms

- Absent federal, uniform ballot access reform, states should all be required to publish in advance all the rules attendant to their election procedures. These should not be allowed to change in the midst of an election year or to be augmented, amended, and then applied retroactively after candidates have turned in their qualifying papers. There can be no secretive, intentionally misleading, and retroactive post hoc legislating by partisan secretary of state offices.
- State and local officials, especially law enforcement, in all offices need to understand that petitioning is a constitutional right not to be confused with loitering or soliciting. Petitioning is one significant way the First Amendment applies in public forums. More than a few public officials appear to confuse the exercise of constitutionally protected rights with antisolicitation ordinances and need to be sent to remedial First Amendment school.
- States with regulations on the books that have provisions declared unconstitutional should bear the burden and expense of justifying their unconstitutional laws, not the candidates trying to access their ballots. Federal election funds should be cut off for any state legislature that is unable to get its state laws into compliance with federal court election law rulings.
- The administrators of the election process should be in accord with the enforcers of state election law such that public officials from different entities or within the same public entity are not openly sparring about how election regulations and procedures are to be interpreted and enforced. If state officials cannot understand their laws, how can candidates?
- All states should permit fusion candidacies to allow third parties and independents more leverage and the ability to bring in more voters.

- State voter registration databases must be (1) centralized; (2) free and accessible to the public, including candidates seeking to ensure the validity of registered voters; (3) complete and accurate; and (4) timely. There should be no cases of candidates who must collect tens of thousands of extra signatures in a state just because the election commission admits it has no unified or accurate database and cannot process its voter registration cards. Federal funding should be cut off for failing to maintain an accurate voter registration database.
- The mechanics of voting must be repaired so that there is a way to verify each vote. Paper on top of a faulty computerized system does not necessarily verify a faulty vote. If this means paper and hand counts, so be it. If ATMs can dispense $20 bills with precision and issue a receipt each time, I think we as a country can figure out how to have a competent paper-verified voting trail in every state.
- Short of an accurate national database of voter registration, at the state level there must be accurate and transparent voting roll purges that are subject to standards, tested, and made public far in advance of the election so that there is time for people wrongfully purged to correct errors.
- Similarly, there needs to be a right to obtain absentee ballots easily and timely so that they can count and be counted in secret. Disenfranchising the military, the sick, students at out-of-state or abroad universities, or even those who happen to be on vacation is unconscionable. If a customer can buy sixteen products online and have them shipped to different recipient addresses and paid for with sensitive credit card information, surely we can figure out as a country how to make absentee ballots available in a fraud-free way.
- If we don't have opt-out federal registration, we should move to same-day registration across the country or a registration cutoff that is close to the election and leaves time for correction. The states with same-day registration have undeniably better turnout.[56]
- States should get rid of "sore-loser" and disaffiliation laws. These laws require individuals to disaffiliate from a prior party by a certain time or ban them from running in the general election if they ran in the primary election under a different mantle. Any supposed state interest served by limiting who can be on a general election ballot is usually already served by the natural disinclination of a candidate to party hop from one party to another mid-election. These laws should

all be removed because they primarily act as barriers to candidates who, after seeing the electoral landscape and being disappointed with the choices, choose to wear a party or nonparty hat to offer more choice.

Short of a uniform federal law, which is the optimal solution, the following should be reformed in state ballot access laws to make access to the ballot for third parties and independents more fair:

- All ballot access deadlines before mid-August of the election year should be pushed later in the year.
- Disparities in the treatment between third-party and independent candidates that treat independents worse than minor parties should not be tolerated.
- Validation procedures that allow any objection, no matter how specious or superficial, without any minimum burden of proof, to invoke automatically a tedious, time-consuming adjudicative process to defend all signatures should be revised.
- Costs and burdens of proof should be borne by those who seek to remove candidates from the ballot, not vice versa, as the move is almost always one sought to enhance a rival candidate's campaign.
- Minutiae such as paper color, paper size, page numbering, placement of the staples, and the spelling of elector names/initials should not operate as material bars to access the ballot.
- Multiple and onerous simultaneous county-by-county or township-by-township turn-in procedures and locations throughout the state for petitions should be eliminated.
- More than one notarization per circulator, per candidate petition, requirements should be removed.
- Excessive (that is, hundreds of dollars) filing fees should be banned.
- Guidelines for determining who is a registered voter should comport with the jurisdictional dictates of the election. For the purposes of senatorial or presidential elections, as long as a citizen is a voter within the state, it shouldn't matter if the voter has moved within the state as long as he or she remains a valid registered voter or eligible elector within the state.
- Requirements for circulators of petitions should be uniform and comport with U.S. Supreme Court rulings. If a circulator meets those standards, no state interest exists in heaping on other standards

for the circulator, such as declaring residency, requiring badges or armbands, or filling in which county he or she lives in on every page of hundreds of pages of petitions.

- The procedures for naming and selecting electors for presidential ballots should be federalized. If not, they should be locally streamlined, as they could not be more confusing in some states, including those that require electors to show up in person at state offices or to be named or written in on each petition and/or write-in ballot; standards for serving as a presidential elector should be federally set and uniform throughout the country.
- The vice-presidential requirements forcing candidates to name VPs on petitions to be circulated even before those VPs are nominated should be revised and federalized and allow for seamless substitution of a vice-presidential candidate once selected.
- States should be federally required to count write-in votes and to have uniform write-in procedures for federal office that do not require, for example, the candidates to sign and notarize forms for every locality or election jurisdiction.
- Finally, every election administration jurisdiction should allow for a limited number of both domestic and international nonpartisan election observers.

The Judiciary

The judiciary has to do its part. It can start by hearing challenges to and reconsidering and overturning most of the decisions addressed in Chapter 5. We need litigation plans to work on those reversals, percolated strategically in state and federal courts across the country, just as the civil rights and the women's movements did to remove discriminatory barriers.

If you think this impossible, just remember that eighty years ago the Supreme Court and the Democratic Party in Texas were in a decades-long duel about the rights of African Americans to vote in what is known as the "White Primaries." Texas passed a law saying that "in no event shall a negro be eligible to participate in a Democratic party primary election held in the State of Texas." The U.S. Supreme Court struck it down in *Nixon v. Herndon* (1927) and *Nixon v. Condon* (1932), but then the Texas Democrats just rewrote the law to say that party membership was restricted to whites, which then the U.S. Supreme Court said was permissible—in *Grovey v. Townsend* (1935)—as the parties were not state actors, just private organizations.[57] The NAACP, with Thurgood Marshall as lead counsel, eventually got the *Grovey* decision overturned another decade later in *Smith v. Allwright* (1944). This case in turn set the stage *another* ten years later, ending "white-only" private parties when once again Marshall and the NAACP brought the seminal *Brown v. Board of Education* (1954) to finally overturn more than half a century of "separate but equal" from the nineteenth century's *Plessy v. Ferguson*.[58]

The history of the Texas cases indicates that just because the Supreme Court finds nothing constitutionally objectionable in one decade does not mean the Supreme Court is always right—or that that is the last word on the matter. If we can go from Jim Crow to President Obama in half a century, we can elect a third-party president as well—once the bigoted barriers are brought down. This is why in Chapter 5 I suggest *strategically* going after the cases that are rotten for third parties and independents, as they provide the undue life support for the two parties and the license to discriminate against third parties and independents but are not necessarily right for our country.

The judiciary must also remain an independent branch of government not seeking to do the bidding of one party or another, or one branch of government or another. When judges make political contributions to partisan political candidates and then sit and interpret the law as it applies to the competitors of their donees, the judiciary as well as the electoral process is compromised. At minimum, judges who make donations for candidates in the elections they are being asked to rule on should recuse themselves and states should adopt much stronger recusal standards.[59]

Winged Thoughts

As I finish this book, I am listening to Giuseppe Verdi's "Va pensiero," the chorus of Hebrew slaves on the banks of the Euphrates in the third act of *Nabucco*, the opera that made him famous. I first heard this opera live in 1984, sitting in the Baths of Caracalla outdoors in Rome. "Va pensiero" is not a dirge but a song of redemption, of rising up.

When Verdi died, the Italians lined the streets of his funeral, singing this song. We too need a Risorgimento, not just lone election reformers but a full chorus contemplating national redemption for our electoral system.

For as long as I have been alive, Americans have considered regimes such as the former Soviet Union—where only one party was allowed to exist or control government—to be undemocratic. Today, we see the opposition parties complaining that for the first time in post-Soviet Russia, Vladimir Putin has so arrayed the election rules "against all other parties" that the leader of its Republican Party, Vladimir A. Ryzhkov, calls it "'selection before election.'"[60] We condemn other countries that oppress political choice, be it a second, third, fourth, or even fifth party, because the fundamental human rights violation exists in the oppression of free political choice. How shall we now—as the United States of America moves through the twenty-first century—categorize ourselves among the nation-states of the world, with an incumbent two-party regime that so tilts the electoral rules that, *de facto*, it allows for only two parties—and increasingly at the congressional and state levels, for just one?

We don't need to agree on all the reforms, but we need to agree that there are injustices that must be redressed by beginning the process of remolding our electoral processes. As Alan Dershowitz (an opponent of the Nader 2000 campaign) explains in his exploration of where rights come from: "It is enough to agree on what constitutes the kinds of injustices that are sufficiently wrong to occasion a system of rights designed to prevent their recurrence."[61] I would suggest, as I have tried to demonstrate in this book, that we have arrived at this point with the manifestly unjust way third parties and independents are treated today in our electoral system and the overall dysfunction of our electoral processes now administered at the state level. I have proposed a list of reforms, and others have also made suggestions. The point is that we have to have the purposeful conversation at a national level.

What are the consequences of doing nothing? This is no place to recount all the substantive injustices of this country, but if you can name your top offenders, then you can probably trace the lack of progress on these problems, or the worsening of them, back to the two-party tyranny of our elections—the political contributors that control them and the best politicians money can buy and return to office, election after election after election, with little or no competition.[62]

As a favor to yourself, make a list of the top ten problems you believe face our nation. Mine includes poverty, the failing educational system, foreign and domestic violence, oil and energy dependence and global warming, corporate crime and abuse, lack of access to affordable health care, crumbling public infrastructure and mass transit, gross civil rights and civil liberties violations, regressive taxation policies, and of course, the poorly crafted and administered electoral system. Some of these problems have been around for half a century or more. Solving these problems requires a series of steps, including recognizing a problem exists, discussing plans to address the situation, finding leaders and legislators who will champion solutions, implementing a plan for execution, and evaluating the results. On many of our greatest national problems, we are not even at step one because members of neither major party will expend the political capital to recognize or discuss the full range of issues and solutions during our elections, much less between them.

The larger conversation for electoral reform starts at kitchen tables, in book clubs, in political parties, at the water cooler, in organizations, on blogs, in all the ways that Alexis de Tocqueville exclaimed was our unique American character. We do not wait for the government to propose the solution. We take matters into our own hands. As Thomas Jefferson, near death, said, "[B]urst the chains" and "assume the blessings and security of self-government,"[63] by getting together as a people to fix the problems. When the political institutions of entrenched institutional actors will not act to upset a system that benefits them, the people must.[64]

Notes

Introduction

1. Theresa Amato, William G. O'Neill, and Lawyers Committee for Human Rights, *A Childhood Abducted: Children Cutting Sugar Cane in the Dominican Republic* (New York: Lawyers Committee for Human Rights, 1991).

2. *See generally* Alexander Keyssar, *The Right to Vote: The Contested History of Democracy in the United States* (New York: Basic Books, 2000).

3. *See* Jamin B. Raskin, "A Right-to-Vote Amendment for the U.S. Constitution: Confronting America's Structural Democracy Deficit," *Election Law Journal* 3 (2004): 564: "There are 570,898 taxpaying, draftable U.S. citizens living in the District of Columbia who lack any voting representation in the U.S. Congress. . . . There are 4,129,318 American citizens living in the federal Territories of Puerto Rico, Guam, American Samoa and the U.S. Virgin Islands who have no right to vote for president and no voting representation in Congress. . . . There are approximately 3,900,000 citizens disenfranchised, many of them for the rest of their lives, in federal, state and local elections as a consequence of a felony criminal conviction" (citation omitted).

See also Bob Fitrakis and Harvey Wasserman, "Supreme Court Stabs Another GOP Knife into US Democracy by Upholding Ex-Felon Vote Ban," Nov. 16, 2005 (*available at* www.freepress.org/departments/display/19/2005/1574): "In Florida and other states where ex-felons are permanently or partially disenfranchised, fully 25% of the black male population cannot cast a ballot" (citing the Sentencing Project).

4. Alexander Kirshner, "The International Status of the Right to Vote," Democracy Coalition Project (*available at* www.demcoalition.org/pdf/International_Status_of_the_Right_to_Vote.pdf).

5. Some countries have mandatory voting, including Singapore, Cyprus, Austria, Belgium, and Australia, which fines citizens for nonvoting. *See* Norman Ornstein, "Vote—or Else," *New York Times*, Aug. 10, 2006.

6. *See, e.g.*, Editorial, "Mr. Mubarak's Concession," *Washington Post*, Feb. 28, 2005, A16.

7. The Federal Election Commission does not award matching funds for the general election unless the candidate receives 5 percent of electoral votes. *See generally* "General Election Funding: How General Election Funding Works" (*available at* www.fec.gov/info/chtwo.htm).

8. *See generally* Brennan Center for Justice et al., "Deterring Democracy: How the Commission on Presidential Debates Undermines Democracy" (*available at* www.opendebates.org/documents/REPORT2.pdf). The Commission on Presidential Debates, a private corporation, does not allow any participant in the presidential debates unless the candidate has 15 percent or more support in the average of five polls.

9. North Carolina makes third parties collect approximately 70,000 verified signatures to get on the ballot, but if they fail to get at least 10 percent of the vote in the election, they have to start all over again before the next election. *McLaughlin v. North Carolina Bd. of Elections*, 65 F.3d 1215 (4th Cir. 1995) (interpreting N.C. Gen. Stat. Ann. §§ 163–96, 163–97 [1994]), *cert. denied*, 517 U.S. 1104 (1996).

10. *See, e.g.*, E.E. Schattschneider, *Party Government* (New York: Holt, Rinehart & Winston, 1942), 85 ("It is difficult to imagine anything more important than the tendency of the parties to avoid extreme politics"); *see also* Larry J. Sabato and Bruce Larson, *The Party's Just Begun: Shaping Political Parties for America's Future* (Glenview, IL: Scott, Foresman, 1988), 5 ("The two parties serve as vital, umbrella like, consensus-forming institutions that help counteract the powerful centrifugal forces in a country teeming with hundreds of racial, economic, social, religious, and political groups"); Richard L. Hasen, "Entrenching the Duopoly: Why the Supreme Court Should Not Allow the States to Protect the Democrats and Republicans from Political Competition," *Supreme Court Review* (1997): 347–50 (explaining how "responsible party government scholars" support the two-party system by advancing arguments that fall into three categories, "political stability, antifactionalism, and voting cue," as benefits; *e.g.*, "The second great perceived benefit of the two-party system is its tendency to minimize the power of factions or special interest groups"); *see also* Samuel Issacharoff and Richard H. Pildes, "Politics as Markets: Partisan Lockups of the Democratic Process," *Stanford Law Review* 50 (1998): 652: "Indeed, one of the great unappreciated ironies of the original constitutional vision is that although the Framers were exquisitely sensitive to the need to create formal checks and balances between governmental organizations, they failed to see the need to ensure sufficient competition between political organizations. In the absence of a clear constitutional conception and textual basis for ensuring such competition, American courts have been tentative and hesitant—as well as politically unsophisticated—in recognizing when partisan political markets have been captured or are appropriately 'free.' "

11. Anita S. Earls, "Election Reform and the Right to Vote" (presented at Right to Vote Amendment Roundtable, Washington, DC, Nov. 21, 2003), 1 (citing "The States Tackle Election Reform," National Conference of State Legislatures, Oct. 7, 2003, *available at* www.ncsl.org/programs/legman/elect/taskfc/03billsum.htm).

12. George Washington's 1796 farewell address stated that "there is an opinion that parties in free countries are useful checks upon the administration of the government and serve to keep alive the spirit of liberty. This within certain limits is probably true; and in governments of a monarchical cast, patriotism may look with indulgence, if not with favor, upon the spirit of party. But in those of the popular character, in govern-

ments purely elective, it is a spirit not to be encouraged." *Available at* The Avalon Project at Yale Law School, http://avalon.law.yale.edu/18th_century/washing.asp.

13. "None [of the developed democracies] mandates primaries, imposes strict rules about party labels, or regulates access to the ballot to the extent the United States does." Dennis F. Thompson, *Just Elections: Creating a Fair Electoral Process in the United States* (Chicago: University of Chicago Press, 2002), 67 (citing Leon Epstein, *Political Parties in the American Mold* [Madison: University of Wisconsin Press, 1986], 158; and Samuel Issacharoff, Pamela S. Karlan, and Richard H. Pildes, *The Law of Democracy: Legal Structure of the Political Process* 2d ed. [Westbury, NY: Foundation Press, 2001], 398).

14. Paul S. Herrnson, "Minor Party Candidates in Congressional Elections," in Michael P. McDonald and John Samples, eds., *The Marketplace of Democracy: Electoral Competition and American Politics* (Washington, DC: Brookings Institution, Cato Institute, 2006), 109 (citation omitted).

15. Maurice Duverger, "The Two-Party System and the Multiparty System," excerpted from his *Political Parties: Their Organization and Activity in the Modern State* (New York: John Wiley & Sons, 1954), in Peter Mair, ed., *Oxford Readings in Politics and Government: The West European Party System* (Oxford: Oxford University Press, 1990), 285–90.

16. Excerpted from Giovanni Sartori, "A Typology of Party Systems," in *Parties and Party Systems: A Framework for Analysis* (Cambridge: Cambridge University Press, 1976) and reprinted in Mair, *Oxford Readings in Politics and Government*, 316–49.

17. Ibid., 340, 342–43: "The rarity of the case suggests that two-party systems are 'difficult.' But the emphasis is mostly on the view that two-party systems represent a paradigmatic case, an optimal solution. The claim has generally been—until recent discontents—that two-party systems obtain beneficial returns for the polity as a whole. More precisely, two-party systems always 'work,' whereas the more parties there are, the more we find 'less working' solutions and, ultimately, non-viable systems. The claim is not unwarranted; but it cannot be warranted by pointing to the countries in which twopartism happens to work. Indeed, these countries are so few that one may well argue that all of the more-than-two party systems are such precisely because the two-party solution either did not endure, or did or would prove to be unworkable. The retort could be, then, that twopartism generally fails or would fail if attempted." *See also* Alan Ware, *Political Parties and Party Systems* (Oxford: Oxford University Press, 1996), 162–63.

18. *See, e.g.*, Richard W. Soudriette and Andrew Ellis, "Electoral Systems Today: A Global Snapshot," *Journal of Democracy* 17 (2006): 80–81; list of political parties by country (*available at* http://en.wikipedia.org/wiki/Lists_of_political_parties_by_country).

19. Micah L. Sifry, *Spoiling for a Fight: Third-Party Politics in America* (New York: Routledge, 2002), 5 (citing Theodore Lowi, "The Party Crasher," *New York Times Magazine*, Aug. 23, 1992).

20. Soudriette and Ellis, "Electoral Systems Today," 78, 83.

21. Robert A. Dahl, *How Democratic Is the American Constitution?* 2d ed. (New Haven, CT: Yale University Press, 2003), 41; Lisa Jane Disch, *The Tyranny of the Two-Party System* (New York: Columbia University Press, 2002), 11 ("Casually attributed to the United States in everyday conversation, media analysis, American government textbooks, and even specialized studies of electoral politics, the two-party system is typically represented as original, immutable, and a measure of progress toward democracy that should be a model for the world").

22. Louis Massicotte, André Blais, and Antoine Yoshinaka, *Establishing the Rules of the Game: Election Laws in Democracies* (Toronto: University of Toronto Press, 2004), 11.

23. *See* Why Tuesday? (*available at* www.whytuesday.org); Massicotte, Blais, and Yoshinaka, *Establishing the Rules of the Game*, 117.

24. Massicotte, Blais, and Yoshinaka, *Establishing the Rules of the Game*, 81.

25. Richard Winger, "BALLOT ACCESS: A Formidable Barrier to Fair Participation," *Ballot Access News* (*available at* www.ballot-access.org/winger/fbfp.html).

26. Daniel Lazare, *The Velvet Coup: The Constitution, the Supreme Court, and the Decline of American Democracy* (London: Verso, 2001), 6.

27. Steven J. Rosenstone, Roy L. Behr, and Edward H. Lazarus, *Third Parties in America*, 2d ed. (Princeton, NJ: Princeton University Press, 1996), 8.

28. A. James Reichley, *The Life of the Parties: A History of American Political Parties* (Lanham, MD: Rowman & Littlefield with Free Press, 2000), 5.

29. Theodore J. Lowi, "Deregulate the Duopoly," *Nation*, Dec. 4, 2000 (*available at* www.thenation.com/doc/20001204/lowi).

30. Ibid.

31. Ibid.

32. Alan Ware, *The Logic of Party Democracy* (London: Macmillan 1979), chap. 3 (citing Albert O. Hirschman, *Exit, Voice and Loyalty* [Cambridge, MA: Harvard University Press, 1970]).

33. Rosenstone, Behr, and Lazarus, *Third Parties in America*, 39 (citing examples of electorate beliefs regarding George Wallace and John Anderson).

34. Ibid., 40.

35. Ibid., 46–47.

36. Peter H. Argersinger, "A Place on the Ballot: Fusion Politics and Antifusion Laws," *American Historical Review* 85 (1980): 289 (citations omitted).

37. *See generally* Office of the Clerk of the U.S. House of Representatives (*available at* http://clerk.house.gov/art_history/house_history/party-Div.html); U.S. Senate, Art & History, Party Division in the Senate 1789–Present (*available at* www.senate.gov/pagelayout/history/one_item_and_teasers/partydiv.htm). In the prior election cycle in the House (1897–99, the 55th Congress), twenty-two Populists had been elected.

38. Bradley A. Smith, "Judicial Protection of Ballot-Access Rights: Third Parties Need Not Apply," *Harvard Journal on Legislation* 28 (1991): 170 (citing David A. Shannon, *The Socialist Party in America* [New York: Macmillan, 1955], 5).

39. *See generally* 63rd Congress (1913–15), Office of the Clerk of the U.S. House of Representatives (*available at* http://clerk.house.gov/art_history/house_history/party Div.html).

40. Richard Winger, "Can United States Voters Still Recruit Someone to Run for President as an Independent After the Identities of the Major Party Presidential Candidates Are Known?" *University of Arkansas at Little Rock Law Review* 29 (2007): 764–65.

41. Smith, "Judicial Protection," 174.

42. Rosenstone, Behr, and Lazarus, *Third Parties in America*, 22–23 (citations omitted).

43. Ibid., 23.

44. Richard Winger, "The Supreme Court and the Burial of Ballot Access: A Critical Review of *Jenness v. Fortson*," *Election Law Journal* 1 (2002): 236.

45. Winger, "Can United States Voters Still Recruit Someone," 769.

46. Ibid., 770–73 and n.53 (citing the ten states of Alabama, Arizona, Colorado, Illinois, Indiana, New Mexico, North Carolina, Oklahoma, South Dakota, and Texas).

47. *See* ibid., 764.

48. *E.g.*, in *Timmons v. Twin Cities Area New Party*, 520 U.S. 351, 367 (1997), the U.S. Supreme Court approved antifusion laws allowing states to "favor the traditional two party system" even though in two earlier cases, in 1968 and 1980, the Court virtually rejected that the two parties needed protection. *See Williams v. Rhodes*, 393 U.S. 23, 32 (1968); *Anderson v. Celebrezze*, 460 U.S. 780, 802 (1983); *see also* Hasen, "Entrenching the Duopoly," 334–35.

49. According to Richard Winger in an email conversation with the author, the four George Wallace ballot access cases are: *Application of American Party v. Secretary of State*, 444 P.2d 465 (Okla. 1968); *McLin v. Miller*, Civ. No. 68–158 (Sup. Ct. 1st Dist. Aug. 30, 1968) (Alaska) (unpublished); *Williams v. Rhodes*, 393 U.S. 23 (1968); *American Independent Party v. Cenarrusa*, 92 Idaho 356, 442 P.2d 766 (1968).

50. Ibid. The twenty-two Eugene McCarthy cases are: *McCarthy v. Askew*, 540 F.2d 1254 (5th Cir. 1976); *McCarthy v. Austin*, 423 F. Supp. 990 (W.D. Mich. 1976); *McCarthy v. Briscoe*, 429 U.S. 1317 (1976); *McCarthy v. Contessa*, 40 N.Y.2d 629, 357 N.E.2d 968 (1976); *McCarthy v. Exon*, 424 F. Supp. 1143 (D. Neb. 1976); *McCarthy v. Garrahy*, 460 F. Supp. 1042 (D.R.I. 1978); *McCarthy v. Noel*, 420 F. Supp. 799 (D.R.I. 1976); *McCarthy v. Hardy*, 420 F. Supp. 410 (E.D. La. 1976); *McCarthy v. Kirkpatrick*, 420 F. Supp. 366 (W.D. Mo. 1976); *McCarthy v. Slater*, 553 P.2d 489 (Okla. 1976); *McCarthy v. Tribbitt*, 421 F. Supp. 1193 (D. Del. 1976); *McCarthy v. Secretary of the Commonwealth*, 359 N.E.2d 291 (Mass. 1977); *McCarthy v. Evans*, Civ. No. 76–565P (D.N.M. Feb. 23, 1977) (unpublished); *McCarthy v. Andrus*, No. 1-76-191 (D. Idaho Nov. 12, 1976) (unpublished); *McCarthy v. Eu*, No. C172816 (Cal. Super. Ct. Los Angeles County Oct. 7, 1976) (unpublished); *McCarthy v. Hassler*, No. A-7991-II (Chancery Ct. Nashville Tenn. Sept. 22, 1976) (unpublished); *McCarthy v. Lunding*, No. 76-C-2733 (N.D. Ill. Sept. 7, 1976) (unpublished); *McCarthy v. Mandel*, No. Y-76-1495 (D. Md. Oct. 13, 1976) (unpublished); *McCarthy v. Rampton*, No. C76-303 (D. Utah Oct. 6, 1976) (unpublished); *McCarthy v. Salmon*, Civ. No. 76–213 (D. Vt. Oct. 7, 1976) (unpublished); *McCarthy v. Shanahan*, No. 76-237-C6 (D. Kan. June 17, 1976) (unpublished); *Anderson v. Poythress*, No. C80-1671A (N.D. Ga. Sept. 26, 1980) (unpublished).

51. Ibid. The eleven John Anderson ballot access cases were: *Anderson v. Celebrezze*, 460 U.S. 780 (1983); *Anderson v. Davis*, 419 A.2d 806 (Pa. Commonw. Ct. 1980); *Anderson v. Firestone*, 499 F. Supp. 1027 (N.D. Fla. 1980); *Anderson v. Hooper*, 498 F. Supp. 898 (D.N.M. 1980); *Anderson v. Mills*, 664 F.2d 600 (6th Cir. 1981); *Anderson v. Morris*, 636 F.2d 55 (4th Cir. 1980); *Anderson v. Poythress*, 271 S.E.2d 834 (Ga. 1980); *Anderson v. Quinn*, 634 F.2d 616 (1st Cir. 1980); *Kromko v. State*, 132 Ariz. 161, 644 P.2d 897 (1982); *Anderson v. Babb*, 632 F.2d 300 (4th Cir. 1980); *Anderson v. Indiana Election Commission*, Civ. No. S680-1157 (Ind. Sup. Ct. Marion County Sept. 16, 1980) (unpublished).

52. Ralph Waldo Emerson, *Journals of Ralph Waldo Emerson 1836–1838*, Edward Waldo Emerson and Waldo Emerson Forbes, eds. (Boston: Riverside Press, Cambridge, 1910), 427.

53. Nonprofits dedicated, at least in part, to reforming the electoral system include the American Civil Liberties Union (ACLU), Campaign Legal Center, Campaign Finance Institute, Democracy 21, National Voting Rights Institute, Voter Action, Public Citizen, Reform Institute, Common Cause, Demos, FairVote, Coalition for Free and Open Elections (COFOE), Center for Competitive Democracy, BlackBoxVoting,

Brennan Center for Justice at New York University School of Law, Velvet Revolution, Free and Equal, The Brookings Institution, The American Enterprise Institute, Public campaign, NAACP, the League of Women Voters, James Madison Center for Free Speech, Center for Competitive Politics, Voter Voice, and *Ballot Access News*, in addition to most established third parties and many foundations, including The Joyce Foundation, The Pew Charitable Trusts, and The Annenberg Foundation.

54. Sam Smith, "Getting Through the Bad Times," *Progressive Review*.

Chapter 1: Ballot Access Laws Since the Time of Cholera

1. Alexander Keyssar, "Reform and an Evolving Electorate," *New York Times*, Aug. 5, 2001, 3.

2. United States General Accounting Office GAO-02-3 Elections, "Perspectives on Activities and Challenges Across the Nation," Oct. 2001, at 10.

3. Alexander Keyssar, *The Right to Vote: The Contested History of Democracy in the United States* (New York: Basic Books, 2000), 6 (citation omitted): "[A]side from property qualifications, there were no firm principles governing colonial voting rights, and suffrage laws accordingly were quite varied. Not only Catholics and Jews, but also Native Americans, free blacks, and nonnaturalized aliens could vote in some places and not in others."

4. Yes, the United States still has territories: Guam (organized), American Samoa (unorganized), and the Virgin Islands (organized).

5. U.S. Department of Commerce, Economics and Statistics Administration, Census Bureau, "Voting and Registration in the Election of November 2004," Mar. 2006, 1–2, *available at* www.census.gov/prod/2006pubs/p20-556.pdf.

6. R. Michael Alvarez, Co-director, Caltech/MIT Voting Technology Project, "Voter Registration: Past, Present and Future" (written testimony prepared for the Commission on Federal Election Reform, Pasadena, CA, June 17, 2005), 3, citing data from the 2000 census and concluding that because local governments usually administer election activities, "when a registered voter moves from one county to another within a single state, there often is no simple and efficient way for both counties to simultaneously update their voter registration database for that voter, unless the voter takes the initiative to update her voter registration status in both counties." *See also* Commission on Federal Election Reform, *Building Confidence in U.S. Elections* (Washington, DC: Sept. 2005), 9—stating that about 41.5 million Americans moved each year, on average, during the last decade: "Of those, about 31.2 million moved within the same state, and 8.9 million moved to a different state or abroad. Young Americans (aged 20 to 29), representing 14 percent of the U.S. population, moved to a different state at almost three times the rate of the rest of the population" (citing Jason P. Schachter, "Geographical Mobility: 2002 to 2003," *Current Population Reports*, Mar. 2004 [*available at* www.census.gov/prod/2004 pubs/p20-549.pdf]).

7. Commission on Federal Election Reform, *Building Confidence in U.S. Elections*, 33.

8. Tex. Elec. Code Ann. § 192.032 (d), (f) & (g)(2) (West 2008). In some states, like Minnesota, the petition signers have to promise not to vote in an upcoming primary.

9. *See* Clothilde Ewing, "Nader's Tough Road Ahead," *CBS News*, Apr. 30, 2004.

10. Michael Richardson, *Voter Voice*, "'Footnote state' update" Oct. 2005, at 3 ("footnote states" at the time included Pennsylvania, Texas, North Carolina, Arkansas, Wisconsin, and Maryland), on file with author.

11. Ohio Rev. Code Ann. § 3513.261 (West 2004).

12. In Delaware, where we collected the requisite 5,182 signatures—Del. Code Ann. tit. 15, § 3002 (b) (West 2008)—we were told that the state's Department of Elections insisted on both candidates, president and vice president, filing a declaration stating that they had not been affiliated with any political party for at least three months before the filing of the declaration. (*See* letter dated May 20, 2004, from Mirlande Hector, Office of the State Election Commissioner, to Michael Richardson, on file with author.) Ralph was an independent, but Peter Camejo didn't want to give up his Green Party registration, so we had to find another way to get on the ballot. The Delaware Independent Party filed regular financial reports with the state, but the "party" was dicey because the officers were never elected, bylaws were never adopted or followed, a convention was never convened, and delegates were not selected to a nominating convention. The party corrected this in record time and nominated Ralph and Peter, three electors, and its gubernatorial and vice-gubernatorial candidates.

13. *For example*, Karen Sanchirico was the VP in Montana, which prohibited any candidate with an affiliation to be the VP on an independent party petition, and Sandy Kucera was the VP in Oregon because of a similar state-based prohibition.

14. *See, e.g.*, Ala. Code § 17-9-3(a) (West 2008); email from election administrator Ed Packard to Trey Granger, counsel to Secretary of State Nancy Worley of Alabama, dated Oct. 22, 2004, on file with the author; and Idaho Code Ann. § 34-708A (West 2008).

15. *See* Illinois State Board of Elections, "Excerpt of the Meeting held on the 1st day of September, 2000," Springfield, Illinois (transcript of proceedings, Sept. 1, 2000).

16. On August 8, 2004, Michael Richardson informed the campaign that we "could statutorily substitute Peter Miguel Camejo for Jan Pierce," but doing so would cost us one day of petitioning. The substitution provision of the Ohio Election Code—Ohio Rev. Code Ann. § 3513.31(F) (West 2008)—operates through a vacancy. The petitions are due seventy-five days before the election (August 19). The vacancy committee has only until seventy-six days before the election to fill vacancies (August 18), so petitions must be turned in for substitutions to be made. Gretchen Quinn, the secretary of state's legal counsel, had been advising the Ohio legislature each session to fix this problem, but the legislature had failed to act by the 2004 election.

17. *Bush v. Gore*, 531 U.S. 98, 104 (2000) (citing U.S. Const., art. II, § 1). All of the states award their electoral votes in a winner-take-all fashion except for Nebraska and Maine, which allocate their electors based on the winners of congressional districts, and the winner of the most districts statewide gets the extra two electoral votes.

18. Neb. Rev. Stat. §§ 32-1038 & 32-620 (1) (West 2008).

19. New Hampshire requires 1,500 valid signatures from each of its two congressional districts. N.H. Rev. Stat. Ann. § 655:42 (West 2008). Virginia requires at least 400 valid signatures from each congressional district. Va. Code Ann. § 24.2-543 (West 2008).

20. Idaho Code Ann. § 34-606 (West 2008).

21. N.J. Stat. Ann. §§ 19:3-5, 19:13-4, & 19:13-9 (West 2008).

22. Mo. Rev. Stat. §§ 115.327, 115.347 (West 2008).

23. *Nader v. Brewer*, No. 06-16251 (9th Cir. July 9, 2008); *Nader v. Blackwell*, 545 F.3d 459 (6th Cir. 2008).

24. *Frami v. Ponto*, 255 F. Supp. 2d 962 (W.D. Wis. 2003).

25. W. Va. Code § 3-5-23(d) (West 2000).

26. *McClure v. Manchin*, 301 F. Supp. 2d 564 (N.D. W. Va. 2003).

27. Justice Byron White, writing for the Supreme Court, said so in *Storer v. Brown* (1974). Justice White wrote that "the political party and Independent candidate approaches to political activity are entirely different and neither is a satisfactory substitute for the other." *Storer v. Brown*, 415 U.S. 724, 745 (1974). According to Richard Winger, the failure of states to have procedures for both parties and independents was the basis of all of Eugene McCarthy's winning lawsuits in 1976, including those reported: *McCarthy v. Askew*, 540 F.2d 1254 (5th Cir. 1976); *McCarthy v. Austin*, 423 F. Supp. 990 (W.D. Mich. 1976); *McCarthy v. Briscoe*, 429 U.S. 1317 (1976); *McCarthy v. Exon*, 424 F. Supp. 1143 (D. Neb. 1976), *aff'd*, *Exon v. McCarthy*, 429 U.S. 972 (1976); *McCarthy v. Slater*, 553 P.2d 489 (Okla. 1976); and *McCarthy v. Tribbitt*, 421 F. Supp. 1193 (D. Del. 1976).

28. ALASKA STAT. §§ 15.30.026, 15.15.030 (West 2008). Finally, in 2005, after years of bills repeatedly dying in committee, the governor signed HB 94, which established the state's first set of procedures to allow an independent presidential candidate to get on the ballot (with a petition signed by 1 percent of the votes cast in the last presidential election). Other states like Pennsylvania—with at least six different election laws, still on the books, that are out of date or that have been declared unconstitutional—just continue to ignore their problems (*see*, *e.g.*, 25 PA. CONS. STAT. § 2936 [West 2008]). Pennsylvania was also the only state in 2004 that still hadn't published its election statutes on its Web site.

29. ARIZ. REV. STAT. ANN. § 48-265 (West 2008).

30. CAL. ELEC. CODE § 9209 (West 2002).

31. District of Columbia Nominating Petition of Registered Voters for Elector of President and Vice President of the United States in the Election of November 2, 2004, on file with author.

32. *PruneYard Shopping Ctr. v. Robins*, 447 U.S. 74 (1980); memorandum from Jason Kafoury to Ralph Nader and Theresa Amato dated May 26, 2006, on file with author.

33. N.Y. ELEC. LAW § 6-138(1) (West 2008). Indeed, Missouri's petition says: "It is a felony for anyone . . . knowingly to sign his or her name more than once to the same petition." MO. REV. STAT. § 115.325 (2) (West 2008). If a signer signs both the Libertarian Party's petition and the Green Party's petition, then whichever party turns it in first gets those signatures to count, while the other party is just out of luck, based on where it was in line to turn in its petition!

34. NEB. REV. STAT. § 32-628(1) (West 2008); ALASKA STAT. § 15.07.060 (a)(2) (West 2008); VA. CODE ANN. § 24.2-418 (West 2008); HAW. REV. STAT. § 11-15(a)(2) (West 2008).

35. OHIO REV. CODE ANN. §§ 3513.05, 3513.261 (West 2008).

36. WASH. REV. CODE § 29A.20.140 (West 2008).

37. NEV. REV. STAT. §§ 293.200(2) & 293.102 (2 & 3) (c) (West 2008).

38. The Nader 2000 Primary Committee, Ralph Nader, and others sued Pennsylvania to remove these unconstitutional laws with the assistance of John Bonifaz and Brenda Wright (then both of the National Voting Rights Institute), Professor David Kairys, and Jordan Yeager. The cases were *Bullock v. Carter*, 405 U.S. 134 (1972), and *Lubin v. Panish*, 415 U.S. 709 (1974). Judge A. Richard Caputo, U.S. District Court of the Middle District of Pennsylvania, declared the Pennsylvania law (25 P.S. § 2873) unconstitutional in *Belitskus v. Pizzingrilli*, 243 F. Supp. 2d 179 (M.D. Pa. 2001), *aff'd in part, rev'd in part, vacated in part, remanded*, 343 F.3d 632 (3d Cir. 2003).

39. Nev. Rev. Stat. § 293.200 (1)(a) (West 2008); Or. Rev. Stat. § 249.740 (3) (West 2008).

40. N.H. Rev. Stat. Ann. § 655:17-b (West 2008); R.I. Code, §§ 17–14-1, 17-14.12 (West 2008).

41. Nev. Rev. Stat. § 293.12757 (West 2008); Mich. Comp. Laws § 509x (West 2008).

42. N.J. Stat. Ann. § 19:13-5 (West 2008); Miss. Code Ann. § 23-15-785 (1) (West 2008); Iowa Code § 45.1(1) (West 2008).

43. Minn. Stat. § 204B.11(2)(a); Wis. Stat. §§ 8.15(6)(a), 8.20(4) (West 2008).

44. N.C. Gen. Stat. § 163-122 (a)(1) (West 2008).

45. Cal. Elec. Code § 8400 (West 2008).

46. Tex. Elec. Code § 192.032 (c), (d), (f), & (g) (1)–(2) (West 2008).

47. Wyo. Stat. Ann. §§ 22-5-301(a), 22-5-304 (West 2008).

48. Okla. Stat. tit. 26, § 10-101.1 (1) (West 2008).

49. Editorial, "Oklahoma's Most Wanted," *Wall Street Journal*, Nov. 19, 2007 (querying whether this was "the latest news from Pakistan") (*available at* www.opinionjournal.com/editorial/feature.html?id=110010882).

50. Cal. Elec. Code § 8400 (West 2008).

51. Cal. Elec. Code §§ 8403 (a)(2), 8454 (b) (West 2008).

52. Editorial, "Denying the Vote," *New York Times*, Sept. 11, 2006: "[F]elony disenfranchisement is an enormous obstacle to voting for black people in the Deep South. These laws are the worst in the free world. The process for restoring rights for people who have been convicted of crimes can be so byzantine that officials don't know who is eligible. The confusion bars some eligible voters from the polls for life."

53. Pam Belluck, "States Face Touchy Decisions on Who Is Mentally Fit to Vote," *New York Times*, June 19, 2007, A1, A16.

54. United States Government Accountability Office GAO-06-450 Elections, *The Nation's Evolving Election System as Reflected in the November 2004 General Election*, at 51. Nine states didn't request one—either because they had met the deadline (Alaska, Arizona, Georgia, Hawaii, Kentucky, Minnesota, South Carolina, South Dakota, and West Virginia) or because they were already in compliance with HAVA's requirements (Kentucky).

55. Doug Chapin, "Election Preview 2004: What's Changed, What Hasn't and Why," Electionline.org, 2004, 23 (*available at* www.pewcenteronthestates.org/uploadedFiles/Election.preview.2004.report.final.update.pdf).

56. National Commission on Federal Election Reform, *To Assure Pride and Confidence in the Electoral Process*, Charlottesville, VA, Aug. 2001, 29 (*available at* www.reformelections.org/data/reports/99_full_report.pdf). Since most registered voters get a driver's license (about 92 percent), the 1993 Motor Voter law means that the local Department of Motor Vehicles (DMV) is where most voter registration is done. Indeed, the Carter-Ford Commission concluded that the DMV database was considered more reliable and more comprehensive than the U.S. Postal Service.

57. Gretchen A. Quinn, Ohio Assistant Elections Counsel, Conversation with author, Sept. 7, 2004.

58. United States Government Accountability Office GAO-05-478 Elections, *Additional Data Could Help State and Local Elections Officials Maintain Accurate Voter Registration Lists*, June 2005; GAO-05-997 Elections, *Views of Selected Local Election Officials on Managing Voter Registration and Ensuring Eligible Citizens Can Vote*, Sept. 2005; GAO-06-247 Election Reform, *Nine States' Experiences Implementing Federal Requirements for Computerized Statewide Voter Registration Lists*, Jan. 2006.

59. "Assorted Rolls: Statewide Voter Registration Databases Under HAVA," Electionline.org, 2005, 4–7 (*available at* www.pewcenteronthestates.org/report_detail.aspx?id=35430). The GAO in 2001 estimated that 46 percent of all election jurisdictions nationwide had problems with Motor Voter, "including incomplete, illegible, and late applications forwarded to election offices by the motor vehicle authority" and "voters who claimed to have registered through the motor vehicle authority but whose applications *never arrived* in the election office." And this was true despite only 64 percent of jurisdictions nationwide using this information. More than two-thirds of the jurisdictions using Motor Voter information had problems with it. *See* GAO-02-3 Elections, *Perspectives on Activities and Challenges Across the Nation*, Oct. 2001, at 7, 11 (emphasis added).

60. GAO-06-450 Elections at 83 (emphasis added).

61. Ibid., 81–82.

62. *See* ibid., 98.

63. Justin Levitt, Wendy R. Weiser, and Ana Muñoz, "Making the List: Database Matching and Verification Processes for Voter Registration" (Brennan Center for Justice at New York University School of Law, Mar. 24, 2006), ii–iii (*available at* http://brennan.3cdn.net/96ee05284dfb6a6d5d_j4m6b1cjs.pdf). *See also* Myrna Pérez, "Voter Purges," Brennan Center for Justice at New York University School of Law, 2008, at 1–2 (emphasis added) ("No state reviewed in this report uses purge practices or procedures that are free from risk of error or manipulation . . .").

64. Ben Ysursa and Matthew Dunlap, "Never Too Late to Vote," *New York Times*, May 11, 2007.

65. *See United States v. New York State Board of Elections*, Civ. No. 06-CV-0263 (N.D.N.Y. Mar. 1, 2006).

66. *See United States v. Alabama*, Case No. 2: 06-CV-392-WKW (M.D. Ala. July 21, 2006).

67. In 2004, more than 1.6 million voters received provisional ballots, but only about 1 million were counted. *See* Chapter 9.

68. *See* Steven J. Rosenstone, Roy L. Behr, and Edward H. Lazarus, *Third Parties in America*, 2d ed. (Princeton, NJ: Princeton University Press, 1996), 19. *See also* Bradley A. Smith, "Judicial Protection of Ballot-Access Rights: Third Parties Need Not Apply," *Harvard Journal on Legislation* 28 (1991): 176: noting that "forty-nine states required a third-party candidate for U.S. Senate in 1988 to gather signatures, with an average signature requirement of 17,281, while only nineteen states required a major-party candidate to submit any signatures, with the average requirement being just 1243" (citing HR 1582, 101st Cong., 1st sess., sec. 29a)[7][1989] [congressional findings included in the Fair Election Act]).

69. John McCain challenged those laws and won in *Molinari v. Powers*, 82 F. Supp. 2d 57 (E.D.N.Y. 2000).

70. In DC, the "Elections 2004 District of Columbia Candidate Qualification and Ballot Access Guide" at 34 (on file with author) says: "Section 2 of the U.S. Constitution leaves the manner of selecting electors up to the individual states. The first of these affects only the major parties in the District. Since the Democratic and Republican parties have both had a presidential candidate elected to that office, the executive committee of the party selects that party's candidates for elector and submits the names to the Board of Elections and Ethics by September 1st (Title 3 DCMR § 1509) of the presidential election year. The second affects the independent and minor political party candidates. Independent and minor political party candidates for president

must petition to nominate their electors. Information concerning this process is in the 'Getting your name on the Ballot' section of this guide."

71. Dmitri Evseev, "A Second Look at Third Parties: Correcting the Supreme Court's Understanding of Elections," *Boston University Law Review* 85 (2005): 1278 n.4 (citing Samuel Issacharoff and Richard H. Pildes, "Politics as Markets: Partisan Lockups of the Democratic Process," *Stanford Law Review* 50 [1998]: 687 [describing the large financial burden faced by minor-party candidates seeking to challenge ballot access restrictions]). *See also* Richard Winger, "The Supreme Court and the Burial of Ballot Access: A Critical Review of *Jenness v. Fortson*," *Election Law Journal* 1 (2002): 235 (showing that it costs hundreds of thousands to millions of dollars for a minor-party candidate to appear on all states' ballots).

72. Katharine Q. Seelye, "Democrats' Legal Challenges Impede Nader Campaign," *New York Times*, Aug. 19, 2004, A24 (quoting ballot access expert Richard Winger). Winger on his Web site *Ballot Access News* in an article titled "Ballot Access: A Formidable Barrier to Fair Participation" (*available at* www.ballot–access.org/winger/fbfp.html) notes that in Georgia: "[t]he legislature passed a law in 1943 requiring that new party and independent candidates submit a petition signed by 5% of the number of registered voters in order to get on the ballot for any office. Previously, any party could get on the ballot just by requesting it. The result has been that since 1943, there has not been one third party candidate on the Georgia ballot for U.S. House of Representatives."

Chapter 2: To Third Party or Not?

1. Louis Menand, "The Unpolitical Animal," *New Yorker*, Aug. 30, 2004, 95.

2. "Bush Still Wins Florida in Newspaper Recount," *Inside Politics*, Apr. 4, 2001 (*available at* http://archives.cnn.com/2001/ALLPOLITICS/04/04/florida-recount.01).

3. *See* Donna Brazile, *Cooking with Grease* (New York: Simon & Schuster, 2004), chap. 16.

4. Jeffrey Toobin, *Too Close to Call: The Thirty-Six-Day Battle to Decide the 2000 Election* (New York: Random House, 2001), 276.

5. The *New York Times* reported that "under any of seven single standards," *when two out of three coders had to agree* on the ballot review, "and combined with the results of an examination of overvotes, Mr. Gore would have won, by a very narrow margin." Ford Fessenden and John M. Broder, "Examining the Vote: The Overview; Study of Disputed Florida Ballots Finds Justices Did Not Cast the Deciding Vote," *New York Times*, Nov. 12, 2001, A1.

6. John Fund, *Stealing Elections: How Voter Fraud Threatens Our Democracy* (San Francisco: Encounter Books, 2004), 34.

7. A consortium of eight media outlets conducted a recount of the undervotes and the 113,000 "overvotes," where ballots had more than one mark that could be interpreted as a vote for president. Of the overvotes, 75,000 chose Gore and a minor candidate, whereas only 29,000 chose Bush and a minor candidate. Fessenden and Broder, "Examining the Vote." It was impossible to tell who those voters wanted because all the minor candidates received anywhere from 22,968 to 35,631 votes in this situation.

8. Menand, "The Unpolitical Animal," 94 (citing Princeton political scientists Christopher Achen and Larry Bartels).

9. *See* Sam Smith, "Why Democrats and the Media Should Stop Beating Up on Ralph Nader," *Progressive Review*, Apr. 2004 (*available at* www.web.gpnys.com/?p=48)

(citing CNN's exit poll showing Bush at 49 percent and Gore at 47 percent, without Nader in the race, and noting that "sixty-two percent of Nader's voters were Republicans, independents, third-party voters and nonvoters").

10. Solon Simmons, "One in Ten Thousand: Ralph Nader Takes on the Presidency," *Wisconsin Political Scientist* 10.2 (Summer 2004): 4.

11. Robert C. Fellmeth, "Why Democrats Should Thank Nader," *San Diego Union-Tribune*, Nov. 12, 2000.

12. Third parties generally try to build themselves, not take down another party. Barry C. Burden, at the time an associate professor at Harvard University, studied the campaign's media buys and itineraries to prove that Nader's 2000 campaign sought to maximize the 5 percent vote threshold to get FEC financing. Barry C. Burden, "Ralph Nader's Campaign Strategy in the 2000 U.S. Presidential Election," *American Politics Research* 33 (2005): 672–99.

13. Micah Sifry's book shows the difficulty of third-party building and attempts to get to the inner workings of the third parties for the decade of the 1990s through a postmortem of the 2000 elections. *See* Sifry, *Spoiling for a Fight: Third Party Politics in America* (New York: Routledge, 2002).

14. Ibid., 302 (citing phone interview with David Cobb on Feb. 9, 2001).

15. James L. Sundquist, "Needed: A Political Theory for the New Era of Coalition Government in the United States," *Political Science Quarterly* 103.4 (1988): 615 (citing *The Federalist*, particularly no. 10 but also no. 47, no. 48, and no. 62).

16. Ibid., 615–16.

17. Ibid., 616.

18. James Madison, no. 10 and no. 51, in Clinton Rossiter, ed., *The Federalist Papers* (New York: New American Library, 2003), 71, 317.

19. John J. Coleman, "Party Organizational Strength and Public Support for Parties," *American Journal of Political Science* 40 (1996): 806 (citing Louis Harris study number 921105, July 1992, question D4. N=1256).

20. L. Sandy Maisel, ed., *The Parties Respond: Changes in American Parties and Campaigns*, 3d ed. (Boulder, CO: Westview Press, 1998), xv.

21. Zogby International, "U.S. Constitution Wearing Well in Modern America: But Zogby Newsletter Poll Shows Wide Majority Feels the Two-Party Political System Is Not Working Well; Most Want More Options," July 2, 2007 (*available at* www.zogby.com/news/ReadNews.cfm?ID=1332) (poll surveyed 5,651 respondents and was conducted June 19–21, 2007, with margin of error of +/– 1.3 percentage points).

22. Joel H. Silbey, "From 'Essential to the Existence of Our Institutions' to 'Rapacious Enemies of Honest and Responsible Government': The Rise and Fall of American Political Parties, 1790–2000," in Maisel, *The Parties Respond*, 3, 19 (citing Austin Ranney, *The Federalization of Presidential Primaries*. Washington, DC: American Enterprise Institute, 1978 at 24).

23. A. James Reichley, *The Life of the Parties: A History of American Political Parties* (Lanham, MD: Rowman & Littlefield with Free Press, 2000), 3.

24. *See* Steven Hill, *Fixing Elections: The Failure of America's Winner Take All Politics* (New York: Routledge, 2003). *Also see* William Poundstone, *Gaming the Vote: Why Elections Aren't Fair (and What We Can Do About It)* (New York: Hill & Wang, 2007). Poundstone, who seems to go out of his way to string together colorful and wild anecdotes about the Nader campaigns to magnify his view of "spoilers" in history, has nevertheless added to the discussion with his recent book favoring range voting.

25. Hill, *Fixing Elections*, xv.

26. Ibid., 82–91; *see also* Austin Levitt with Bethany Foster, "A Citizen's Guide to Redistricting," the Brennan Center for Justice at New York University School of Law, New York, 2008 at 10.

27. Hill, *Fixing Elections*, at 75 (emphasis in the original).

28. *See, e.g.*, Gene Weingarten, "None of the Above," *Washington Post Magazine*, Oct. 31, 2004, 21; *see also* Robert M. Stein, Jan Leighley, and Christopher Owens, "Who Votes, Who Doesn't, Why, and What Can Be Done?" A Report to the Federal Commission on Electoral Reform (Washington, DC: June 10, 2005): 6 (including election administration among the three factors influencing voter turnout).

29. *See* Lisa Jane Disch, *The Tyranny of the Two-Party System* (New York: Columbia University Press, 2002), chap. 2; and at 35: "If the political party is an American tradition, it is only in the manner of democracy itself: as an innovation *contrary* to the design of the Constitution" (emphasis in original).

30. Lani Guinier, *The Tyranny of the Majority: Fundamental Fairness in Representative Democracy* (New York: Free Press, 1994), 4.

31. Range voting proponent Warren D. Smith suggests that range voting is superior to IRV for third parties. *See* the Center for Range Voting, which is a Web site located at http://rangevoting.org, providing useful information about the virtues of range and approval voting.

32. *See* Steven J. Rosenstone, Roy L. Behr, and Edward H. Lazarus, *Third Parties in America*, 2d ed. (Princeton, NJ: Princeton University Press, 1996), 16.

33. Douglas J. Amy, *Real Choices/New Voices: The Case for Proportional Representation Elections in the United State*s (New York: Columbia University Press, 1993), 7–8.

34. Fair Vote, "Faithless Electors," (*available at* www.fairvote.org/e_college/faithless.htm#4). Roger L. MacBride, an elector pledged to the Republican Party of Virginia, cast his votes for the Libertarian candidates, John Hospers (president) and Toni Nathan (vice president).

35. American Political Science Association, "Toward a More Responsible Two-Party System: A Report of the Committee on Political Parties," *American Political Science Review* 44.3 (Sept. 1950): 1–96.

36. *See* John Kenneth White, "E.E. Schattschneider: A 50-Year Retrospective and the Responsible Party Model," *PS: Political Science and Politics* 25.2 (June 1992): 167.

37. American Political Science Association, "Toward a More Responsible Two-Party System," 1.

38. Ibid., 22.

39. Ibid., 14, 95.

40. Ibid., 18.

41. Gerald M. Pomper, "Toward a More Responsible Two-Party System? What, Again?" *Journal of Politics* 33 (1971): 916, 918.

42. Ibid.

43. Paul S. Herrnson, "Why the United States Does Not Have Responsible Parties," *Perspectives on Political Science* 21.2 (Spring 1992): 91 (*available at* www.apsanet.org/~pop/APSA1950/Herrnson1992.html) (citations omitted).

44. Reichley, *The Life of the Parties*, 3.

45. Louis Menand, "Postcard from Stanford, Permanent Fatal Errors," *New Yorker*, Dec. 6, 2004, 54.

46. "Third Party Running," *Hill*, July 13, 2006 (900 surveyed on July 11 by Fox News–Opinion Dynamics; margin of error: +/– 3 percent).

47. Kirk Johnson, "In Southwest, a Shifting Away from Party Ties," *New York Times*, Oct. 24, 2006, A20.

48. Other candidates, like the late Senator Eugene McCarthy, who opted to run principled independent campaigns, were limited in how many ballots they could get on because of these discriminatory laws and, as a result, were hampered by the structural barriers. In 2008, Nader ran as the nominee of seven different parties: the Peace Party (OR), the Independent Party (HI, NM, MD), the Ecology Party (FL), the Independent Party (DE), the Independent Party (CT), the Peace and Freedom Party (CA), and the National Law Party (MI) and as an Independent elsewhere.

49. *See* Rosenstone, Behr, and Lazarus, *Third Parties in America*, 24 (citations omitted): "George Wallace qualified for every ballot except the one in the predominantly black District of Columbia, but he was forced to run under six different party labels. Eugene McCarthy secured a spot on only twenty-nine state ballots; fifteen of these required court battles to win his position. . . . John Anderson won positions on all fifty-one November ballots but only after a costly effort. The campaign spent more than half of the $7.3 million it raised between April and September on petition drives and legal fees."

50. Sifry, *Spoiling for a Fight*, 2–3.

51. Howie Hawkins, ed., *Independent Politics: The Green Party Strategy Debate* (Chicago: Haymarket Books, 2006).

52. *See, e.g.*, Jeffrey St. Clair, "Suicide Right on the Stage: The Demise of the Green Party," published on www.counterpunch.org, July 2, 2004, reproduced in ibid., 172–77, 177: a vote for Cobb is "also a vote for political self-annihilation. David Cobb is the Jim Jones of the Green Party. Form a line and pass the Kool-Aid." *See also* Edward Walsh, "Nader Rejects Green Party Backing: Run for Presidency Still Possible as Independent Candidate," *Washington Post*, Dec. 23, 2003, A5 (discussing three-part division at summer 2003 meeting).

53. *See, e.g.*, Hawkins, *Independent Politics*, 30–31 (describing the tension).

54. David Cobb, "Green Party 2004 Presidential Strategy" (presented at the National Committee meeting in Washington, DC, July 2003), reproduced in ibid., 96–98.

55. Hawkins, *Independent Politics*, 31.

56. Carol Miller and Forrest Hill, "Rigged Convention, Divided Party: How David Cobb Became the Green Nominee Even Though He Only Got 12 Percent of the Votes," published on www.counterpunch.org, Aug. 7, 2004, and reprinted in ibid., 184.

57. James Chace, *1912: Wilson, Roosevelt, Taft and Debs—The Election that Changed the Country* (New York: Simon & Schuster, 2004), 157–58.

58. Forrest Hill, "Reexamining the Green Party Nominating Convention: A Tactical Analysis," in Hawkins, *Independent Politics*, 271.

59. *See, e.g.*, Alan Maass, "The Green Party's Step Backward," *Socialist Worker*, July 2, 2004, in Hawkins, *Independent Politics*, 154–60; Peter Miguel Camejo, "Cut and Run: The Green Party 2004 Convention," Aug. 17, 2004, in Hawkins, *Independent Politics*, 197.

60. Joshua Frank, "David Cobb's Soft Charade: The Greens and the Politics of Mendacity," published on www.counterpunch.org, Aug. 6, 2004, reprinted in Hawkins, *Independent Politics*," 222–24.

61. Mike Feinstein with Richard Winger, *Ballot Access News*, from the Green Party Web site at www.gp.org, citing Richard Winger's "States in Which One Can Register

Green—and Be Counted" (*available at* http://web.greens.org/stats/): "States in which people can register Green . . . and the government keeps a tally are: AK, AZ, CA, CO, CT, DE, DC, FL, KY, LA, ME, MD, MA, NE, NJ, NV, NM, NY, OR, PA, UT, and WV. If the Greens were on the ballot in IA and RI, their registrations would be counted. States in which people can register Green but the government presently won't tally are: KS, NH, NC, OK, SD, WY." *See also* Richard Winger, *Ballot Access News*, "Early 2008 Registration Totals," 23.11 March 1, 2008 (*available at* www.ballot-access.org/2008/030108.html); and Richard Winger, *Ballot Access News*, 24.8 at 3, December 1, 2008.

62. Conversation with David Wilcox of the Campus Greens, Feb. 17, 2006.

63. *For example*, in a fax dated May 27, 2004, three individuals affiliated with the Socialists started circulating a sign-on open letter to Ralph Nader and Nader campaign activists titled "Reject the Reform Party Ballot Lines," on file with author.

64. Ronald B. Rapoport and Walter J. Stone, *Three's a Crowd: The Dynamic of Third Parties, Ross Perot, and Republican Resurgence* (Ann Arbor: University of Michigan Press, 2005), 233.

65. Sifry, *Spoiling for a Fight*, 215.

66. Ibid., 109.

67. *See, e.g.*, articles in the *Neo-Independent* 3.2 (Winter 2006): 26–31.

68. Christopher Hitchens, "Unsafe on Any Ballot," *Vanity Fair*, May 2004.

69. Letter from Lenora B. Fulani to the Honorable Elijah Cummings, dated May 2, 2004 (*available at* www.blackelectorate.com/print_article.asp?ID=1113).

70. *See* Robert Roth, *A Reason to Vote: The Natural Law Party* (New York: St. Martin's Press, 1998), 6.

71. Ibid., 27.

72. Email letter from Ralph Nader to John Hagelin, dated August 23, 2004, on file with author.

73. Katharine Biele, "Third Party Growing Pains: Breaking Two-Party Hegemony May Be Tough, But It's Also About the Pursuit of Happiness," *Salt Lake City Weekly*, Apr. 8, 2004, City Beat section. She wrote that "the party states that Personal Choice is its mission statement, and the Party shall make no group decisions on specific issues. No person shall be authorized to speak for the Personal Choice Party on any specific issue. Each Person is free to develop and express their own personal opinions. Apparently, there will be a state convention, although no one will be required to come. And it also says that no official business will be transacted anywhere at any time outside the state convention. The PCs take consensus decision-making to a whole new level. They even allow their candidates to choose whatever kind of smiley face they like for their literature."

74. Johnson, "In Southwest," A20 (citing "Election Data Services, a nonpartisan consulting company that tracks election information").

75. David W. Rohde, "Political Command and Control," *New York Times*, Nov. 18, 2006, A27.

76. *See* Elizabeth Daniel, "Unity08 Scales Back, Co-Founders Split for Draft Bloomberg Committee," *Daily News*, The Daily Politics Blog, Jan. 10, 2008 (*available at* www.nydailynews.com/blogs/dailypolitics/2008/01/unity08-scales-back-cofounders.html and www.unity08.com).

77. *See generally* Alan Ware, *Political Parties and Party Systems* (Oxford: Oxford University Press, 1996), 2–7.

Chapter 3: Suffer or Sue: Searching for a Level Playing Field

1. Jonathan Groner, "Girding for Another Bush v. Gore: With Nader's Decision to Run Adding Urgency, the Parties Are Mobilizing in the Event of a November Electoral Showdown," *Legal Times*, Mar. 1, 2004 (parenthetical added).

2. *See* a partial list of these suits at www.ballot-access.org/special/appendix.html.

3. Arizona: *Shultz et al. v. Nader et al.*, CV2004-11969 (Sup. Ct. Maricopa County Ariz. July 2, 2004) (unpublished); *Nader et al. v. Brewer et al.*, CV2004-16880 (D. Ariz. Sept. 10, 2004) (unpublished), *aff'd per curiam*, 386 F.3d 1168 (9th Cir. 2004); *Nader v. Brewer*, No. 04-1699 (D. Ariz. June 8, 2006), U.S. Dist. LEXIS 38500, *rev'd*, 531 F.3d 1028 (9th Cir. 2008) (declaring Arizona's out-of-state circulator prohibition and early deadline unconstitutional), *cert. denied* March 9, 2009. Arkansas: *Linda Chesterfield et al. v. Charlie Daniels et al.*, No. CV 2004-9755 (Cir. Ct. Pulaski County Ark. Sept. 20, 2004) (unpublished), *vacated, Populist Party of Arkansas, Ralph Nader and Peter Miguel Camejo et al. v. Linda Chesterfield and Democratic Party of Arkansas*, 359 Ark. 58, 195 S.W.3d 354 (Ark. 2004). Colorado: *Pakiefer et al. v. Davidson*, 04-CV-7546, *Colorado Democratic Party et al. v. Davidson*, No. 04-CV-7547 (consolidated) (Denver D. Ct. Sept. 17, 2004) (unpublished). District of Columbia: *Nader v. McAuliffe*, 549 F. Supp. 2d 760 (E.D. Va. 2008); *Nader v. McAuliffe*, No. 08-0428 (D.D.C. Jan. 7, 2009); *Nader v. DNC*, 555 F. Supp. 2d 1137 (D.D.C. 2008); *Nader v. DNC*, No. 1:08-CV-589 (D.D.C. Dec. 22, 2008); *Linda Serody et al. v. Ralph Nader*, CA 003385 F (D.C. Super. 2007) (attachment proceedings initiated May 16, 2007; remains pending). *See also* MUR 6021 *available at conclusion*, www.fec.gov. Florida: *Harriet Jane Black et al. v. Glenda Hood et al.*, No. 04-CA-2140, *Harriet Jane Black et al. v. The Reform Party of Florida et al.* No. 04-CA-2141 (consolidated) (Leon County Ct. Sept. 9, 2004) (unpublished); *Glenda Hood v. Harriet Jane Black et al.*, No. 1D04-4136, *The Reform Party of Florida et al. v. Harriet Jane Black, et al.*, No. 1D04-4050 (D. Ct. App. 1st Dist. Sept. 13, 2004) (determination to not rule, but to send to Florida Supreme Court), *rev'd and vacated trial court decision, The Reform Party of Florida et al. v. Harriet Jane Black et al.; Glenda Hood v. Harriet Jane Black et al.*, 885 So. 2d 303 (Fla. 2004) (per curiam). Hawaii: *Nader et al. v. Yoshina*, 04-611 (D. Haw. Oct. 13, 2004), *aff'd* (Cir. Ct. Apr. 5, 2005) (unpublished), *Nader v. Yoshina*, *Peroutka v. Yoshina* (consolidated), 17 Haw. 323, 179 P.3d 1050 (Haw. 2008); *Nader et al. v. Cronin*, Civ. No. 04-00611 (D. Haw. Feb. 7, 2008) (unpublished); *Peroutka et al. v. Cronin*, *Nader et al. v. Cronin*, Civ. No. 04-00611 (D. Haw. May 1, 2008), *appeal filed* May 30, 2008. Idaho: *Nader v. Ysursa*, CV-OC-04-7234 (4th Dist. Ada County) (dismissed from bench Oct. 6, 2004, subsequent decision unpublished); *Nader et al. v. Navarro*, CV-OC-04-8074 (4th Dist. Ada County) (Idaho 2004), *withdrawn*. Illinois: *Tully v. Nader et al.*, No. 04 SEB GE 504 (election board hearing decision Aug. 19, 2004); *Ralph Nader et al. v. Illinois State Bd. of Elections, Keith et al.*, 354 Ill. App. 3d 335, 289 Ill. Dec. 348, 819 N.E.2d 1148 (2004); *Nader v. Keith*, No. 04 C 4913 (N.D. Ill. Aug. 23, 2004), *aff'd*, 385 F.3d 729 (7th Cir. 2004); *see also Skinner v. Madigan*, 2004-CH-15757 (Cook County Ch. Ct. Oct. 15, 2004) (FOIA records request for state personnel records). Iowa: Findings of Fact, Conclusions of Law, Decision and Order, *In the Matter of the Objection to the Nominating Petition of Ralph Nader and Peter Miguel Camejo for the Office of President and Vice President* (Aug. 30, 2004) (administrative decision, 3-0, on file with author). Maine: *Dorothy Melanson v. Dan Gwadosky, Secretary of State, et al.*, Civ. No. AP-04-68 (Sup. Ct. Kennebec County Sept. 27, 2004) (unpublished), *aff'd*, 2004 Me. 127, 861 A.2d 641 (2004). A second challenge was brought by Benjamin Tucker. Maryland: *Nader For President*

2004 v. Maryland State Board of Elections, 383 Md. 216, 858 A.2d 483 (2004) (per curiam), *rev'd*, 399 Md. 681, 926 A.2d 199 (2007). Michigan: *Deleeuw et al. v. Board of State Canvassers et al.*, 263 Mich. App. 497, 688 N.W.2d 847 (2004); *Deleeuw et al. v. Board of State Canvassers et al.*, 693 N.W.2d 179 (Mich. App. 2004); *Nader v. Land*, No. 04-72830 (E.D. Mich. 2004) (unpublished); *Nader v. Land*, 115 Fed. Appx. 804 (6th Cir. 2004); *Nader v. Land*, No. 04-2428 (6th Cir. Jan. 10, 2006). Mississippi: Transcript In the Matter of: Presentation of Candidates and Challenges to Candidates' Political Parties for November, 2004 Election, Board of Election Commissioners for the State of Mississippi, Tuesday, September 7, 2004, 9:06 a.m., Jackson, Mississippi (administrative decision, 3-0, on file with author). Nevada: *Petition for Writ of Mandamus and Challenge to Candidacy of Ralph Nader*, Civ. 04-01187A, Transcript and Order (1st Dist. Ct. Carson City Sept. 1, 2004); *McKinley v. Heller*, 131 P.3d 622 (Nev. 2004). New Hampshire: Decision of the Ballot Law Commission on the Petition in Objection to Ralph Nader for President Nominating Petitions (administrative decision, 5-0, September 24, 2004). New Mexico: *Griego et al. v. Vigil-Giron*, CV 2004-5952 (Bernalillo County Sept. 17, 2004, *withdrawn* by Judge Wendy York, then reheard and reordered Sept. 20, 2004 by Judge Teresa Baca), *rev'd*, *Nader v. Griego*, Civ. No. 28900 (N.M. Sept. 28, 2004) (unpublished); *see also Gladstone v. Vigil-Giron*, CV-04-1078 (D.N.M. Sept. 28, 2004) (unpublished federal court decision victory). North Carolina: *Nader v. Bartlett*, No. 1:04-CV-00793 (M.D.N.C. Sept. 2, 2004) (unpublished); *Nader v. Bartlett*, No. 5:04-CV-675 (E.D.N.C. Sept. 24, 2004) (unpublished). Ohio: *Blankenship v. Blackwell*, 2:04-CV-965 (Ohio 2004) (Oct. 12, 2004) (unpublished); *Blankenship v. Blackwell*, No. 04-4259 (6th Cir. Oct. 18, 2004) (denial of injunctive relief), *aff'd per curiam*, *Blankenship v. Blackwell*, 103 Ohio St. 3d 567, 817 N.E.2d 382 (Ohio 2004), *cert. denied*, 543 U.S. 951 (2004) (denial of stay); *Blankenship v. Blackwell*, 341 F. Supp. 2d 911 (S.D. Ohio 2004), *appeal dismissed for want of jurisdiction*, 429 F.3d 254 (6th Cir. 2005); *Nader et al. v. Blackwell*, Civ. No. C2-04-1052 (Nov. 2, 2004) (unpublished) (denial of write-in votes); *Nader v. Blackwell*, Civ. No. 06-00821 (S.D. Ohio Sept. 19, 2007) (unpublished), *aff'd*, 545 F.3d 459 (6th Cir. 2008) (in analyzing § 1983 claim, court declared Ohio's circulator laws unconstitutional but denied relief because of immunity). Oregon: *Kucera et al. v. Bradbury and Democratic Party of Oregon et al.*, CC 04C18259, SC S51756 (Sept. 22, 2004), 337 Or. 384, 97 P.3d 1191 (2004), *cert. denied*, 544 U.S. 1056 (2005). Pennsylvania: *In re Nomination Paper of Nader*, 858 A.2d 1167 (Pa. 2004); *In re Nomination Paper of Ralph Nader and Peter Miguel Camejo v. Linda S. Serody et al.*, 865 A.2d 8 (Pa. Commw. Ct. 2004), *aff'd*, *In re Nomination Paper of Nader*, 580 Pa. 134, 860 A.2d 1 (Pa. 2004), *cert. denied*, *Nader v. Serody*, 543 U.S. 1052 (2005); *In re Nomination Paper of Ralph Nader*, 588 Pa. 450, 905 A.2d 450 (2006); *In re Nomination Paper of Nader*, No. 568 M.D. 2004 (Pa. Commw. Ct. Dec. 4, 2008) (unpublished) (appealed December 15, 2008, No. 94 MAP 2008). Texas: *Nader v. Connor*, 332 F. Supp. 2d 982 (W.D. Tex. 2004), *aff'd*, 388 F.3d 137 (5th Cir. 2004), *cert. denied*, 544 U.S. 921 (2005). Washington: *Washington State Democratic Central Comm. et al. v. Reed*, 04-2-1822-3 (Sup. Ct. Thurston County Sept. 15, 2004); a second suit was filed September 3, 2004 by Ken Valz, *Appeal of Determination of Candidacy Certification*, No. 04-2-01805 (Sup. Ct. Thurston County) and similarly dismissed. West Virginia: *State of West Virginia v. Ralph Nader*, Civ. No. 04-MISC-332 (Kanawha County W. Va. Sept. 2, 2004), *aff'd*, No. 041616 (W. Va. Sept. 9, 2004) (unpublished). Wisconsin: *Democratic Party of Wisconsin v. State Board of Elections*, Civ. No. 04-CV-2971 (Dane Co. Cir. Ct. Sept. 28, 2004), *rev'd*, *State of Wisconsin ex rel. Ralph Nader v. Circuit Court for Dane County et al.*, Civ. No. 04-2559-W (Wis. Sept. 30, 2004) (unpublished). We also had three administrative hearings—in Iowa, Mississippi, and New Hampshire—all brought by Democrats or the party's allies. The Nader 2008 campaign did not have to file a single suit because neither party went after them—and all resources were focused on ballot access.

4. The only possible exception would be the Communist Party in the 1940s.

5. Brian Faler, "Nader Criticizes Effort to Keep Him Off Ballot, Blames Kerry," *Washington Post*, Sept. 22, 2004, A8.

6. Letter from Ralph Nader to John Kerry, dated August 19, 2004, on file with author.

7. *See* J. David Gillespie, *Politics at the Periphery: Third Parties in Two-Party America* (Columbia: University of South Carolina Press, 1993), 35–36. "In the fifteen elections from 1920 through 1976 no third-party or independent campaign mastered all requirements to place its presidential candidate on the ballots of every constituency. Progressive nominee Robert La Follette in 1924 made all but one of the forty-eight state ballots, but his name appeared in the forty-seven under four different party labels. By grace of the Supreme Court, a body he often condemned for 'judicial tyranny,' George Wallace cracked all fifty state ballots (not that of Washington, D.C.) though under six different labels." Ibid., 35.

8. Steven J. Rosenstone, Roy L. Behr, and Edward H. Lazarus, *Third Parties in America*, 2d ed. (Princeton, NJ: Princeton University Press, 1996), 257–60 (citations omitted).

9. *Anderson v. Celebrezze*, 460 U.S. 790 (1983).

10. Samuel Issacharoff, Pamela S. Karlan, and Richard H. Pildes, *The Legal Structure of the Political Process* 3d ed. (New York: Foundation Press, 2007), 297 ("*Anderson* is largely disregarded in subsequent court opinions").

11. Richard Winger, "An Analysis of the 2004 Nader Ballot Access Federal Court Cases," *Fordham Urban Law Journal* 32 (2005): 572.

12. Texas moved its deadline from July to May in 1986; Arizona moved its deadline from September to June in 1993; and Illinois moved its deadline from August to June in 1999. *See* ibid., 571–73.

13. *See, e.g*, ibid., 571–78.

14. Tex. Elec. Code Ann. § 192.032 (c) (2004).

15. *Compare* Tex. Elec. Code Ann. § 192.032 (a), (b)(3)(A), (c), and (d) with §§ 181.005 (a) and 181.006 (b) (2004) (requiring independent candidates for president in Texas to present petition signatures totaling 64,077 or 1 percent of the vote in the last presidential election in Texas on or before May 10, 2004, while new political parties in Texas may get on the ballot by presenting only 45,540 signatures or 1 percent of the total vote in the last gubernatorial election in Texas on or before May 24, 2004).

16. *See* Winger, "An Analysis of the 2004 Nader Ballot Access," 574–75 and nn.79, 81–83 (citing Tex. Elec. Code Ann. §§ 192.032 (c) and (d), 181.006 (b)(2), and 142.007 (1) (2004)).

17. My in-house calculations were that we were going to spend more than $125,000 on ballot access in Texas alone.

18. *See* Winger, "An Analysis of the 2004 Nader Ballot Access," 575 and n.85 (citing *Cromer v. South Carolina*, 917 F.2d 819, 824 (4th Cir. 1990); *Greaves v. N.C. Bd. of Elections*, 508 F. Supp. 78, 83 (E.D.N.C. 1980); *McCarthy v. Kirkpatrick*, 420 F. Supp. 366, 375 (W.D. Miss. 1976)).

19. Email from Wes Benedict, state volunteer coordinator, Libertarian Party of Texas Ballot Access Committee, to Jason Kafoury, Apr. 27, 2004, on file with author.

20. *See, e.g.*, *Initiative & Referendum Inst. v. U.S. Postal Serv.*, 417 F.3d 1299 (D.C. Cir. 2005).

21. Memo from Cheryl Rohrick, volunteer petitioner from May 1, 2004, to May 9, 2004, Dallas, TX, titled "Documentation on Nader Petitioning Efforts in Dallas and Getting Asked to Leave," on file with author.

22. Texas Democratic Party, yellowdog@txdemocrats.org, email to Nader campaign supporter, "The Political Week in Review from the Texas Democratic Party, Friday, May 7, 2004," on file with author.

23. *Nader v. Connor*, 332 F. Supp. 2d 982, 985 (W.D. Tex. 2004).

24. James C. Linger, Esq., from Oklahoma, and he was assisted by local counsel John Kitchens, Esq.

25. As the May 10 deadline passed, the press was already spinning that we wouldn't be on the ballot. Nick Anderson, then from the *Los Angeles Times*, wrote a story on May 12, 2004, titled "Nader Won't Be on Ballot in Texas." Winger wrote Anderson an email dated May 11, 2004, on file with author, arguing the merits of our position: "Texas requires 41% more signatures for an independent presidential candidate, than it does for an independent candidate for US Senate, Governor or any other statewide office. Also, Texas requires 41% more signatures for an indp. pres. Candidate than to establish a new party. The Texas law is not even rational. The purpose of ballot access laws is to keep the ballot from being too crowded. A new party has the right to nominate someone for every partisan office in the state, so a single new party can have a big impact on the ballot. A single independent candidate takes up very little room on the ballot. All the precedents say that states cannot be tougher on independent presidential candidates, than on new parties. There are 5 on-point precedents, from North Carolina, South Carolina, Alabama, Florida and Missouri. They are all on Nader's side. There are no precedents on the other side. The US Supreme Court said in *Anderson v. Celebrezze*, 460 U.S. 780 (1983) that the states have less interest in keeping independent presidential candidates off their ballots, than independent candidates for other office. Texas law is absolutely backwards. In addition to all that, Texas says independent presidential candidates must file their petitions two weeks before new parties. The Secretary of State of Texas told the press that the Texas laws have been upheld in court before. No independent presidential candidate has ever filed a lawsuit against these Texas laws. The laws did not discriminate against independent presidential candidates, relative to other independent candidates, until 1977. So the law is not really very old. Also the petition deadline was always in July for independent presidential candidates, until 1987 when it was moved to May. The Texas deadline is an entire month earlier than the state with the 2nd earliest Independent presidential petition deadline (Arizona)."

Nick Anderson, to his credit, responded that he did not write the headline.

26. *Nader v. Connor*, 332 F. Supp. 2d 982, 992 (W.D. Tex. 2004).

27. Id. *See also* Winger, "An Analysis of the 2004 Nader Ballot Access," 575–76 and n.87 (citing Tex. Elec. Code Ann. § 181.031) (noting the judge made a major factual error regarding the filing prerequisites, claiming we had failed to file a form that applied only to state candidates). For example, Michael Badnarik, the 2004 Libertarian Party presidential candidate, did not file one in Texas and was on the ballot.

28. *Nader v. Connor*, 388 F.3d 137 (5th Cir. 2004).

29. The statute in Arizona just says: "A person who files a nomination paper pursuant to this section for the office of president of the United States shall designate in writing to the secretary of state at the time of filing the names of the candidate's vice

presidential running mate, the names of the presidential electors who will represent that candidate and a statement signed by the vice presidential electors and the designated presidential electors that indicates their consent to be designated. A nomination paper for each presidential elector designated shall be filed with the candidate's nomination paper." ARIZ. REV. STAT. ANN. § 16–341 (H) (2004).

30. We lost our first challenge in federal court for preliminary relief. *Nader v. Brewer*, No. 04-1699 (D. Ariz. Sept. 10, 2004), *aff'd*, 386 F.3d. 1168 (9th Cir. 2004) (affirming the denial of injunctive relief to get on the ballot).

31. The flipside of the petition has "Instructions for Circulators" in a box that says the following:

1. All petitions shall be signed by circulator.
2. Circulator must be qualified to register to vote in this state.
3. Circulator's name shall be typed or printed under such person's signature.
4. Circulator's residence address or, if no street address, a description of residence location shall be included on the petition.

The instructions do not say you *must* put in the county. So for failure to put in a county or the correct one, we lost another 1,349 signatures, well more than the amount we needed to put us over the top and on the ballot.

32. *See Nader v. Brewer*, Order No. CV-1699, June 8, 2006, *rev'd and rem'd*, No. 06-16251 (9th Cir. July 9, 2008) (recommended for publication).

33. Karen Tumulty, with reporting by Perry Bacon Jr., "The Nader Effect: How Worried Should the Democrats Be That the 2000 Spoiler Won't Quit?" *Time Magazine*, May 31, 2004, 36.

34. The Honorable Frederick J. Martone, a U.S. district judge, denied our claims, stating that the filing deadline is not more burdensome than necessary, as many of the concerns presented twenty years ago in the *Anderson* case were now reduced, given the earlier primaries. He said we had 107 days and that was enough to collect the signatures, as the state needed a full 113 days to get the ballots printed before early voting began before the election. He also concluded that the residency requirement was reasonable, given that the state had an interest in finding circulators through subpoena powers since there had been a history of circulator fraud in Arizona elections. We appealed to the Ninth Circuit in early July 2006, the case was argued in mid-2008 by Robert Barnes of the Bernhoft Law Firm on appeal, and we won in a unanimous decision, No. 06-16251 (9th Cir. July 9, 2008), *cert. denied*, March 9, 2009.

35. *See* Katharine Q. Seelye, "Democrats' Legal Challenges Impede Nader," *New York Times*, Aug. 19, 2004.

36. David Jackson and Ray Long, "Barack Obama: Showing His Bare Knuckles," *Chicago Tribune*, Apr. 4, 2007, 1.

37. *E.g.*, in 2002, independent Marsellis Brown appeared on the gubernatorial ballot even though he filed just his own signature when he was required to file 25,000 valid signatures.

38. On July 6, 2004, Patrick Martin, on the World Socialist Web site, wrote an article titled "Illinois Democratic Officials Use Legislative Staffers to Attack Third-Party Campaigns," stating: "On June 30—two days after the Democrats and Republicans filed their challenges against the SEP [Socialist Equality Party], the Greens, Nader and the Libertarians—the two parties joined forces to pass legislation to put Bush on the ballot. The Democrats were rewarded for this favor with perks of their own, including, re-

portedly, the effective dismissal of as much as $1 million in fines for campaign law violations." (*Available at* www.wsws.org/articles/2004/jul2004/illi-job.shtml.)

39. 10 Ill. Comp. Stat. §§ 5/10-3, 10-4, and 10-6 (West 2008). 10 Ill. Comp. Stat. 5/10-2 requires the signatures of "1% of the number of voters who voted at the next preceding Statewide general election or 25,000 qualified voters, whichever is less."

40. In Illinois, anyone can object to any candidate's nominating paper. 10 Ill. Comp. Stat. § 5/10-8 (West 2008).

41. Michael Kasper's legal profile says that he was Illinois counsel to former President Bill Clinton, to the Clinton/Gore campaigns in 1992 and 1996, and to the 2000 Gore/Lieberman campaign and that he represents "[m]ore than 50 members of the Illinois House of Representatives, including Speaker of the House, Michael J. Madigan" and "[s]eventeen members of the Illinois Senate." "[He] is currently the General Counsel and Treasurer of the Democratic Party of Illinois." (*Available at* www .hinshawlaw.com/64/mkasper.) Michael Kreloff has over thirty years of experience in election law in Illinois, including supervising the Election Law Unit for the Cook County State Attorney's Office. He was paid $12,000 by Ballot Project, Inc., for legal consulting, apparently as part of its global campaign to get us off the ballot. *See* Ballot Project, Inc., IRS Form 8872, for the period of July 1, 2004, to September 30, 2004, two expenditures of $5,000 each for Michael Kreloff for "consulting service—legal fees" on July 14, 2004, and August 3, 2004; and IRS Form 8872, for the period October 14, 2004, to November 22, 2004—expenditure of $2,000 on October 29, 2004.

42. *Nader 2000 Primary Comm., Inc. v. Illinois State Bd. of Elections*, No. 00-C-4401 (N.D. Ill. 2000): "The members of the Illinois State Board of Elections are ordered to accept the supplemental petitions of Ralph Nader and Winona LaDuke for President and Vice President of the United States presented to the State Board in Springfield on or before 9:30 a.m. on August 29, 2000, that were notarized on or before August 7, 2000."

43. "Request to Examine Records," dated June 23, 2004, by Peter Senechalle, on file with author.

44. Visitor Register, June 23, 2004, City of Chicago Board of Election Commissioners, on file with author.

45. Letter from Michael Mahoney, clerk of the Illinois House of Representatives, to Christina Tobin, dated July 20, 2004, on file with author.

46. *See Critical Montages* (*available at* http://montages.blogspot.com/2004/07/democrats-put-bush-on-ballot-while.html): "Democrats Put Bush on the Ballot While Fighting to Keep Nader Off It," July 19, 2004 (citing "Nader Campaign Says Madigan Staffers Used to Challenge Petitions," *Illinois Leader*, *formerly at* www .illinoisleader.com/news/newsviews.asp?c=17747, July 19, 2004).

47. Bernard Schoenburg, "State Elections Board Moves Against Unqualified Candidates," *Copley News Service*, July 19, 2004.

48. 10 Ill. Comp. Stat. § 5/9-25.1 (b) (West 2008).

49. Objector Tully's Motion to Dismiss at paragraph 9, filed Aug. 4, 2004, in *Nader v. Keith*, 2004 WL 3338651 (N.D. Ill. 2004).

50. Id. at para. 24.

51. Id. at para. 8.

52. Id. at para. 9.

53. Id. at para. 10.

54. Brief of the Plaintiffs-Appellants at 26 in *Nader v. Keith*, No. 04-3183.

55. *Nader v. Keith*, 385 F.3d 729, 734 (7th Cir. 2004).

56. Winger, "An Analysis of the 2004 Nader Ballot Access," 578.

57. Illinois also has another onerous law that requires more than 95 percent of the signatures on a referendum to be placed on the ballot to be valid! *Protect Marriage Illinois v. Orr*, 463 F.3d 604, 607 (7th Cir. 2006) (interpreting 10 ILL. COMP. STAT. § 5/28–11–12). Someone should sue to overturn this too.

58. Letter from Alexander McC. Peters, special deputy attorney general to Judge Bullock, dated June 2, 2004 (citing *Nader 2000 Primary Comm. Inc. v. Bartlett*, No. 5:00-CV-348-BR3 (E.D.N.C. Aug. 9, 2000), *aff'd*, 230 F.3d 1353 (2000)).

59. *See* N.C. GEN. STAT. § 163–122 (a)(1) (West 2008).

60. N.C. GEN. STAT. § 163–96 (a)(2) (West 2008).

61. N.C. GEN. STAT. § 163–96 (a) & (b)(1) (West 2008).

62. *Delaney v. Bartlett*, 370 F. Supp. 2d 373 (M.D.N.C. 2004).

63. Id.

64. *See* letter from Ralph Nader, independent candidate for president, to the Honorable Frank W. Bullock Jr., U.S. District Court judge, Middle District of North Carolina, dated May 21, 2004, on file with the author.

65. *Delaney*, 370 F. Supp. 2d at 385.

66. *McCarthy v. Briscoe*, 429 U.S. 1317, 1322–23 (1976).

67. Letter from Theresa Amato, campaign manager, to Gary O. Bartlett, executive secretary-director, North Carolina State Board of Elections, Aug. 11, 2004 (citing *McCarthy v. Briscoe*, 429 U.S. 1317, 1322 (1976), on file with author).

68. Id.

69. Defendants' Brief in Opposition to Plaintiffs' Motion for Preliminary Injunction, filed in U.S. District Court for the Middle District of North Carolina, 1-04-CV-793, Sept. 8, 2004.

70. *See* Winger, "An Analysis of the 2004 Nader Ballot Access," 584 and n.144.

71. MD. CODE ANN. ELEC. LAW § 4–102 (b) (2) (i) (West 2008). The state requires 10,000 signatures for a new party to be on the ballot but 1 percent of the registered voters or approximately 30,000 for an independent or "unaffiliated" candidate. MD. CODE ANN. ELEC. LAW § 5–703(e) (West 2008). We believed that making it more difficult for an independent or unaffiliated candidate to qualify than a third-party candidate, just like in Texas, was unconstitutional. We didn't have time, though, to bring that suit, but it too should be brought.

72. *Nader for President 2004 v. Maryland State Bd. of Elections*, No. C2004-100210 (Cir. Ct. Anne Arundel County Md. Sept. 14, 2004) (unpublished).

73. MD. CODE ANN. ELEC. LAW § 6–203(b) (West 2008).

74. *Nader for President 2004 v. Maryland State Bd. of Elections*, No. C2004-100210 (Cir. Ct. Anne Arundel County Md. Sept. 14, 2004) (unpublished).

75. Id.

76. Douglas E. McNeil, director of Marylanders for Democracy, "A Short History of Nader for President 2004 v. State Board of Election, 383 Md. 216 (2004)," 2006, on file with author; *Nader for President 2004 v. Maryland State Bd. of Elections*, 858 A.2d 483 (Md. 2004).

77. On June 21, 2007, the highest court of Maryland, the State Court of Appeals, voted 4 to 3 to say that if a registered voter is registered anywhere in the state, the signature is good for petition purposes, in large part because the state has a statewide database (a consequence of HAVA) and could easily verify this. *See Nader for President 2004 et al. v. Maryland State Bd. of Elections*, 399 Md. 681, 926 A.2d 199 (Md. 2007).

78. Id.

79. Or. Rev. Stat. § 249.735 (2) (West 2008).

80. Or. Rev. Stat. § 249.740 (1) (West 2008).

81. Or. Rev. Stat. § 249.722 (1) (West 2008); Or. Rev. Stat. § 249.720 (1)(e) (West 2008).

82. We had similar problems in Maine, Delaware, and Montana. Kentucky had relented by this point. Maine would eventually, but not Delaware, which forced us to go with the Independent Party nomination, even though we had indeed collected the requisite signatures there. An Oregon lawyer suggested that, contrary to Winger's analysis, a challenge to Oregon's ballot access requirement of disaffiliation for independents would not succeed for two reasons: first, we should have gone to get a declaratory judgment; and second, "the overwhelming weight of authority on the constitutional issues does not support the challenge." In *Storer v. Brown*, 415 U.S. 724 (1973), this disaffiliation requirement withstood challenges both on First and Fourteenth Amendment grounds and on adding of qualifications to the Constitution for federal office. State courts in Georgia, Colorado, and Massachusetts have all upheld the constitutionality of disaffiliation requirements.

83. *See, e.g.*, Letter from Margaret Olney to [petitioner], dated Aug. 12, 2004, on file with author.

84. Letter from Theresa Amato to Margaret Olney, dated Aug. 13, 2004, on file with author; Or. Rev. Stat. § 260.575 (West 2008).

85. 42 U.S.C. § 1971(b) (West 2008).

86. From the Aug. 2004 affidavit of an Oregon circulator, on file with author.

87. Letter from Margie Franz, compliance specialist, Office of the Secretary of State, to Ralph Nader, dated Sept. 2, 2004, on file with author.

88. Dan Meek, "The Unwritten Rules of the Duopoly: How Democrats Kicked Nader Off the Oregon Ballot," *CounterPunch*, Sept. 28, 2004 (*available at* www.counterpunch.org/meek09282004.html).

89. Opinion and Order, *Kucera v. Bradbury*, Sept. 9, 2004, No. 04C18259 (Cir. Ct. Oregon, Marion County).

90. *Kucera v. Bradbury*, 337 Or. 384, 398, 97 P.3d 1191, 1199 n. 7 (2004).

91. Email from Anne Martens to "Boz," dated Oct. 26, 2004—subject: Re: Dirty Tricks, on file with author.

92. *Kucera*, 337 Or. at 400, 97 P.3d at 1200 (2004).

93. Id. at 409, 97 P.3d at 1204-05 (2004).

94. *Kucera v. Bradbury*, 542 U.S. 963 (2004).

95. Petition for *Writ of Certiorari* at 30; *Kucera v. Bradbury*, 544 U.S. 1056 (2005).

96. *Available at* http://williamgillis.blogspot.com/2004, Aug. 16, 2004, posted by William Gillis.

97. SEIU Press Release, "Widespread Forgery Shown on Nader for President Petitions," media advisory announcing August 16, 2004 press conference (*available at* www.blueoregon.com/2004/08/nader_ballot_fr.html).

98. Ibid.

99. Kari Chisolm, "Nader Ballot Fraud," August 15, 2004 (*available at* www.blueoregon.com/2004/08/fraud_and_forge.html).

100. Peter Wong, "Nader to Be Listed on Ballot. Judge Rules Officials Erred. The State Says It Will Appeal Order," *Statesman Journal* (Salem, OR), Sept. 10, 2004.

101. Editorial, "A Lesson from Nader Fiasco," *Albany Democrat Herald*, Sept. 6, 2004 (*available at* www.dhonline.com/articles/2004/09/06/news/opinion/edit01.txt).

Chapter 4: Democrats Fighting the Last War

1. Janice D'Arcy, "Anti-Nader Forces Coordinate Strategy," *Hartford Courant*, July 27, 2004, A1 (reporting how the "Democratic party's political elite gathered to re-shape their anti-Nader campaign" at the Four Seasons Hotel during the DNC's convention in Boston, quoting Toby Moffett, Anti-Nader 2004 Ballot Project coordinator).

2. Fla. Stat. § 103.021(3) (2008).

3. Fla. Stat. § 99.097(4) (2008).

4. *See* Fla. Stat. § 103.021(4)(a): "A minor party that is affiliated with a national party holding a national convention to nominate candidates for President and Vice President of the United States may have the names of its candidates for President and Vice President printed on the general election ballot by filing with the Department of State a certificate naming the candidates for President and Vice President and listing the required number of persons to serve as electors. Notification to the Department of State under this subsection shall be made by September 1 of the year in which the election is held. When the Department of State has been so notified, it shall order the names of the candidates nominated by the minor party to be included on the ballot and shall permit the required number of persons to be certified as electors in the same manner as other party candidates."

5. Since 1999, the law in Florida appeared to be that parties just had to nominate someone at a national convention. Indeed, in 2000, the Green Party got on, even though it wasn't an official FEC-recognized party, because it had a nominating convention and nominated Nader. Neither the Socialist Workers nor the Workers World parties had a convention, and their candidates both got on in 2000. It seemed very easy to get on in Florida if you were a party or even claimed to be a party. If you weren't, and ran as an independent, you had to collect 93,024 valid signatures to get on the ballot.

6. Three law firms were on the papers: Podhurst Orseck (with three lawyers, Stephen F. Rosenthal, Michael S. Olin, and Maria Kayanan) and Richard B. Rosenthal (of the Law Offices of Richard B. Rosenthal, P.A), both from Miami, and Mark Herron (of Messer, Caparello & Self, P.A.) from Tallahassee. More lawyers would enter appearances in the next few days, including Joel S. Perwin of Podhurst Orseck in Miami and Thomas Findley of Tallahassee, along with Laurence Tribe of Cambridge, Massachusetts.

7. *Wilson v. Hood*, Plaintiff's Motion for Preliminary Injunction, filed Sept. 3, 2004 (emphasis in original).

8. We hadn't received any of these papers. These plaintiffs were represented by Edward S. Stafman of Stafman Law Offices in Tallahassee; M. Stephen Turner and Kelly Overstreet Johnson, David K. Miller, and Brooke E. Lewis of Broad and Cassel in Tallahassee. The Ballot Project, Inc., according to IRS reports, paid Broad and Cassel $150,000 for their participation in the Florida lawsuit. The Ballot Project, Inc., Form 8872, Report for the Period 7/1/2004 to 9/30/2004, showing multiple payments totaling $150,000 to Broad and Cassel.

9. The court wrote the following footnote: "The Court is very concerned with the due process rights of Defendants Nader and Camejo. While the injunctive relief is not sought against them, the Court recognizes their interests are directly affected by this proceeding. However, given the exigent circumstances which all parties acknowledged, this Court determined that the only appropriate course was to proceed with the emergency hearing." The Honorable P. Kevin Davey, Order Granting Preliminary In-

junction, Sept. 9, 2004, Case Nos. 2004-CA-2140, 2141, consolidated *Black v. Hood*; *Wilson v. Hood*; at 5, n. 2.

10. Transcript of September 8, 2004, before the Honorable P. Kevin Davey, in the Second Judicial Circuit in and for Leon County, Florida, at 251–52.

11. For example, during the initial phone "hearing," the Democrats argued that they would be "irreparably harmed." When I asked Maddox why—what precisely was the harm they were claiming if Nader/Camejo were on the ballot—he claimed, under oath, "As I testified earlier, the Democratic Party would have a different campaign strategy, would allocate resources differently than if it were a simple head-to-head contest between two candidates." I pointed out that this rationale would then suggest he should have challenged all the other minor-party candidates certified for the ballot and asked if he had done so. He said, "No, I have not personally." I asked, "Has the Democratic Party challenged any other minor party certification on the ballot?" "No." (Transcript of September 8, 2004, before the Honorable P. Kevin Davey, in the Second Judicial Circuit in and for Leon County, Florida, at 93–94.) This challenge was all about removing Nader.

12. Transcript of September 8, 2004, before the Honorable P. Kevin Davey, in the Second Judicial Circuit in and for Leon County, Florida, at 256.

13. In retrospect, we should have had counsel lined up well in advance for Florida, but we did not believe that the Reform Party nomination was challengeable after the in-person nomination convention. With the existing lawsuits in at least fifteen places and five more on the way, it was hard just to make sure every courtroom was covered. (To put this in perspective, at this point in the 2004 campaign, we had lawsuits we were defending in Ohio, New Mexico, Colorado, Arkansas, Washington, Wisconsin, Maryland, Pennsylvania, New Hampshire, and Maine all in the hopper that also needed urgent attention, not to mention our affirmative lawsuits in a dozen states.)

14. The $10,000 was more than we had to spend. Ralph didn't want to spend anything on lawyers, much less big firm ones, much less Republican ones, and I knew we were going to be going into debt, massively, across the country on all this litigation. But I said yes. Sukhia was extremely talented and the right man for the job. I had no idea at the time I hired him that he participated in the 2000 recount for Bush regarding the military ballots. If I had, I probably still would have hired him.

15. Richard Winger, "January 2004 Registration Totals," *Ballot Access News*, 19.10, Feb. 1, 2004 (*available at* www.ballot-access.org).

16. Bill Cotterell, "Nader Off the Ballot in Florida," *Tallahassee Democrat*, Sept. 9, 2004.

17. Brief of Respondent-Appellee at 2, 32, *Reform Party of Florida v. Black*, 885 So. 2d 303, No. 04-CA-2141 (Fla. Sept. 16, 2004).

18. Id. at 12.

19. Id. at 19 (italics in original).

20. There were a host of reasons for this, including a massive debt the FEC claims the party has with the FEC. Anyone with rudimentary knowledge of FEC law knows that a party committee that owes the federal government money cannot terminate itself without government permission.

21. Brief of Respondent-Appellee at 20, 34, *Reform Party of Florida v. Black*, 885 So. 2d 303, No. 04-CA-2141.

22. Id. at 22. There is a distinction between which groups the FEC officially recognizes to have "national party committee status" and those the FEC considers to be a "political party." In 2000, Ralph was the nominee of the Green Party before the

Greens were an FEC-recognized political party. The Greens then were two separate associations, one called the Association of State Green Parties and the other the Green Party USA. Indeed, one group had been denied FEC recognition earlier as a party because of disputes between these two factions and for not having met all the requirements, not the least of which was to hold a nominating convention for president. They cured the failure to hold a national convention in June 2000 by having Ralph Nader and Winona LaDuke nominated as their presidential and vice-presidential nominees. But the Greens did not successfully apply for national party committee status from the FEC until mid-2001, long after the 2000 election. There is no definition of a *political party* in the relevant chapter of the Code of Federal Regulations beyond the following: "an association, committee, or organization which nominates or selects a candidate for election to any Federal office, whose name appears on an election ballot as the candidate of the association, committee, or organization." (11 C.F.R. § 100.15.) That is it. So I asked the FEC Information Division Hotline, "Do you mean that three people in a closet can be a political party if they select a candidate for office and the name appears on the ballot?" Response: "Yes."

The "party" issue becomes complicated for FEC purposes only after money becomes involved. The raising and spending of money (not membership or other criteria) triggers reporting and disclosure requirements for regulatory purposes, not philosophical or political science purposes of what constitutes a party. Even those who are not "parties"—indeed, even just individuals—have to engage in reporting and disclosure once certain levels of money are raised or spent.

23. Brief of Respondent-Appellee at 23, *Reform Party of Florida v. Black*.

24. FLA. CONST. art. VI, § 1.

Article VI—Suffrage and Elections

> Section 1: regulation of elections.—All elections by the people shall be by direct and secret vote. General elections shall be determined by a plurality of votes cast. Registration and elections shall, and political party functions may, be regulated by law; however, the requirements for a candidate with no party affiliation or for a candidate of a minor party for placement of the candidate's name on the ballot shall be no greater than the requirements for a candidate of the party having the largest number of registered voters.

25. Order, September 9, 2004, Case Nos. 2004-CA-2140 and 41 consolidated, at 1–2.

26. Bill Cotterell, "Ballots Are Certified Without Nader; Elections Supervisors Wring Hands over Potential Mess," *Tallahassee Democrat*, Sept. 10, 2004.

27. On September 10, 2004, we filed an emergency motion for stay, pending review in the Florida Court of Appeals for the First District, Editorial, "The Return of Katherine Harris," *New York Times*, Sept. 17, 2004.

28. Steve Bousquet, "Judge Deals Florida Ballot Setback to Nader," *St. Petersburg Times*, Sept. 10, 2004 (*available at* www.sptimes.com/2004/09/10/State/Judge_deals_Florida_b.shtml).

29. Lesley Clark, "Judge Boots Nader Off Fla. Ballot," *Miami Herald*, Sept. 10, 2004.

30. Steve Bousquet, "Did Bush Camp Err on Ballot Papers? Democrats Say the President May Have Missed Florida's Filing Deadline, But Say They Don't Plan a Challenge," *St. Petersburg Times*, Sept. 11, 2004 (*available at* www.sptimes.com/2004/09/11/Decision2004/Did_Bush_Camp_err_on.shtml).

31. IRS reports show that the Ballot Project, Inc., paid more than $20,000 for Lichtman's attendance at the trial and expenses. The Ballot Project, Inc., IRS Form 8872, Pre-election report for the period 10/1/2004 to 10/13/2004, Schedule B, showing expenditure for Mr. Lichtman at $20,534.

32. It showed in the quality of brief we filed; we sought to extend the timeline by two hours to file an amended brief, but that was denied. I was up most of the night fixing our statement of facts, putting in citations by going through the record, leaving the Florida law part to the Florida lawyers. It is hard to believe that the national campaign manager had to find transcript citations in the middle of the night to keep us on the Florida ballot. But that is an indication of how thinly stretched we were, how overwhelming all the litigation was, and how few lawyers in the United States would come to our defense.

33. Fla. Stat. § 97.021(17) (2008).

34. Amended Initial Brief of Petitioner-Appellants at 46–47, *Reform Party of Florida v. Black*, 885 So. 2d 303, No. SC04–1755; DCA Case No. 04–4050.

35. Hugo Torres, "Tribe Argues to Keep Nader Off Florida Ballot," *Harvard Law Record*, Sept. 30, 2004.

36. Ibid.

37. Ibid.

38. Ibid.

39. The *per curiam* decision stated, "In making our decision in this case we are guided by the overriding constitutional principles in favor of ballot access and our recognition of the plenary authority of the Legislature to direct the manner of selecting Florida's presidential electors." (*Reform Party of Florida v. Black*, 885 So. 2d at 304.)

The court focused on the legislative history of the statute and on how to define the terms that had no legislative definition. It noted, for example, that Hawaii defines a national party as "a party established and admitted to the ballot in at least one state other than Hawaii or one which is determined by the chief election officer to be making a bona fide effort to become a national party." (Id. at 313 [referencing Haw. Rev. Stat. § 11-113(b) (1993)].) It also looked at Iowa, which states the party must be a political party "in at least twenty-five other states." (Id. [referencing Iowa Code § 68A.102(16) (2003)].) It cited Puerto Rico, which defines a national party as "every political party that nominates and participates in the election of candidates for the offices of President and Vice-President of the United States of America." (Id. [referencing 16 P.R. Laws Ann. § 1322 (1987)].) In 2005, the Florida legislature made clear: "As used in this section, the term 'national party' means a political party established and admitted to the ballot in at least one state other than Florida" (Fla. Stat. § 103.021 (4) (a) (2008)), thus reaffirming its commitment to ballot access for minor parties.

The court concluded that "there is no consensus on what constitutes a national party, even among the few states that define the term." (*Reform Party of Florida v. Black*, So. 2d at 304.) It declined to use the FEC term for national committee status. The court also noted that even the trial court found some sort of "affiliation" and that a meeting of some type occurred. (Id. at 314.) It therefore concluded that absent "[any] more specific statutory criteria or guidance from the Legislature we are unable to conclude that a statutory violation occurred." (Id.) The next day I learned that a clerk of the U.S. Supreme Court had called our counsel that prior afternoon to give him a fax number to send "any kind of filing to" over the weekend. The U.S. Supreme Court appeared ready—for once—to take on one of our ballot access cases. Too bad their enthusiasm didn't extend to some of the federal court decisions everywhere else in the country.

40. Joshua Green, "In Search of the Elusive Swing Voter," *Atlantic Monthly*, Jan.–Feb. 2004.

41. Alan Greenblatt, "Battleground, Neck and Neck Around the Country," *New York Times*, Oct. 26, 2004, 9.

42. Ibid.

43. The pressure was tremendous and irrational, akin to the naturalists and the purists of the P.K. Dick short story "The Chromium Fence." Philip K. Dick, "The Chromium Fence," in *The Philip K. Dick Reader* (New York: Citadel Twilight, 1997), 298.

44. Having seen the Colorado, Mississippi, and Florida challenges, John Blare, the Reform Party ballot access liaison and the liaison to the Nader campaign, corresponded with the Kansas SOS throughout September to make sure that there would be no similar challenge there.

45. ME. REV. STAT. ANN. TIT. 21-A, § 354(5)(A) (West 2008).

46. ME. REV. STAT. ANN. TIT. 21-A, § 354(8)(A) (West 2008).

47. The other was by Benjamin J. Tucker.

48. Letter from Julie L. Flynn, deputy secretary of state, to Ralph Nader et al., dated Aug. 24, 2004, on file with the author.

49. Tucker, the other complainant, hired James T. Kilbreth of Verrill & Dana, LLP, and their challenges included most of Melanson's and a few more for good measure. For example, "on information and belief," they claimed that some circulators fraudulently concealed the identity of the candidate from signers of the petition and then misled the registered voters into signing. They also claimed that Nader for President 2004 "likely" received direct or in-kind contributions to fund the signature collection in violation of the Federal Election Commission Act (FECA) by accepting these "illegal contributions." And they claimed that Rosemary Whitaker, one of our electors, had unenrolled on January 22, not January 1, 2004, and was therefore ineligible to be an independent elector—even though the deadline for unenrollment was actually March 1.

50. Transcript of Testimony from Dorothy Melanson, chairwoman of Maine Democratic Party, Public Hearing Before the Bureau of Corporations, Elections and Commissions, Augusta, ME, Aug. 30 and 31, 2004.

51. Report of the Hearing Officer, for the Public Hearing held Pursuant to ME. REV. STAT. ANN. TIT. 21-A., § 356(2)(B) on the Challenges . . . at III.A.(1).

52. Id. at (2).

53. Id. at III.(C) and IV.

54. Dorothy M. Melanson, Benjamin J. Tucker v. Ralph Nader, Peter Miguel Camejo, et al., Secretary of State's Decision on Report of the Hearing Officer, dated Sept. 8, 2004, citing ME. REV. STAT. ANN. TIT. 21-A, § 356(2)(D).

55. Justice S. Kirk Studstrup, Decision on Appeal, Sup. Ct. Civ. No. AP-04-68, slip op. at 7, dated Sept. 27, 2004.

56. *Melanson v. Secretary of State*, 2004 Me. 127, 861 A.2d 641 (2004).

57. W. VA. CODE § 3-5-23(a) & (c) (West 2008).

58. W. VA. CODE § 3-5-23(a) (West 2008).

59. *See McClure v. Manchin*, 301 F. Supp. 2d 564 (N.D. W. VA. 2003).

60. W. VA. CODE § 3-5-23(b) (West 2008).

61. Deposition of Jennifer Breslin in the State of West Virginia, by Darrell V. McGraw Jr., Attorney General, Civ. No. 04-Misc.-332, dated Aug. 29, 2004, at 8–9.

62. *See* W. VA. CODE § 3-5-23(b) (2004) (stating that solicitors of signatures "must first obtain from the clerk of the county commission credentials which must be exhibited to each voter canvassed or solicited").

63. Deposition of Jennifer Breslin in the State of West Virginia, by Darrell V. McGraw Jr., Attorney General, Civ. No. 04-Misc.-332, dated Aug. 29, 2004, at 38–39.

64. *See, e.g.*, "Nader Camp Admits Hiring Controversial Firm," *Charleston Gazette* (WV), July 20, 2004, 1.

65. Editorial, "Tangle: Nader Petition Complexities," *Charleston Gazette* (WV), July 20, 2004, A4.

66. Deirdre Purdy, Gary Collias, Phil Hancock, Karen Coria, and Norris Light.

67. *State ex rel. Deirdre Purdy, Gary Collias, Phil Hancock, Karen Coria, and Norris Light v. The Honorable Joe Manchin, Secretary of State for the State of West Virginia*, filed Aug. 16, 2004, in the Supreme Court of Appeals for the State of West Virginia, at 4.

68. Paul J. Nyden, "Barring Order, Manchin Will Not Release Nader Petitions," *Charleston Gazette*, Aug. 3, 2004.

69. W. VA. CODE § 3-5-23(e) (West 2008).

70. As a footnote to support this assertion, he claimed that fives states "have already officially rejected Nader nominating petitions," citing Arizona, Virginia, Maryland, Illinois, and Missouri as some sort of validation of the West Virginia effort to suddenly revisit our certification. (*The State of West Virginia v. Ralph Nader*, Civ. No. 04-MISC-332, at 2.)

71. We were to appear by telephone for a status conference at 8:30 the next morning. Since we had no lawyer yet, I appeared. I informed the court I was a licensed attorney but not licensed in West Virginia and that I had not had an opportunity to secure counsel yet on behalf of the campaign. The Honorable Tod J. Kaufman directed the state to supply me with affidavits and told the campaign to be prepared to present our case in West Virginia in five days.

72. Complaint, *State of West Virginia v. Ralph Nader*, Civ. No. 04-MISC-332 (Kanawha County W. Va. 2004) at 3.

73. In the meantime, I had to find counsel to defend Breslin's deposition, scheduled by phone for Sunday, August 29, in Washington, DC. We also had to take two depositions of witnesses who would not be available at the hearing in West Virginia the next day. A local lawyer named Haig V. Kalbian, who knew little about our campaign, graciously volunteered on short notice. He hit pay dirt by establishing that neither deponent knew whether the circulators they complained about were actually working for our campaign. (*See* deposition transcripts of Jennifer Narog Taylor at 14 and Deirdre H. Purdy at 15, Aug. 20, 2004, in *State of West Virginia v. Ralph Nader*, Civ. No. 04-MISC-332 [Kanawha County, W. Va. 2004], on file with author.)

74. Recollections of Harry Kresky to Theresa Amato, dated October 27, 2005, on file with author.

75. Findings in *State of West Virginia v. Ralph Nader*, Civ. No. 04-MISC-332, dated Sept. 2, 2004.

76. Petition for Injunction, *State of West Virginia v. Ralph Nader*, Civ. No. 04-MISC-332, In the Supreme Court of Appeals of West Virginia, at 6.

77. Order, West Virginia Supreme Court of Appeals dated Sept. 9, 2004, *State of West Virginia v. Ralph Nader*, No. 041616.

78. Editorial, "Nader's Complaint," *Wall Street Journal*, Sept. 14, 2004, A20.

79. The secretary of state said that we turned in 52,398 signatures. The Commonwealth Court of Pennsylvania claimed that the number was 51,273. (*See* Decision of the Commonwealth Court of Pennsylvania, No. 568 M.D. 2004, Consolidated Findings, Opinion and Order, dated Oct. 13, 2004, at 3 n.3.)

80. John Fund, "A Rich History of Corruption," *Wall Street Journal*, Apr. 13, 2006.

81. *Buckley v. American Constitutional Law Foundation, Inc.*, 525 U.S. 182 (1999); *Morrill v. Weaver*, 224 F. Supp. 2d 882 (E.D. Pa. 2000); Letter from Pedro A. Cortes, Secretary of the Commonwealth, to Theresa Amato, dated July 14, 2004, attaching an Attorney General letter dated Apr. 26, 2002, to Elizabeth Daniel of the Brennan Center for Justice at New York University School of Law.

82. 25 Pa. Stat. Ann. §§ 2911(b), 2913(c), superseded by Consent Decree in *Hall v. Davis*, Civ. No. 84-1057, June 15, 1984.

83. 25 Pa. Stat. Ann. §§ 2911, 2911.1 (West 2008).

84. Tom Barnes, "Petitions Submitted to Put Nader on Pa. Presidential Ballot," *Post-Gazette Harrisburg Bureau*, Aug. 3, 2004.

85. Bill DeWeese, "PA Stays Blue Despite Repeated Bush Visits, DeWeese/Veon Weigh Nader Factor," Press Release, Harrisburg, Nov. 5, 2004 (*previously available at* www.billdeweese.com/newsite/articles/11-5-04.php but since removed, on file with author).

86. *See* Dick Polman, "America Votes: Spurned by Friends, Nader Labors to Get on State Ballots," *Philadelphia Inquirer*, July 4, 2004, A3; *see also* www.heinz.org.

87. The Ballot Project's filing of Form 8872 with the IRS for the period of July 1, 2004 to Sept. 30, 2004, shows that Mongtomery, McCracken, Walker & Rhoads was paid $6,000 for reimbursed expenses on Aug. 3, 2004.

88. Ira Lefton, Chris Walters, Barbara Kiely, Melissa J. Oretsky, James P. Williamson, Milind Shah, Jeremy Feinstein, Jeffrey J. Bresch, Mark Tambury, John M. McIntyre, James Doerfler, Lisa M. Camploi, Andreas Simonson, Kim Watterson, and Cynthia Kernick, all of Reed Smith.

89. *See* Brown, "Policing Ballot Access," 193 n.201 (citing *In re Nader*, 856 A.2d 8, 12 (Pa. Commw. Ct. 2004) [listing names of twenty-one attorneys from Philadelphia and Pittsburgh who represented the objectors]).

90. "Nader's Campaign Files Petitions in Pa.," UPI, Harrisburg, PA, Aug. 3, 2004.

91. *In re Nader*, 856 A.2d 908, 910 & n.3.

92. Katharine Q. Seelye, "Democrats' Legal Challenges Impede Nader," *New York Times*, Aug. 19, 2004 (*available at* http://query.nytimes.com/gst/fullpage.html?res=9A03E7DB1E3FF93AA2575BC0A9629C8B63).

93. Ibid.

94. Ibid.

95. *In re Nader*, 856 A.2d at 910 (Pa. Commw. Ct. 2004).

96. *See In re Nomination Paper of Ralph Nader and Peter Miguel Camejo*, 858 A.2d 58 (Pa. 2004).

97. *See In re Nomination Petition of Flaherty*, 770 A.2d 327 (Pa. 2001); *In re Nomination Petition of Silcox*, 674 A.2d 224 (Pa. 1996).

98. Brief of the Appellants, Ralph Nader and Peter Camejo, Supreme Court Docket No. 154 MAP 2004, at 45.

99. *In re Nomination Paper of Ralph Nader*, 858 A.2d 1167 (Pa. 2004).

100. Id.

101. *Not* to be included in the review were "the names and addresses which may be a variable form of the name or addresses on the registration"—such as nicknames or missing initials. *See* Brief of Appellants, In the Supreme Court of Pennsylvania, No. 182 MAP 2004, *In re Nomination Paper of Ralph Nader*, at 11.

102. Peter Jackson, "Multiple Judges May Consider Nader Challenge in Pa.," *AP Newsbreak*, Aug. 11, 2004.

103. We also asked the court to amend its order because it improperly focused in the hearings on the voter registration status rather than the voting qualifications, that is, whether signatories were properly registered, rather than qualified to vote. The Commonwealth Court denied our motion on the same day. Immediately after that denial, we also sought an application for extraordinary relief to the Pennsylvania Supreme Court, arguing that the hearings were improperly focused on whether the signatories were registered voters rather than merely qualified electors. This was denied in an order dated October 1, 2004. (*In re Nomination Paper of Nader* ("Nader II"), No. 171 MM 2004 (filed Oct. 1, 2004) (per curiam) [with Justice Thomas G. Saylor filing a concurring and dissenting statement arguing that our position had "arguable merit"].)

104. *See* John A. Murphy, "Political Profiling in Pennsylvania, Keeping Nader Off the Ballot," *Counterpunch*, June 28, 2005 (*available at* www.counterpunch.org/murphy 06282005.html).

105. *See, e.g.*, Tim Ferrick Jr., "Cash and Carry (the City)," *New York Times*, Apr. 22, 2008 (describing legal "street money": "In Philadelphia, it is a mandatory fee for most Democratic candidates.") (*available at* www.nytimes.com/2008/04/22/opinion/22 ferrick.html?).

106. *See* Reply to the Order of the Court filed by Louis Lawrence Boyle, Deputy Chief Counsel for the Secretary of the Commonwealth and the Bureau of Commissions, Elections and Legislation, dated Aug. 24, 2004, in No. 568 M.D. 2004, *In re Nomination Paper of Ralph Nader and Peter Miguel Camejo v. Serody et al.*

107. *In re Nomination Paper of Ralph Nader and Peter Miguel Camejo*, Brief in Support of Motion to Intervene, In the Supreme Court of Pennsylvania, Middle District, Case No. 171 MD 2004, at 3.

108. *In re Nomination Paper of Ralph Nader*, 865 A.2d at 18 (Pa. Commw.), *aff'd*, 840 A.2d 1 (2004), *cert. denied sub. nom.*, *Nader v. Serody*, 543 U.S. 1052 (2005).

109. *Nader v. Serody*, 865 A.2d at 18.

110. Darcy G. Richardson, "The Untold Story of the 2004 Presidential Election: Fewer Voices, Fewer Choices," *Rumor Mill News*, Aug. 31, 2004 (*available at* www .rumormillnews.com).

111. 25 PA. STAT. ANN. § 2911 (West 2008).

112. 25 PA. STAT. ANN. § 2911(c) (West 2008).

113. Brief of Appellants, In the Supreme Court of Pennsylvania, No. 182 MAP 2004, *In re Nomination Paper of Ralph Nader and Peter Miguel Camejo*, at 24, citing § 102 (t) of the Election Code, 25 PA. STAT. ANN. § 2602 (emphasis added).

114. *Morrill v. Weaver*, 224 F. Supp. 2d at 899–900 (citations omitted).

115. 25 PA. STAT. ANN. § 1326 (b).

116. Brief of Appellants at 12–18 & n.5, *In re Nomination Paper of Nader*, 860 A.2d 1 (Pa. 2004).

117. Id.

118. Id. at 17 & n.8.

119. Id. at 54, n.16 (citations to respondents' exhibits omitted).

120. *In re Nomination Paper of Nader*, 860 A.2d 1, 2 (Pa. 2004) (Saylor, J., dissenting) (citing Act of June 3, 1937, P.S. 1333 (as amended, 25 PA. STAT. ANN. §§ 2600-3591 [the "Election Code"])).

121. Id. at 6, n.4 (providing examples from the Election Code).

122. Id. at 14–15.

123. Id. at 14.

124. Brown, "Policing Ballot Access," 198–200, also noting: "the three judges who initially disqualified Nader were responsible for striking more signatures (over 20,000) than all the other judges combined."

125. Memorandum from Monna J. Accurti, Commissioner, Bureau of Commissions, Elections and Legislation, to All County Contact Persons for Elections, re: Presidential Electors—Write-in Votes, dated Oct. 26, 2004, on file with author.

126. *Nader v. Serody*, 543 U.S. 951 (2004); and *Nader v. Serody*, 543 U.S. 1052 (2005).

127. *In re Nomination Paper of Nader*, 905 A 2d. 450, 455 (Pa. 2006). Two justices, Saylor and Eakins, dissented, but Justice Eakins found that another uncited provision of the court's "Internal Operating Procedures" allowed for the ordering of the court reporters' costs. (Id. at 460 (Saylor, J., dissenting) (Eakins, J., concurring and dissenting).)

128. Our Petition for a *Writ of Certiorari* filed November 17, 2006, stated that "between June and September of 2004, seventeen state Democratic Parties either sued or materially supported lawsuits filed against Petitioners," with the help of "[a]t least eighty-nine lawyers from forty-eight law firms nationwide," at 3. The actual number of suits or challenges was greater but involved different circumstances, such as in West Virginia, where the Democrats got the government to do their work, or in secondary suits, with "citizen" challengers that just materialized, often with the help of Democratic firms.

129. Petition for a *Writ of Certiorari* at 3–4, *Nader v. Serody*, 543 U.S. 1052 (2005).

130. *Bullock v. Carter*, 405 U.S. 134, 149 (1972).

131. During the campaign, our researcher Steve Conn wrote as part of a larger piece: " 'In a recent edition of the *American Lawyer*, Reed Smith's DC based anti-trust specialist (and lobbyist) . . . crowed about a decision his firm's pro-bono committee made to remove Ralph Nader, from the Pennsylvania ballot. A dozen Reed Smith attorneys, including seven partners' (as of Oct. 1) [put in] 1,300 nonbillable hours on the fight. 'As Carlyn Kolker put it in *American Lawyer*, "[o]ver at Reed Smith, the project is billed as charity, although keeping Nader out of the election isn't quite feeding the poor or representing a death row inmate." Carlyn Kolker, "Anti-Nader Raiders: a Massive Pro Bono Effort Works to Block a Third Party Ballot Spot in the Keystone State," *American Lawyer*, Oct. 1, 2004.' "

132. Dennis B. Roddy and Tracie Mauriello, "E-mails Show How Dems Tied Staffers' Bonuses to Campaign Work," *Pittsburgh Post-Gazette*, Dec. 16, 2007 (*available at* www.post-gazette.com/pg/07350/842079-85.stm).

133. Presentment on file with author. *See also* Nader Complaint to the FEC, MUR 6021 (*available at* the close of the matter at fec.gov); *see, e.g.*, Angela Couloumbis, "Former Aide Implicates Top House Democrat in Bonusgate," *Inquirer* (Harrisburg Bureau), Oct. 8, 2008 (*available at* www.philly.com/philly/hp/news_update/20081008_Bonusgate_defendant_may_cooperate_with_authorities.html).

134. Eugenio Montale, *Collected Poems 1920–1954*, rev. bilingual ed., trans. and annotated Jonathan Galassi (New York: Farrar, Straus & Giroux, 2000), 47.

135. The only ACLU affiliates to give any response were the Atlanta ACLU affiliate, which was already conflicted because of a prior representation, and the Florida ACLU, which from the sidelines watched us struggle but showed some interest in the outcome.

136. *See* Katharine Q. Seelye, "Convictions Intact, Nader Soldiers On," *New York Times*, Aug. 2, 2004, A14 (describing polling efficacy of Republican money smear); Jonathan Finer and Brian Faler, "Nader Still Unsure of Ballot Spot in Many States," *Washington Post*, Aug. 24, 2004, A9 (citing that direct contributions as of late August show only 4 percent from those who also gave to Bush).

137. Eric M. Appleman, "Efforts to Stop Nader," (*available at* www.gwu.edu/action/2004/nader/antinader.html); *see, e.g.*, Up for Victory Press Release, "The New Nader Raiders: Latest FEC Reports Show More Evidence of GOP Support to Nader," Oct. 27, 2004 (*available at* www.commondreams.org/news2004/1027–06.htm). At most, they claimed to have found $125,000 of contributions that came from Republicans, including people that Ralph had long worked with like Jack and Laura Dangermond and Jeno and Lois Paulucci. Of course, this represented less than 4 percent of all the money we had raised, but the Democrats wanted to make hay out of this because it fit their poll-tested smear.

138. Prominent Democrats such as Barbra Streisand ($1,000), attorney William Lerach ($5,000), and Wes Boyd ($5,000), developer of MoveOn.org who even had dinner with Ralph in Connecticut, gave to the Progressive Unity Voter Fund. The Progressive Unity Voter Fund also got money from the American Federation of State, County and Municipal Employees (AFSCME) ($5,000); the Association of Trial Lawyers of America PAC ($5,000); MoveOn.org PAC ($5,000); SEIU Committee on Political Education ($5,000); and Planned Parenthood Action Fund PAC ($5,000). This group launched as "Ralph Don't Run" was set up initially by John Pearce, Kathy Cramer, and Paul Erskine. The strategic adviser was Gloria Totten of Progressive Majority. They changed, after Ralph announced, into "Don't Vote Ralph" and spent more than $8,000 at the end of October alone against Ralph, according to their Federal Election Commission filings.

139. The United Progressives for Victory group included Bob Brandon, Heather Booth, Bob Borosage, Deb Callahan, Peter Edelman, David Halperin, Roger Hickey, Liz Holtzman, Ginny Hunt, Patricia Ireland, Amy Isaacs, Toby Moffett, Karen Mulhauser, Ralph Neas, Bill Oldaker, Ellie Smeal, Gloria Steinem, and Gloria Totten, among others. Their main effort was to put out targeted statements by progressives, urging Ralph to drop out in late October.

140. Uniting People for Victory, IRS Form 8872, Report for period 7/21/2004 to 9/30/2004.

141. Uniting People for Victory, IRS Form 8872, Reports for periods throughout 2004.

142. Joanna Weiss, "Knocking Out Nader Becomes a Campaign, Democratic Activists Adopt Hard-line Tactics," *Boston Globe*, May 26, 2004, A3.

143. In their initial report to the IRS, the NaderFactor.com people show on their May 2004 expenditure statement that they started May 4 and that David Jones immediately paid himself $45,000 the next day, and Tricia Enright, $7,500, though she apparently resigned early on. They paid $10,000 for polling with Harstad Strategic Research, a Democratic/progressive firm, as early as May 5. They later paid $25,000 to Greenberg Research for more polling. They made some ads and got union money—mainly money that had been contributed to Americans for Jobs, Jones's prior vehicle (also including a lot of union money)—that was then rolled over into the National Progress Fund.

144. The Ballot Project, Inc., "527" Political Organization Filing Information (*available at* www.campaignmoney.com/political/527/the_ballot_project_inc.asp). Like United Progressives for Victory, the Ballot Project was also housed at 1730 Rhode Island Avenue, Suite 712. Its initial directors were William Oldaker, Ginny Hunt, and Tom Shakow. It in turn got money from Communications Workers of America–Committee on Political Education (CWA-COPE) ($25,000); Uniting People for Victory ($30,000); United Food and Commercial Workers (UFCW) ($25,000); and Max Palevsky ($25,000). Who works at 1730 Rhode Island Avenue,

Suite 712? That would be again Robert M. Brandon & Associates, a progressive public affairs firm claiming to be "working in the public interest." The Ballot Project, cochaired by former Nader Raiders and public officials Liz Holtzman and Toby Moffett, was recruiting lawyers to file challenges everywhere including Pennsylvania, North Carolina, and Illinois. Moffett admitted to the *Connecticut Post* that his effort to remove Ralph from the ballot was a "bare-knuckled" effort being "backed in part by Moffett's former employer, Monsanto CEO Bob Shapiro." Peter Urban, "Angry Dems battle to keep Nader off ballot," *Connecticut Post*, Aug. 15, 2004 (article in which Moffett identifies himself as a full-time volunteer with United Progressives for Victory). Monsanto? That would be the corporation of the genetically engineered and hormone-injected foods that Ralph and organizations he has founded have challenged.

145. Ballot Project, Inc., Form 8872 to the IRS lists Greenberg Research as an expenditure of $10,000 on 7/14/2004 for "consulting fees—political research."

146. Seelye, "Convictions Intact"; *see also* Urban, "Angry Dems."

147. Finer and Faler, "Nader Still Unsure of Ballot Spot," A9.

148. David Postman, "Nader Foes Seek Funding from Democratic Donors," *Seattle Times*, July 28, 2004, A1.

149. Seelye, "Convictions Intact."

150. Ibid.

151. Ibid. One can see how money flowed among these groups just from one report filed in 2005 after the election (when no one pays attention to these things). On the contributions side to Uniting People for Victory, in their IRS statement are the following donors: AFSCME ($2,500); Democratic National Committee ($10,000); and United Progressives for Victory ($2,289). Ballot Project, Inc. (which was loaned $30,000), gave $13,796; Grassroots Campaign, Inc., gave $5,000; National Education Association (NEA) Fund gave $3,000; CWA-COPE, PCC, gave $5,000; and lo and behold, Friends of John Kerry, Inc., gave $5,000. Brandon pulled out another $10,000 and Mulhauser another $5,000 in consulting fees for themselves in 2005.

152. D'Arcy, "Anti-Nader Forces Coordinate Strategy," A1.

153. Ibid.

154. Steve Terrell, "Fears of Nader Keep Dems on Offensive," *Santa Fe New Mexican*, July 29, 2004, A4.

155. Ibid.

156. Julian Borger, "Fasten Your Seatbelts," *Guardian (U.K.)*, Dec. 7, 2004 (*available at* www.guardian.co.uk/world/2004/dec/07/usa.uselections2004).

Chapter 5: The Courts and Third Parties: "Delphic," Hostile, and MIA

1. Richard Winger, "An Analysis of the 2004 Nader Ballot Access Federal Court Cases," *Fordham Urban Law Journal* 32 (2005): 567.

2. Ibid., 568.

3. Mark Brown, "Policing Ballot Access: Lessons from Nader's 2004 Run for President," *Capital University Law Review* 35 (2006): 231.

4. *See Deleeuw v. State Bd. of Canvassers*, 688 N.W.2d 847 (Mich. Ct. App. 2004), where the Michigan Court of Appeals granted our *writ of mandamus* to place Ralph Nader's name on the Michigan ballot as a presidential candidate. On February 8, 2008,

the federal court upheld the constitutionality of Hawaii's statute requiring more petition signatures for independent candidates than for new political parties and granted summary judgment to the state on the grounds that (1) the statute (HAW. REV. STAT. § 11-113 (2004)) does not violate the First Amendment, as Hawaii's statute is narrowly tailored and fulfills the compelling state interest of minimizing potential confusion on the ballot; and (2) Hawaii's statute does not violate the equal protection clause of the Fourteenth Amendment since the different requirements Hawaii imposes for placement on the general ballot between so-called new party candidates and independent candidates do not amount to invidious discrimination. The district court determined that while the plaintiffs failed under summary judgment, they could proceed to trial on the issue of whether the actions of the chief election official in, first, determining that the Peroutka/Baldwin campaign's petition did not contain the required number of signatures and, subsequently, serving as the hearing officer at the administrative hearing challenging the decision were improper. We argued that the officer was, in effect, reviewing his own previous decisions, but lost. (*See Nader v. Cronin*, 2008 WL336746 (D. Haw. 2008).) At publication, these decisions are on appeal.

5. *Williams v. Rhodes*, 393 U.S. 23 (1968); *Anderson v. Celebrezze*, 460 U.S. 567 (2000); Dmitri Evseev, "A Second Look at Third Parties: Correcting the Supreme Court's Understanding of Elections," *Boston University Law Review* 85 (2005): 1287 (citing Bradley A. Smith, "Judicial Protection of Ballot-Access Rights: Third Parties Need Not Apply," *Harvard Journal on Legislation* 28 [1991]: 187 [discussing the history of Supreme Court election law jurisprudence since *Jenness v. Fortson*, 403 U.S. 431 (1971)]).

6. Laurence H. Tribe, *American Constitutional Law*, 2d ed. (Mineola, NY: Foundation Press, 1988), 1106.

7. *See, e.g.*, Todd J. Zywicki, "Federal Judicial Review Of State Ballot Access Regulations: Escape From The Political Thicket," *Thurgood Marshall Law Review* (1994): 89 ("where the Supreme Court has intervened, its decisions have been essentially random, both with regards to the level of review to be applied, and with regard to how the various fact patterns are related").

8. Samuel Issacharoff and Richard H. Pildes, "Politics as Markets: Partisan Lockups of the Democratic Process," *Stanford Law Review* 50 (1998): 646 (citation omitted).

9. Evseev, "A Second Look at Third Parties," 1280–81.

10. Robert Barnes, "Roberts Supports Court's Shrinking Docket," *Washington Post*, Feb. 2, 2007, A6 (*available at* www.washingtonpost.com/wp-dyn/content/article/2007/02/01/AR2007020102213.html).

11. *Timmons v. Twin Cities Area New Party*, 520 U.S. 351, 358 (1997).

12. *Anderson v. Celebrezze*, 460 U.S. 780, 788 (1983).

13. *See* Richard L. Hasen, "Entrenching the Duopoly: Why the Supreme Court Should Not Allow the States to Protect the Democrats and Republicans from Political Competition," *Supreme Court Review* (1997): 347–50.

14. Evseev, "A Second Look at Third Parties," 1280 (case citations omitted).

15. Ibid.

16. Hasen, "Entrenching the Duopoly," 371.

17. Richard L. Hasen, *The Supreme Court and Election Law: Judging Equality from Baker v. Carr to Bush v. Gore* (New York: New York University Press, 2003), 12–13.

18. *Lubin v. Panish*, 415 U.S. 709, 716 (1974): "The right of a party or an individual to a place on a ballot is entitled to protection and is intertwined with the rights of voters." *Bullock v. Carter*, 405 U.S. 134, 143 (1972): "The rights of voters and the rights

of candidates do not lend themselves to neat separation; laws that affect candidates always have at least some theoretical, correlative effect on voters."

19. *Jenness*, 403 U.S. at 438.

20. According to Richard Winger, publisher of *Ballot Access News*, there were two independent candidates (1964, 1982) who succeeded under different deadlines and conditions, as have special election candidates where such petitioning requirements are not in play.

21. *Jenness*, 403 U.S. at 442.

22. *Gaffney v. Cummings*, 412 U.S. 735, 738 (1973).

23. Id. at 781 (Brennan, J., dissenting).

24. *Storer v. Brown*, 415 U.S. 724, 735 (1974).

25. Id. at 730 (citing *Dunn v. Bumstein*, 405 U.S. 330, 348 (1972)).

26. Id. at 756 (Brennan, J., dissenting).

27. Id. at 758.

28. *American Party of Texas v. White*, 415 U.S. 767, 780–81 (1974).

29. Id. at 798–99 (Douglas, J., dissenting).

30. *Munro v. Socialist Workers Party*, 479 U.S. 189, 196–97 (1986).

31. Richard Winger, "How Many Parties Ought to Be on the Ballot?: An Analysis of *Nader v. Keith*," *Election Law Journal* 5 (2006), Appendix C, 188.

32. Id. at 201 (Marshall, J., dissenting).

33. Id. at 202–3.

34. *Burdick v. Takushi*, 504 U.S. 428, 433 (1992).

35. Id. at 438.

36. Id. at 441.

37. Id. at 442 (Kennedy, J., dissenting).

38. Id. at 444.

39. *See generally* Peter H. Argersinger, "A Place on the Ballot: Fusion Politics and Antifusion Laws," *American Historical Review* 85 (1980): 287–306.

40. *Timmons*, 520 U.S. at 366–67.

41. Id. at 378 (Stevens, J., dissenting).

42. Id. at 384 (Souter, J., dissenting).

43. *Arkansas Educ. Television Comm'n v. Forbes*, 523 U.S. 666, 670 (1998).

44. Id.

45. Id. at 676.

46. Id.

47. Id. at 684–85 (Stevens, J., dissenting with Ginsburg, J., and Souter, J.).

48. *Clingman v. Beaver*, 544 U.S. 581, 594 (2005) (quoting brief for the Petitioners, citation omitted); *Tashjian v. Republican Party of Conn.*, 479 U.S. 208, 225 (1986).

49. *Clingman*, 544 U.S. at 599 (O'Connor, J., concurring in part and concurring in judgment).

50. Id. at 603.

51. Id.

52. Id. at 616–17 n.8 (Stevens, J., dissenting with Ginsburg, J., joining, and Souter, J., in Parts I, II, and III) (citing generally John Aldrich, *Why Parties? The Origin and Transformation of Political Parties in America* [Chicago: University of Chicago Press, 1995]).

53. Id. at 620 (Stevens, J., dissenting with Ginsburg, J., joining Part IV).

54. *Clements v. Fashing*, 457 U.S. 957 (1982).

55. *New York State Bd. of Elections et al. v. Lopez Torres et al.*, 128 S. Ct. 791 (2008).

56. Samuel Issacharoff, Pamela S. Karlan, and Richard H. Pildes, *The Law of Democracy: Legal Structure of the Political Process*, 3d ed. (New York: Foundation Press, 2007), 246.

57. Hasen, *The Supreme Court and Election Law*, 95.

58. Jamin B. Raskin, *Overruling Democracy: The Supreme Court vs. the American People* (New York: Routledge, 2003), 116.

59. *Lassiter v. Northampton County Bd. of Elections*, 360 U.S. 45 (1959).

60. United States Government Accountability Office, GA0-05-956 Elections, *Federal Efforts to Improve Security and Reliability of Electronic Voting Systems Are Under Way, But Key Activities Need to Be Completed*, Sept. 2005, 5–6.

61. The Appleseed Center for Electoral Reform and the Harvard Legislative Research Bureau, "A Model Act for the Democratization of Ballot Access," *Harvard Journal on Legislation* 36 (1999): 451.

62. Id. at 452–55.

63. *See, e.g.*, HR 2320 (1985); HR 1582 (1989); HR 1941 (2003) (the first two by Congressman John Conyers and covering all federal offices; the last by Congressman Ron Paul and applying to those running for the House of Representatives).

64. National Voter Registration Act of 1993 (NVRA), 42 U.S.C. §§ 1973gg-gg10.

65. *Oregon v. Mitchell*, 400 U.S. 112 (1970).

66. Help America Vote Act of 2002, HR 3295, 107th Cong. § 302(a) (2002).

67. *See* United States General Accounting Office GAO-01-470 Elections, *The Scope of Congressional Authority in Election Administration*, Mar. 2001.

68. One added benefit of a uniform law could be to make it easier for absentee and military ballots to be timely disbursed across the country, free from petition signature litigation.

69. Alexander Keyssar, "Reform and an Evolving Electorate," *New York Times* on the Web, Aug. 5, 2001 (*available at* http://query.nytimes.com/gst/fullpage.html?res=9E02EFDA123CF936A3575BCOA9679C8B63).

70. *See* John C. Culver and John Hyde, *American Dreamer: The Life and Times of Henry A. Wallace* (New York: W.W. Norton, 2000).

Chapter 6: Regulations, Regulations: Beware of the Code

1. Editorial, "Replace the FEC," *Washington Post*, May 18, 2002, 22.

2. Federal Election Commission, *Performance and Accountability Report*, Fiscal Year 2007, 1 (hereafter cited as *PAR*) (*available at* www.fec.gov/pages/budget/fy2007/par_2007.pdf).

3. Interview with Anton E. Reel III, executive assistant to former Vice-Chairman Michael E. Toner, Nov. 30, 2005, at the FEC (hereafter cited as Reel interview).

4. 11 C.F.R. § 110.11(a)(1) (2006).

5. 11 C.F.R. § 110.11 (c)(2)(ii) & (iii) (2006).

6. 11 C.F.R. § 110.11(c)(3) & (4) (2006).

7. *See, e.g.*, 11 C.F.R. § 114.4 (c)(7) (2006).

8. *See, e.g.*, 11 C.F.R. § 110.20 (2006).

9. *See, e.g.*, 11 C.F.R. § 102.9(d) (2006).

10. I had called to ask about something I saw another grassroots campaign doing, thinking it was a good idea and that we should try it; but my questions were about the legality. I saw the idea on another candidate's Web site and asked if it was okay. The

information specialist told me that what the campaign did was not really kosher. That shut that idea down, much to the frustration of some campaign supporters.

11. Reel interview.

12. *PAR* at 1.

13. Federal Election Commission Strategic Plan FY 2008–2013, Federal Election Commission, 1 (*available at* www.fec.gov/pages/budget/fy2009/FECStrategicPlan 2008–2013.pdf). Even with all this information, however, problems and gaps still exist. For example, POGO, the Program on Government Oversight, put out a report in 2001 that showed how some things just don't add up in all the disclosures, and there doesn't seem to be an easy way to reconcile them. One of POGO's main examples was the glaring discrepancy between what PACs reported giving to candidates for Congress and what candidates in the House and Senate reported as having received from PACs. According to POGO, looking only at incumbents, these discrepancies were more than $12 million of PAC money given but not reported as received in just one election cycle. Indeed, POGO reported that only six incumbent candidates (out of the entire Congress) matched up in both databases regarding donated PAC monies and received PAC monies. *See generally* "At the Federal Election Commission Things Don't Add Up," Project on Government Oversight (POGO), Mar. 28, 2001 (*available at* www.pogo.org).

14. *Buckley v. Valeo*, 424 U.S. 1 (1976).

15. J. David Gillespie, *Politics at the Periphery: Third Parties in Two-Party America* (Columbia: University of South Carolina Press, 1993), 32 (citing *Buckley v. Valeo*, 424 U.S. 1 (1976)).

16. *NAACP v. Alabama ex rel. Patterson*, 357 U.S. 449 (1958).

17. Regular audits are not likely for other political committees; most of them will never get audited as there are only about 40 auditors and they are consumed with the presidential audits.

This wasn't always the case. Once upon a time the FEC would conduct random audits of congressional committee campaigns; Congress put a stop to that and curtailed the time frame in which any audit could be conducted by eliminating the budget for random audits and starving the audit division of staff. Even today there may be only up to fifty nonpresidential audits, up from ten or fifteen in the 1980s and 1990s, but the number of committees has doubled. Reel interview.

That represents an audit of only about one-half of 1 percent of all the committees filing. Still, in each category of committee—candidates committees, corporate PACs, union PACs, political party PACs, unconnected PACs—someone will get audited. This is *an improvement* in randomness over years past when only the most heinous violators got audited. Back then, if you were only wantonly noncompliant, your committee could skate. The recent Administrative Dispute Program and the automatic fines program have helped the FEC bring into compliance small but persistent violators who before thought that they were too small to get the notice of any FEC employee.

18. *PAR* at 9. If a campaign still has debt or possible outstanding payments to make, a committee can't be terminated, except with special permission. In 2008, the Reform Party of 2000 is still waging those battles with the FEC. The Buchanan 2000 committee is still reporting on its debts from the 2000 campaign. In 2004, even though we finished the audit early, we had debts to repay and ongoing litigation, so we too were still open years after the fact.

19. Harry Browne, *The Great Libertarian Offer* (Great Falls, MT: Liam Works, 2000), 24.

20. Steven J. Rosenstone, Roy L. Behr, and Edward H. Lazarus, *Third Parties in America*, 2d ed. (Princeton, NJ: Princeton University Press, 1996), 25–26.

21. Ibid., 26.

22. Editorial, "Big Decal, Why is the FEC Wasting Time on Bumper Stickers?" *Washington Post*, Dec. 29, 2006, A26; Bradley Smith, "The Speech Police," *Wall Street Journal*, June 27, 2007 (*available at* http://online.wsj.com/article/SB118290892610549503.html?mod=Letters).

23. Smith, "The Speech Police."

24. Ibid.

25. Ibid.

26. *See* "Federal Election Commission Makes Legislative Recommendations," FEC News Release, Apr. 12, 2007 (*available at* www.fec.gov/press/press2007/20070412meeting.shtml). (The FEC-recommended higher expenditure level for individuals is probably still too low at $1,000.)

27. In the last few election cycles, the only one has been Ralph Nader.

28. The IRS has said as much with a clarification of its definition of permissible business activity that does not constitute political intervention by a nonprofit. *See* IRS, Fact Sheet "Election Year Activities and the Prohibition on Political Campaign Intervention for Section 501(c)(3) Organizations," FS-2006-17, Feb. 2006 (*available at* www.irs.gov/newsroom).

29. James V. Grimaldi, "Nader Had Campaign Office at Charity," *Washington Post*, A1, June 13, 2004.

30. Editorial, "Who Is CREW?" *TheHill.com*, Mar. 30, 2005 (*available at* http://thehill.com/editorials/who-is-crew-2005-03-30.html). CREW's board, filled with Democrats, including Bill and Hillary Clinton's former pollster Mark Penn and other major donors to the Democrats or their allies, seems to file nearly all of their complaints against Republicans or "Democratic irritants." *See* Brody Mullins, "In Washington, Watchdogs Bear Watching, One of DeLay's Severest Critics Isn't as Nonpartisan as It Purports to Be," *Wall Street Journal*, May 10, 2008. Mullins quotes its executive director Melanie Sloan as saying, "Since I started, the main thing I wanted to do was to go after Tom DeLay. . . . DeLay is my top target." This is not necessarily a bad mission, but ask, is such a mission appropriate for a supposedly nonpartisan, nonprofit 501(c)(3) watchdog organization?; Complaint by CREW, MUR 5475, *available at* www.fec.gov.

31. Complaint by CREW, Count I, MUR 5489, *available at* www.fec.gov (for FEC resolutions, *see* www.fec.gov enforcement query system).

32. MUR 5489, Complaint dated July 20, 2004, at para 9.

33. Id. at para 14. Jeff Mapes, "Nader Getting Support From Unlikely Voters," *Oregonian*, June 25, 2004, A1.

34. *See* www.fec.gov, MUR 5475, certification 02/10/2005; and MUR 5489, 5581, 5513, 5533, certification 06/23/2005.

35. *See* www.fec.gov, MUR 5581, certification 04/21/2006.

36. Jeffrey H. Birnbaum, "Election Commissioner Is a Lonely Voice," *Washington Post*, Oct. 3, 2005, D1 (*available at* www.washingtonpost.com/wpdyn/content/article/2005/10/02/AR2005100201585.html).

37. Center for Public Integrity, "527s in 2004 Shatter Previous Records for Political Fundraising," Dec. 16, 2004 (*available at* www.publicintegrity.org/527/report.aspx ? aid=435).

38. Ibid.

39. Editorial, "Finally 527s," *Washington Post*, Dec. 18, 2006 (*available at* www.washingtonpost.com/wp-dyn/content/article/2006/12/17/AR2006121700684.html); *see also* Helen Dewar, "Bill Would Curb '527' Spending, No Action Expected Before Elections," *Washington Post*, Sept. 23, 2004, A27 (*available at* www.washingtonpost.com/wp-dyn/articles/A43103-2004Sep22.html).

40. *Shays-Mechan v. FEC*, Civ. No. 04-1597, March 29, 2006. *See* Kate Phillips, "Election Panel Won't Issue Donation Rules," *New York Times*, June 1, 2006 (*available at* www.nytimes.com/2006/06/01/washington/01fec.html?_r=1&oref=slogin).

41. Kate Phillips, "Settlements Including Fines Are Reached in Election Finance Cases of Three Groups," *New York Times*, Dec. 14, 2006, A26 (*available at* www.nytimes.com/2006/12/14/us/politics/14fec.html). *See also* Editorial, "Finally 527s," *Washington Post*, Dec. 18, 2006. In 2007, the FEC settled with Progress for America Voter Fund for $750,000 for failure "to register and file disclosure reports as a Federal political committee" and accepting "contributions in violation of Federal limits and source prohibitions." (FEC Press Release Feb. 28, 2007); the FEC also settled with the Soros- and Lewis-backed America Coming Together and Media Fund, for $775,000 and $580,000, respectively, "for expenses that should have been paid with funds raised within the federal contribution limits and prohibitions" (FEC Press Release dated Aug. 29, 2007) and for failure "to register and file disclosure reports as a federal political committee and knowingly accepted contributions in violation of federal limits and source prohibitions" (FEC Press Release dated Nov. 19, 2007).

42. Birnbaum, "Election Commissioner Is a Lonely Voice," D1, quoting Lawrence M. Noble.

43. Testimony of Donald J. Simon, Carter-Baker Commission on Federal Election Reform, June 30, 2005, 2 (citing a *Washington Post* editorial).

44. Birnbaum, "Election Commissioner is a Lonely Voice," A1 (quoting Scott E. Thomas).

45. Testimony of Donald J. Simon, Carter-Baker Commission on Federal Election Reform, June 18, 2005. (But at least one employee I spoke with at the FEC noted that about 94 percent of the FEC's decisions are majority decisions, not 3–3 splits, and that within the 3–3 splits half of those are not along party lines.)

46. "FEC Assessed a Record $6.2 Million in Penalties in 2006," *Washington Post*, Dec. 29, 2006 (quoting Fred Wertheimer, Democracy 21).

47. Simon Testimony, June 18, 2005, at 2.

48. Campaign Finance Institute, "So the Voters May Choose . . . Reviving the Presidential Matching Fund System," Apr. 2005, 8–17 (*available at* www.cfinst.org (proposing a three-to-one match on the first $100 of donations from donors, which is a great incentive, but then only permitting this match for qualified candidates, requiring them to raise five times as much in any state to be able to qualify—a criterion likely to disqualify nearly all third-party and independent candidates).

49. Ibid., 21.

50. Spencer A. Overton, "The Donor Class: Campaign Finance, Democracy and Participation," *University of Pennsylvania Law Review* 153 (2004): 102–5.

51. Glen Justice, "Concerns Grow About Role of Interest Groups in Elections," *New York Times*, Mar. 9, 2005 (quoting Senator McCain, who went on to say that "that should alarm every federally elected member of Congress"). *See also* Morton Mintz, "Corporate Campaign Finance Elephant," *Progressive Populist*, June 15, 2007, at 17 (suggesting questions for U.S. Supreme Court nominees regarding campaign finance, corporations, and political speech).

52. Jeffrey Rosen, "The Right to Spend: Has the Age of Campaign-Finance Reform Come to an End?" *New York Times Magazine*, July 8, 2007, 11 (*available at* www.nytimes.com/2007/07/08/magazine/08wwln-lede-t.html).

53. The Center for Public Integrity, the Center for Responsive Politics, the National Institute on Money in State Politics, "State Secrets: A Joint Investigation of Political Party Money in the States," June 25, 2002.

54. Conversely, third parties historically have been more receptive to women candidates. *See* Kathleen A. Dolan, *Voting for Women* (Boulder, CO: Westview Press, 2004), 32–33.

Chapter 7: The Corporate Fourth Estate

1. Robert F. Kennedy Jr., "Was the 2004 Election Stolen?" *Rolling Stone*, June 15, 2006, quoting MSNBC news anchor Keith Olbermann.

2. Joe Klein, *Politics Lost: How American Democracy Was Trivialized by People Who Think You're Stupid* (New York: Doubleday, 2006), 21 (recounting a conversation with Bob Shrum in which he discussed Harry Truman's 1948 nomination acceptance speech referencing Turnip Day in Missouri).

3. "Number of Acceptable Things Candidates Can Say Now Down to Four," *Onion*, Issue 44.19, May 12–18, 2008.

4. Andrew Gumbel, *Steal This Vote: Dirty Elections and the Rotten History of Democracy in America* (New York: Nation Books, 2005), 317.

5. Eric Boehlert, "The Pelosi Smear: Stupid—But Kind of Entertaining," Media Matters for America, Feb. 13, 2007 (*available at* http://mediamatters.org/columns/200702130007) (emphasis in original).

6. Ibid.

7. Michael Kinsley, "Electio ad Absurdum," *Washington Post*, Oct. 31, 2004, B7 (*available at* www.washingtonpost.com/wp-dyn/articles/A10802-2004Oct29.html).

8. Steven Hill, *Fixing Elections: The Failure of America's Winner Take All Politics* (New York: Routledge, 2002), 190.

9. Howard Kurtz, "The Candidate's 'Catch Me If You Can': Reporters Following Hillary Clinton on the Campaign Trail Are Covered in Dust," *Washington Post*, Nov. 30, 2007 (*available at* www.washingtonpost.com/wp-dyn/content/article/2007/11/29/AR2007112902165.html).

10. *See* Luciano Rebay, ed., *Introduction to Italian Poetry* (New York: Dover Publications, 1991), 75.

11. *See, e.g.*, Robert Roth, *A Reason to Vote: Breaking the Two-Party Stranglehold—and the Remarkable Rise of America's Fastest Growing New Political Party: The Natural Law Party* (New York: St. Martin's Griffin, 1999), 13.

12. Dana Milbank, "My Bias for Mainstream News," *Washington Post*, Mar. 20, 2005, B1, B3 (*available at* www.washingtonpost.com/wp-dyn/articles/A48952-2005Mar19.html).

13. Leonard Downie Jr., "A Strict Separation," *Washington Post*, Oct. 27, 2004, A25 (*available at* www.washingtonpost.com/wp-dyn/articles/A706-2004Oct26.html).

14. *See* Howard Kurtz, "For the Candidates, Not Just Any Brand of Soapbox Will Do," *Washington Post*, Aug. 13, 2007 (*available at* www.washingtonpost.com/wp-dyn/content/article/2007/08/12/AR2007081201201.html).

15. Ibid.

16. Peter Hart, "Clear the Stage: Media Have Little Time, Tolerance for 'Second-Tier' Candidates," *Extra!*, July–Aug. 2007, quoting Howard Kurtz (*available at* www.fair.org/index.php?page=3148).

17. Ibid.

18. Ibid.

19. Clarence Page, "Ron Paul Big on 'Net, But Media Don't Notice," *Chicago Tribune*, Aug. 8, 2007, 25 (*available at* http://archives.chicagotribune.com/2007/aug/08/opinion/chi-oped0808pageaug08); *see also* FAIR Media Advisory, "More than a Two-Person Race, Corporate Media Largely Ignores Other Presidential Candidates," Oct. 21, 2008 (*available at* www.fair.org/index.php?page=363) (discussing media's "refusal to open up the political conversation").

20. Hart, "Clear the Stage."

21. John F. Bibby and L. Sandy Maisel, *Two Parties—or More?: The American Party System*, 2d ed. (Boulder, CO: Westview Press, 2003), 22.

22. As cited in Roth, *A Reason to Vote*, 12.

23. Alan Keyes, "Elections, Media, and Money, Part 3 of the Crisis of the Republic," Renew America, May 9, 2007 (emphasis in original) (*available at* www.keyesarchives.com/crisis/070509.php).

24. Clark Hoyt, "The Campaign and the Horse Race," *New York Times*, Nov. 18, 2007, 14 (*available at* www.nytimes.com/2007/11/18/opinion/18pubed.html?partner=rssnyt&emc=rss), citing the Project for Excellence in Journalism and the Joan Shorenstein Center on the Press, Politics and Public Policy, Harvard University.

25. Editorial, "Mr. Nader's Misguided Crusade," *New York Times*, June 30, 2000. *See also* Editorial, "Mr. Nader's Electoral Mischief," *New York Times*, Oct. 26, 2000; Editorial, "Al Gore in the Home Stretch," *New York Times*, Nov. 3, 2000; Editorial, "The Power of the Undecideds," *New York Times*, Nov. 5, 2000. In the 2008 race, the *New York Times* would keep it up with Eleanor Randolph writing in the Editorial Notebook, "Ralph Nader: Going, Going, Not Gone," Feb. 26, 2008 (*available at* www.nytimes.com/2008/02/26/opinion/26tue4.html?_r=1&oref=slogin): "The real question about Ralph Nader's political nadir is this: are we there yet?"; Jim Naureckas, "Nader and the Press: Condescension Turns Nasty," *Extra*!, Oct. 2000 (*available at* www.fair.org/index.php?page=1047).

26. Howard Kurtz, "Four . . . More . . . Years? The Left Contemplates the Unthinkable," *Washington Post*, Oct. 25, 2004, C1, C3.

27. Daniel Okrent, "Is the New York Times a Liberal Paper?" *New York Times*, July 25, 2004.

28. Daniel Okrent, "How Would Jackson Pollock Cover This Campaign?" *New York Times*, Oct. 10, 2004.

29. Eric Boehlert, "What Haircut Stories Tell Us About the Press," *Progressive Populist*, June 1, 2007, 20 (reprinted from http://mediamatters.org).

30. Brian Boyd, news analyst, *Esquire's 'Monica's View' of Bill; CBS's Clayson Pleaded for Nader to Drop Out; NBC's Prime Time Drama Advanced Gore's Agenda*," Media Research Center, October 30, 2000, 5: 219. CyberAlert Extra (*available at* www.mrc.org/cyberalerts/2000/cyb20001030_extra.asp).

31. Ibid.

32. Stephen J. Farnsworth and S. Robert Lichter, *The Nightly News Nightmare: Network Television's Coverage of U.S. Presidential Elections, 1988–2000* (Lanham, MD: Rowman & Littlefield, 2007), 81.

33. Roth, *A Reason to Vote*, 11–12.

34. Roger Cohn, "Editor's Note," *Mother Jones*, May–June 2000, 4.

35. Thomas E. Patterson, *The Vanishing Voter: Public Involvement in an Age of Uncertainty* (citation omitted) (New York: Knopf, 2002), 168.

36. Farnsworth and Lichter, *The Nightly News Nightmare*, 80.

37. Ibid., 83.

38. Campaign Legal Center, Media Policy Program, FAQ about "Our Democracy, Our Airwaves Act" (*available at* www.campaignlegalcenter.org/attachments/1435.pdf).

39. Christopher Drew, "Democrats Try to Rein in Fees on Consulting," *New York Times*, Dec. 25, 2007, A1.

40. Ibid.

41. *See* William G. Hillsman, *Run the Other Way: Fixing the Two-Party System, One Campaign at a Time* (New York: Free Press, 2004), 184.

42. Erika Falk and Sean Aday, "Are Voluntary Standards Working? Candidate Discourse on Network Evening News Programs," Annenberg Public Policy Center, University of Pennsylvania, Dec. 20, 2000, 4 (Table 2: Average Amount of Candidate-Centered Discourse per Night) (*available at* www.annenbergpublicpolicycenter.org).

43. Hill, *Fixing Elections*, 180–82.

44. Paul Taylor, "TV's Political Profits," *Mother Jones*, May–June 2000, 31.

45. National Association of Broadcasters, Wirthlin Worldwide, the Association of RTNDA Electronic Journalists, "Nationwide Poll Finds Broad Voter Approval of Broadcast Election Coverage," Press Release, Oct. 30, 2002.

46. Annenberg Public Policy Center of the University of Pennsylvania, "Legislative Issue Advertising in the 108th Congress," Mar. 2005, 3 (*available at* www.annenbergpublicpolicycenter.org/Downloads/Political_Communication/LegIssueAds108Congree/Report_IssueAds108thCongressMarch2005.pdf).

47. Candidates are supposed to be charged the "lowest unit charge," but this rate can be trumped by anyone paying full freight that comes along and wants to advertise in the candidate's time slot. A free airtime bill would prohibit that trumping so that candidates do not have to pay the full freight to be absolutely assured they will not have their ads bumped. The bill would have the broadcast companies accept the vouchers as cash, then turn them over to the FCC for cash. *See* Campaign Legal Center, describing "S. 1497: Our Democracy, Our Airwaves Act" of 2003, introduced but never passed, *available at* www.campaignlegalcenter.org. The organization absorbed the prior Alliance for Better Campaigns and provides multiple fact sheets describing how this could work.

48. The Annenberg Public Policy Center, "Internet as Political Information Tool Popular, But Television Still Dominates, Annenberg Survey Finds," News Release, Mar. 28, 2008 (89% of adults get presidential race information from broadcast or cable television). *See also* Froma Harrop, "If Young Citizens Voted," *Progressive Populist*, June 1, 2007, 6 (only 15 percent of the eighteen- to twenty-nine-year-old set read newspapers regularly anyway; a full 26 percent of them "get their news from Comedy Central's *The Daily Show* or *The Colbert Report*").

49. Mark Crispin Miller, "None Dare Call It Stolen: Ohio, the Election, and America's Servile Press," *Harper's Magazine*, Aug. 2005, 39–40.

50. Mark Crispin Miller, *Fooled Again: The Real Case for Electoral Reform* (New York: Basic Books, 2007), 202.

51. Nicholas D. Kristof, "No More Sham Elections," *New York Times*, Nov. 20, 2004.

Chapter 8: "The Debate Commission Sucks"

1. As transcribed in Institute of Politics at Harvard University, ed., *Campaign for President: The Managers Look at 2000* (Hollis, NH: Hollis, 2002), 162.

2. Ibid., 167.

3. Ibid., 166.

4. Ibid., 169.

5. Ibid., 170.

6. 11 C.F.R. § 110.13 (2005) provides:

> (b) Debate structure. The structure of debates staged in accordance with this section and *11 CFR 114.4(f)* is left to the discretion of the staging organization(s), provided that:
> (1) Such debates include at least two candidates; and
> (2) The staging organization(s) does not structure the debates to promote or advance one candidate over another.
>
> (c) Criteria for candidate selection. For all debates, staging organization(s) must use pre-established objective criteria to determine which candidates may participate in a debate. For general election debates, staging organization(s) shall not use nomination by a particular political party as the sole objective criterion to determine whether to include a candidate in a debate. For debates held prior to a primary election, caucus or convention, staging organizations may restrict candidate participation to candidates seeking the nomination of one party, and need not stage a debate for candidates seeking the nomination of any other political party or independent candidates.

7. George Farah, *No Debate: How the Two Major Parties Secretly Ruin the Presidential Debates* (New York: Seven Stories Press, 2004), 6–10.

8. Ibid., 9–10.

9. Ibid., appendix B (reprinting News from the . . . Democratic and Republican National Committees Press Release, "RNC and DNC Establish Commission on Presidential Debates," Feb. 18, 1987). *See also* Newton N. Minow and Craig L. Lamay, "Inside the Presidential Debates," 74 (Chicago: University of Chicago Press, 2008) (claiming bipartisan beginnings with nonpartisan rules) (emphasis added).

10. Farah, *No Debate*.

11. Ibid., 33 (quoting Nancy Neuman, former president of the League of Women Voters, explaining their withdrawal of the sponsorship of the debates whose terms were dictated by the two parties in 1988).

12. Deposition of Frank J. Fahrenkopf Jr., co-chair of the CPD, Dec. 5, 2001, at 18, lines 10–14, attached as Exhibit 3 to the complaint filed on Feb. 11, 2004, before The Honorable Henry H. Kennedy Jr., *Hagelin et al. v. FEC*, 332 F. Supp. 2d 71 (D.D.C. 2004), and taken in the matter of *Nader v. Comm'n on Presidential Debates et al.*, Case No. 00-12145-WEY (D. Mass. 2000).

13. Id. at 19, lines 8–11.

14. Id., lines 14–17.

15. Farah, *No Debate*, 57–58 (citing John F. Kennedy School of Government Institute of Politics, *Campaign for President: The Managers Look at '96*, ed. David Broder [Hollis, NH: Hollis, 1997], 162).

16. In 2000, seven candidates, including Ralph Nader, John Hagelin, Pat Buchanan, Howard Phillips, and Harry Browne, would have all been mathematically eligible to win the election.

17. *Larry King Live*, "Buchanan and Nader Discuss Their Political Agendas," transcript of Oct. 2, 2000 *(available at* http://transcripts.com/TRANSCRIPTS/0010/02/lkl.00.html).

18. In 1997, even the then–FEC counsel Lawrence Noble argued, in a thirty-seven-page memorandum, that the "nonpartisanship" of the CPD was worthy of investigation. His call was rejected, 6 to 0, by the Democrats and Republicans of the FEC. *See* Farah, *No Debate*, 7.

19. Ibid., 72 (citing George Stephanopoulos and William Daley, Gore's campaign chairman—interviews with the author in 2001).

20. Mark Shields, on jacket cover of Ralph Nader's *Crashing the Party: Taking on the Corporate Governments in an Age of Surrender* (New York, St. Martin's Press: 2002).

21. 11 C.F.R. § 110.13(a)(1) (2006) provides: "Nonprofit organizations described in 26 U.S.C. 501(c) (3) or (c) (4) and which do not endorse, support, or oppose political candidates or political parties may stage candidate debates in accordance with this section and 11 CFR 114.4 (f)." 11 C.F.R. § 114.4 (f)(1) (2006) provides that "a nonprofit organization described in 11 CFR 100.13(a)(1) may use its own funds and may accept funds donated by corporations or labor organizations under paragraph (f)(3) of this section to defray costs incurred in staging candidate debates held in accordance with 11 CFR 100.13."

22. *Chevron U.S.A. Inc. v. Natural Resources Defense Council, Inc.*, 467 U.S. 837 (1984).

23. *See Becker v. FEC*, 112 F. Supp. 2d 172 (D. Mass. 2000).

24. *Becker v. FEC*, 230 F.3d 381 (1st Cir. 2000), *cert. denied sub. nom. Nader v. FEC*, 532 U.S. 1007 (2001).

25. *Id.* at 397.

26. *John Hagelin et al. v. Federal Election Commission*, 411 F.3d 237, 239 (D.C. Cir. 2005) (citing *FEC v. Democratic Senatorial Campaign Comm.*, 454 U.S. 27, 37 [1981] [citations omitted]).

27. *See* Ann Bartow, "Likelihood of Confusion," *San Diego Law Review* 41 (2004): 809–10 n.315 (citing Mark Hamblett, "Judge Backs Nader's Parody of MasterCard Ad," *New York Law Journal*, Sept. 13, 2000).

28. *MasterCard Int'l v. Nader 2000 Primary Committee, Inc. et al.*, 70 U.S.P.Q.2d 146 (2004).

29. The Honorable Jesse Jackson Jr., Press Release, "Open Presidential Debates Energize Electoral Process" (*available at* www.jessejacksonjr.org/query/crendpr.cgi?id="001500"), July 28, 2000.

30. Deposition of Mr. Lewis Loss, Washington, D.C. General Counsel to the CPD, dated Oct. 25, 2001, at 57, lines 19–22, attached as Exhibit 2 to the complaint filed on Feb. 11, 2004, before the Honorable Henry H. Kennedy Jr., *Hagelin et al. v. FEC*, 332 F. Supp. 2d 71 (D.D.C. 2004) and taken in the matter of *Nader v. Comm'n on Presidential Debates*, Case No. 00-12145-WEY (D. Mass. 2000).

31. Deposition of Frank J. Fahrenkopf, Jr., Dec. 5, 2001, at 42, lines 15–17.

32. Oct. 25, 2001, deposition of Mr. Lewis Loss, at 50, lines 10–13.

33. From the recollections of a conversation George Farah had with Dan Beckman on Oct. 16, 2000.

34. Ibid.

35. Email from Fred Volkmann, the vice-chancellor for public affairs at Washington University in St. Louis, Oct. 23, 2000, on file with author.

36. In Massachusetts, there is a civil rights law, called the Massachusetts Civil Rights Act (MCRA), that permits a civil action "[w]henever any person whether or not acting under color of law, interfere[s] by threats, intimidation or coercion, or attempt[s] to interfere by threats, intimidation or coercion with the exercise of enjoyment by any person . . . of rights secured by the Constitution or laws of the United States" or the commonwealth of Massachusetts. MASS. GEN. LAWS Ch. 12 § 11(H) & (I) (West 2008). We filed under both Massachusetts law and the Federal Civil Rights Act, 42 U.S.C. § 1983.

37. The court did grant summary judgment for state police officer McPhail.

38. *Buchanan v. FEC*, 112 F. Supp. 2d 58, 72–73 (D.D.C. 2000).

39. MUR 5378 (*available at* http://eqs.sdrdc.com/eqsdocs/000012C2.pdf).

40. Federal Election Commission Certification, In the Matter of John Hagelin; Ralph Nader; Patrick Buchanan; Howard Phillips; Winona LaDuke; Natural Law Party; Green Party of the United States; Constitution Party, dated March 18, 2004 (*available at* www.fec.gov).

41. *Hagelin*, at 80.

42. "Candidates Arrested at Debate: Libertarian, Green Party Nominees Tried to Serve Commission," *WorldNetDaily.com*, Oct. 9, 2004 (*available at* www.worldnetdaily.com/news/article.asp?ARTICLE_ID=40843).

43. *See, e.g.*, Chuck Todd and Nicholas Felton, "Clocking the Candidates," *New York Times*, Dec. 28, 2007, A23 (*available at* www.nytimes.com/2007/12/28/opinion/28todd.html).

44. In 1992, when Perot was included, 100 million people watched the network debates. In 1996, when he was excluded, the network audience dropped to 42 million.

45. Thomas E. Patterson, *The Vanishing Voter: Public Involvement in an Age of Uncertainty* (New York: Knopf, 2002), 15, 165.

46. Lisa De Moraes, "'West Wing' Candidates to Face Off in Live Debate," *Washington Post*, Oct. 15, 2005, C1, C7 (*available at* www.washingtonpost.com/wp-dyn/content/article/2005/10/14/AR2005101401982.html).

47. Alessandra Stanley, "Voting Rights Drive 'Idol,' Not the Abuse or the Hair," *New York Times*, Apr. 4, 2007, B1 (*available at* www.nytimes.com/2007/04/04/arts/television/04watc.html?_r=18&oref=slogin).

48. *See* Clarence Page, "Idol Minds of American Voters," *Chicago Tribune*, May 28, 2006, 7 (citing stats from Committee for the Study of the American Electorate, www.broadcastingcable.com, Scripps Howard News Service, and Washington-based Pursuant Inc.).

49. Ibid.

50. David S. Broder, "Open Up the Debates," *Washington Post*, Sept. 30, 2004, A25 (*available at* www.washingtonpost.com/wp-dyn/articles/A60972-2004Sep29.html).

51. Norman J. Ornstein, "Moderation in Excess," *Wall Street Journal*, Apr. 3, 2007 (*available at* www.aei.org/publications/filter.foreign,pubID.25887/pub_detail.asp).

52. Marvin Kalb, "Nine Ways to Elect a President," *New York Times*, May 5, 2007 (*available at* www.nytimes.com/2007/05/05/opinion/05kalb.html).

Chapter 9: One Person, One Vote. Or Maybe None. Or Maybe Two.

1. Editorial, "In Search of Accurate Vote Totals," *New York Times*, Sept. 5, 2006 (*available at* www.nytimes.com/2006/09/05/opinion/05tue1.html). *See also* Christopher Drew, "Overhaul Plan for Vote System Will Be Delayed," (July 20, 2007) (describing Congressional Democrats caving to local pressure and delaying sweeping changes until *2012*!) (*available at* www.nytimes.com/2007/07/20/washington/20vote.html).

2. *See* Jo Becker and David Finkel, "Now They're Registered, Now They're Not; Election Officials Express Dismay at Extent of Misinformation, Variety of Tricks Targeting Voters," *Washington Post*, Oct. 31, 2004, A22: describing fliers telling Democrats to vote "on Wednesday" or coming from the bogus "Milwaukee Black Voters League" targeting black neighborhoods and saying, "If you've already voted in any election this year, you can't vote in the presidential election" and "If you violate any of these laws, you can get ten years in prison and your children will get taken away from you." "In South Carolina, Charleston County election officials warned voters Friday to ignore a fake letter that purports to be from the NAACP. The letter threatens voters who have outstanding parking tickets or have failed to pay child support with arrest" (*available at* www.washingtonpost.com/wp-dyn/articles/A12514-2004Oct30.html). *See also* John Harwood, "Block the Vote; as a Final Gambit, Parties Are Trying to Damp Turnout," *Wall Street Journal*, Oct. 27, 2004, A1: "Voter suppression is 'a dirty little secret,' says Shanto Iyengar, a Stanford political scientist who believes that negative campaign information damps turnout. 'Both campaigns' rhetoric is being tailored to peel off the weak layers of would-be opponents. It's much easier to get those voters not to turn out than to switch over to your guy.'" And at A12: "In Ohio, Republicans plan to place recruits inside polling places to challenge the credentials of voters they consider suspicious . . ." (*available at* http://pcl.stanford.edu/press/2004/wsj-block.html). *See also* Bob Fitrakis and Harvey Wasserman, "Twelve Ways Bush Is Now Stealing the Ohio Vote," *Free Press*, Oct. 27, 2004: "*The Columbus Dispatch* (which has endorsed Bush) and WVKO Radio have both documented phone calls from people impersonating Board of Elections workers and directing registered voters to different and incorrect polling sites."

3. The Illinois Campaign for Political Reform's Web site (*available at* www.ilcampaign.org/issues/campaign_finance/index.asp) states: "Illinois is widely considered the wild west of campaign finance. No other state has quite the same combination of unregulated, unsupported political campaigns as the Land of Lincoln. Candidates in Illinois, from dog catcher on up to governor, are free to take as much money from whomever will give it to them—state vendors, state employees, regulated professionals and businesses, lobbyists, corporations, unions, trade associations, foreign nationals. Nor does Illinois offer any substantial public support—in the form of public financing, tax deductions or credits for small contributions, voters guides, or the like—to help candidates or parties to opt out of the special interest rat race."

4. Peggy Boyer Long, "Ethics Seem to Be on the Agenda. But, Remember, Our Roster of Political Scoundrels Dates to Statehood," *Illinois Issues OnLine*, June 2003 (*available at* http://illinoisissues.uis.edu/editor/ethics.html).

5. Dennis Byrne, "The Sorry State of Illinois," *Chicago Tribune*, Apr. 23, 2006, 7. The three governors were Dan Walker (D) after he left office, Otto Kerner (D), and George Ryan (R). This of course does not include the indicted city workers, aldermen, county officials, statewide officials, or judges. *See, e.g.*, Todd Lighty and Dan

Mihalopoulus, "We'll Keep Chasing Them, U.S. Wins Round Against Graft, but Fight Isn't Over," *Chicago Tribune*, Apr. 18, 2006, Sec. 1, 13.

6. 42 U.S.C. § 1973gg (b)(1)(3); NVRA, P.L. 103-31.

7. Christi Parsons, "Motor Voter Opposition Is Dropped by Edgar," *Chicago Tribune*, Oct. 3, 1996, Metro DuPage. Then Governor Jim Edgar and the Republicans instead created a confusing, costly, dual registration system that was in place until October 1996, when litigation finally ended.

8. *See* Hal Dardick, "Motor Voter and GOP Take Us to Deep South," *Press Publications* (Elmhurst, IL), Feb. 7, 1996 (describing yellow placard in Elmhurst City Hall, confusion).

9. Ironically, the *Tribune* carried a quote by Cook County clerk Democrat David Orr, noting that Florida had registered "roughly 1 million voters" through Motor Voter, while Illinois had only registered 220,000 in the same time period. Parsons, "Motor Voter Opposition" at 2.

10. They were filed by the League of Women Voters, by ACORN (Association of Community Organizations for Reform Now) and Equip for Equality, and by the U.S. Department of Justice.

11. This was true and made the behavior even more nefarious because for years the drivers license facilities and clerks offices had people trained already on staff to register for all the offices. David Bailey, "Two-Tier 'Motor-Voter' Law Challenged in Suit," *Chicago Daily Law Bulletin*, Oct. 30, 1995, 1.

12. Sue Ellen Christian, "Officials Preparing for Chaos," *Chicago Tribune*, Feb. 5, 1996, 7.

13. *See, e.g.*, Editorial, "State's 'Motor Voter' Law Is a Deception," *Kane County Chronicle*, July 8, 1995, A4 (emphasis in original): "Once again our glorious state of Illinois has embarrassed itself in front of the nation with its political games and lack of leadership. . . . The Illinois motor voter law is a sham. It will most likely be challenged in federal court, and is just another reason for the nation to point to Illinois and ridicule it for its corrupt election process. Our state lawmakers and Edgar should be ashamed for bringing this blight upon Illinois citizens." *Also see* Editorial, "Voting Wrong," *Naperville Sun*, Sept. 29, 1995: "Forty states have successfully implemented this law with no evidence that it is too costly or opens the system to fraud. Nor has there been evidence that there is an advantage to one party by so doing—a major, if unstated, Republican objection. . . . This kind of voter discrimination is little more than a throw-back to poll taxes and closed primaries."

14. David Bailey, "State Officials Weigh Another Appeal in Wake of Decision Voiding 2-Tier Voter Registration System," *Chicago Daily Law Bulletin*, Sept. 27, 1996, 1.

15. Bailey, "Two-Tier 'Motor-Voter' Law Challenged in Suit," 1 (citing Cook County clerk David Orr's attorney David R. Melton, who brought the lawsuit to stop two-tier registration as illegal).

16. Ibid., 18.

17. Bailey, "State Officials Weigh Another Appeal," 1 (citing *Orr v. Edgar*, 283 Ill. App. 3d 1088, 670 N.E.2d 1243 (1st Dist. 1996)).

18. Laurie Cohen, Todd Lighty, and Dan Mihalopoulos, "Trading Services for Votes," *Chicago Tribune*, July 30, 2006, 1.

19. *See, e.g.*, "Democrats, Leave DuPage County to Republicans: No Challengers Surface for Countywide Offices," *Chicago Tribune*, June 6, 2006, sec. 2, at 2 (citing that the "Democrats failed to produce anyone to oppose them [the Republicans] in

November" and that "[n]o Democrat has won since at least World War II" for a countywide race).

20. *See* DuPage County Election Commission (*available at* http://www.dupage elections.com/pages.asp?pageid=208): "The DuPage County Election Commission is unique within the State of Illinois, since it is the only countywide election commission. Legislation passed in 1973 provided for the formation of this independent bipartisan agency in January 1974. The Election Commission is charged with the conduct of all federal, state, county and local elections occurring within its boundaries."

21. Editorial, titled "Barriers to Student Voting," *New York Times*, Sept. 28, 2004, stated that "the truth is . . . local elections officials often discourage students from registering and voting from their campus addresses, even though the Supreme Court has ruled that they have the right to do so." The *Times*, noting that "only about 37 percent of citizens between the ages of eighteen and twenty-four voted," said that this "was often attributed to apathy" but that "a lack of support, and sometimes outright hostility, from elections officials is a significant factor" (*available at* www.nytimes .com/2004/09/28/opinion/28tue1.html).

22. Thomas Hargrove, "Unearthing the Undervote," *American Journalism Review*, Oct.–Nov. 2004 (*available at* www.ajr.org/article_printable.asp?id=3752).

23. Douglas Holt and Michael J. Berens, "State Worst in Ballot Errors; City, Cook Lead Illinois to Dubious Mark," *Chicago Tribune*, Apr. 29, 2001 (*available at* www .jessejacksonjr.org/query/creadpr./cgi?id=3349); *see also* Paul J. Quirk, James H. Kuklinski, and Philip Habel, "The Machinery of Democracy: Voting Systems and Ballot Miscounts in Illinois," *Institute of Government and Public Affairs* (Chicago: 2002): 3 (*available at* www.igpa.uiuc.edu/system/files/VotingSystems.pdf): "In the election of 2000, more than 190,000 ballots, almost 4 percent of all ballots, were miscounted in the state. . . . About one-quarter of all jurisdictions had miscount rates higher than 3.5 percent in 2000; several had rates higher than 6 percent."

24. Greg Palast, "Lost Votes," *ZNet*, *Third Party*, June 20, 2004 (*formerly available at* www.zmag.org/content/print_article.old/itemID=5744§ionID=33). *Also see* R. Michael Alvarez, "Voter Registration: Past, Present and Future, Written Testimony Prepared for the Commission on Federal Election Reform," Caltech/MIT Voting Technology Project, June 2005, 2 (*available at* www.votingtechnologyproject.org/ media/documents/wps/vtp_wp30.pdf): "First, between 1.5 and 2 million were not counted because they were unmarked spoiled or ambiguous. . . . Second, we found that between 500,000 and 1.2 million votes were lost due to polling place operations, like long lines, inconvenient hours of operation, or poor location of poll sites. . . . Third, and most significant . . . we found that between 1.5 and 3 million ballots were lost due to problems with voter registration. These problems included errors in voter registration databases, problems handling voter registration applications, or difficulties updating voter registration information following a move."

25. Jo Becker and Dan Keating, "Problems Abound in Election System," *Washington Post*, Sept. 5, 2004, A1 (*available at* www.washingtonpost.com/wp-dyn/articles/ A62468-2004sept.4.html). *See also* "Voting: What Is, What Could Be," Caltech/MIT Voting Technology Project, July 2001, 8 (*available at* www.votingtechnologyproject .org/media/documents/july01/July01_VTP_Voting_Report_Entire.pdf).

26. United States General Accounting Office, GAO-02-122 Elections, *Statistical Analysis of Factors that Affected Uncounted Votes in the 2000 Presidential Election*, Oct. 2001, 3.

27. *Compare* Ginger Thompson, "After Volatile Election, a Smooth Vote Count in Haiti," *New York Times*, Feb. 9, 2006, A10, *and* John McCormick and Gary Washburn,

"Week Later, Almost All Ballots from Primaries Are Counted," *Chicago Tribune*, Mar. 29, 2006, 3: "Suburban Cook County election officials said Monday that they had finished counting polling place ballots, nearly a week after the primary election was thrown into confusion by new and problem-plagued voting equipment that many election judges were not trained to operate. In Chicago, roughly 25 precincts remain to be counted, a job likely to be done Tuesday [a week after the election]."

28. Ralph Nader and Theresa Amato, "Towards a More Vital Democracy," Feb. 2001, "Concrete ways that state and local officials can strengthen the democratic process," on file with author; Ian Urbina, "Voting Officials Face New Rules to Bar Conflicts, Politics and Cash at Issue," *New York Times*, Aug. 1, 2007, A12. Part of the problem is that in most states there are virtually no rules that prohibit elections officials from highly public partisanship, lending an appearance of bias, whether real or imagined. The *New York Times* reported that secretaries of state in Arizona, Kansas, Michigan, Missouri, and Ohio were also the chairmen of George Bush's reelection campaign in their states. Worse, "secretaries of state in at least seven states have overseen races for governors' offices or Congress in which *they* were candidates." Ibid. (emphasis added).

29. Nader and Amato, "Towards a More Vital Democracy," Feb. 2001: The Duval County ballot (Jacksonville, FL) had presidential candidates stretched over two pages. Democratic election workers distributed a sample ballot to people before voting with the instructions to "vote every page." In Duval County 21,855 people overvoted, that is, voted for more than one presidential candidate, including 6,935 who voted for Gore on page one and another candidate on page two! Clifford A. Jones, "Out of Guatemala?: Election Law Reform in Florida and the Legacy of *Bush v. Gore* in the 2004 Presidential Election," *Election Law Journal* 5 (Nov. 2, 2006): 124–25.

30. Gerald Ford, Jimmy Carter, *et al.*, Co-Chairs of the National Commission on Federal Election Reform, "Letter to the American People," in *To Assure Pride and Confidence in the Electoral Process*, Aug. 2001, 1 (*available at* www.reformelections.org/data/reports/99_full_report.pdf).

31. Ibid.

32. Ibid., 6, 8.

33. Ibid., 5–14.

34. Ibid., 19–20 (emphasis added).

35. White House Press Release, "President Signs Historic Election Reform Legislation into Law," Oct. 29, 2002 (*available at* www.whitehouse.gov/news/releases/2002/10/20021029-l.html). "Each state will be required to maintain a clean and current and accurate statewide list of registered voters, making it easier to register and easier to detect fraud. Under this law people registering to vote are required to prove that they are who they say they are, with appropriate identification. First-time voters who register by mail will be asked to provide identification when they cast their ballots. This law also creates new criminal penalties for providing false information, and punishes anyone guilty of conspiracy to deprive voters of a fair election.

"Each polling place must have at least one voting machine accessible to persons with disabilities. When people show up at the polls, and their voting registration is in doubt, they should not be turned away, but allowed to cast a provisional ballot so their vote can be counted if it is later verified that they are properly registered.

"And every state must have a fair procedure for hearing and resolving voter complaints. Under these reforms, training and education will be provided to poll workers and voters, reducing the possibility of confusion and error at the polls.

"Along with the resources come high standards for the integrity of elections. States must ensure that voting systems have minimal rates of error and allow voters a reasonable opportunity to review their ballots and correct any mistakes before a vote is cast." Ibid.

36. Ibid.

37. Election Assistance Commission, *Annual Report*, Jan. 2005, 3 (reports for 2003–07 *available at* www.eac.gov/about/operations/annual=reports).

38. Ibid. Worse, the EAC itself became embroiled in partisan crosshairs about whether it was changing research about voter fraud at the behest of the Justice Department. *See* Zachary A. Goldfarb, "Panel Faces Partisanship Allegations," *Washington Post*, June 22, 2007 (explaining how a report produced in August 2006 finding nearly "nonexistent" voter fraud was rewritten and released in December 2006 claiming there was "debate" on the issue, after arguably inappropriate influence from the Justice Department) (*available at* www.washingtonpost.com/wp-dyn/content/article/2007/06/21/AR2007062102103.html/?tid=informbox). *See also* Tova Andrea Wang, "A Rigged Report on U.S. Voting?" op ed., Aug. 30, 2007 (*available at* www.washingtonpost.com/wp-dyn/content/article/2007/08/29/AR2007082901928.html).

39. *See, e.g.*, Adam Cohen, "Where the Action's at for Poll Watchers: Ohio as the New Florida," *New York Times*, Oct. 31, 2004, A10: "[T]he legacy of Florida 2000 was public knowledge of a secret that election officials had long kept to themselves: that every year millions of eligible voters are wrongly prevented from voting, and millions of votes are thrown out. . . . Reckless voting-roll purges are still throwing eligible voters off the rolls. . . . More voters are disenfranchised every year by incompetent or malevolent election administrators than anything else." Becker and Keating, "Problems Abound in Election System,": quoting the Bureau of Elections director of New Mexico saying, "God help us if the election is close," and the governor of Pennsylvania's spokesperson saying, "[W]e're trying to prevent chaos." *Also see* Adam Liptak, "Expect Bush v. Kerry, the Chadless Sequel," *New York Times*, Oct. 27, 2004, A14; Jackie Calmes, "November Butterflies: as Election Nears, Counting the Vote Faces New Pitfalls," *Wall Street Journal*, Oct. 5, 2004, A1 (documenting multiple discrepancies among the states on what would count concerning provisional votes); Jo Becker, "Behind the Scenes, Officials Wrestle Over Voting Rules," *Washington Post*, Oct. 10, 2004, A10 (discussing how partisan elections officials were waging battles about various rules even as they chaired presidential efforts in their state).

40. Tim Renneberg, letter to the editor, "How America Votes, and How We Can Do Better," *New York Times*, Oct. 31, 2004, A10.

41. The Commission on Federal Election Reform, *Building Confidence in U.S. Elections*, Sept. 2005, 1 (citing Adam Nagourney and Janet Elder, "Late Poll Still Shows Sharp Split in U.S. Vote," *International Herald Tribune*, Nov. 1, 2004) (*available at* www.american.edu/ia/cfer/report/full_report.pdf).

42. Ibid. (citing the Pew Research Center for the People and the Press, "Voters Liked Campaign 2004, But Too Much Mud-Slinging," Nov. 11, 2004, [*available at* http://people-press.org/reports/display.php3?ReportID=233]). *See also* Editorial, "Lessons of the Ballot Box," *New York Times*, Nov. 4, 2004, A30 (*available at* www.nytimes.com/2004/11/04/opinion/04thu2.html); Mark Crispin Miller, "None Dare Call It

Stolen: Ohio, the Election, and America's Servile Press," *Harper's Magazine*, Aug. 2005, 39 ("on Election Day, twenty-six state exit polls incorrectly predicted wins for Kerry, a statistical failure so colossal and unprecedented that the odds against its happening, according to a report last May by the National Election Data Archive Project, were 16.5 million to 1"); Robert F. Kennedy Jr., "Was the 2004 Election Stolen?" *Rolling Stone*, June 2006; Steven Rosenfeld, Bob Fitrakis, and Harvey Wasserman, *What Happened in Ohio: A Documentary Record of Theft and Fraud in the 2004 Election* (New York: The New Press, 2006).

43. Adam Liptak, "Voting Problems in Ohio Set Off an Alarm," *New York Times*, Nov. 7, 2004 (quoting professor Heather K. Gerken) (*available at* www.nytimes.com/2004/11/07/politics/campaign/07elect.html).

44. House Judiciary Committee Democratic Staff, *Preserving Democracy: What Went Wrong in Ohio*, Status Report, Jan. 5, 2005, 6 (*available at* www.nvri.org/about/ohio_conyers_report_010505.pdf). *See also* Tova Andrea Wang, "More Trials and Tribulations for Ohio," The Century Foundation, Dec. 30, 2004 (*available at* www.tcf.org) (summarizing reports of voting system failures in Ohio).

Now, had the Republicans lost the election because of a state in which the secretary of state was a Democrat, as in Oregon, West Virginia, or New Mexico, the same hearings probably would have been held and investigations done by Republicans, with similar reports issued. Matt Bai wrote, "Our politics, not our voting machines, are imperiling the idea of a fair election" and that "no matter which man, George W. Bush or John Kerry, gets the nod from the networks on election night, we have already been warned to expect angry recrimination, demands for recounts and litigation filed by some of the hundreds of lawyers who will spend Tuesday on call, ready to jet off to battle in counties they never knew existed." Bai explained that "in the rush to address the country's electoral confusion after the 2000 debacle, Congress—try to contain your surprise here—appears instead to have made it worse." Matt Bai, "Another Contested Contest? Our Politics, Not Our Voting Machines, Are Imperiling the Idea of a Fair Election," *New York Times Magazine*, Oct. 31, 2004, 17.

45. Commission on Federal Election Reform, *Building Confidence in U.S. Elections*, iv (emphasis added).

46. FairVote, "Presidential Election Inequality: The Electoral College in the 21st Century," Fairvote.org (2006), 33 (*available at* www.fairvote.org/media/perp/presidentialinequality.pdf).

47. Ronald B. Rapoport and Walter J. Stone, *Three's a Crowd: The Dynamic of Third Parties, Ross Perot, and Republican Resurgence* (Ann Arbor: University of Michigan Press, 2005), 115 (citing Paul R. Abramson, John H. Aldrich, and David R. Rohde, *Change and Continuity in the 1996 Elections* [Washington, DC: Congressional Quarterly Press, 1998], 199).

48. Ronnie Dugger, "Counting Votes," *New Yorker*, Nov. 7, 1988, 40.

49. *Ryan v. DuPage County Bd. of Election Commissioners*, No. 2-92-1393 (Ill. App. Jan. 11, 1995) (Petition for Rehearing *en banc* filed to overturn the reading of Illinois's public records statute to exempt all software from disclosure, and Petition for Leave to Appeal filed Feb. 14, 1995).

50. *See* William A. Wright, "Public Access to Vote-Counting Software," *University of Chicago Legal Forum* (1995), 548 (arguing contrary to the FEC for greater public access that would instill public confidence in the vote-counting software). Bill Wright, a former University of Chicago law student, was part of the first team of fantastic law school interns at the Citizen Advocacy Center in the summer of 1994; we worked

together on the *Ryan v. DuPage County Board* appeal for public access to vote counting software.

51. United States Government Accountability Office, GAO-06-450 Elections, *The Nation's Evolving Election System as Reflected in the November 2004 General Election*, Washington, D.C., June 2006, 48, 295–300. Since 2000 there has been a definite shift from lever and punch card use to direct recording equipment, or "DRE." Optical scan voting, not DREs, are the most cost-effective and reliable, and they have a better paper trail (that the voter fills out rather than a DRE-machine receipt). Why are the vendors and their lobbyists running around election administrators to push DREs when they are more hackable than other machines? Because they are expensive, cost a lot to store, and need to be replaced often, ensuring more corporate profits for the industry to which we have outsourced our elections. *See* Editorial, "Virtues of Optical-Scan Voting," *New York Times*, Mar. 9, 2005, A26; Jeanne Cummings, "Reversing Course on Electronic Voting," *Wall Street Journal*, May 12, 2006 (citing New Mexico's and Maryland's decision to curb problems related to electronic voting machines). Some 98 percent of election jurisdictions use some kind of equipment involving technology, either punch card, optical scan, lever machine, or direct recording electronic equipment—or some mix. About 2 percent do it by hand—with paper ballots. What does this mean? Well, paper ballots mean a voter marks his or her vote on paper and puts it in a sealed box, and then someone counts it. Lever means a voter pulls a lever next to the name or issue to be voted on, and the machine records and tallies the vote by using a counting mechanism. Punch card means a voter uses computer-readable card boxes and you punch out your votes, which are then read by a computerized machine that computes the holes punched. Optical scan means that a voter votes on a computer-readable paper ballot that then gets tabulated by computerized machine. DRE means a voter pushes a button or touches a screen on a machine or computer screen, and then the vote is stored in a computer memory chip, which is then tallied by reading the chip. In 2000, 5 percent of the GAO-studied jurisdictions used multiple voting systems. In 2004, that number had jumped to 21 percent. (GAO-06-450 Elections at 301.) According to Electionline.org, as of October 2008, seven states still had no paper record of a vote, relying instead exclusively on electronic equipment. Pew Center on the States, www.electionline.org, "Election Preview 2008, What if We Had an Election and Everyone Came?" at 4, Oct. 2008 (*available at* www.pewcenteronthestates.org/uploadedfiles/election%20preview%20final.pdf).

52. GAO-06-450 Elections at 7–8 (emphases added). The report then lists "challenges" in voter registration, absentee voting, Election Day activities, vote counting, voting technology, early voting, overseas voting, provisional voting, and voting systems. The GAO spends 377 pages explaining and documenting these challenges, with another 150 pages of appendixes. And after you wade through this polite tome about the electoral system of the United States of America, remember that these are the results of our nation having spent the years since the 2000 fiasco ostensibly *trying to fix our elections* through HAVA and state statutes.

53. GAO-02-3 Elections at 18, Oct. 2001.

54. *See* ibid., 224, comparing Ohio, which does not count a vote with three corners attached, to Nevada, which insists that a chad with three corners attached be counted.

55. HAVA, Public Law 107-252, 42 U.S.C. § 15481, Sec. 301. Voting Systems Standards (1) (a), Oct. 29, 2002.

56. HAVA, Public Law 107-252, Subtitle B—Voluntary guidance. Sec. 311. Adoption of Voluntary Guidance by Commission.

57. GAO-06-450 Elections at 345.

58. Ibid. *See also* GAO-05-956.

59. GAO-02-3 Elections at 221.

60. Ibid., 216.

61. James Fallows, "Electronic Voting 1.0, and No Time to Upgrade," *New York Times*, Nov. 28, 2004.

62. Zachary Goldfarb, "As Elections Near, Officials Challenge Balloting Security," *Washington Post*, Jan. 22, 2006.

63. Andrew Gumbel, in his book *Steal This Vote: Dirty Elections and the Rotten History of Democracy in America* (New York: Nation Books, 2005), tells how Sancho, when given by Katherine Harris a special list in 2000 of the "felons" who were supposed to be purged, had the good sense to examine the 694 names on his list and realize that only 33 were actually criminals (at 213).

64. Goldfarb, "As Elections Near."

65. Ibid., quoting Bev Harris, a Black Box Voting activist.

66. Peter Whoriskey, "Election Whistle-Blower Stymied by Vendors," *Washington Post*, Mar. 26, 2006.

67. Others have found problems in electronic touch-screen systems. A Carnegie Mellon University professor who was studying Pennsylvania's electronic systems told the *New York Times*, "It's the most severe security flaw ever discovered in a voting system," referring to a risk in the Diebold Election Systems touch-screen voting machines. In the same article, a Johns Hopkins University professor who studied the latest problem said: "I almost had a heart attack. The implications of this are pretty astounding." Monica Davey, "High Tech Voting Machines Stir Debate over Security," *New York Times*, May 12, 2006 (quoting, respectively, Michael I. Shamos at Carnegie Mellon and Aviel Rubin at Johns Hopkins). Diebold "minimized the significance of the risk," ibid., and claimed that certain alleged scenarios could not occur in elections with procedures in place. Anne Marie Squeo, "Make-or-Break Balloting," *Wall Street Journal*, Oct. 25, 2004, B6. Shortly before the November 2006 election, the Republican governor of Maryland, Robert L. Ehrlich, suggested that state offer all voters paper ballots. Ian Urbina, "Bill Would Reimburse States for Printing Alternate Ballots," *New York Times*, Sept. 27, 2006. He had to. Maryland had spent some $106 million on its voting technology in the four years prior to the election, but the citizens in all 238 precincts in sophisticated Montgomery County couldn't vote on time, if at all, because someone forgot to pack the secret plastic card to make the electronic machines work. Jamin Raskin, the candidate and victor for state senator, described to the press the primary in Maryland as "chaos": "It was Florida. It was Mexico. It was your worst nightmare," he told the *Post*. Eric Rich, "Voting Problems Could Spark Legal Challenges to Results," *Washington Post*, Sept. 13, 2006. In June 2006, the Brennan Center for Justice at NYU Law School issued a report that concluded it might only take *one person* with the right knowledge and access to alter the outcome of an election. "A Single Person Could Swing an Election," *Washington Post*, June 28, 2006 (citing "The Machinery of Democracy: Protecting Elections in an Electronic World," June 27, 2006, *available at* www.brennancenter.org/content/resource/machinery_of_democracy_protecting_elections_in_an_electronic_world/).

68. Cameron W. Barr, "Security of Electronic Voting Is Condemned," *Washington Post*, Dec. 1, 2006.

69. Daniel Wolfe, "Security Watch, Exposures," *American Banker*, Aug. 8, 2007, at 5. On top of that, Ciber Inc., the *tester* of the machine software, itself was "unable

to meet federal quality standards that will take effect later this year." (Editorial, "Testing the Testers," *New York Times*, Jan. 8, 2007.) What is more, the testers are paid by the voting machine manufacturers. The *Times* notes, "The [testing] labs, which see themselves as working for the voting machine companies, do not tell the public when they find problems or what those problems are." The only good news in all this is that in 2002 only two states required votes to have verified records, whereas by 2006, twenty-eight states required a paper record, and twelve more are moving in that direction with proposed legislation not yet passed. (*Yes! Magazine*, *Yes!* Graphic, Fall 2006 at 14, citing www.verifiedvoting.org.) Despite all the glitches reported from 2004 and 2006 elections, the EAC has not imposed a federal requirement that states use only voting machines that have independently verifiable paper trails or result auditing. "U.S. Panel Rejects Plan for Paper Ballots," *New York Times*, Dec. 5, 2006.

70. United States General Accounting Office, GAO-02-52 Elections, *Voting Equipment Standards*, Oct. 2001, 2 (emphasis added and citation omitted).

71. Ibid., 6 n.7, 7.

72. Ibid., 12.

73. Ibid., 16.

74. GAO-06-450 Elections at 270.

75. Electionline.org, "Recounts: From Punch Cards to Paper Trails," *Briefing*, Oct. 2005, 10 (*available at* www.pewcenteronthestates.org/uploadedfiles/ERIPbrief12.sb370updated.pdf).

76. Voter Action, "Did Crimes Occur?" Aug. 15, 2007 (*available at* www.voteraction.org).

77. Ian Urbina, "New Laws and Machines May Spell Voting Chaos," *New York Times*, Oct. 19, 2006, A1, A16.

78. Ibid., A16.

79. Ian Urbina, "Panel Altered a Draft Report on Vote Fraud," *New York Times*, Apr. 11, 2007, A1, A18 (citing Electionline.org as the source of data for voter ID map *available at* www.electionline.org).

80. *Crawford et al. v. Marion County Elec. Bd. et al.*, 128 S. Ct. 1610 (2008).

81. Joyce Purnick, "Stricter Voting Laws Incite Latest Partisan Divide," *New York Times*, Sept. 26, 2006 (quoting Russell K. Pearce, a Republican state representative and ID proponent in Arizona).

82. Eric Lipton and Ian Urbina, "In 5-Year Effort, Scant Evidence of Voter Fraud," *New York Times*, Apr. 12, 2007, A1.

83. Michael Waldman and Justin Levitt, "The Myth of Voter Fraud," *Washington Post*, Mar. 29, 2007.

84. Editorial, "The Acorn Indictments," *Wall Street Journal*, Nov. 3, 2006.

85. The law was declared unconstitutional by state law judge the Honorable T. Jackson Bedford Jr. of the Fulton County Superior Court in September 2006. He said the Georgia state constitution didn't allow for this voting requirement. *See* Darryl Fears and Jonathan Weisman, "Georgia Law Requiring Voters to Show Photo ID Is Thrown Out," *Washington Post*, Sept. 20, 2006.

86. Adam Cohen, "American Elections and the Grand Old Tradition of Disenfranchisement," *New York Times*, Oct. 8, 2006.

87. "Ohio ID Law Suspended for Absentee Voting," *Washington Post*, Oct. 27, 2006, covering U.S. District Court judge the Honorable Algenon L. Marbley's restraining order.

88. "Florida: Voter Registration Law Challenged," *New York Times*, Sept. 18, 2007, 21.
89. Purnick, "Stricter Voting Laws Incite Latest Partisan Divide."
90. Ibid.
91. Ibid., A20.
92. GAO-02-3 Elections at 14.
93. GAO-06-450 Elections at 114.
94. Ibid., 144.
95. U.S. Government Accountability Office, GAO-06-521 Elections, *Absentee Voting Assistance to Military and Overseas Citizens Increased for the 2004 General Election, but Challenges Remain*, Washington, D.C., April 2006, 1.
96. Ibid., 4–5.
97. Ibid., 5.
98. Electionline.org, "Overseas Voting—Challenges and Innovation," *Briefing*, Oct. 2007 (*available at* www.pewcenteronthestates.org/reportdetail_aspx?id=34082) (citing U.S. Election Assistance Commission, *UOCAVA Survey Report Findings* [Sept. 2007]).
99. Tova Andrea Wang, "Soldiering Voters," *Century Foundation*, Oct. 8, 2004, www.tcf.org, quoting the *New York Times* (*available at* www.nytimes.com/2004/10/08/politics/campaign/08vote.html).
100. Josh White, "80% of Military Voted or Tried to," *Washington Post*, Dec. 7, 2005 (*available at* www.washingtonpost.com/wp-dyn/content/article/2005/12/06/AR2005120601556.html).
101. Ian Urbina, "Casting Ballot from Abroad Is No Sure Bet," *New York Times*, June 13, 2007, A1 (*available at* www.nytimes.com/2007/06/13/washington/13overseas.html?/top/reference/timestopics/people/u/Urbina/Ian).
102. Ibid.; *see also Associated Press*, "New Help for Overseas Voters," *Washington Post*, Sept. 12, 2006; Blake Hulnick and Daniel O'Brien, "Viewpoint: Using Technology to Improve UOCAVA" AEI-Brookings Election Reform Report, Nov. 7, 2007 ("only 5.5% of UOCAVA voters successfully cast a ballot").
103. *Available at* www.fvap.gov.
104. Formerly at http://fvap.gov/link/politicallinks.html; April 2006 printout of old site, on file with author.
105. *Available at* http://memory.loc.gov/ammem/ndlpedu/features/election/partysys.html.
106. An amendment to UOCAVA, Pub. L. No. 108–375, § 566 (2004), allowed military personnel even in the United States to use the emergency federal write-in absentee ballots.
107. GAO-06-521 at 18.
108. Ibid., 20.
109. GAO-06-521 at 21, citing Pub. L. No. 107–252, § 706 (2002), and Pub. L. No. 107–107, § 1606 (2001), respectively.
110. Ibid.
111. Letter from Richard Winger to Oregon state senator Kate Brown, dated Mar. 29, 2005, urging passage of SB 1015 to provide for presidential tallies of write-in votes, on file with author.
112. Ibid.
113. Ibid. According to Richard Winger: "[I]n 1964, [in New Hampshire] Henry Cabot Lodge won the Republican presidential primary on write-ins. He wasn't even a candidate, but people just wanted to write him in, and he won. In 1968, Lyndon Johnson won the Democratic presidential primary on write-ins. He didn't get his name on

the ballot because he wasn't sure if he wanted to run for re-election (later that year he declined to run). Everyone thinks that Eugene McCarthy won. Actually McCarthy was the only name on the ballot and Lyndon Johnson still beat him on write-ins, but it was fairly close, so history recorded it as a 'defeat' for the person who won and won the hard way. It's all expectations. Seven times, someone has been elected to Congress in the general election by write-in votes, three times in California alone; also in Oregon, New Mexico, Arkansas, South Carolina."

114. Richard Scammon, Rhodes Cook, and Alice McGillivray, *America Votes 26: 2003–2004, Election Returns by State* (Washington, DC: Congressional Quarterly, 2005), 10.

115. Ralph Nader; Nader; Ralph; Raph Nader; Ralph Nadir; Ralph Nadur; Raph; Nadur; Nadir; Nadr; Nadurr; Ralphie; Raph Nadir; Raph Nadur; Raph Nadurr; R. Nader; R. Nadir; R. Nadur; R. Nadr; Raff; Raf; Rolf; Rolph; Nader/Camejo; Nader/Camjo; Nader/Comejo; Ralph Nader/Peter Miguel Camejo; R. Nadir/P. Camejo; R. Nader/P. Comejo; R. Nadur/Peter Camjo; R. Nadr/Peter Cumejo; R. Nadir/Peter Cemejo; R. Nader/Peter Miguel Camjo. Kevin Shelley, California Secretary of State, "Certified List of Write-in Candidates for the November 2, 2004 General Election," dated Oct. 22, 2004.

116. Email from Larry Sparrow to Mike Richardson, dated Dec. 10, 2004, on file with author.

117. *Nader et al. v. Blackwell*, No. 04-1052 (S.D. Ohio Nov. 2, 2004) (unpublished).

118. *See Ballot Access News*, 16.8 (Nov. 16, 2000); and *Phillips v. Hechler*, 120 F. Supp. 2d 587 (S.D. W. Va. 2000).

119. GAO-06-450 Elections at 216 (citing U.S. Census Bureau, *Voting and Registration in the Election of November 2000* [Washington, DC: Department of Commerce, Feb. 2002]).

120. United States General Accounting Office, GAO-02-90, Elections, *A Framework for Evaluating Reform Proposals*, 2001, 27.

121. Century Foundation, *Balancing Access and Integrity: The Report of The Century Foundation Working Group on State Implementation of Election Reform* (Washington, DC: Century Foundation, July 25, 2005), 31–32 (citation omitted).

122. Ibid.

123. Ibid., 213–48.

124. Ibid., 231.

125. Even vote order depends on where you live. Did you know that how your federal candidates appear on your ballot and whether they are allowed by your given state to call themselves a member of a party or an independent or any other appellation all depend on state laws? Jon A. Krosnick, a professor of communication, political science, and psychology at Stanford, wrote a compelling op-ed in the *New York Times* in November 2006, explaining the bias of ballot order. The candidate on the top of the ballot votes will always get an advantage of about two percentage points than if he or she had been listed later. If your name begins with *A* or *Z* or if you are a Republican or Democrat, you might want to pay attention to how your state runs vote ordering. Krosnick points out that in some states Democrats are always listed alphabetically by party and thus always precede Republicans. Jon A. Krosnick, "In the Voting Booth, Bias Starts at the Top," *New York Times*, Nov. 4, 2006 (*available at* www.nytimes.com/2006/11/04/opinion/04krosnick.html).

126. A report by FairVote states that between 1980 and 2006, out of an annual average of 250 to 300 statewide elections, "there was less than one statewide recount a

year." Monideepa Talukdar and Rob Richie, "A Survey and Analysis of Statewide Election Recounts. 1980–2006," *Fairvote.org*, July 27, 2007, 2 (*available at* http://fairvote.org).

Article 1, Section 5, of the U.S. Constitution contemplates contested elections, and the Federal Contested Elections Act of 1969 provides procedures on how to go about certifying contested elections for the House of Representatives. According to the Congressional Research Service (CRS), from 1933 to 2000, there have been 102 contested elections for the United States House of Representatives. *See* GAO-02-3 Elections at 237, citing CRS Report, *House Contested Election Cases: 1933 to 2000*, CRS 98-194A (updated Nov. 3, 2000).

127. Richard Boudreaux, "Thousands Demand Mexico Recount," *Chicago Tribune*, July 17, 2006 at 8 (describing the scene of López Obrador's supporters in Mexico).

128. Andrés Manuel López Obrador, "Recounting Our Way to Democracy," *New York Times*, Aug. 11, 2006, A19.

129. Richard Boudreaux, "Mexico's Election Dispute a Crucial Test of Country's Stability," *Chicago Tribune*, July 16, 2006, 20.

130. *See* GAO-02-3 Elections at 232.

131. GAO-06-450 Elections at 277–80.

132. Ibid., 284–85.

133. Electionline.org, "Recounts," 5.

134. GAO-06-450 Elections at 259.

135. Ibid., 261.

136. *See* GAO-02-3 Elections at 231.

137. GAO-06-450 Elections at 269.

138. Ibid.

139. Electionline.org, "Recounts," 4.

140. *See* GAO-02-3 Elections at appendix VII, 407–11.

141. GAO-06-450 Elections at 268.

142. Joan Indiana Rigdon, "The Help America Vote Act Four Years Later," *Washington Lawyer*, Oct. 2006, 26.

143. Lois Romano and Jim VandeHei, " 'That's It': A Two-Year Quest Ends," *Washington Post*, Nov. 4, 2004, A27.

144. N.H. Rev. Stat. Ann. § 660:2(III) (West 2008).

145. Memo from Rob Cirincione to Ralph Nader and Theresa Amato, Nov. 19, 2004, RE: NH Recount, Thursday, Nov. 18, 2004, Washington, DC, on file with author: "All the ballots reviewed (except absentee) were cast on November 2 by filling in a circle next to the candidate's name. If the Diebold machine could not count the ballot properly (or if a write-in vote was filled), it was separated from the automatically counted ballots for human review.

"Prior to the start of the recount, ballots were transported from the local county wards to the Department of State in Concord (where the recount was being conducted). Ballots were stored and transported either in sealed cardboard boxes or padlocked containers.

"Recounts for state senate and president were conducted simultaneously. At several tables (5–8, depending on the time of day), two representatives from the Secretary of State's office were stationed to sort and count ballots. In the presence of a Republican, Democrat, and Nader representative the "straight-ticket" ballots were first segregated. For the purposes of this round a straight-ticket ballot is considered any ballot with votes for 'straight-Republican' only, 'straight-Democratic' only, Bush & Martel, or Kerry & Gelanis. Accordingly, ballots were placed into three piles: straight-Republican, straight-Democratic and split, which included all other ballots.

"During this initial segregation no challenges were accepted, as the votes were not being counted. Separating the straight-ticket ballots first is a procedural tool used to speed up the recount. Almost two-thirds of the ballots were straight-ticket votes.

"Once the ballots had been separated into straight-ticket and split votes the straight-ticket votes were officially counted. Straight-Republican ballots were counted in the presence of a Democrat and a Nader observer. Straight-Democratic ballots were counted in the presence of a Republican and Nader observer. As each ballot was placed in front of the observers they were allowed to challenge for any reason, in which case the ballot was set aside in a 'challenged—president and senate' pile.

"After all the straight-Republican and straight-Democratic ballots had been observed the unchallenged ones were counted and placed in stacks of 25 by each of the state representatives. When the stack of 25 had been counted and a final number of straight-Republican or straight-Democratic votes had been tabulated the state representatives exchanged piles (of Democratic or Republican straight-tickets), and the count was double checked.

"Next, the split ballots were counted, first for the senate race and then for the presidential. During the senate count, observers from the Martel and Gelanis campaigns watched as the state representatives placed each ballot in a pile for Martel or Gelanis. Objections from either observer set the ballot aside in a pile marked 'challenged—senate, not counted for president.'

"Once the state senate ballots had been separated into Martel and Gelanis piles they were counted in the same manner as the straight-tickets. All unchallenged split ballots were then collected and the process was repeated for president, this time with an observer from the Bush, Kerry, and Nader campaigns present. Objections from the observers set the ballots aside in a pile marked 'challenged—president, counted for senate.' Again, the unchallenged ballots were counted in stacks of 25 and then double-counted for accuracy.

"At various times during the day the Secretary himself ruled on the challenged ballots. Chief representatives from all campaigns observed the Secretary's decision. Upon hearing how a specific ballot would be counted presidential or state senate representatives were able to lodge a formal protest, which sends the Secretary's decision to the Ballot Law Commission for appeal. . . .

"By the end of the day only 3 wards had been completely recounted—Litchfield and Manchester wards 6 and 7. None of these recounted wards showed any significant deviation between the reported vote totals and the recount numbers. . . . At no time did we witness or hear about any questionable handling of the ballots. . . . While we haven't finished looking at all 11 wards, if the trend from the first three continues the recount will have confirmed the November 2 totals."

146. Ibid.

147. Michael Richardson, VoterVoice, "Legislative Report," Oct. 2005, at 3.

148. Richard Winger, *Ballot Access News*, 21.6, Oct. 2005, "More Lawsuit News, New Mexico." *Cobb v. State Canvassing Board*, 2006-NMSC-034, 140 N.M. 77, 140 P.3d 498 (2005), at 3.

149. National Voting Rights Institute, "Seeking a Fair Democratic Process," June 12, 2006 (*available at* www.nvri.org/about/ohio_recount.shtml).

Conclusion

1. Woodrow Wilson's Seventh State of the Union Address, Dec. 1919.

2. Samuel P. Huntington, *The Third Wave: Democratization in the Late Twentieth Century* (Norman: University of Oklahoma Press, 1993), 3.

3. Richard Winger, "Can United States Voters Still Recruit Someone to Run for President as an Independent After the Identities of the Major Party Presidential Candidates Are Known?" *University of Arkansas at Little Rock Law Review* 29 (2007): 784 and n.115.

4. Huntington, *The Third Wave*, 174–92.

5. The United States ranks 139th out of 172 countries for voter participation. That puts us below Bangladesh, Uganda, and Iran. International Institute for Democracy and Electoral Assistance, *Turnout in the World: Country-by-Country Performance (1945–1998)* (*available at* www.idea.int/vt/survey/voter_turnout_pop2.cfm) (ranking countries on elections since 1945).

6. *But see* Douglas E. Schoen's contrary conclusions in *Declaring Independence: The Beginning of the End of the Two-Party System* (New York: Random House, 2008), which, though encouraging, reads as a solicitation to Mayor Michael Bloomberg to enter the fray of the 2008 election. He cites his firm's poll, saying that "61 percent of voters say the two parties are failing and that having an independent on the ballot in the 2008 presidential election would be good for America." Introduction at xvii.

7. *See* FairVote's report by Christopher Pearson *et al.*, *The Shrinking Battleground*, 2008, 2–3 (*available at* www.fairvote.org/media/perp/Shrinking_Battleground_Final.pdf). And if you don't live in a battleground state, the major-party presidential campaigns will not spend one penny to curry your favor or vote after the primaries are over, unless they want your donations.

8. James E. Campbell, "The Stagnation of Congressional Elections," in Michael J. Malbin, Campaign Finance Institute, ed., *Life After Reform: When the Bipartisan Campaign Reform Act Meets Politics* (Lanham, MD: Rowman & Littlefield, 2003), 142.

9. Michael P. McDonald and John Samples, eds., *The Marketplace of Democracy: Electoral Competition and American Politics*: Brookings Institution, Cato Institute (Baltimore, MD: Brookings Institution Press 2006), 3.

10. Micah L. Sifry, *Spoiling for a Fight: Third-Party Politics in America* (New York: Routledge, 2003), 5 (citations to FairVote omitted).

11. Dan Balz, "Partisan Polarization Intensified in 2004 Election," *Washington Post*, Mar. 29, 2005, A4 (*available at* www.washingtonpost.com/wp-dyn/articles/A7793-2005Mar28.html). *See also* David S. Broder, "No Vote Necessary: Redistricting Is Creating a U.S. House of Lords," *Washington Post*, Nov. 11, 2004, A37 (*available at* www.washingtonpost.com/wp-dyn/articles/A41304-2004Nov10.html): In Florida, five of the twenty-five representatives to the U.S. House had no opposition; four of them also ran unopposed in the primary. *They were not even on the November ballot*. In Florida they were "'automatically reinstated in Washington'" after they won the primary election!

12. Balz, "Partisan Polarization," A4.

13. Organization for Security and Co-Operation in Europe, Preliminary Report, Election Observation Mission, "United States of America, 2 November 2004 Elections," Washington D.C.: Nov. 4, 2004 at 3.

14. David Lublin and Michael P. McDonald, "Is It Time to Draw the Line?: The Impact of Redistricting on Competition in State House Elections," *Election Law Journal* 5 (2006): 157.

15. IGPA University of Illinois, *Illinois Assembly on Political Representation and Alternative Electoral Systems* (Spring: 2001), 7, Chicago: "[A] good three-fourths of all 2000 House elections had either no or only token competition. In five of every ten districts, voters had no choice in either the primary or general election." Id. at 18.

16. *See* Office of the Clerk, U.S. House of Representatives, *available at* http://clerk.house.gov/art_history/house_history/partyDiv.html.

17. McDonald and Samples, *The Marketplace of Democracy*, 18.

18. Paul S. Herrnson, "Minor Party Candidates in Congressional Elections," in ibid., 118–19.

19. Ibid., 118.

20. Richard Winger, *Ballot Access News*, 23.8, Dec. 2007.

21. Richard W. Soudriette and Andrew Ellis, "Electoral Systems Today, a Global Snapshot," *Journal of Democracy* 17 (2006): 84.

22. Ibid.

23. "Comparison of Selected Electoral Systems," in IGPA University of Illinois, *Illinois Assembly*, appendix A, 29.

24. Dennis F. Thompson, *Just Elections: Creating a Fair Electoral Process in the United States* (Chicago: University of Chicago Press, 2002) (citing Jefferson to John Wayles Eppis, 24 June 1813, [13:270], and citing Thomas Jefferson to Samuel Kercheval, July 12, 1816, both in *The Writings of Thomas Jefferson*, ed. Andrew A. Lipscomb and Albert Ellery Bergh, memorial ed. [Washington, DC: Thomas Jefferson Memorial Association, 1903–04]).

25. Of course, these are not just my reforms, as they have all been proffered or championed by other scholars, activists, and institutions, some for decades, but they are the ones that I find persuasive or that at least should be considered as part of a national reform effort.

26. A. James Reichley, *The Life of the Parties: A History of American Political Parties* (Lanham, MD: Rowman & Littlefield with Free Press, 2000), 4.

27. *See, e.g.*, Tara Ross, *Enlightened Democracy: The Case for the Electoral College* (Dallas, TX: Colonial Press, L.P., 2004); Dr. George Grant, *The Importance of the Electoral College* (San Antonio, TX: Vision Forum Ministries, 2004).

28. *See, e.g.*, George C. Edwards III, *Why the Electoral College Is Bad for America* (New Haven, CT: Yale University Press, 2004); FairVote, "Presidential Election Inequality: The Electoral College in the 21st Century," 2006 (*available at* www.fairvote.org).

29. The year 1824 (John Q. Adams over Andrew Jackson); 1876 (Rutherford B. Hayes over Samuel J. Tilden); 1888 (Benjamin Harrison over Grover Cleveland); and 2000 (Bush over Gore).

30. Monideepa Talukdar, Rob Richie, and Ryan O'Donnell, "Fuzzy Math: Wrong Way Reforms for Allocating Electoral College Votes," FairVote, Aug. 9, 2007, 16–17 (*available at* http:fairvote.org). *See also* Alan B. Morrison, "A Better Way?" *National Journal*, 35:1 at 24 (Jan. 4, 2003) (discussing proportionate allocation and instant-runoff voting).

31. Talukdar *et al.*, "Fuzzy Math," 6, 16–17.

32. Ibid., 16–17.

33. Ibid., 3.

34. Richard E. Berg-Andersson, "To the Spoils Goes the Victor, Proposals and Prospects for Electoral College Reform," *The Green Papers Commentary*, Jan. 23, 2001 (*available at* www.thegreenpapers.com/PCom/20010123-0.html).

35. For more information, *see* www.nationalpopularvote.com. As of Nov. 2008, Maryland, New Jersey, Hawaii, and Illinois have signed it into law. States could of course change their minds, based on who controls them, about whether or not they are participating. If there are always enough states representing 270 electoral votes, no problem. If not, the way we elect the president could change every four years, which would be inconsistent but, arguably, not much more problematic than now. It sure would shake up the monopoly of certain battleground states and force the presidential campaigns to deviate beyond their standard game plans. But I also think that it doesn't do third parties or independents much good in being able to attract substantial constituencies because those voters that thought they lived in a "safe" state will now have their vote counted and may be even less willing to cast that vote for a third-party or independent candidate. In a 2008 conversation with Rob Richie, executive director of FairVote, he pointed out that it could help third parties by removing the "spoiler" stigma. Ultimately, the question would be how all voters in a particular state would react, whether they could break out of the state geography identity if their electoral votes all go to someone who did not win the popular vote in their state but did nationally.

36. *Yick Wo v. Hopkins*, 118 U.S. 356, 370 (1886) (right to vote is "a fundamental political right . . . preservative of all rights").

37. *Available at* www.house.gov/jackson/VotingAmendment.shtm.

38. *See* John F. Bibby and L. Sandy Maisel, *Two Parties—or More?: The American Party System*, 2d ed. (Boulder, CO: Westview Press, 2003), 77. They argue that Americans like single-member legislative districts (districts with just one representative) and the direct presidential primaries. True enough. But other institutional arrangements, even if disliked, such as the Electoral College, the ballot access laws, and the FEC Act which "perpetuate the status quo," just don't "generate the public interest or displeasure required for major changes that could benefit third parties. The prospects for institutional reforms that could aid third parties are therefore bleak." Ibid.

39. *See U.S. Term Limits, Inc. v. Thornton*, 514 U.S. 779 (1995).

40. Joseph P. Harris, *Election Administration in the United States* (Washington, DC: Brookings Institution, 1934), 1.

41. Alexander Hamilton, "Federalist 59, Concerning the Power of Congress to Regulate the Election of Members" in *The Federalist Papers*, Clinton Rossiter, ed. (NY: New American Library, 1961), 360–61 (emphasis in original).

42. For example:

1. Same-Day Voter Registration Act of 2007 (HR 2457)
2. Vote by Mail Act of 2007 (HR 1667; S 979); Universal Right to Vote by Mail Act of 2007 (HR 281)
3. Ballot Integrity Act of 2007 (S 1487)
4. Provisional Ballot Fairness in Counting Act of 2007 (HR 4145)
5. Vote Integrity and Verification Act of 2007 (S 559)
6. Count Every Vote Act of 2007 (S 804; HR 1381)
7. Voter Freedom Act of 2007 (HR 3600)

43. At the 2008 conference of the National Association of Secretaries of State, which I attended, some secretaries seemed to openly berate the EAC for its lack of competence.

44. Michael J. Malbin, "Rethinking the Campaign Finance Agenda," *Forum* 6.1 (2008): Article 3 (*available at* www.bepress.com/forum/vol6/iss1/art3).

45. Hank Kalet, "Cleaning Up Campaigns," *Progressive Populist*, June 1, 2007, 16–17 (discussing a 126-page report from the Maine Commission of Governmental Ethics and Election Practices, April 2007).

46. Campaign Finance Institute, *Large Donors Dominate Record-Setting Presidential Fundraising*, Oct. 17, 2007 (*available at* www.cfinst.org/pr/prRelease.aspx?ReleaseID =164) (showing Kucinich, Gravel, and Huckabee to be the exception to these trends).

47. Paul S. Herrnson, "Minor Party Candidates," 118–19.

48. Thomas E. Patterson, *The Vanishing Voter: Public Involvement in an Age of Uncertainty* (New York: Knopf, 2002), 149. Many people are never engaged. Patterson conducted 90,000 interviews with Americans, with many responding that they disliked the nominating system because it "was too long," "too costly," and "unfair."

49. Derek Cressman, "PACs for the People," *TomPaine.com*, Apr. 11, 2005 (*available at* www.tompaine.com/articles/pacs_for_the_people.php?dateid=20050415).

50. *See* Rob Richie, letter to the editor, "Electoral Lessons from Australia," *Washington Post*, Dec. 21, 2007 (*available at* www.fairvote.org).

51. Editorial, "Prisoners and Human Rights," *New York Times*, July 31, 2006, A20 (*available at* www.nytimes.com/2006/07/31/opinion/31mon2.html).

52. Erik Eckholm, "States Are Growing More Lenient in Allowing Felons to Vote," *New York Times*, Oct. 12, 2006 (*available at* www.nytimes.com/2006/10/12/us/12felons.html?scp=3&sq=&st=nyt).

53. Bradley A. Smith, "Block the Vote, Abusing Election Laws to Prevent Competition," *Washington Post*, Aug. 20, 2006 (*available at* www.washingtonpost.com/wp-dyn/content/article/2006/08/18/AR2006081801 25.html).

54. *See* HR 3600, Sept. 19, 2007, 110th Cong.

55. David S. Broder, "Why Vote on Tuesdays?" *Washington Post*, Nov. 10, 2005, A29; *see also* www.whytuesdays.org.

56. Joan Indiana Rigdon, "The Help America Vote Act Four Years Later," *Washington Lawyer*, Oct. 23, 2006, 29 (*available at* www.dcbar.org/for_lawyers/resources/publications/washington_lawyer/october_2006/hava.cfm) (citing the New York nonprofit Demos: "states with Election Day registration reported an average voter turnout of 74 percent in 2004, compared with 60 percent for states without").

57. *Nixon v. Herndon*, 273 U.S. 534 (1927); *Nixon v. Condon*, 286 U.S. 73 (1932); *Grovey v. Townsend*, 295 U.S. 45 (1935).

58. *Smith v. Allwright*, 321 U.S. 649 (1944); *Plessy v. Ferguson*, 163 U.S. 537 (1896); *Brown et al. v. Board of Educ. of Topeka* (KS), 347 U.S. 483 (1954).

59. *See* James Sample, David Pozen, and Michael Young, "Fair Courts: Setting Recusal Standards," Brennan Center for Justice at NYU School of Law, New York, 2008 (*available at* www.brennancenter.org).

60. Clifford J. Levy, "With Tight Grip on Ballot, Putin Is Forcing Foes Out of Parliament," *New York Times*, Oct. 14, 2007 (*available at* www.nytimes.com/2007/10/14/world/europe/14russia.html). *See also* C.J. Chivers, "Gorbachev, Rebuking Putin, Criticizes Russian Elections," *New York Times*, Jan. 29, 2008 (*available at* www.nytimes.com/2008/01/29/world/europe/29russia.html) (quoting Gorbachev: "Something is wrong with our elections, and our electoral system needs a major adjustment."); C.J. Chivers, "Russia Bars Opposition Candidate from March 2 Ballot," *New York Times*, Jan. 28, 2008 ("the Russian government . . . denied an opposition leader's application

to appear on the March 2 presidential ballot, clearing a path for the Kremlin's favorite candidate to run all but unchallenged.") (*available at* www.nytimes.com/2008/01/28/world/europe/28russia.html).

61. Alan Dershowitz, *Rights from Wrongs: A Secular Theory of the Origin of Rights* (New York: Basic Books, 2004), 85.

62. Harvard professor Alexander Keyssar argues in a paper called "The Project of Democracy" that political choice has been narrowed by the "increasing institutionalization of the two-party system" and that "the two major political parties operate within a narrow, ideological spectrum; [where] the programmatic differences between candidates often are difficult to discern; the core social and economic policies of both parties are shaped largely by the desire to foster economic growth and therefore to satisfy the business and financial communities. Ideas and proposals that might appeal to the poor and are commonplace in other nations such as national health insurance or laws enhancing job security-have been beyond the pale of modern American political discourse." Alexander Keyssar, "The Project of Democracy," National Initiative for Democracy, Feb. 2002, 4 (*available at* http://demofound.org/symposium/library/keyssarpaper.pdf).

63. Joseph J. Ellis, *Founding Brothers: The Revolutionary Generation* (New York: Vintage Books, 2000), 246 (citing letter of Thomas Jefferson to Roger C. Weightman, June 24, 1826, Paul Leicester Ford, ed., *The Writings of Thomas Jefferson*, 10 vols. [NY: 1892–1899] 10:390–92).

64. This is my email address: theresa@amatomain.com. If you want to start or join a national conversation or provide feedback on this book, please contact me. Resources and links to many great organizations, Web sites, and individuals helping to advance the larger discussion of electoral reform as well as additional proposed reforms can be found on our Web site: amatomain.com. We need a mass-based citizen movement along with our civic institutions to undertake this work—funded by individuals, organizations, and foundations—to start, fuel, and sustain a massive electoral reform drive.

Index